Dodie NORTON

INFANTS IN MULTIRISK FAMILIES

Case Studies in Preventive Intervention

Clinical Infant Reports
Series of the National Center for Clinical Infant Programs

INFANTS IN MULTIRISK FAMILIES

Case Studies in Preventive Intervention

Editors

Stanley I. Greenspan, M.D.

Serena Wieder, Ph.D.   Robert A. Nover, M.D.

Alicia F. Lieberman, Ph.D.   Reginald S. Lourie, M.D

Mary E. Robinson, M.Ed.

International Universities Press, Inc.

Madison ● Connecticut

Library of Congress Cataloging-in-Publication Data

Infants in multirisk families.

(Clinical infant reports)
Includes bibliographies and index.
1. Infants—Diseases—Prevention—Case studies.
2. Infant health services—Maryland—Case studies.
3. Clinical Infant Development Program (Prince Georges County, Md.) I. Greenspan, Stanley I. II. Clinical Infant Development Program (Prince Georges County, Md.)
III. Series. [DNLM: 1. Child Development Disorders—prevention & control—case studies. 2. Child Health Services—Maryland. WA 310 I43]
RJ102.5.M3154 1987   362.1′9892′0009752   86-84
ISBN 0-8236-2645-8

Manufactured in the United States of America.

This volume is dedicated to the mothers, fathers, and children who let us reach them and opened the doors to new knowledge and services for others.

Thank you.

The National Center for Clinical Infant Programs is a non-profit, tax-exempt corporation. It was established in 1977 by representatives from the fields of mental health, pediatrics, child development, and related fields, as well as community leaders, in order to improve and support professional initiatives in infant health, mental health and development.

Contents

Preface

This volume is the third in the series of Clinical Infant Reports published by the National Center for Clinical Infant Programs. The series is designed especially for practitioners in the new and growing multidisciplinary field of infant health, mental health and development.

Each volume in the series addresses an identified gap in the professional literature. Of special interest to the series are theoretical inquiries, empirical investigations, and in-depth case studies which relate to the challenges of clinical work with infants, young children and their families. The current volume well illustrates this focus by exploring diagnostic and therapeutic issues and methods through detailed case studies and by evolving from these studies new theoretical foundations for further clinical practice and research.

The Editorial Board
National Center for
Clinical Infant Programs

Acknowledgments

It is difficult, if not impossible, to summarize the appropriate expression of appreciation for the years of intensive work undertaken by the staff of the Clinical Infant Development Program (CIDP). The CIDP began as a National Institute of Mental Health (NIMH) program in collaboration with a community agency, the CIDP at Family Service of Prince Georges County, Maryland, where the intervention took place. These mental health and community perspectives were enriched by subsequent collaboration with the Infant and Child Clinical Development Services Program, Division of Maternal and Child Health, Health Resources and Services Administration (HRSA). The commitment and devotion of the staff helped us to learn that the "hard-to-reach" are, in fact, available and responsive if we persist and find new ways to understand and work together.

From the anxious beginnings in 1977 to the completion of the intervention phase of the project in 1983, the staff dedicated itself to the demanding and difficult work this segment of our population required, with crises at all times of the day and many nights. The case studies in this volume will convey the energy, skill, creativity, and caring each staff member invested in our participant families, often in heroic efforts. The tremendous impact this had on the lives of the parents and their babies will be self-evident. Only 4 of the intensive treatment cases could be included in this volume. They are representative of the efforts everyone, including the primary clinicians, the infant specialists, and the infant–parent center and support staffs, made on all the cases.

The staff of the CIDP not only affected the lives of the participants, but each other, learning and growing together. There were shared fears and hopes, failures and successes, conflicts and alliances, disappointments and joys. Most of all, we wish to acknowledge the families, whom we will always remember, who let us into their lives, and taught us so much. For all of this, we are very grateful.

Below is a list of all the staff members who participated at various intervals, and for different periods of time, in the CIDP between 1977 and 1983. Secretaries, drivers, and students who worked in the program for short periods of time also deserve our thanks. Many CIDP staff members have gone on to work in infant programs throughout the country. The most special tribute that can be made to the parents and the staff is continuation of the programs and use of the knowledge gained. A direct outgrowth of the CIDP is the Regional Center for Infants and Young Children of Washington, Maryland, and Virginia, a nonprofit organization which now serves many more families in a model program of comprehensive clinical, research, training, and education services.

Program Staff

Clinicians
Maurice Apprey
Euthymia Hibbs
Eva Hollingsworth
Kathy O'Leary
Carol Pollack
Ruth Reynolds
Edward Turner
Delise Williams

Infant Specialists
Joan Castellan
Diana Denboba
Delois Ward

Infant Center Staff
Patricia Findikoglu
Judy Hubert
Jan Perini

Research Staff
Christopher Anderson
Mary Batcher
Griff Doyle
Pirkko Graves
Julie Hofheimer
Katherine Jacobs
Mahmoud Jahromi
Michael Jasnow
Victoria Levin
Alicia Lieberman
Mary Pharis
Billie Press
Mary Ann VandeLoo
Debby Williams
Elizabeth Zinner

Supervisors and Consultants
Patricia Allison
Stanley Greenspan
Reginald Lourie
Robert Nover
Mary Robinson
Alfred Scheuer
Milton Shore
Serena Wieder

Audio-Visual Staff
G. G. Esch
Curtis Powell

Support Staff
Betty Albaugh
Darlene Butler
Ethel Gurtz
Norma Klein
Jeanne Lopez

*Administrative Structure
Family Service, of
Prince Georges County*

Nathan Nackman, Executive Director

Serena Wieder, Clinical Research Director, CIDP; currently Director, The Regional Center for Infants and Young Children, Rockville, Maryland

Members of the Editorial Board of the National Center for Clinical Infant Programs have been individually and collectively supportive of our work. Special thanks are due to Emily Schrag, NCCIP's Associate Director for Publications and Public Policy, who edited this volume and helped us convey to others what we learned.

Contributors

Joan M. Castellan, M.A. Pediatric Nurse Practitioner at the Regional Center for Infants and Young Children, Rockville, Maryland.

Patricia Findikoglu, M.A. Teacher–therapist and supervisor of The Therapeutic Pre-School at The Regional Center for Infants and Young Children.

Nancy Thorndike Greenspan, M.A. Formerly Chief, Economic and Long-Range Studies Branch, Office of Research and Demonstrations, Health Care Financing Administration, and currently an author on books for parents on the health and development of children.

Stanley I. Greenspan, M.D. Chief, Infant and Child Clinical Development Services Program, Division of Maternal and Child Health, Department of Health and Human Services, Rockville, Maryland.

Euthymia D. Hibbs, Ph.D. Clinical Research Psychologist, Child Psychiatry Branch, National Institute of Mental Health, Intramural Research Program, Rockville, Maryland.

Eva L. Hollingsworth, M.S.W., L.C.S.W. Clinical Social Worker, The Regional Center for Infants and Young Children.

Judy Hubert. Day Care Supervisor, Broadcaster's Day Care Center, Washington, D.C.

Michael Jasnow, Ph.D. Associate Research Scientist, Department of Psychiatry, College of Physicians and Surgeons, Columbia University.

Alicia F. Lieberman, Ph.D.   Associate Professor in Residence at The University of California at San Francisco, Department of Psychiatry, and Staff Psychologist with the Infant–Parent Program at San Francisco General Hospital.

Reginald S. Lourie, M.D.   Medical Director at The Regional Center for Infants and Young Children.

Robert A. Nover, M.D.   Associate Clinical Professor of Psychiatry and Child Health Development, George Washington University School of Medicine. Formerly, Research Psychiatrist at The Clinical Infant and Child Development Research Center of the Division of Maternal and Child Health and NIMH, Rockville, Maryland.

Mary E. Robinson, M.Ed.   Early Childhood Educator, Division of Maternal and Child Health, Department of Health and Human Services.

Alfred Q. Scheuer, M.D.   Fellow, American Academy of Pediatrics. Formerly, Consulting Developmental Pediatrician, CIDP.

Milton Strauss, Ph.D.   Professor of Psychology at The Johns Hopkins University in Baltimore, Maryland.

Delois B. Ward, M.A.   Mental Health Therapist, Fairfax City, Virginia Department of Mental Health.

Serena Wieder, Ph.D.   Director of The Regional Center for Infants and Young Children.

Delise Williams, A.C.S.W.   Adoption Worker, placing special-needs children. Homes for Black Children, Washington, DC

Introduction

Everyone knows multirisk families—doctors, social workers, ambulance drivers, welfare administrators, teachers, police officers, and volunteers, all of whom struggle valiantly, though seldom successfully, to help such families cope with the chaos that for them is daily life.

At a case conference organized around a multirisk family's latest crisis, one is likely to see representatives from the half-dozen community agencies involved with the family. Each participant will have a file several inches thick, with entries sometimes going back several generations. It was multirisk families that Buell was describing when he estimated, more than 30 years ago, that approximately 6 percent of the population uses 50–75 percent of all public health, mental health, and social services in a community, usually seeking help only when a crisis threatens survival itself.

What do we know about multirisk families? For example, how are poor coping capacities in such families transferred from one generation to another? This has only rarely been the focus of systematic research. Even less effort has been devoted to figuring out how to interrupt this cycle.

In a 1969 study of some 50 preschool children in 13 multiproblem families in Boston, Pavenstedt and her colleagues (1967) found that between the ages of 3 and 6, most children in these families already showed emotional disturbance. Their emotions and behavior were fragmented, asocial, or antisocial. Their personality development reflected deficits

1

in such basic areas of functioning as reality testing, impulse regulation, maintenance of self-esteem, and ability to concentrate and learn. A more recent study of the impact of multiple risk factors in infancy on later development demonstrated for the first time that even when socioeconomic class was held constant family and interactive patterns predicted maladaptive functioning at age 4. Furthermore, when all risk factors, including interactional ones, were considered, children in families with more than four risk factors were 25 times more likely to show poor cognitive patterns at age 4 than children in families with only a few risk factors. Similar, though less dramatic, predictions of behavioral problems were possible (Sameroff, Seifer, Barocas, Zax, and Greenspan, in press).

Pavenstedt (1967) and her colleagues emphasized the importance of learning how such patterns unfolded, from prenatal development through the earliest months of infancy and into the second and third years of life. They hoped that an understanding of the origins of maladaptive behavior would lead to the development of preventive intervention strategies, to be employed early enough in a child's life to reverse the antecedents of disturbed behavior.

While the Pavenstedt study looked at children whose environments failed to support healthy development, other researchers investigating infants born with biological or constitutional vulnerabilities found that, in a *proper* environment, these youngsters could overcome their potential for disability to a significant degree. Infants born with biological vulnerabilities living in chronically *unsupportive* circumstances, however, would be likely to experience successive developmental failures, as environments insensitive to their individual differences and special needs tended not only to undermine development at one stage, but to continue to do so at each subsequent stage in life.

These studies present a compelling challenge. Can special patterns of care help youngsters with and without constitutional vulnerabilities, living in multirisk families, to build on existing strengths and coping capacities or to create compensatory strengths? The establishment of successful programs of diagnosis and preventive intervention for such children would signal a major advance in reducing the large number of children, adolescents, and adults who show severe, and costly, disturbances in their social, emotional, and cognitive development.

With these public health challenges in mind, the Clinical Infant Development Program of the National Institute of Mental Health (now the Clinical Infant and Child Development Research Center, Division of Maternal and Child Health, HRSA, and the National Institute of Mental Health, Public Health Service, U.S. Department of Health and Human Services) undertook a study beginning in 1977, to look simultaneously at the following:

1. How psychopathology develops, and in what patterns and configurations, in infants from multirisk as well as other types of families,
2. What ideal combinations of clinical techniques and service delivery models would be needed to have even a chance of reversing maladaptive patterns,
3. Which clinical techniques and service system approaches were effective for specific problems, examined on a case by case basis,
4. A comparison between comprehensive and less intensive intervention approaches and treatment outcomes, and
5. The relationships among perinatal risk patterns, the formation of therapeutic relationships, and subsequent development in the children and their families.

The goal of this volume will be to present clinical descriptions and analytic formulations which, together with our earlier work (Greenspan, 1981) reflect on the first three of the questions outlined above. The descriptions of the workings of our clinical research project, known as the Clinical Infant Development Program (CIDP), the four case studies, and the analytical chapters which follow document the ways in which our program tried to meet the challenges we set ourselves.

Because of the exploratory nature of our study and because the people we were serving were difficult to know, our glimmers of understanding, insights, and eventual attempts to conceptualize what we learned came to us slowly, over a period of many years of intense involvement with the families of the study.

When we began our study, we had available neither many models for understanding infant psychopathology, nor the framework for describing disturbed infant functioning. We hoped that our project would lead to a more explicit description of the patterns of disorders experienced by infants and families. We also hoped to integrate, on behalf of multirisk families, two traditions of human services, one involving coordination of the social support system and the establishment of an ongoing, trusting human relationship, and the other employing highly technical medical and psychiatric approaches.

We assembled a core staff and planned outreach and therapeutic approaches which our previous knowledge of multirisk families suggested would be effective. During the course of the project, however, we continuously modified our interventions on the basis of new information, sometimes changing approaches to a particular family, sometimes finding new ways to use resources such as our Infant Center. Providing staff with enough stimulation, satisfaction, and support to sustain them during years of work of unrelenting challenge also demanded flexibility and mutual respect. We have presented the four case studies which form the core of this volume in an unusual degree of detail in order to provide what we believe represents essential data for the relatively new field of comprehensive clinical preventive approaches for infants and their families. The analytic chapters present the conceptual fruits of our labors: findings on antecedent psychosocial factors in mothers in multirisk families; a model for comprehensive preventive intervention services; a new formulation of dimensions and levels of the therapeutic process; a developmental diagnostic approach for infants, young children, and their families; and theoretical and clinical perspectives on research regarding psychopathology and preventive intervention in infancy. In a future work, we will present the quantitative trends (now being analyzed) which characterize the developmental process, therapeutic experience and outcomes of the multirisk families described from a clinical perspective in these pages.

Part I: The Clinical Infant Development Program: Basic Organization and Case Studies

1

Staffing, Process, and Structure of the Clinical Infant Development Program

Serena Wieder, Ph.D.
Stanley I. Greenspan, M.D.

In this chapter we will describe the underlying process
and structure of the Clinical Infant Development Program
(CIDP); that is, our attempts to identify and engage multirisk
mothers and then to figure out what to do, who could do it,
and what the role of clinical research should be in the program.
We tried to work with mothers whose lives were full of difficulty and pain to help them create an opportunity to grow
emotionally and to learn to care for their infants with tenderness and intimacy, even though they had never experienced such a relationship themselves. While CIDP started
with the clearly defined objectives of offering preventive intervention to high-risk multiproblem families while studying
the unfolding, amelioration, and prevention of psychopathology in their infants, it was primarily a descriptive, exploratory study. Intensive work with participants permitted
a teasing out of the hidden needs, the often difficult to observe
psychopathology, and most important, the special abilities and
strengths of each family, which led to a model for comprehensive intervention services.

9

The Families: An Overview

Since multirisk families tend to remain outside the traditional human services system, rarely coming for appointments and generally distrusting traditional service providers,
they are even less likely to volunteer for research studies. To
recruit participants for our study, therefore, we launched an
extensive outreach effort. We stationed clinicians at prenatal
clinics, called on social service agencies and courts, and
alerted service providers to send us their most difficult and
challenging cases. Soon calls came in from prenatal clinics
regarding mothers who had missed appointments, appeared
confused, or were not adequately following medical guidance,
and from protective service and court workers involved with
families in which an older child appeared neglected and the
mother was pregnant again.

The mothers who participated in the CIDP had anywhere
from two to six children, lived in communities ranging from
urban to rural, and were mostly married or involved in an
ongoing relationship with the fathers of their children. There
were no significant differences in our group between the distribution of white or black families or between those receiving
and not receiving public assistance. We discovered that the
high-risk mother can be young or middle-aged, a high-school
dropout or a college graduate, married or single.

More significantly, we discovered that our mothers had
had difficult lives and many problems before their children
were born, and that these difficulties did not go away. These
women, however, did not seek psychiatric help (short of hospitalization) for their problems, nor were they responsive to
traditional mental health services. The wealth of information
about our mothers' lives, which emerged only gradually during our many years of contact, is elaborated in Chapter 7.
When we began our study, however, our chief focus was on
maternal functioning. We were most concerned about the
impact of their multiple problems on participants' capacity to
rear their children.

It was useful, we found, to think in terms of primary maternal functions (the ability to provide physical care and protection, the basic ability to read an infant's signals of pleasure or displeasure, and the minimum emotional basis for a human attachment between mother and infant); and secondary maternal functions (the ability to discern a child's changing developmental needs during the course of the first two years of life and the capacity to respond promptly, effectively, and empathically to the signals). The mothers we looked for as participants in CIDP were those who:

- had already clearly shown severe difficulties in providing one of the primary or all of the secondary maternal functions for an older child;
- were pregnant; and
- seemed likely to repeat the pattern with the new infant.

All the families were offered either comprehensive services, including evaluations and treatment by CIDP, or periodic evaluations and referral to community agencies for needed services. The evaluations included detailed histories, observations, and standardized assessment at a child's birth, every four months during the first year, and every six months thereafter.

In order to form the beginnings of a therapeutic alliance with a new participant, who had never before been offered services, our staff had to develop techniques of engaging and working with them in ways they found possible to use. In most cases, continued reaching out by an interested person willing to hear about and try to understand the difficulties a mother, father, or family was experiencing eventually met with a response, however slight, indirect, or cautious it might be. We learned that each family, like each baby, could respond if our overtures were persistent, respectful, and sensitive. (Chapter 3, 4, 5, and 6 provide extensive case material on four mothers and their children which illustrate the range of intervention strategies needed to effect the changes achieved. These four mothers represented the most difficult cases in our program.)

Essential Components of Our Intervention

As we looked back on the major strategies we used to help our participants cope with different aspects of their lives, we identified three major components in our intervention approach.

1. We had to support basic survival and meet concrete needs. This meant searching for apartments with participants who were facing eviction, making clinic appointments, and providing transportation so that the appointments would be kept, and delivering emergency food and diapers. This also meant working with the other agencies and authorities who affected our families' lives.

2. We had to develop some regularity and continuity in our contacts in order to build trust and a healing relationship. We needed to consider both the nature of the pathology involved and the impact of our mothers' past relationships as we persisted in outreach in the face of patterns of avoidance which frequently lasted for months.

3. We had to develop the special patterns of care suited to the highly varied constitutional capacities of the babies we were dealing with—our infants ranged from the very vulnerable, with unique tactile or auditory sensitivities, to those who were resilient. As our contacts with participants stabilized and attachments formed, our goal became to bring our mothers to higher developmental levels, helping them to relate to their children's individual vulnerabilities, strengths, and emerging capacities for human interaction, from early reciprocal interchanges to later representative-symbolic elaborations.

Staffing the Clinical Infant Development Program: The Team Approach[1]

Shortly after recruiting our program's first families (see Chapter 7), we realized that we would need a team approach, with at least two staff assigned to each family as well as the support of the Infant Center. This was necessary for several reasons. First, the sheer number of things to be done, agencies to involve, and children in the families of multirisk mothers often required the energies of more than one person for an adequate response. Second, the emotional stress of working with multirisk families was difficult to tolerate alone. Faced by many early rejections as we pursued our participants, team members could support each other. Later in the work, when a mother might be angry at one team member, the other usually retained enough good will to be accepted. By the same token, if one member of the team became too angry or despairing to be effective, the other partner could take over. Forming teams of people with different skills and professions was useful in this respect: a mother might, for example, feel more comfortable with a nurse than with a social worker. Finally, and most important, giving attention equally to the infant, to the family, and to the mother required a team. We found that mothers often competed with or used their infants in relation to the program. A team approach permitted more differentiation and greater access to infant and mother. For example, while a mother worked through painful conflict with the clinician, the infant specialist could have less emotional sessions with the mother which focused on the baby: these would permit the work of understanding the baby's unique

---

[1]CIDP staff were called "primary clinicians" and "infant specialists" in order to reflect our program's difference from more traditional services and to avoid the stigma or fear our families might attach to more traditional titles such as "therapist." For brevity, all staff will be referred to as clinicians in this work unless specific functions or roles need to be elaborated. It should also be noted, mothers in the program were called "participants" rather than "patients" or "clients." This practice reflected our decision not to diagnose mothers nor require them to identify a problem or need for help as a condition of joining the CIDP.

capacities and new developmental requirements to proceed with relatively little interruption. If, as sometimes happened, the mother was unable to focus on her infant and the clinician was still in the process of trying to help the mother with her patterns of avoidance, the infant specialist could provide the baby with crucial experiences until the mother was more available. With those mothers who felt most comfortable with the baby and the infant specialist, the more intense therapeutic process emerged in the mother–infant specialist relationship, while the clinician focused more on the infant. For other cases, reaching both mother and infant proved so difficult that the additional services of the Infant Center, described in the next chapter, were needed to maintain progress.

Who Could Do the Work

Reaching out to mothers typically identified as "unmotivated," "uninterested," or "unavailable" required a commitment and skills different from those needed in an environment of regular appointments in counseling offices or therapy rooms. From the start of the CIDP, we told new and prospective staff that our program was unique, that we would be trying to do something not done before, and that we would work together to make it happen. We wished to convey the sense that we all had to figure out together how to reach our objectives and that we would learn by doing. In the course of six years, only 2 of 16 clinical staff left the CIDP because of difficulties in doing the work. This remarkable absence of burnout was related both to the support built into the program in the form of supervision and conferences and to the selection of clinicians committed to developing innovative approaches to work with families whom traditional service programs had failed.

Our ability to identify the characteristics of staff which enabled them to engage in this type of work increased as CIDP progressed. We learned that first, staff had to be able to tolerate rejection and flight by participants not only initially, but again and again, without withdrawing or retaliating. Phone calls, letters, and knocks on the door—representing countless hours of staff time—would go unanswered. Staff would have to function like detectives, interviewing agencies, visiting participants' neighbors, waiting in clinics, driving long distances to make contact, and yet maintain the sense that this persistent reaching out was not intrusive or invasive.

Second, staff had to be willing to provide concrete services in order, on one level, simply to ensure survival, and on another, to provide the foundation for a relationship with the mothers. Searching for housing, waiting at social service agencies, getting emergency food and diapers, driving to the hospital, or picking up a check could all be involved. The hours and miles often seemed endless, the thanks often nil. Yet this modality was crucial: concrete help could be measured by our mothers in ways "interest" and "talking" could not.

Third, staff needed the ability to tolerate participants' lack of gratitude and their own feeling of failure over long periods of time. Participants were often so guarded and afraid of contact that they maintained distance and tested offers of help repeatedly, habitually reacting in negative and rejecting ways. If staff could not provide a ride the same morning, if we could not arrange baby-sitting, if a taxi voucher was not forthcoming, we could expect silence, anger, and flight. Some participants could not delay, or wait, or accept anything less than what they demanded or needed. Precisely because we *were* there, we often became the target of their reactions to disappointment, deprivation, and fear. Other participants grabbed whatever they could get, demanding more and more once a response to their dependency needs was available.

Whether one could not do enough because of clinging and helplessness or because of anger and disappointment, staff members' experience of participants' dependency was both intense and relentless. While working toward trust, a mother who could never be satisfied could become threatening and indeed overwhelming. The CIDP clinical staff varied in their

ability to absorb these feelings. Some staff offered total availability, tolerating calls at home or late night crises again and
again. On occasion these staff members became possessive of
"their" participants, using program services but limiting identification with the program. Other staff consistently presented
themselves as part of the CIDP, presenting resources through
the program, and referring families to the on-call staff in
emergencies. With this group, the degree to which a participant became integrated into the overall program often provided a measure of the relationship between participant and
clinician and between clinician and program. These choices
reflected personal characteristics and needs of the clinicians.
The former pattern resulted in more team, staff, and program
conflict, while the latter generated more staff and program
support. Both approaches appeared to work in helping participants and their infants.

Our staff consisted of social workers, psychologists,
nurses, educators, and paraprofessionals. Although we had
hoped to recruit more male staff in order to study the effects
of male versus female intervenors, with the exception of one
male social worker we had an all-female clinical staff. As the
program progressed, it became apparent that a personal ability
to tolerate the various stresses in the work was more important
than background in a particular discipline. Successful staff,
regardless of previous training, were individuals who learned
in the course of our program about subtle individual differences in infants and how these expressed themselves in infant–caregiver patterns of interaction. An especially sensitive
infant who found mother's voice noxious, for example, required a staff member who could work with the mother on
trying special patterns of holding, touching, and vocalizing
with the infant while at the same time empathizing with the
mother's feelings of defectiveness, rejection, and often anger.
Although professional background in a particular discipline
proved not essential, several years of prior experience in some
forms of outreach or community-based work did seem a pre-

requisite to effectiveness. The two staff members who left the program had come from academic settings in which their authority was derived in part from that of the institution. For these clinicians it was especially challenging to function "outside," where they had to represent themselves, alone, without direct backing, for long periods of time and where "teaching" postures were less effective.

Although the difficulties of our work were evident and real, an effort that included outreach and innovative approaches offered important advantages to staff as well. The work was varied and could be experienced as an adventure. Moving about and meeting participants in their own world was dramatic, far more challenging than routine office appointments, especially for clinicians who had had the experience of attempting to work with populations of patients who do not *keep* office appointments. Home visits also gave clinicians a sense of participants' experience which most of the mothers could not have conveyed in words. This was particularly important in the beginning of the program when few of the participants could articulate their feelings or talk about their lives. They had not sought and could not respond to traditional treatment, but staff members using sensitivity and intuition in ways other than those used in traditional therapy were able to enter and understand their lives.

There was a lack of traditional patient–therapist boundaries between CIDP participants and clinicians, who needed the capacity to tolerate a certain degree of merging, out of which differentiation could occur. This intimacy took very concrete forms, as clinicians joined the struggle for survival, experienced the fears and fury of participants, and became the nurturant figures who slowly helped create some order and organization in the lives of participants and their children, a necessary foundation for growth and development.

Supervision and Other Supports for Clinical Staff

It was the continuous supervision, conferences, and team effort which helped relieve the stress of working in the CIDP.

In hallway discussions, as well as scheduled meetings, it was possible to absorb staff reactions against the participants, to acknowledge often heroic efforts, identify avoidance and helplessness, and to refuel energies so that staff could return to and persist in the intervention. It was crucial to take time to identify problems, to understand dynamics, and to determine next possible moves.

At some stages, as much time was spent in supervision and support as in direct contacts with CIDP participants. We needed a highly experienced clinical supervisory staff who could pay close attention to the impact of the work both on participants and staff members. Each clinician had a weekly session with an individual supervisor. Team meetings, which periodically included the CIDP psychologist and developmental pediatrician in addition to the team members and supervisor, were held every other week. Where needed, interagency meetings were also organized on a regular basis. Finally, all members of the clinical staff, administrative supervisors, and program directors participated in a weekly case conference, which permitted the regular review of all families following each assessment interval.

The critical underlying task in all of these meetings was dealing with the reactions, or countertransference, stirred up by the difficult work with participants. These reactions typically took three forms: (1) the tendency to overidentify with the mothers and lose sight of program objectives; (2) the tendency, when feeling angry, despairing, or exhausted from tremendous efforts, to retaliate and reject participants; and (3) the tendency to become concrete, misinterpreting participants' troublesome behavior as a sign that "they don't want help" rather than continuing to seek understanding of families' fears or other underlying patterns. Achieving and maintaining a balanced identification with the infants and their caregivers also posed challenges. Staff members might feel anger at a mother for "not caring" or, less often, anger at a child, particularly a toddler, for stressing his mother. The team meeting often helped to integrate awareness of the families' real needs and played an important role in helping clinicians learn to use their "identifications" and accompanying anger to facilitate understanding and balanced empathy.

Precisely because contacts with participants were often irregular at the beginning of the program, the CIDP's support structure needed to be regular and predictable in order to sustain the work. Individual, team, and staff conferences all gave us an opportunity to learn about our participants and our objectives for them; to share information; to ventilate day-to-day frustration, anger, or disappointment; to share pleasure in progress made and receive acknowledgment for effort, and to get new ideas and increase our understanding. Refreshments and a staff development program were the other elements of the program's crucial nurturance of its staff.

Limited caseloads can be seen as another element of support for staff. Typically, each clinician could only carry five or six intensive cases, following about the same number in the comparison (community referral) group. A clinician's caseload was primarily determined by the amount of effort needed to work with the families involved rather than by an absolute number. Fortunately, even the most difficult cases usually stabilized around the infant's first birthday and we would sense a consolidation of our efforts and a shift to easier stages of intervention. As some cases achieved regularity and stability, clinicians could take on new participants; thus during CIDP's first years, caseloads increased slowly, as the stage of work with each participant was assessed.

The Role of Research

The research aspect of the CIDP turned out to be both an arena for resistance and confrontation within the program and (although not initially and not so apparently) a source of support for staff. Clinicians responded with ambivalence to the time-consuming, demanding requirements to report every step taken, obligations which involved narrative reporting,

completing contact forms, and conducting specific assessments at set intervals. Reporting a step often took as much
time as the step itself. On the other hand, it was the research
component of CIDP which provided a structure and time in
which to record the details, review, and reflect on our efforts.
Because our ultimate goal was to learn from these efforts how
to work with families to help their children get a better start
in life, the research gave importance to every step and also
helped us to transcend the immediate success or failure of
what we tried.

Potential conflict between the two roles of clinician and
data gatherer which each staff member assumed was an important issue for our program. Given our unusual group of
participants, it was clear that only experienced clinicians could
do this type of work. We therefore recruited experienced
clinicians who, for the most part, had not worked in research
before but who were willing to enter the difficult and painful
lives of mothers and children who were failing in life. These
clinical requirements were often experienced as being at odds
with such research demands as completing forms or pressing
for assessments on schedule.

In order to foster staff identification with the research
effort more systematically, we met regularly to discuss the
nature and impact of our work *as a group*, focusing on staff
efforts rather than individual cases. Nevertheless, the staff
was only variably successful in its identification with the research. Some clinicians felt uncomfortable being scrutinized
and needed to control their cases. Others experienced research requirements as difficult, demanding too much of staff
resources and energy, which were already strained by arduous
clinical work. There was also an inherent source of potential
conflict in the issue of who would receive credit for the work
done. We needed to develop ways, as in this volume, of
acknowledging the contributions of both clinicians and researchers.

The program's comparison cases, which received periodic

evaluations and referrals as needed to existing community services, at first presented a source of conflict as staff struggled over just how much help the CIDP should be offering this group. As time went on, clinicians welcomed the lower levels of intervention involved in these cases, despite the difficulty in keeping them engaged, simply because they required less effort than the families receiving comprehensive services.

As the CIDP neared its end, the research effort became more significant to all staff members. We realized that the research would extend the life of our program, defining what was learned through clinical description and statistical analysis, and allowing our work to be of value to others both at the clinical case and program development level.

2

The Infant Center: A Developmentally Based Environment to Support Difficult Lives

Serena Wieder, Ph.D.
Patricia Findikoglu, M.A.

The Purposes of the Infant Center

Our early contacts with project families quickly confirmed our hypothesis that many of our mothers could not provide an appropriately responsive environment for their infants. We recognized, too, that many of our mothers would be slow to respond to treatment but that their infants could not wait to have their developmental needs addressed. We felt that a center-based program in a familiar "home away from home" could provide timely help for babies while the mother's treatment continued. For example, bringing one such mother and her baby who was at risk for failure to thrive, to the Infant Center daily allowed us to nurture them both as treatment proceeded. The infant in another family, left with a series of inadequate baby-sitters, was deteriorating rapidly. By bringing the baby to the center and having his mother join the child after work, we could provide the infant with the intervention he urgently needed while we persisted in our efforts with his mother.

The Infant Center allowed mothers, as well as babies, to

experience a responsive and nourishing environment. As we got to know the lives of our participants, we saw how many felt imprisoned in their noisy, crowded, dingy, and comfortless apartments. The Infant Center provided a warm, friendly setting for these women when they needed it, along with a small, sensitive staff who knew each family and could cushion the otherwise difficult reality of their lives. In an atmosphere which program participants came to trust, the Infant Center also provided individualized therapeutic programs for infant and caregiver; therapy groups for mothers and children; workshops on nutrition, birth control, toys, and driver education; a high-school equivalency program; and trips and celebrations of birthdays and holidays.

Within this nurturant milieu a structure existed to meet the specific goals identified for each family. This structure consisted of criteria or elements which were considered in planning each family's use of the Infant Center.

1. The stage specific needs of the infants, such as establishing homeostasis by helping mothers develop effective caregiving routines which permitted alert periods of interest in the world as well as comfortable eating and sleeping cycles;
2. Each child's individual differences, such as tactile or auditory hypersensitivities which required special techniques of care and handling;
3. The emotional or psychological problems of the mother which resulted in distortions interfering with her nurturing of her child; these might involve attributing aggression to the baby's dependency needs or rejection to the baby's autonomous strivings; and
4. The supportive elements needed to meet day-to-day needs for social companionship, a hot lunch, skills training, or a place to rest and not be alone.

These four elements were essential in keeping the work focused and organized in a setting which had to be responsive to so many families coming and going over five years.

The Infant Center also served as a "holding place" at times of emergency. These were frequent, especially in the early phases of our work with families before we could help them stabilize basic services and anticipate needs. We used the Center as an "emergency day home" when families were evicted, when other family members needed emergency care and there was nowhere to leave an infant, when mothers had urgent appointments, when there was no other way to wash clothes and the diapers were gone, and when the cupboards at home were bare. We offered friendly territory for estranged couples and a neutral meeting ground for natural parents and their children in foster care.

Finally, the Infant Center provided private, quiet settings for individual therapy once mothers could accept meeting alone with the therapist or infant specialist. Participants' homes were often too noisy, crowded, or chaotic to allow the kind of conversation which involves examining one's situation or focusing on a baby. Clinicians and infant specialists tried to schedule their meetings with mothers on the same day at the Infant Center. Before, between, or after sessions, the Center provided a setting in which mothers and infants could socialize and children could play.

By understanding the life situation and capacities of participants at different stages of intervention, Center staff were able to maintain a flexible approach, whose definition came through providing a variety of successful experiences to the participants. We were a treatment and assessment center with a host of therapeutic services. We were also a place to spend the day, use the telephone, or do the laundry.

The Infant Center Approach

Because we were reaching out to multirisk families long dependent on various agencies for meeting their needs, we anticipated negative, suspicious attitudes when we offered our help. Because our families had often experienced conflict, anger, resentment, and frustration in dealing with agency regulations, we did not expect mothers to accommodate to a new set of rules we might develop. At the same time, our theory of structural development (see Chapter 10) suggested that the first goal in treating high-risk mothers was to establish some form of homeostasis. The Infant Center was designed to provide regularity and predictability and establish rhythms of intervention with the families we served.

Combining regularity with sensitivity to mothers' needs and capacities, we made the Infant Center available to them from 8 A.M. to 5 P.M., but made its regular use a treatment *objective* rather than a *requirement*. We decided not to schedule participation for set times and days, thus imposing more rules on families, but rather to respond as best we could to the availability of our mothers, recognizing that their inner emotional turmoil often manifested itself outwardly in an inability to adhere to scheduling and routines. Mothers and babies could come to the Infant Center throughout the day. The times at which they came might be a function of the treatment team's schedule, the availability of transportation, scheduling of a special program, or their need to "get away" and drop in on us. In the Infant Center's early days, participants expressed needs (from which we took our cues in planning Center services) which were often concrete and immediate. One mother, on the brink of abuse, might come to the Center to be free of responsibility for her children for a few hours. Another might come to make sure that her family had lunch. Some came so overwhelmed by depression as to be almost unable to speak. Others came, as eventually all mothers did to some extent, for a bit of socializing.

The role of the Infant Center staff, consisting of two or three full-time staff, an infant educator and assistants, and trainees, was to provide a milieu which would be responsive to participants and staff alike. We tried to be different from others in the participants' lives and to avoid reacting against mothers' provocations and incompetencies. Our task was to identify those aspects of the Center program mothers could make use of at any given time, and to build on those aspects as mothers progressed. The Infant Center staff and the team of clinicians and infant specialists complemented each other in providing responsive interaction for program participants.

Running the Center

Because the Infant Center served so many purposes and had to meet so many needs, which varied from day to day, it was crucial to establish a stable and predictable schedule to serve as the structure of the program. This schedule was known to everyone and allowed staff and participants to take advantage of the Center to meet their numerous individual needs. The schedule also prevented the Center from disintegrating into chaos even on the busiest of days as families came and went and inevitable crises occurred. The Center day began with free time in the morning when families arrived, mothers helped themselves to coffee, or fed their children breakfast; and children, infants, and siblings played freely. This period was followed by one or two staff-led activities, geared to the ages of the children present, which mothers could join or observe. Then came a snack, which provided an opportunity to feed the children who arrived later in the morning. Outdoor play followed in our small playground, which had a large sandbox, wading pool, benches, and equipment for children of every age. Mothers knew lunch would always be served around 11:30 A.M. and, in fact, they helped with the preparation and clean-up. Staff planned the menus until one mother assumed this responsibility in a job-training program we developed for her (see Chapter 6). After lunch, children could play freely; some children who stayed for the full day took naps. Afternoons were often used for special activities, such as simultaneous group therapy for mothers and children, both separately and together.

For the most part the Infant Center was organized around the children's activities and modeling adult–child interactions throughout the day. Mothers and infants had individual appointments with their therapists at various times during the day, but would usually be brought to the Center early enough to have a chance to socialize with other mothers and the staff, and to participate in the routine activities at the Center. In addition, high-school equivalency classes were conducted twice a week; children participated in the Infant Center activities or were seen by infant specialists while their mothers attended these classes or other special workshops.

Each of the 27 families invited to use the Infant Center had individual, changing needs and treatment plans which also changed with time. Because we provided transportation, we were able to schedule mothers' visits in advance and maintain considerable control over the schedule. We also found that once mothers had established a pattern of regular contacts with their clinicians, their use of the Center could be planned. Some mothers and children, for example, came to the Center several full mornings each week; during this time, mothers saw their therapists individually and attended high school equivalency classes. Other mothers came to the Center two afternoons per week for group therapy and marital counseling, bringing their children on the same days for therapeutic children's groups or individual treatment. Some mothers who did not feel comfortable using the Center with other families or who had conflicting family responsibilities came only once a week or, in some cases, only for periodic assessments or special workshops.

Despite the efforts of the Infant Center staff to plan for the number of families and to coordinate the use of the Center with the program clinicians, unexpected demands on Center staff and resources occurred frequently. These were usually related to crises in which mothers needed extra support. Some of the most difficult moments for staff involved incidents of child abuse which required immediate handling, days when a mother was so depressed that all she could do was lie on the sofa, and physical battles between a mother and her boyfriend that required staff intervention. Thefts of money and purses occurred several times. And when parents were full of rage that could not be quieted, their young children, too, were often out of control. In the midst of the chaos of participants' lives, the daily routine of the Infant Center helped to keep the staff organized and able to respond to unanticipated needs and emergencies.

The Patterns of Involvement with the Infant Center

About halfway through the program we identified different patterns of utilization among the mothers which appeared to correspond primarily to their developmental level or needs.

The first group consisted of mothers (see Chapter 7) who, after initial pursuit and wooing, turned themselves over to the program, becoming extremely dependent and needing intensive, sometimes daily contact. These mothers were extremely depressed at first and desperately needed to be nurtured and cared for before they could begin to meet even the basic needs of their children. Before they joined us, their lives were often chaotic and unpredictable, hardly environments which could support their newborn infants. Once these mothers became engaged, they permitted us to help; by bringing them into the Center we could help stabilize daily life for them. Their individual treatment was totally compatible and synchronized with the Infant Center routines and the Infant Center staff became primary intervenors along with the primary clinician and infant specialist. (The story of Madeline, presented in chapter 6, best represents this group.)

The second group consisted of mothers who eventually established relationships with their therapists but could not integrate their therapeutic work with the needs of their infants, having at best very ambivalent attachments. These mothers, represented by Louise (Chapter 3) and Mrs. M. (Chapter 5), were usually driven to pursue their own needs and would try to work and "hustle," often at the expense of their infants. As a result, their infants were left with a series of inadequate baby-sitters, had unpredictable care, and began to deteriorate rapidly. These makeshift arrangements also meant that program clinicians did not have regular access to the babies and could not intervene as we hoped. But these infants could not wait, so we offered regular day availability to several of these children in order to prevent further deterioration. The mothers continued to see their therapists individually at home or at the Infant Center.

The mothers in this second group were initially less interested in meeting with the infant specialists, as this would mean confronting their ambivalence toward their children and feelings of failure related to their children's difficulties or delays, with which they identified. As the children improved and these mothers progressed in treatment, however, they became more amenable to discussing issues involving their infants and did not appear to experience as much competition or rejection as they had earlier. These mothers did get intensely involved with the Infant Center staff, on whom they became very dependent on a day-to-day basis. Not unexpectedly this dependency was fraught with many intense, conflicting feelings, not all grateful. These mothers made us feel at times that they were doing us a favor by letting us care for their children, and they required great patience and understanding on the part of the staff.

For the children, attendance at the Infant Center provided an opportunity to make up quickly for the experiences they missed early in life and to benefit from the special techniques of intervention we had developed. Each child was assigned to one particular caregiver. A comforting, dependable routine helped him establish homeostasis. Only later did children proceed to form attachments and catch up on their development. For some of these children individual play therapy was also added beginning at 18 months. These children had to cope with the coming and going of other families throughout the day while the routine schedule kept their days stable. We learned from this group that a therapeutic nursery designed specifically for partial day support and parent work on a regular basis and specific parent activities would be the more appropriate intervention modality.

By far the largest number of mothers fell into the third group. These were mothers who came to the Center once or twice a week on a regular basis and were also typically seen regularly at home by either the clinician or infant specialist. The nature of their involvement at the Center always dovetailed with and complemented their individual treatment plans. During their time at the Center they would usually meet individually with one or both of their clinicians, socialize, or have lunch, and attend an Infant Center activity such as group therapy, a parent workshop, or school. Because their attendance was predictable, their children could also benefit from the various routines of special activities, such as play therapy, organized for small groups.

This group of mothers would also come in more frequently when certain developmental issues such as severe separation difficulties needed to be worked through. The Infant Center offered a comfortable and supportive setting which enabled the mother and child to practice separation and play out feelings and concerns. Some of these mothers came in when special needs arose, such as monitoring new medications, or when they were feeling particularly needy and dependent. During such periods they would spend a great deal of time at the Center, but after these needs were satisfied they could assume more regularly scheduled participation. This flexibility in use of the Center represented one way we could adapt the general program to the developmental needs of the mothers. All the mothers in this group were able to take advantage of the various programs and parties at the Center and could acknowledge how much it offered them. Most got to know each other and even formed friendships, but only a few had contacts outside the Center. A few, however, were never able to accept the Center for themselves: they always made a point of telling us how much their children liked to come and gave their children as the reason for their own attendance.

In the last group were the mothers who often attended the Infant Center but did not become integrated into any of the special services it had to offer. These were the same mothers who also found it difficult to stabilize their contacts with their individual therapists, tending to meet intensively for a while and then take flight until another crisis or persistent pursuit brought them back to the program. Interestingly, most of these mothers were somewhat more autonomous in the outside world than other project participants and would work, drive, or make use of other systems in an effort to meet their endless needs. They were also more educated, articulate, and identified with groups of higher socioeconomic status than their own. These mothers, we came to realize, used their infants to manipulate their unhappy relationships with the fathers and felt especially ambivalent about their children. These were the mothers about whom we often felt most helpless. They seemed to "organize" their lives around crises and rescue missions, invariably disappointed and angered by others who failed them, including us. We later realized that these women were uncomfortable with and mistrustful of dependency; they probably experienced our project as too enveloping. Their children, however, benefited from any intervention we could offer, when we were permitted contact.

The Challenges

The nature of the Infant Center and its multiple undertakings required continual day-to-day and even moment-to-moment decision making.

Whether to intervene in mother–child interaction was always a question. The Infant Center staff frequently witnessed undesirable child-rearing techniques. For example, one moment a mother might slap her child for accidentally spilling his milk; the next moment she might be roughly jerking the child's arm while putting on a coat. Although one might be tempted to intervene in each episode, this was unlikely to be productive. On the other hand, ignoring these behaviors might be interpreted as condoning the behavior.

Few of our mothers could respond to educational approaches, such as a discussion of discipline as a child-rearing issue. Those mothers who could already "say all the right things" were unable to match their behavior to their ideology. Again and again our mothers had the opportunity to watch our interactions with their children, experience tenderness and care through their interactions with staff, and try out new patterns of care and closeness with uncritical support.

Another challenge for staff was attempting to moderate the interaction between participants at the Infant Center. Many of our mothers were volatile. Like most of us, they saw their children as extensions of themselves. However, this tendency was so strong that mothers often took personally toy grabbing and squabbles between their children and began to direct hostility toward each other. Toward the end of the six-year program, when mothers knew each other quite well and most had made significant gains in their development, inappropriate interaction was less of an issue. In fact, some participants very clearly used the Center to practice newly acquired social skills. For example, a mother who early on in the program seemed a bundle of rage, slamming doors or failing even to respond to a "hello" from another mother after a difficult session, eventually was able to announce to the other mothers, after a painful therapy session, "I'm so mad at my therapist today." As one might expect, by the end of the program those mothers who were in a therapy group together tended to be the closest to each other, and also showed the most empathy for each other outside of the group.

The continued difficulty of balancing attention between adults and children represented a third challenge to staff. Mothers could be as demanding as children, and yet there were parts of the day, such as the children's story time, when we wanted to protect both parties. Good coordination among the Center's staff helped to deal with this issue. For example, one of us would announce, "I'm going to read a story," and take the children to a corner far from the door; the second

staff member would then avoid any intense one-to-one play
or deep conversations for a time, but rather remain available
to greet people, moderate "hassles," and spread her attention
generally.

Staff also faced the challenge of protecting the children
from what we call "the revolving door." With so many individuals coming and going, the Infant Center could become
noisy and chaotic. We tried hard to protect the children from
disruptions by means of careful scheduling and the presence
of consistent caregivers. We also found that when mothers
were dealing with difficult treatment issues and avoiding their
clinicians, they continued to come to the Center, which always
maintained its integrity and unique position in the total treatment program. The availability of the Center not only allowed
the child's treatment to continue but also was often the bridge
for the mother back to the clinician. Seeing the Center as
neutral territory, "the grandmother you could always come
back to," mothers often first shared information or problems
with the staff. Of course the staff had to be careful never to
lead the participant to believe that there could be secrets
among the staff, so when the participant shared something
with an Infant Center staff, most of them understood that
eventually that information was going to get back to the clinician. In fact, that was probably why they were telling us.

Two challenges proved particularly difficult for staff. One
was constant exposure to the suffering of the children. Painful
as this was, however, it was also the main impetus to get on
with the work. The other most difficult challenge was to maintain our responsiveness and flexibility in the fluctuating world
of our participants. How could we be sure that the responses
we offered would keep pace with the participant and her stage
in individual treatment? We needed to gauge, for example,
when it was time to expect a particular mother to bathe her
own child, bring her own diapers, or keep an appointment
without three prior phone calls. When was it appropriate to
introduce the idea of a child's need for special education or

to expect more involvement in child-care decisions from a mother? How could we avoid missing these opportunities for growth? We risked falling into a pattern of intervention because that intervention had worked in the past. We did not want to be like a mother who might very appropriately cuddle her 3-month-old baby for long periods but be "stuck" repeating this behavior when the child was 6 months old and needed time to explore on the floor. With this hypothetical baby, the Infant Center staff would have known enough about child development and reading cues to know when to put the baby down. Working with adults whose lines of development were less clear, we also needed to read cues, to be sensitive to what mothers were doing and saying. For example, at one point, a few of our mothers seemed capable of getting to the Center on their own, without Center-supplied transportation. The staff had first to recognize this capacity and then to suggest this step toward autonomy to the mothers, offering sufficient support to get them on their way. The mothers had to be taught how to use the Metro (subway) system and had to be walked through the system. In this case, the hunches of the staff proved correct and several of these mothers continued to be able to use the system alone.

Reacting to the participant on the basis of our own feelings and reactions was another problem staff sought to avoid. Periodically, individual staff members would become so distressed over a child's condition that they would feel the mother was "hopeless" and that removal from the mother offered the only hope for the child. Discussion often revealed that staff came to this conclusion because of our own current feelings toward the mother rather than on the basis of the child's condition. Anger toward a participant might surface when staff felt unappreciated; not wanting to deal with that mother, staff might tend to slacken its heroic efforts to get her into the Center. Sometimes feelings of being manipulated would arise, or fatigue might lead to a staff decision that it was not so important that this participant be picked up and given a ride to the doctor. The challenge in all of these situations was to be sensitive to what it was that we were feeling so that we would be sure to respond rather than react.

The human issue of competition among team members for recognition, for control, and for credit also needed to be faced. Team discussions and supervision were essential to understanding these processes.

In order to assure that we were responding to participants in a way that promoted growth, we used team meetings, case conferences, supervision, and informal discussions to evaluate constantly our intervention through the Infant Center, just as we monitored other aspects of the intervention. We monitored our feelings about the work closely, because our feelings provided the best cues as to what was really going on and what processes underlay the problems we saw.

The most concrete yet most crucial challenge involved transportation, without which participants would not have been able to attend the program. We learned that it would be better to set up infant centers which serve smaller geographic areas. The cost and coordination would be attenuated. Mothers would be more able to attend on their own and would have the opportunity to develop outside friendships. We also learned how crucial auxiliary staff were by observing our drivers. It was only with our third and last driver that we were able to find a sensitive individual who was able to listen politely and tactfully suggest that a mother take up pressing issues with her clinician. Like other staff members, the driver needed to be integrated into the clinical team and offered supervision.

Conclusion

The Infant Center demonstrated the need for a developmentally based environment which can support infants and mothers together during the crucial early years of development. The joint focus, essential in order to strengthen the mother–baby dyad, required expertise and sensitivity in understanding the challenges each may face. While the milieu approach provided the context for growth, and supported the staff in their efforts, it was the definition of specific objectives in each case that organized the effort and work to be done. For example, some mothers were helped to understand and respond to the tactile sensitivities their children were born with before they concluded their distressed infants were rejecting them. Others were first pursued, then nurtured until they were able to woo their infants with a more stable attachment. At later stages, the object was for children involved to learn symbolic play and pretend behavior. Whenever possible the work involved mothers and babies together in a day treatment context which responded to multiple needs through the variety of interventions described earlier. At other times the work needed to proceed independently in order to provide the infants with crucial developmental experiences until their mothers were more emotionally available and able to respond to their needs. We learned that both approaches were necessary. Therapeutic programs need individualized and milieu treatment capacities in order to design and implement interventions which respond to the unique constellation of needs, readiness, functioning, and capacities of mother, of infant, and of the dyad and family in interaction.

3

A Case of Double Vulnerability for Mother and Child: Louise and Robbie

Delise Williams, A.C.S.W.
Robert A. Nover, M.D.
Joan M. Castellan, M.A.
Stanley I. Greenspan, M.D.
Alicia F. Lieberman, Ph.D.

AN INTRODUCTORY NOTE TO THE CASE STUDIES: It is hoped the case studies in this chapter and Chapters 4, 5, and 6 will convey the clinical challenges and insights that emerged from this unique opportunity to work with infants and their families. Chapter 7 will describe how aspects of the mother's complex clinical experiences can in part also be quantified. Part II will reflect the ongoing process of conceptualization and systematization that challenging indepth clinical experience both stimulates and demands.

The case of Louise and her son, Robbie, illustrates our work with a mother–infant dyad in which each of the partners had difficulty in establishing early regulatory and attachment patterns.

Louise's chaotic childhood had been marked by psychological rejection, physical abuse, and abandonment. She had a long history of psychiatric disturbance as well; records from a mental health clinic she contacted a few years before starting our program show a diagnosis of "schizoid personality with paranoid features and periodic transient psychotic states." Louise's initial hostility and intense suspiciousness toward the CIDP clinician, combined with the disorganization of her thinking under stress and her difficulties with impulse control, made us consider very seriously the possibility that this diagnosis was indeed accurate. This worrisome picture was compounded by Louise's overt ambivalence, first toward the pregnancy and later toward her child; her feeling that the baby's birth interfered with her working; and her warnings to us that she became depressed when she stayed at home. In the context of Louise's own experience of rejection and abuse as a child, these feelings conveyed to us Louise's fears that she could not nurture her child, and her fears became our concerns.

When Louise's son, Robbie, was born, it became apparent that this baby would make difficult demands even on a mother with unconflicted nurturing resources. Robbie became easily irritable and was not readily consoled. Though cuddly, he had tense musculature and many tremors and startles. He showed poor orientation to face and voice, and gaze aversion was noted as early as the first month of life. Given Louise's suspiciousness and already intense ambivalence, we feared that she would interpret her baby's behavior as a rejection of her as a mother, setting up a dangerous cycle in which the mother's pain and anger led to rejection and withdrawal from the child.

This appraisal led us to formulate a treatment plan in which a clinician engaged in psychotherapy with the mother and an infant specialist worked directly with the child. We adopted this strategy because we thought that Louise's own primitive neediness was of such proportions that she would feel rejected and jealous whenever a single therapist's attention would be addressed to the baby instead of to herself.

Such feelings could lead our intervention to a hopeless stale-mate. Having her "very own" therapist helped the mother feel value in her own right, and gradually, though unsteadily, she was able to become the clinician's ally on behalf of her child. At the same time, the infant specialist provided the baby with specially designed patterns of care and relaxed in-terpersonal experiences, when his mother could not yet do so to facilitate his coping capacities and help him achieve early developmental milestones. Later, treatment included daily intervention implemented at our infant center in order to provide Robbie with some stability in the midst of a chaotic and unpredictable environment to which he was very reactive. The treatment plan evolved into complex and multiple inter-ventions with Louise and with her child over the next few years.

The First Stage of Treatment: The Prenatal Period

Louise expressed interest in participating in our program in the course of a prenatal health clinic visit when one of our clinicians was recruiting participants by describing our work with parents and infants to the expectant mothers in the wait-ing room. An attractive black woman in her midtwenties, Louise was then five months pregnant with her second child; she already had a 6-year-old daughter, Terry. Louise stressed that her primary motive in joining the program was to help us in our stated goal of better understanding parent–infant relationships; she did not mention any personal problems or concerns. However, the clinician became alerted to the pos-sible presence of personal difficulties by Louise's overall flat affect, suspicious glances, evasiveness in responding to ques-tions, fleeting eye contact (as part of an overall lack of relat-edness), halting, yet sarcastic speech, and the tension expressed by her fidgeting hands. It also became quickly apparent that when she spoke about herself and her life, Louise's thinking was tangential with occasional loose associations, often con-nected to the theme of being "hurt."

Louise lived with her daughter in a small apartment. She was single, but had dated the same man, the father of both Terry and the unborn baby, for eight years. However, this relationship was a chaotic one, involving stormy fights followed by threats on both sides to end the relationship. Louise could not rely on her boyfriend, "Big Robert," for either financial or emotional support.

The beginnings of our intervention were unpromising. In spite of her professed interest in helping us with our study, Louise failed to keep appointment after appointment. She was either not at home or refused to open the door to our clinician, even though clear noises betrayed her presence to the therapist standing at the door. Yet Louise phoned regularly, often calling after a missed appointment to request yet another one (which she also failed to keep). We interpreted this pattern as an expression of her simultaneous wish for contact and fear of closeness. She seemed to be testing whether the clinician's interest in her would persist in spite of her elusiveness.

The clinician's interest did persist, and long phone conversation eventually gave way to appointments that were kept. It is possible that as the time of delivery approached, Louise felt more keenly the need for support, since she "permitted" more regular appointments and several home visits about six weeks before her due date.

In these initial sessions Louise was frequently angry and withdrawn. She sullenly refused to speak about the pregnancy and showed no joyous anticipation of the new baby. She curtly commented that she "would be glad when the baby came" because she could then go back to work. Louise was most communicative when expressing anger, which she did in long tirades. She raged against the baby's father for his failure to provide financial and emotional support. She complained bitterly about the indifference of social workers who were supposed to help her with Aid to Families with Dependent Children (AFDC) and food stamps, but failed to do so. She expressed indignation at being deemed ineligible for unemployment compensation because she quit work due to her advanced pregnancy. While anger often seemed justified under the circumstances, Louise gave the impression of struggling with barely controlled rage. At these times the clinician sympathized with the intensity of Louise's feelings and also tried to provide boundaries for her anger by making suggestions about concrete steps that Louise could take to feel more in control of the situation. The anger often turned toward the clinician, and Louise spent many sessions either challenging every question the clinician asked or sullenly refusing to be engaged in conversation. For example, Louise would tell the clinician that her questions did not make sense, say she did not feel like talking, or limit herself to responding with desultory movements of the hands or head when the clinician tried to engage her in conversation. She often smoked for long periods of time while staring into space, as if the clinician was not there.

Occasionally, however, Louise was touchingly open about her feelings of warmth toward the clinician. At these times she said openly that it felt good to have such a reliable visitor. She also showed a surprising ability to respond to the clinician's cautious attempts at emotional exploration. While Louise herself chose to discuss concrete things and shied away from talking about feelings, she could be very receptive to the clinician's efforts to discuss a current incident in the light of the feelings it had elicited. At one point, Louise even volunteered that the events in her past had "made it hard to trust people now, and that is bad." She also expressed her wish to understand her feelings better. Although rare, these moments of reflection gave us hope that Louise could be helped to have better control over the feelings that so troubled her.

The main task of these prenatal sessions was to establish a stable availability to the clinician and to facilitate the development of a therapeutic relationship that would eventually permit emotional exploration. The clinician patiently absorbed Louise's outbursts of anger, encouraged the verbal expression of disappointment and anger felt toward her, and kept appearing, week after week, regardless of Louise's behavior. The surprise and relief often present in Louise's face when she saw the clinician at the door were an eloquent testimony to the repeated absence of such sustained relationships in Louise's past.

Slowly, Louise began to confide the many fears that plagued her daily life. She was afraid of using the bus system because she considered buses to be dangerous places where she could be attacked. As a result she was severely limited in her freedom of movement. The darkness terrified her because she thought that dangerous figures lurked there, and she needed a night light to fall asleep. Even with this light, however, she did not sleep well because she saw unidentified "things" moving in her room, and she feared being attacked and hurt by them. These experiences, Louise feared, signified that she was "crazy." The clinician assured Louise that she could deal with these fears. Perhaps most importantly, the clinician kept coming to visit, a concrete proof for Louise that this emerging information would not scare the clinician away.

Louise's History: The Past

As Louise began to trust the clinician, she became more willing to unveil her past. The following story unfolded in the course of many sessions.

Louise was conceived out of wedlock by her mother, who was married to a Filipino man by whom she had six children. Louise's father was black, and she looked very different from her half-siblings, who resembled their Filipino father. Louise was 6 months old when her mother gave her up to friends, the Burtons, who lived nearby. Louise continued to see her mother, stepfather, and half-siblings, and could not understand as a child why she did not live with them. Remembering this period of her life, she said poignantly: "Imagine how it feels never to feel that you belong."

As she recounted it, Louise's life with the Burtons was polarized between the warmth and affection she received from Mr. Burton and the harsh physical punishment meted out by his wife. Louise described Mrs. Burton as a "sneaky, cruel" woman who was "all smiles" when Mr. Burton was present but who mistreated Louise when they were alone, hitting her almost daily with a belt or a stick for what Louise felt to be no apparent reason. Mr. Burton, on the other hand, was loving and accepting in Louise's eyes. Louise thought of him as her real father, and referred to him as such.

Mrs. Burton died of cancer when Louise was 8 years old, and Mr. Burton's sister and her husband came to live with them soon afterwards. Louise remembers feeling relief at Mrs. Burton's death, particularly because her new "mother," Mrs. Carson, was an affectionate woman who treated Louise with tenderness. Unfortunately, Mrs. Carson died one year before Louise's present pregnancy. Louise's eyes still filled with tears when she spoke of this "aunt" who was, in her words, the only loving "mother" she had known.

Louise did not reveal much about her adolescence, but some scattered remarks indicated that this time was characterized by feelings of isolation, by a sense of being different and unwanted, and by pronounced suspiciousness of people's motives when somebody approached her or was friendly to her.

It is not surprising, then, that there were many concerns, both on Louise's part and on our own, about her capacity to nurture her baby. Louise's biological mother had given her up without explanation but continued to live nearby with her other children, keeping open for Louise the question of why she had been singled out as the sole unwanted child. Rejection by her biological mother had been followed by abuse at the hands of her surrogate mother, Mrs. Burton, thus confirming Louise's fears that she was "no good" and deserved abandonment and punishment. We can surmise that Louise felt not only relief but also guilt at Mrs. Burton's death. Because of her anger at her surrogate mother she most probably wished secretly for her surrogate mother's demise and, when it occurred, it might well have compounded her perception of herself as an evil child. Not until she was 8 years old did Louise have what she considered to be a "mother." By this time the early images of the mother as a rejecting and punishing figure and of herself as a "bad" child had been intensely experienced. And even this "loving mother" had abandoned Louise through death.

Louise was 20 years old when her biological mother revealed to her that she was the product of an adulterous relationship. Louise had already suspected this because she looked so different from her siblings. Nevertheless, she reported feeling "numbed" by the news, shocked yet "unable to feel anything." It is noteworthy that only a few months later Louise contacted a mental health clinic for the first time. The clinic records show that she was experiencing "growing agitation, irritability, sleeping difficulties, and suspiciousness." It is then that the diagnosis of schizoid personality with paranoid features was made. Louise had sporadic contacts with the clinic's social worker for the following two years and was given a variety of medications—Mellaril, Thorazine, Sinequan. She said that she could "turn the symptoms on or off" depending on whether or not she wanted to obtain medication. (Thorazine she considered a sedative; Sinequan helped her to "keep going.") It is unclear to what extent this was objectively true and to what extent it was a perception that helped Louise feel more in control of her symptoms than she really was.

Mrs. Carson, the loving "aunt," died a year later, when Louise was 21. Two months after her death, Louise asked to be admitted to a mental hospital because she felt confused by her sudden mood swings and her difficulty in controlling her emotions. She was hospitalized for two weeks and signed herself out because she thought that "being doped out" was not the way she would solve her problems. Upon her release she

got herself a job and, by her account, had been working steadily as a clerk. (Later on there was reason to doubt Louise's
account of her steady employment. During the treatment
period she changed jobs often, and there was some indication
that she had been engaged in prostitution after her hospital
discharge.)

This was Louise's story as we could reconstruct it from
many sessions. There are still many gaps in our knowledge,
and we remain uncertain about many details. Louise's thought
was often disorganized, particularly when she was experiencing strong emotion, and the same episode was often described
differently on different occasions. There were aspects of her
life that she only hinted at: having been a prostitute, having
used drugs and alcohol, repeated suicidal attempts "which did
not work," and venereal disease during her pregnancy with
Robbie. Careful probing by the clinician only produced suspicion and withdrawal, and the decision was made to work
with the facts that Louise could tell us rather than risk shaking
her precarious psychic balance by attempting to elicit premature revelations.

During the prenatal phase, another important aspect of
the clinician's work consisted of helping Louise pay attention
to her nutritional state and avail herself of prenatal medical
care. This was no easy task, given Louise's despondence, her
repeated statements that she wished the pregnancy were over
so that she could resume her previous life, and the complete
absence of any statements that might indicate a beginning
attachment to her unborn baby. Louise seemed to deal with
the pregnancy by letting it unfold without her cooperation:
she saw no point in improving her diet (which was deficient
in calcium and protein) and in keeping regular medical appointments. She answered the clinician's urgings by saying
that she never had much appetite, that she felt well enough,
and that there was no need to see a doctor. Only gradually
did she begin to drink more milk and to keep her prenatal
appointments more regularly.

Over the course of four months' contact with Louise, the clinician was able to engage and establish regular contacts through her persistent reaching-out efforts. The missed appointments and closed door gave way to face-to-face contacts following a period during which long phone conversations, safer and more in Louise's control, formed a bridge to the clinician. The willingness of the clinician to come to Louise on her terms and accept whatever she could offer, was crucial to the development of this regularity. But this too was no easy task for the clinician, who often sat hour after hour with Louise as they both smoked through tense and distant periods of silence. At other times, the clinician absorbed Louise's rage while attempting to provide boundaries and empathize with Louise's feelings through calls and home visits.

Until Louise's relationship patterns became more evident, the clinician often felt intrusive and uncertain about what she should be doing, what would happen next, and what her involvement meant to Louise. Although we could not know this at the time, the early pattern of coming to Louise on her terms came to characterize the work with her. Needless to say, Louise's preference to be in control, while respected, raised many intense feelings of frustration, annoyance, and rejection in the clinician.

Toward the end of her pregnancy, Louise also agreed to meet with the infant specialist, who taught her breathing and relaxation techniques. This contact provided another way of getting to know Louise while helping her prepare for the birth.

Robbie's Birth and the Prenatal Period: Infant, Mother, and Their Interaction

Robbie was born approximately four months after Louise joined the program. She had been meeting the clinician in regular weekly sessions for about six weeks. The delivery presented no medical complications. Robbie was of average weight and length and his Apgar scores were 8/9. The Parmelee Obstetrical Index, postnatal indices, and Ponderal Index were in the normal range.

However, there were some worrisome features. Robbie had difficulty orienting to his environment. Although cuddly, he could not be readily consoled, and his own attempts at self-quieting (for example, by taking his hand to his mouth) were mostly unsuccessful. There were tremors and startles, although not enough to be a cause of worry in their own right. These observations were documented in the Brazelton Neonatal Behavioral Assessment Scale.

Observation one month later was not encouraging. In the 30-day administration of the Brazelton Scale, which was part of CIDP's regular evaluation procedure, Robbie showed even more difficulty orienting than before—a reversal from the expectation that a baby would orient better with increased maturity. We began to observe gaze aversion. Robbie had also become less cuddly and his muscles had become tense and stiff. It was quite clear that this baby's initial interactions with his environment had not helped him and might even have caused some deterioration in the areas of concern observed at birth. Such relative deterioration in an infant's capacity for regulation and interest in the world (homeostasis) we have found, in most cases, to be an extremely worrisome early sign.

The interaction between Robbie and his mother was certainly far from optimal, and we hypothesized that this was an important factor in Robbie's failure to become more organized in his behavior. Louise had difficulty looking at her baby and showed little spontaneous pleasure in him. She held Robbie in a wooden posture, with a striking lack of accommodation to the baby's body. These features of the interaction seemed to be mirrored in Robbie's behavior. Louise could not look at her son, and Robbie showed gaze aversion and poor orientation; Louise held the baby rigidly, without helping him to mold, and Robbie was now less cuddly and showed tense musculature. Our forebodings about a vicious cycle of interaction between this mother and baby were beginning to be confirmed. The low intensity of Louise's affect, which we had experienced earlier, could now be seen in relation to her child.

It should be noted that since the clinician was out of town at the time of Robbie's birth, the therapeutic intervention had been disrupted. Although the infant specialist remained involved through calls and home visits, Louise only turned to her with requests for concrete supplies such as diapers and milk.

When the clinician returned after two weeks of absence, Louise greeted her joyfully and displayed her new slim figure proudly, obviously enjoying the clinician's warm praise for herself and her baby. As the session progressed, however, she spoke bitterly of her anger at Big Robert, who had not visited her at the hospital and had not bothered to meet his new son until the baby was about 10 days old. Anger and hurt alternated as Louise spoke of her intention to break up with Big Robert. As the clinician listened, Louise went on to speak about her fear that she was becoming too dependent on Big Robert. She would no longer allow herself to remain dependent, Louise announced; being dependent only meant that "you felt let down when people betrayed you." The clinician suggested that perhaps Louise also felt she was becoming too dependent on the clinician. Louise agreed. Was she afraid the clinician would let her down? the clinician asked. Louise hesitated before confessing to this fear, but she hotly denied the clinician's further suggestion that she felt betrayed by the clinician's absence when Robbie was born. In spite of this denial, Louise's feelings were apparent, and she acted them out in the ensuing sessions. She reverted to her old pattern of not being at home or of not answering the door when the clinician arrived for scheduled appointments.

The theme of rejection thus became the focus of the intervention. When there was no answer, the clinician returned until she had succeeded in meeting Louise for that

week. During these sessions, Louise limited herself to re-
questing concrete services; she particularly wanted help in
persuading the local social services agency that she needed
housing assistance. While providing this assistance, the clinician also brought up at different times the issue of separation
and the feelings people experienced when others go away.
Louise tended to ignore these remarks or protest angrily that
she did not know what the clinician was talking about. However, in her characteristic way of conveying feelings through
actions, she began to be at home whenever an appointment
had been scheduled.

In the following few months, Louise showed increasing
willingness to talk about her fears of rejection, illustrated by
her repeated statements that she feared being abandoned by
people she felt dependent on, such as Big Robert and the
clinician. In the meantime, it became clear through our observations that these fears were only too graphically expressed
in Louise's relationship to Robbie. She spoke of her conviction
that the baby would leave her and would prefer to live with
his father when he grew up.

There was much documentation in our records of Louise's
own rejection of Robbie and of the impairment of such basic
functions as her ability to comfort Robbie; to help him regulate
his pattern of feeding, sleeping, and elimination; and to make
herself and the world interesting to Robbie, as the first step
in the development of intimacy. On one home visit, for example, the baby was observed drinking voraciously a watery
fluid which turned out to be whole milk diluted with an equal
amount of water. Louise seemed unconcerned, although she
knew that this was insufficient nutrition for the baby. On other
occasions, Robbie was left to scream for 25 minutes or so while
Louise behaved as if nothing were happening. Louise once
commented that sometimes she liked to see him cry; he made
such funny faces that they made her laugh. In addition, his
diapers were often drenched and smelled sour. Louise often
stared at the baby with icy detachment while smoking a cig-

arette. Her need to nurture herself even took precedence over the baby's feeding: on one occasion she tried rather clumsily to balance a cigarette, the baby, and a baby bottle all at the same time, and she casually accepted the infant specialist's offer to take over the feeding while she finished smoking.

At the same time, there were moments when Louise held Robbie tenderly, nuzzled his neck, responded promptly to his cues and spoke of her love for him. There were also times when the baby looked clean, well fed, and carefully dressed. Unfortunately, these moments did not seem to be sustained enough to promote Robbie's development, and the baby was deteriorating visibly. Although he continued to grow physically, he did not look at his mother even when she attempted to engage him. Instead, he seemed to lock his gaze on objects that were at a distance. When held, he was in constant motion and pushed away from the person holding him, whether it was his mother, the clinician, or the infant specialist. He was fretful and seemed unable to get in a comfortable position; the muscles in his arms and legs were often stiff.

Robbie's avoidance of human relationships, even when "wooed," the constant movement, and the tense musculature were quite worrisome, since under optimal circumstances we would expect a 4-month-old to be relaxed, socially alert, gleefully involved with his primary caregiver, and beginning to have organized reciprocal exchanges involving a range of affects and multiple sensomotor schemas.

We gradually learned that the periods of greatest detachment between Louise and her baby occurred when Louise was feeling rejected or exploited by Big Robert, the baby's father. Louise remarked that she did not like the baby's name and wished she had named him differently, but that she would "get killed" by Big Robert if she now decided to change the name. However, she emphatically denied a connection between her feelings toward Big Robert and her ability to take care of Robbie, and the clinician had to postpone exploration of this very sensitive, yet central issue.

Robbie's Father

Most of what we knew about Big Robert was through Louise. Through her, we had invited him to participate in our program, but this invitation did not receive a response. Since Louise herself was lukewarm about his involvement in the program and about the possibility of couples' therapy, it is possible that she never transmitted our invitation to him.

Unlike many of the husbands and boyfriends of mothers in our program, Big Robbie had no objection to Louise's participation. He neither encouraged nor discouraged her involvement. When he happened to be present during the clinician's house visits, he was quite charming toward her.

Big Robert was a "con artist." He had a booth where he sold jewelry, but there were some indications that he was also a pimp. He represented himself as a congenial, friendly, easygoing man. He made many promises that he did not keep: to Louise, he promised money, food, help with the children. To Robbie, as he grew up, he promised a dog, a bicycle, toys. Sometimes he did not keep the promises, sometimes he kept them months later. However, he consistently came through when Louise was able to ask him for something directly.

As a father, Big Robert was equally unpredictable. He was proud of having a son and was friendly and warm to Little Robbie when the clinician was present. However, he visited once a week at most, although he occasionally took the baby to his own mother's house. When his relations with Louise were stormy, he visited even less. Thus, Little Robbie had, at best, an uneven relationship with his father.

Developmental Intervention with Robbie: The First Four Months

Our ongoing observations of Louise's interaction with Robbie made it clear that her painstaking efforts to cope with her fear of rejection and with her view of the world (including especially, Big Robert and presumably Robbie as well) as malevolent and dangerous were not yet being translated into a greater ability to integrate her positive and negative feelings about her baby and to provide him with more consistently nurturing experiences. Therefore, we began direct intervention with Robbie during home visits.

The infant specialist identified three main areas where Robbie's development was worrisome: his gaze aversion and overall rejection of the human world; the paucity of his vocalizations; and his stiff, tense body posture. Since these behaviors were being influenced by the unpredictable and often abrupt quality of Robbie's interpersonal experiences, the infant specialist decided to address them in the context of warm and playful interactive games. The intervention consisted of specific exercises developed with the goal of encouraging Robbie to engage in eye contact, to vocalize, to relax his muscles, to integrate across his sensory modes and his sensory and motor capacities. But these exercises were never mechanical: they were unobtrusively built into affectionate social exchanges with the baby. The goal of these procedures was to encourage both internal regulation and interest in the world, specifically in the interaction with human partners, in order to build the bases for human attachments.

In attempting to reverse Robbie's persistent gaze aversion, the infant specialist noticed that Robbie avoided eye contact with people but gazed at inanimate objects for long periods of time. Capitalizing on this observation, she drew a face on a piece of paper that she wore as a mask, enticing Robbie to follow with his eyes as she slowly moved her head up and down in front of him. After several such trials, she lowered the mask and greeted Robbie with eye contact, smiling and talking to him softly. At first Robbie shifted his eyes. Slowly he was able to sustain this eye contact, but only for a few seconds. As this game took place again and again, in various forms—such as playing peekaboo in different contexts with different masks—and with much animation, Robbie started responding more and more and appeared to find the human face, first interesting, and, we surmise, eventually pleasurable. It is worth noting that the affective expression of the infant specialist could only gradually be enlarged as initially Robbie found all human, affective exchange frightening.

Vocalization was encouraged in the most natural of ways: by making simple but playful sounds until Robbie could imitate them, then elaborating on the original sound by adding new vowels and consonants. Talking to the baby, greeting him on arrival, and saying good-bye on departure, relating to him as a person who was a legitimate interlocutor for social speech, were also part of the total approach in working with Robbie.

Finally, the stiff muscle tone, uncomfortable posture, lack of cuddliness, and difficulty with cross-sensory and sensory motor integration were addressed through interactive floor games. These games involved, for example, playfully rolling Robbie on the floor, rhythmic extension and flexion of arms and legs while singing or making rhythmic sounds, playing pat-a-cake and other games which encouraged midline reach, playing "This Little Pig Went to Market," and similar games which enticed Robbie to reach for his toes and to play with his feet. The infant specialist's attractive toys were placed slightly out of reach to encourage reaching and holding, which seemed to be restricted by the tightness of the muscles of the shoulder girdle and upper arm, and by the fact that Robbie's hands tended to fist when reaching or when bringing the hands to midline. When Robbie seemed tired after all these activities, he was encouraged to cuddle in the arms of the infant specialist, who sang a lullaby until his body relaxed and/or he fell asleep. Swaddling was successfully used when disorganized body motion interfered with Robbie's ability to fall asleep.

It is apparent from the above description that the intervention with Robbie was neither mechanistic nor focused on global stimulation *per se*. Rather, the infant specialist identified the worrisome aspects of Robbie's functioning and addressed those areas by drawing selectively from the timeless repertoire of songs and games used by generations of adults to delight their children and encourage their development. Yet here these selections were part of an organized program of care with the goal of facilitating related self-regulation and integration; alert, sensible interest in the world; and the formation of a pleasurable human relationship.

Every attempt was made to encourage Louise to participate in these sessions and to take over the infant specialist's role. Louise was told about the reason for the intervention and was asked to participate in the games that she found most congenial. Her reaction varied according to her mood. Sometimes she looked on with much interest and herself entered in the games, getting very involved and showing considerable ability to be in tune with Robbie. At other times she withdrew with a sullen expression and stared through the window. Occasionally she made a comment which reflected some longing to have had in her own childhood the kind of attention Robbie was now receiving. In general, the infant specialist felt that Louise either did not attempt to use these patterns when she was alone with Robbie or found it very difficult to do so. The infant specialist felt worried and discouraged, recognizing Louise was limited in what she could offer her son.

In addition to these types of intervention, Robbie's health and nutritional status were carefully monitored. Many hours were spent serving as advocates for Louise and her baby to ensure that they received food from the special supplemental food program for women, infants, and children (WIC). (Louise had been found ineligible when she applied herself, in spite of the clear absence of a steady source of iron in Robbie's diet—one of the criteria for eligibility.) Appointments were made at the Well-Baby Clinic, and Louise and Robbie were driven there either by the clinician or the infant specialist if no other form of transportation was available. When there was concern about Robbie's persistent hoarseness and the guttural sounds he made, an ear, nose, and throat appointment was made. Fortunately, the results were negative.

Four-month Developmental Assessment

A formal developmental assessment was conducted when Robbie was 4 months old. The semistructured play session showed that, in spite of Louise's ambivalence toward her baby during this session, she tried hard (too hard perhaps) to engage him in interaction. She stood him on her lap and held him very close to her face, speaking to him at very close range. Robbie responded consistently by averting his gaze, and Louise seemed at a loss to improvise other ways of attracting his attention. Her affect became flatter, and she stopped talking and smiling to Robbie, simply allowing him to move rhythmically up and down on her lap while she looked at him silently. While there was an overall absence of synchrony between mother and child, they succeeded, for a brief moment (which we took as an early sign of progress), in being attuned to each other in one lovely sequence when Robbie nuzzled his mother and she immediately nuzzled him back. Nevertheless, at this time, there was a striking contrast between Robbie's response to his mother and to the examiner: he was far more responsive to the examiner's attempts to engage him in play even though he did not know her.

Observations made during the administration of the Bayley Scales showed that Robbie's tactile exploration was entirely limited to mouthing. There were jerky arm and shoulder motions which led to flapping of the arms as he attempted to reach out for a toy. Robbie seemed to be constantly in motion, grunting, stretching, twisting, and flailing his arms and legs whether he was held or not. Vocalizations were very scarce. Robbie's Mental Development Index (MDI) was in the low average range for his age.

Ensuing Intervention: The Therapeutic Infant Center

The results of this assessment confirmed observations made during home visits in the previous weeks, and warranted an intensification of the work with Robbie. However, we were faced with a dilemma. Our ability to work with the baby was curtailed not only by Louise's unwillingness but also by more realistic circumstances. Louise had long working hours. She held two part-time jobs, one of which, in a fast food restaurant, often kept her away until 3:00 A.M. In the mornings, Louise had to get up at 7:00 A.M. to get her daughter Terry ready for school. Although she was often too tired even to attempt to interact with Robbie, she felt she needed the jobs both in order to fend off depression (she said repeatedly that she became depressed when she stayed at home with the children) and because the jobs gave her the sense of personal dignity and self-worth that she longed for. At the same time, the baby-sitting situation for Robbie was often chaotic, with many different adults taking over Robbie's care as needed. His baby-sitters were sometimes unfamiliar women who took care of many children in their homes; at other times they were Louise's acquaintances, recruited often at the last minute when other arrangements had fallen through.

Given this situation, and with Louise's agreement, we implemented a plan in which Robbie spent at least part of the week in our therapeutic Infant Center, where the infant specialist could work with him. In addition, Robbie was cared for by the Infant Center supervisor and assistant, who further reinforced the work of the infant specialist. There were additional consistent adults available to Robbie. Louise sometimes met Robbie at the Infant Center at the end of her working day; she spent some time familiarizing herself with the way Robbie had spent the day, chatting with other mothers and with the infant room staff, and watching what for her were novel ways of interacting with children. This plan remained in effect throughout the treatment, with modifications and interruptions that mirrored the changes in Louise's life. When no baby-sitter was available, for example, Robbie might spend the whole day in the Center, for weeks at a time. When Louise was angry at her clinician, on the other hand, she might "take revenge" by not bringing Robbie in for a few days. During a few months during which he had a baby-sitter who was most nurturing and responsive about helping Robbie to vocalize, reach for objects, and so on, we ourselves reduced the number of hours that Robbie spent at the Center. Thus, Robbie's attendance in the Infant Center, while a central feature of the intervention, was tailored to the changing characteristics of the baby's environment and was also affected, sometimes against our wishes, by the upheavals in Louise's personal life and therapeutic treatment. The time at the Center afforded daily opportunities to engage Robbie in patterns of care, described earlier, which were aimed at helping him relax his muscles, integrate cross-sensory and sensory motor experience, and learn to find satisfaction in human relationships and an ever-increasing range of affective experience.

When Robbie was older, we added a new stage-specific task to his program, consistent with the period of somato-psychological differentiation he was entering. We worked on reading his changing affective signals, providing purposeful (causal) feedback, and facilitating his persistence.

Louise's Treatment: Ongoing Course

Beginning by being available only intermittently, Louise was gradually able to engage in more regular contacts with her clinician. Emotional upheavals still tended, however, to result in Louise avoiding contact and testing her clinician's interest.

In this context Louise began to speak at length about her conflicts with her psychological father, Mr. Burton, the only father she ever knew. Louise lived in a little, cramped annex of her father's apartment. She felt that she needed him and she relied on Mr. Burton for concrete help with many of her needs, particularly for transportation when she needed to go shopping and for last-minute errands when she discovered that she was short of milk or diapers for Robbie. But there were also violent verbal and physical battles between Mr. Burton and Louise, and frequent quarrels during which Louise threatened to leave and Mr. Burton threatened to put her out. The ostensible cause of many of these quarrels was Big Robert; Mr. Burton disliked Louise's boyfriend and did not want to see him in the house. As she described these quarrels, Louise began to acknowledge intense feelings of anger, which she attributed to Mr. Burton's failure to protect her from the mistreatment inflicted on her by his wife when Louise was growing up. Later in the treatment, Louise also remembered a scene with clear sexual overtones—waking up at night to find Mr. Burton silently standing by her bed (the remainder of the scene being "vague").

The clinician believed that Louise's living arrangements encouraged an atmosphere of conflict and violence detrimental to Louise and to her children. For this reason, she supported Louise's initially half-hearted plans to leave her father's house and to find an apartment for herself and her children.

When Louise finally announced her decision to move from her father's apartment, she asked the clinician for help. Not having adequate financial resources, Louise needed assistance from the local housing agency, and she dreaded dealing with this bureaucracy on her own. The clinician agreed to help, and she and Louise went "apartment hunting" together. This experience had many therapeutic implications. It provided a first-hand opportunity to observe how Louise interacted with authority, as represented by personnel of the housing agency, and how she coped with frustration and disappointment as the hoped for "ideal" apartment proved difficult to find. On a different level, it meant that the clinician took on a dual role as a supportive, nurturing figure, and as auxiliary ego. As a nurturing figure, she became a source of emotional as well as concrete support; as an auxiliary ego, she performed for Louise those functions which Louise could not perform on her own without a crippling fear of disintegration. For example, the clinician helped Louise to cope with the anguish she felt in finding that none of the apartments she visited was appropriate by empathizing with Louise's fear and anxiety and reassuring her that an acceptable place would eventually be found. Finally, the success of finding a desirable and affordable apartment gave Louise a sense of achievement that helped to cement the ties with the clinician.

In the many hours spent driving from one apartment to another, the car provided a physical proximity that seemed to promote intimacy without arousing fear. This setting proved to be conducive to revelations: it was in the car, talking about the pressures of finding a place to live, that Louise talked about her wish to be taken care of and her simultaneous fear of getting too close. She illustrated this wish for closeness and her fear of it by speaking of the many men in her past who had given her money, food, clothes, and how she had used them until "they got too close" and then she abruptly told them to leave. Exploration of what "getting close" meant led to Louise's fear that people would become too involved in her "business." She was reluctant to elaborate on the meaning of the term, but we gradually learned that it referred to secrets involving her psychiatric hospitalization, her involvement in prostitution, and her episode of venereal disease while pregnant with Robbie. We surmised that, in turn, these events represented for Louise proof of the dreaded "badness" that she attributed to herself, her deep shame about aspects of her feelings and wishes, and her fear that discovery of these feelings and wishes by others would lead once again to abandonment and rejection. While able to some extent to explore these feelings and withstand the pain they elicited, Louise often turned to intense rage as her most potent defense. When this occurred, the sessions became litanies of anecdotes about the many people who had betrayed her and let her down. Comments, classifications, and attempts at occasional interpretations often led, not to self-observation, but to further illustration of how others had wronged her. On these occasions, Louise often repeated a simple sentence, as if trying to encase in words, and thus get control of, her disorganizing and diffuse anger.

The clinician's approach was to help Louise in her attempts to provide boundaries for her intense feelings. The therapeutic interventions were at first very structured and aimed at clarifying and providing labels for feelings: what did Louise feel, toward whom, for what reasons? As Louise herself became more skillful in these tasks, the clinician could move on to show Louise the common element between the different situations that elicited certain feelings. In this way, Louise became aware of her tendency to set up chaotic external circumstances to escape inner turmoil; of how she used rage as a defense against feelings of helplessness; and of how she tried to fend off rejection by rejecting first. Ultimately, Louise also became aware of her deeply rooted perception of herself as "evil." The prevailing theme in the sessions was a constant reworking of her fear that people would leave her once she exposed her "worst" side, that is, her rage.

This process was filled with turmoil, and there were many moments when we wondered whether Louise had learned more about herself than she could tolerate. However, as this material emerged and the implications for the therapeutic relationship were explored (i.e., Louise was afraid of hurting her clinician or being rejected by her), the bonds with the clinician invariably seemed to become more stable and the therapeutic relationship seemed to provide the support Louise needed for emerging self-exploration and the identification of patterns in her life.

At the same time, an unexpected avenue emerged to explore painful feelings: the soap operas, which Louise watched avidly, often leaving the TV on during a session. Louise identified with different characters and the clinician used this opportunity both to explore Louise's feelings at a greater depth and to show her that those feelings were experienced by many people and were not a sign that Louise was "strange," "crazy," or "stupid," adjectives that recurred in Louise's attempts to clarify to herself who she was. This was a most reassuring experience for Louise, given her early feelings that something had to be unusually wrong with her to prompt others to reject and abuse her as a child. She showed her emerging hope for herself by reflecting that a particularly villainous soap opera character had become virtuous, and saying, with some wonder, that "after all, people can change."

Throughout the treatment, we monitored Louise's relationship with Robbie as an important criterion for her progress, and we noted a marked parallel between Louise's relationship with the clinician and her ability to care for and interact with her son. As Louise began to make use of the clinician as a partner in a stable relationship, as well as an auxiliary ego and a figure for identification, she became more reflective and started to discuss her plans for the future instead of implementing them impulsively. Also, interestingly, she began to imitate the clinician's style of dress. With regard to Robbie, Louise began to express genuine pleasure in his relatedness to herself and to others. She also showed more patience and tenderness toward the baby, responded to him far more promptly and more effectively when he was distressed, cuddled him more often, and spoke to him playfully and lovingly for longer periods of time. We believe that her emerging capacity to establish an enduring relationship to the clinician was directly responsible for her progress in nurturing and interacting with Robbie in a more consistent manner.

A Crisis Ensues

This relatively steady course was interrupted by a series of psychological upheavals involving loss and Louise's sense that she was being rejected by the clinician. First, Louise invited the clinician to Thanksgiving dinner. She declined, and addressed Louise's disappointment and her wish for closeness with her. Louise seemed to accept this clarification.

As the Christmas season approached, the themes of longing and loss became more poignant. Louise revealed her fantasy that this was a time for idyllic family gatherings and simultaneously started speaking with much sadness of her dear "aunt's" death, which had occurred the previous December. She said that she wished this woman were still alive so that they could spend Christmas together as a family. With tears in her eyes she said that Mrs. Carson had been her "true mother" because she had been loving and had not punished her physically.

With these revelations, Louise experienced a reemergence of her old pattern of suspiciousness (approaching delusional proportions) and of the tendency to act out intolerable feelings. Once again she became guarded, sullen, and withdrawn. She threatened to give up Robbie ("You will find him on your doorstep," she said to the clinician) and implied that she would kill herself by saying that she was tired of living. The clinician attempted to address the negative feeling by speaking to Louise's disappointment that she had declined to spend Christmas with her, just as she had earlier declined the Thanksgiving invitation. Louise denied having any negative feelings. Instead, she persistently focused on her anger at her boyfriend and on her need for cheaper housing.

However, Louise did not withdraw completely: she continued keeping her appointments, and she came to the 8-month developmental assessment that had been set up for Robbie. Yet Louise's behavior toward her son depicted graphically how deeply Robbie was still enmeshed in her psychic conflicts. One example stood out: On meeting Robbie after a long working day away from him, Louise stared at her child from a distance as if seething with rage, brushing aside Robbie's hand when he persistently tried to make contact with her.

The clinician attempted to show Louise how her feelings of anger spilled over in her relationship to Robbie, but all such attempts were met by a blank stare and by a refusal to discuss any negative feelings Louise might have toward her baby. All attempts to link Louise's needs to those of her baby were met with a sullen silence. As if to underscore her determination to escape from the feelings that threatened to overwhelm her, Louise moved abruptly from her cozy apartment to a noisy, overcrowded and confusing household, where there were six other adults and children. We had to resign ourselves to observing Louise postpone the integration of her own and her baby's needs. Since this mother could not integrate her own needs with those of her baby, we had to continue a course of intervention that addressed both the infant's and the mother's needs separately at times.

This process led to frustrations and tensions within the intervention team. The clinician was sometimes blamed for not making Louise more responsive and cooperative with the efforts being made for her son. The anger at Louise and the clinician would intensify further when Louise would keep Robbie home from the Infant Center, reacting to a crisis, a negative feeling toward the clinician, or some expectation of the infant team. At such times Louise made it clear that Robbie would attend on her terms or not at all. Meanwhile, the clinician struggled to maintain her alliance with Louise, frequently having to defend both herself and Louise to the staff. Some staff were so angry at both Louise and her clinician that they began withdrawing from their role (e.g., not following up telephone calls). The separate tracks of intervention persisted.

Robbie at 8 Months: The Developmental Assessment and Ensuing Intervention

The most positive finding from the assessment was Robbie's ability to engage in organized and sustained social interactions. Far from averting his gaze from his mother, as he had done in the past, he now sought her out by looking and smiling at her, cooing to her, and grabbing her hand. Louise repeatedly ignored these overtures, and Robbie's persistence in the face of his mother's aloofness was truly touching. He finally was able to elicit some responses from Louise after a great many attempts to gain her attention.

In contrast with her child's impressive persistence in his

social approaches, Louise repeatedly attempted to withdraw from him. For example, she responded to Robbie's offer of a toy by saying, "Oh, you don't want to play."

With the exception of language, the major areas of Robbie's cognitive and sensorimotor function showed adequate development: Robbie was proficient in eye–hand coordination, fine and gross motor development, and in social interaction. Vocalizations had increased noticeably but were still somewhat below age level. A concern that emerged from this assessment was the appearance of perseverative banging of objects, which had a drive-discharge quality and which interfered with manipulation and visual exploration. This, we felt, was another manifestation of the constant body movement we had observed at 4 months.

Robbie's overall performance on the Bayley Scales placed him at the appropriate age level. It seemed, then, that our intensive intervention with Robbie was paying off in the form of a decline in gaze aversion and an increase in his capacity for regulation, for affective interest in his mother and others, and for the new phase-specific tasks of organized reciprocal interaction and social initiative. We attributed this progress not only to his mother's overall progress and our own direct efforts with Robbie, but also to the daily routine that Robbie's current baby-sitter had established for him with the help of the infant specialist. This woman, remarkably warm and affectionate, welcomed the infant specialist's suggestions about games and exercises that would help Robbie to channel his constant and diffused body motion and to relax his tense muscles. (The introduction of a "jolly jumper" proved extremely successful in channeling the body motion in constructive ways.) Thus, there was continuity between the caregiving Robbie received during the day and his activities at the Infant Center, which he now attended only one morning a week. The infant specialist visited at the baby-sitter's a second morning a week to provide guidance and to monitor Robbie's progress.

The positive influence of this environment on Robbie's behavior was illustrated by a fortuitous observation. While visiting the baby-sitter's home one morning when Robbie was 6 months old, the infant specialist noticed that Robbie seemed unusually relaxed and well-coordinated. She soon learned that Louise had not picked her baby up the night before, and that Robbie had thus spent almost two continuous days with the baby-sitter. This observation stressed for us the extent to which Robbie's constitutional traits were accentuated by Louise's often abrupt and unpredictable caregiving. The implications of this observation were troublesome, however: we would not expect a baby in the second half of his first year to be soothed by an overnight separation from his mother, nor would we expect a caring mother to fail to pick up her child. It was apparent that Louise was not yet a primary attachment figure for Robbie and that although he sought her out and responded preferentially to her, she had not yet become for him a uniquely valued love object.

Robbie's vulnerability to environmental stress was again illustrated when he was 9 months old and Louise, as indicated above, moved abruptly to an overcrowded apartment. Robbie now became one more member of a noisy and confused household. Instead of being the only child in the home of a caring and affectionate baby-sitter, Robbie was now cared for by whoever was available. The infant specialist soon noticed that Robbie's activity level had increased and his attention span had declined. He was less available for play, and his vocalizations decreased.

As a result, the decision was made to increase Robbie's visits to the Infant Center once more. He was picked up four mornings a week at his home, brought into the Center for four to six hours, and then returned to his home. Robbie quickly developed affectionate relationships with the Center staff, including the infant room supervisor and the homemaker. They, the support staff, and other mothers and children became the friendly and responsive figures in Robbie's life on a daily basis. Robbie became particularly attached to Judy, the staff member who picked Robbie up and returned him home. On one occasion, when Judy brought Robbie home, the adult who was to take over his care until Louise came back was lying on a couch with his back to Judy and to the baby. He mumbled to Judy that she should leave Robbie on the couch. When Judy did so, Robbie started to cry—he did not want to be left. Even when Louise was present, Robbie left eagerly when Judy came to pick him up. These observations continued to tell us that Louise was still unable to establish a unique relationship with her son.

Treatment Continues: The Ensuing Four Months

Louise's flight to a chaotic household was addressed by the clinician as an attempt to escape from the feelings of disorganization that Louise experienced when she perceived that others abandoned or rejected her. While persistently denying this connection, Louise implicitly confirmed it by beginning to talk about her inability to sustain long-term relationships. She then spontaneously began to speak about her 6-year-old daughter, Terry. She said that she sometimes treated Terry in ways that she did not like—ignoring her, scolding her, or responding abruptly to the child's approaches. Louise showed much awareness of Terry's need for her mother as a source of support, and regretted her own inability to be consistently available to her daughter.

Louise's account made it apparent that she saw herself in her daughter in many ways. Terry had been raised by Louise's "aunt," Mrs. Carson, for her first 3 years of life, and had only afterwards started to live with her mother. While Louise herself had made the decision not to raise her daughter from birth, she saw this arrangement as a form of maternal deprivation for Terry similar to what Louise herself had endured. Mrs. Carson's subsequent death had deprived both Louise and Terry of a beloved figure, and Louise responded to Terry's experience of the loss more like a sibling going through an identical process than like a mother who nurtures her child through a painful experience.

Louise's fear of loss was clearly experienced in relation to Terry. She spoke regretfully about Terry's becoming an adult and leaving her. She sometimes longed to be nurtured by her daughter and expected Terry to anticipate her needs and to respond to them—something that Terry often did. Although this child had in many ways taken on a nurturing role toward her mother, her solicitude seemed often achieved at the cost of her ability to experience negative feelings toward Louise. Nevertheless in spite of her dependence on Terry and the occasional reversal of mother–daughter roles, Louise was often able to empathize with Terry's needs and to respond appropriately to her.

Dealing with Loss and Separation

It was important for our understanding of Louise to listen to her discussion of this relevant thematic area, so central to her life, in the context of the less conflicted relationship she had with her daughter. As Louise began to acknowledge her reliance on Terry's "understanding" of her and her fear that one day the child would leave her to pursue her own life, the clinician pointed out how Louise often retreated from her children in order to forestall the future pain of separation. This contrasted with Louise's earlier complaint that she spent "too much time" with her children. Subsequently, Louise began spending more time with both Terry and Robbie. At the same time, Louise spoke directly about her fondness for the clinician and requested some sort of guarantee that their relationship would continue. The clinician responded to this important event by empathizing with Louise's desire for re-assurance against loss now that she was taking the risk of showing love and concern for her children. Here again, a further sedimentation of her relation to the clinician allowed Louise to become more psychologically available to her children. This process suggested a new level of development for

Louise, in which experiencing and expressing warmth was not too frightening and fears of loss could be verbalized, rather than avoided through preemptive actions. Her therapeutic relationship now appeared to be at a new level, where a stable affective relationship could allow exploration even of painful feelings such as loss, an exploration which in turn bolstered the relationship's stability, affective tie, and depth.

Robbie's 12-Month Developmental Assessment

The important therapeutic progress of the preceding months was vividly reflected in Robbie's 12-month developmental assessment. Louise began the semistructured play episode by speaking to Robbie on the play telephone: "Robbie, are you there?" We interpreted this opening as a symbolic reenactment of Louise's conflicts: a reaching out coupled with fear that he might not be there to respond. But Robbie was very much there. He turned to his mother repeatedly, giving her toys, returning to her for a hug after exploring at a distance from her. Louise was able to allow her son to explore and also to welcome him back when he returned to her. This interactive pattern showed clearly the beginnings of an organized pattern of reciprocal behavior as well as initiative and originality.

During the administration of the Bayley Scales, Robbie's performance remained at age level, as it had in the past. He was also observed to engage in relating schemas, a behavior characteristic of the early second year of life. For example, he used the yellow stick to stir in a cup, showing an understanding of the potential use of objects that was somewhat above age level.

Louise's Treatment: 12–18 Months after Robbie's Birth

In the following six months, Louise began spontaneously to link her ever-chaotic relationship with her boyfriend to her feelings toward her biological mother. She noted a resemblance between her sense of unsatisfied need for Big Robert and her own mother's perennial unavailability. Louise was not yet ready to see how she often triggered Big Robert's prolonged absences through her own paroxysms of rage, in which she yelled at him in a desperate reenactment of her anger at being alone and her fear of closeness. Louise could only see herself as the victim of abandonment, not as an active participant in her internal drama; she also could not perceive herself as someone who made others feel abandoned. This difficulty in seeing herself in an active role greatly interfered with her ability to empathize with Robbie's feelings when she was unavailable to him. In spite of this limitation, the ongoing therapeutic work enabled Louise for the first time to see herself consistently as a mother responsible for the well-being of her children. She spoke now of how her actions would affect her children, and she started to become aware of her children's everyday experiences and her impact on them. She commented, for example, that Terry might find it difficult to start playing with white children now that they were living for the first time in an integrated neighborhood; she also anticipated Robbie's discomfort on being left with a new and unfamiliar baby-sitter. Although she seemed most free in her perceptions of Terry, Louise's new insights were reliably extended also to Robbie. We felt that Louise had moved from absorption in herself to awareness of and empathy for Terry, a child she perceived as similar to herself. She was now moving toward also encompassing Robbie, a child more closely identified with her boyfriend in her expanding awareness. The importance of Louise's ability to see a causal relationship between her feelings and her son's, her actions and his, constituted, we believe, an important milestone in her own development and in her ability to support Robbie's emerging capacities for more organized, purposeful behavior and feelings.

Robbie's Infant Room Experience: 12–18 Months

As Robbie entered the second year of life he faced the task of adapting to the new environment of the Infant Center, but this time the environment he encountered was a stable and responsive one. During the first few months at the Center, his mood varied from day to day, ranging from happy and responsive to irritable and distressed. Sometimes Robbie was so hungry he would eat three or four portions at a meal yet still appear unsatisfied. Similarly, he could hardly tolerate anyone else's eating or sharing anything he wanted. Robbie was very eager to play with all the toys and especially enjoyed sand and water play, but he sometimes had difficulty modulating his energy, becoming overstimulated and disorganized. Each morning the staff awaited his arrival to see if he would be "mellow and even," "upset and withdrawn," or "fighting and aggressive." By the time lunch was over everyone was ready for his nap.

But Robbie could not always let go and separate. At first he cried going to his cot, during his sleep, and each time he awoke. Long sessions of rocking did help him go to sleep and became a very special time for close and tender holding. Very slowly, Robbie established a comforting routine, but this was such a difficult task that every entry in his daily log for more than a year referred to how he got down for a nap. His attachment to Judy also intensified and he frequently sought her out for hugs and holding.

Robbie's days were filled with activities, other children, and consistent adults. Within two months his language began to develop, he attention span increased, and his frustration tolerance improved. He sustained his activities more easily outdoors but also liked puzzles, blocks, and records inside. When the Infant Center acquired a rocking boat, he spent long periods "rowing" back and forth. At 18 months, however, his mood was still variable and it was difficult to decipher why. Robbie would suddenly erupt, throwing things everywhere, and could not be consoled. Sometimes just washing his hands or face triggered an outburst. Pleasure and aggression seemed to intensify simultaneously. For example, Robbie would go up and down the slide, clapping and laughing, but minutes later would be grabbing toys, pulling hair, and attacking other children. Although temper tantrums increased Robbie also became more responsive to limits and to the staff, interacting in a gleeful fashion that was rewarding to them.

The lack of contact with Louise continued to frustrate the staff. This frustration intensified when Robbie came to the Center without breakfast, was sick, or had no one to meet him when we brought him home. Louise moved to train Robbie and stopped his bottle without forewarning or even notifying staff. Yet at other times she agreed to send Robbie to the Center with a favorite toy, understanding that this would help him make transitions and separate.

Robbie responded and reacted to internal and external stimuli we were unaware of, which triggered impulses we could not understand. Although the Infant Center became a critical island of stability and structure for Robbie, we realized that his development was going to take a longer and rockier course than we had envisioned. Despite everything, however, his relationship with Louise developed. In the first half of his second year, Robbie moved from indifference to indicating clearly that his mother was a special person in his life.

Robbie at 18 Months: Developmental Assessment

The 18-month evaluation gave evidence of Robbie's steady improvement. In the semistructured session, mother and son engaged in a pattern of reciprocal interaction that reflected warm, complex, organized interaction, assertiveness and originality. The interaction showed a forthright attempt to deal with earlier and ongoing conflicts adaptively, as part of an organized play sequence. One sequence, a chase game in which Robbie and Louise alternately chased each other, stands out in particular. In the videotaped sequence, Louise chases Robbie, who runs away; she catches him and both laugh. Louise then teases Robbie by going out of the room and closing the door, but knocks on the door to signal to him that she is still there (i.e., this is only a "pretend" desertion);

Robbie attempts to open the door and Louise returns. Louise then leaves again. This time, Robbie does not seek her out but hides instead, under the table. Louise then seeks *him* out, but he flails at her. Louise laughs and hugs him.

We interpreted this sequence as a symbolic enacting of the central conflict in this mother: the theme of abandonment and rejection. Whereas earlier in the treatment, the theme was acted out through all too real threats of abandonment, the persisting conflict was now expressed through a richly organized symbolic game. We also saw an integration, rather than a splitting off of the theme of rejection. In earlier sessions, we often saw unsuccessful one-sided attempts on the part of one partner to woo the other; now Louise and Robbie were literally taking turns at wooing and chasing each other. Finally, we saw a new ability on the part of each partner to recover from rejection and to reach out to the other, instead of withdrawing or becoming disorganized. The ability now to deal with this central conflict at an emerging symbolic level was truly impressive.

A Departure from the Treatment: The Clinician Becomes Pregnant

The course of treatment was altered by the announcement of the clinician's pregnancy when Robbie was 18 months old. Louise's immediate response was to say, "That's why you've been acting so evil." Although she did not elaborate, we interpreted this statement to ourselves as an expression of Louise's fantasies that the clinician, like herself, might have indulged in some "acting out."

The subsequent course of treatment showed that Louise continued to identify with the clinician, but chose caring and nurturance as areas of resemblance. She began to use the sessions to talk about Robbie and to ask for advice about child-rearing issues such as how to respond to Robbie's tantrums. This was a new development, which signaled a growing ability to integrate Robbie's needs with her own, since in the past

Louise had been very reluctant to "share" her therapy time with Robbie by departing from her personal concerns and speaking about her child. It also suggested that her clinician's pregnancy made her a "mother" in reality and this now seemed to allow Louise to be a "mother" too, permitting her to extend the range of her development.

Louise also showed a new, active interest in how Robbie spent his day at the Infant Center; she even suggested that she and the Center staff both keep a baby diary to keep one another informed of the day-to-day happenings in Robbie's routine. This suggestion was, of course, carried out, and was an important indication to the staff that Louise had finally acknowledged their efforts and concerns. Louise was now more tolerant of Robbie when he spilled food or drink or interrupted her conversation—behaviors that had triggered angry yelling at the child in the past. In anticipation of the clinician's absence, Louise started cultivating a relationship with the Infant Center staff and became more involved with and receptive to the infant specialist. This was a sign of a new ability to reach out, instead of fleeing and becoming disorganized at the prospect of conflicts or loss.

As the clinician's pregnancy progressed, Louise became more solicitous toward her, assuring her that she would have an easy delivery. She also began to speak with longing about the clinician's absence and her eventual return. She repeatedly shortened her own estimation of the clinician's absence, reducing it from an original "eight months" to "two or three weeks." Gradually, Louise became aware that these behaviors signaled her sadness at the clinician's anticipated absence and her wish for a speedy reunion. She then became more introspective and started writing down how she felt about loneliness and what friendship meant to her. She also wrote down her "good points" and those aspects of herself that she wished to change. She showed these writings to the clinician and discussed them with her. Louise seemed to be preparing herself for the clinician's absence, trying to organize herself and to set down in writing the insights she had gained in order not to lose them. While an indication of Louise's need to become very concrete to fend off disorganization under stress, this behavior showed also Louise's tremendous progress, since she retained throughout this difficult time an adaptive, realistically optimistic approach to her situation. At no time did she relapse into the angry outbursts and sudden physical and psychological withdrawal that characterized her previous responses to separation or perceived rejection.

When the clinician gave birth, Louise sent a gift for the new baby. She phoned the clinician every week, and these conversations had a regular pattern: Louise asked the clinician how she and the baby were, kept the topic focused on them rather than on herself, and invariably ended the conversation after an appropriate period of time. She waved off the clinician's inquiries about her own life, explaining that the clinician should use those weeks for herself and her baby only. Although this was a poignant example of Louise's enduring need for a concrete presence, it also showed her new ability to take the initiative in establishing contact and in subordinating her own needs to those of somebody else.

During the clinician's absence, Louise kept on good terms with the Infant Center staff and with the infant specialist, whom she saw often. This relationship centered on Robbie and touched only peripherally on Louise's personal life, but its existence kept alive her ties to our program. Her involvement as a "nice and good" person as opposed to a provocative person was needed with the unavailability of her clinician to represent her.

The Clinician Returns

When the clinician returned, the previous therapeutic relationship was reestablished with minimal difficulty. Louise acknowledged doubting whether the clinician would ever return, but seemed realistic in accepting this possibility and spoke of the need to learn how to rely on herself when others could not be there. The pattern of introspective self-examination continued, and many troubled early memories emerged: her surrogate mother locking her in a dark basement, and on another occasion chasing her with a metal hanger; waking up at night to find her father standing next to her bed, looking at her. (This man had been previously described only as warm and protective. Although no sexual abuse seems to have occurred, Louise was obviously aware from an early age of the sexual connotations in her relationship with him.) As she vividly recalled these memories, Louise no longer had "hallucinations" at night, slept better, and seldom used a night light. She had learned to use introspection instead of acting out as a means of protecting herself from disorganization. For example, when she could not sleep, she now thought about the feelings that might be troubling her until she arrived at some understanding that was comforting for her. She found a new freedom of movement: not only could she now use the buses, but she also learned to drive and bought a car, which she used both for necessities and to take her children on family outings.

As Louise began a relationship with a new man, who seemed supportive and nonexploitative, her relationship with Big Robert waned, much to his overt displeasure.

As our program ended, Louise continued to make strides in her relationship with her children. She no longer withdrew from Robbie to the extent she used to. Although she continued to have trouble controlling her anger, she now acknowledged that the source of the difficulty was in herself rather than in her children and actively attempted to find ways of protecting her children from her anger.

Conclusions

In retrospect, the evolving therapeutic relationship with Louise can be understood in terms of a series of stages. Louise's initial distrust and partial avoidance gave way, through the clinician's persistent home visits, to an acceptance of concrete assistance: "milk and diapers." At this second stage, the clinician's untiring availability and her willingness to withstand Louise's demonstrations of rage laid the foundation for the third level of the therapeutic relationship: Louise's acceptance of human relations and her verbalization of her fear of loss. As this fear was acknowledged, Louise gave the therapist implicit permission to address feelings. This made it possible to explore Louise's pattern of alternating availability and withdrawal, and a fourth stage was achieved: the elaboration of Louise's patterns of action in human relationships. This marked the beginning of the fifth stage, characterized by Louise's beginning capacity for self-observation, as evident in her acknowledgment, during the car rides searching for an apartment, that she wished to be taken care of but also was afraid that people would then "mind her business." As this theme was elaborated, a sixth stage emerged: the capacity to recall emotional experiences from the past with full affect, as she relived the pain she experienced when Mrs. Carson died and linked her present unsatisfying relationship to Big Robert with her own mother's perennial unavailability. Finally, Louise was able to live through an experience of loss in the present (the clinician's pregnancy leave) without regression to earlier stages of functioning. This marked the seventh and latest stage in the therapeutic relationship.

It is noteworthy that the early stages in the therapeutic progress were not mirrored by a steady improvement in Louise's relationship with Robbie. While we saw "islands" of improved functioning, it was only in the sixth stage, when she began to reexperience past emotional experiences with vivid affect, that Louise's empathy, first for Terry, and later for Robbie, first began to emerge and to manifest itself in a consistently better integration of her own and her children's needs. Until this integration began to occur, Robbie's developmental progress was facilitated by the infant specialist's direct work with him which, as described, aimed at helping Robbie strengthen his coping capacities. He was able to deal with his mother's mood changes and to be available to help his mother stabilize her gains. (Had Robbie been unavailable, mother may easily have regressed.)

This case, then, illustrates the fruitfulness of a dual intervention in cases of "double vulnerability," where both mother and infant show signs of being at risk for the development of homeostasis and human attachment. In such cases, intervention with only one member of the dyad, mother or child, would be therapeutically incomplete because the persisting vulnerability of the untreated member of the dyad would continue to exert a negative influence on the mother–infant relationship, thus maintaining the potential for disturbances in the dyad's negotiation of the developmental issues facing it.

4

Two Infants, a Family, and the Service System: The Lake Family

Delise Williams, A.C.S.W.
Robert A. Nover, M.D.
Delois B. Ward, M.A.
Joan M. Castellan, M.A.
Stanley I. Greenspan, M.D.
Alicia F. Lieberman, Ph.D.

Our involvement with the Lake family consisted of providing a supportive network to protect the safety and foster the development of two young infants, born in rapid succession to a white, 34-year-old mother with chronic paranoid schizophrenia and a white, 40-year-old deaf father with a borderline personality structure. Due to the pervasiveness and intensity of disturbance in this family, which also included four older children, the physical well-being of each infant and successful negotiation of the earliest developmental tasks were at risk. We were concerned about whether Betty, the first infant in the program, and Phil, born less than a year later, would be properly fed and whether they would achieve homeostasis and form human attachments. Indeed, Betty's pronounced decline in weight, caused by the family's inability to care for her, led to foster care placement during the second month of life. Fortunately, our ability to organize a coordinated interagency collaboration was instrumental in preventing the perpetuation of foster care placement for Betty and later for her younger brother Phil. With the integrated support of community agencies, this schizophrenic mother and borderline father, previously isolated from their families and the general community, were ultimately able to provide adequate care for their two infants.

Background

Mrs. Lake was referred to us by the state mental hospital where she had been hospitalized for the previous four months. She was five months pregnant with her fifth child. Her older children were 16, 14, 12, and 3 years old at the time of referral. Family life was chaotic, marred by physical violence between Mr. Lake and his 14-year-old son and among the children themselves. The two older children were chronic truants and behaved disruptively when they did attend school; they were also involved with the police concerning trespassing, vandalism, and disturbing the peace. Although her psychiatric hospitalization at the time of referral was Mrs. Lake's first, her symptoms were long-standing. She hinted that she had been hearing voices since she was 18 years old, and for the last five years she had had delusions of seeing people she had worked with appear suddenly on the television to warn her of possible harm to herself or her family unless she was careful. She had been diagnosed at the mental hospital as a paranoid schizophrenic, with most of the paranoid ideation consisting of "harm" about to befall the family.

When Mrs. Lake was not under immediate financial or emotional stress, she appeared to be an intelligent woman with the capacity to relate to others in a warm, empathic manner. She had a sarcastic sense of humor, which she did not hesitate to use in teasing her husband or the program staff. She could focus more easily on a troublesome personal issue if the clinician introduced it in a humorous manner. For example, soon after the birth of her fifth child, Mrs. Lake started talking about how much she liked babies. Someone from the staff responded by saying, "Just what you need, Bianca, one more." Mrs. Lake laughed and then talked with some feeling about how much easier it was to care for a baby if one did not have four other children to worry about. When another staff member, in a more direct fashion, attempted to raise the issue of having babies, Mrs. Lake became defensive and inconsistent and denied ever saying she liked babies, adding at the same time that all she wanted was more money to have more babies. When Mrs. Lake became angry, her ability to present herself as the victim of a misunderstanding or abuse by an agency evoked in those working with her a strong desire to protect her. Yet working with Mrs. Lake was often frustrating because of her tangential thinking and loose associations, which often made it impossible to get a direct answer to a request for information or to pursue a topic in an organized fashion.

Mr. Lake, who had been deaf since age 15 as a result of streptomycin therapy following intestinal surgery and a resulting colostomy, had been married to his wife for 17 years at the time of referral to our program. They met at a college where he was a student and she was working in the cafeteria. Although well-educated and intelligent, Mr. Lake had a sporadic work history. At the time of referral, he had not held a steady job for seven years. Mr. Lake's life had been characterized by much physical pain, poor medical care, and many operations. Because he did not take care of his medical needs until they reached crisis proportions and hospitalization became necessary, his own medical problems triggered many family crises.

Although Mr. Lake attempted to present himself to the outside community as the only emotionally healthy member of his family, in fact he appeared isolated, superficially related, and distant. He spoke openly of his wife's "craziness" and berated his three older children for their disobedience. Although he presented himself as struggling unsuccessfully to get others to help the family, he seemed concerned almost exclusively with his own needs and showed little empathy for his wife and children. While his deafness may have played a part in his tendency to isolate himself, Mr. Lake reported having been a "loner" and having had difficulty communicating with people even prior to the onset of his deafness. It is revealing that although he could use sign language, he made virtually no effort to teach it to either his wife or children, who had only a rudimentary knowledge of sign language and used it only sporadically.

Mr. Lake attempted to relieve himself of any responsibility for his family's financial or emotional problems by blaming them all on his wife's psychiatric problems. He did not make use of services which would have enabled him to work. For example, he complained that he could not work unless his medical problems were alleviated. When we made arrangements for appropriate medical treatment, he refused care on the grounds that he was needed at home, when in reality, he spent very little time at home because he volunteered his services to the Community Deaf Club and was there day and night. On another occasion he stated that he did not want to work in the city but could not find living quarters in the country, where he wanted to work. When Mrs. Lake suggested that her mother, who lived in the country, could help them look for housing, he replied that he could not get work because he was too sick. His coping style generated anger in the staff, who felt thwarted in their attempts to help the family by Mr. Lake's ever-shifting but recurrent objections.

Although his deafness made it difficult to evaluate Mr. Lake's mental status formally, his shallow relationships, chronic pattern of unemployment despite education and intelligence, and fluctuating grasp of reality suggested a borderline personality organization.

The relationship between Mr. and Mrs. Lake was characterized by collusion in perpetuating each other's fluctuating grasp of reality. Mr. Lake, for example, helped to maintain his wife's delusions by making no effort to encourage or supervise her intake of psychotropic medication. Mrs. Lake contributed to her husband's withdrawal by not answering his questions and by failing to use sign language to relay comments or information being conveyed verbally by others.

Initial Contacts with the Family

When we first met Mrs. Lake she had been committed to a state mental hospital by her husband, ostensibly because of an increase in delusions that her family was in immediate "danger." She was not interested in our program because she thought that she already knew enough about babies and that a program such as ours would only be helpful to new mothers. However, Mrs. Lake agreed to participate because she thought that her release from the hospital was contingent on her participation. In spite of having been told clearly and repeatedly that her participation was voluntary, her suspicion and feelings of being coerced persisted. We wondered if this was a mechanism that enabled her to participate without feeling guilty about needing help in spite of her already having raised four children.

Although she refused to speak about her childhood or to answer factual questions about her current situation, Mrs. Lake spoke openly about a voice inside her head that controlled her actions and told her who was threatening her family's welfare. She said that "the Voice" told her to watch television, and when she did, her former work supervisor appeared on the screen and warned her that her family was in danger. When the supervisor denied being on television, Mrs. Lake interpreted this to mean that "something was being hidden from her." "The Voice" told Mrs. Lake who was friend and who was foe. "The Voice" also had the power to make Mrs. Lake's children curse and talk back to her. Whenever a family member was aggressive or troublesome, Mrs. Lake attributed this behavior to "the Voice's" control. Mrs. Lake also spoke about the "Portuguese," whom she perceived as trying to get her job and to deprive her family of food. She was convinced these enemies would follow her no matter where she moved: although "the Portuguese" first appeared to her when she was living in Connecticut, she felt they had followed her to Maryland, where they continued to torment her.

The stories of persecution were often difficult to understand and remember because Mrs. Lake's associations were highly personalized and hard to follow. Many times, after listening to Mrs. Lake for as long as 40 minutes and thinking that she had followed her train of thought, the clinician found that she could not remember anything that Mrs. Lake had said. In the early sessions the clinician often found herself feeling confused. However, as she listened closely, she realized that underlying Mrs. Lake's long, rambling discourse was a desire to be protected. Mrs. Lake's feeling that no one was meeting this need generated fear of impending danger to herself and her family. Once the clinician understood this basic theme, she became able to follow Mrs. Lake's conversation much more easily and to respond coherently in a supportive and empathic manner. For example, one of our concerns at this time was Mrs. Lake's lack of interest in talking about pregnancy and in planning for the delivery and for her baby's concrete needs. Mrs. Lake began to speak about "the Voice" whenever the clinician brought up these topics. We interpreted this response as an indication of Mrs. Lake's feelings that she lacked protection and support, and the clinician sought to enlist the family's help in an effort to alleviate these feelings. Although this attempt to build a supportive framework was limited by Mrs. Lake's refusal to meet with us more than once a week, we were able to arrange home and office visits and to see Mrs. Lake by herself, with her husband, and with the entire family.

During the family sessions, the clinician quickly learned that the children addressed their father not directly but only through their mother, and that Mrs. Lake often kept information from her husband by not signing him a message or by not answering his questions. This meant the information available to Mr. Lake, including all the communications between Mr. Lake and his children, were subject to distortion by Mrs. Lake's delusions. Mr. Lake could never know whether the incidents reported by his wife had occurred as she stated them or were being distorted by her. Because Mrs. Lake attributed the children's misbehavior to the power of "the Voice," the children were seldom held accountable for their actions. Mrs. Lake also undermined her husband's half-hearted attempts to discipline the children because she felt that any display of anger was dangerous and part of the master plan to destroy the family.

Even under optimal conditions, our efforts to engage Mr. Lake would have been hampered by the need to write everything we wanted to convey to him. His manifest lack of interest only made matters worse. He spent the sessions complaining about his wife and children. He refused to talk to Mrs. Lake. When the clinician attempted to help the children speak directly to their father, he refused to pay attention. None of the family members wanted to focus on the baby about to be born.

A Complementary Approach: Building a Network of Community Agencies

It quickly became apparent that the Lake family could not be relied upon to give Mrs. Lake adequate emotional and practical support in time for the baby's arrival. Therefore, to our efforts with the family we added active attempts to establish a working relationship and a network of communications among the community agencies already involved with the Lakes. There were several such agencies. At the time we started working with the family, they were already known to the Health Department through the school and the well-baby clinic. In addition, Protective Services had been called by the school authorities three years earlier, when Mrs. Lake had

come to the school to discuss a problem with one of the older
children and commented in passing that her baby, Andrew,
then 9 months old, was covered with bruises. The school
authorities could see no bruises, but they insightfully interpreted Mrs. Lake's remark as an expression of concern and
an appeal for help in warding off potential abuse, and made
the referral to Protective Services.

Although these agencies had been involved long before
our contact with the Lake family, when we started our intervention there was some pressure to have us assume responsibility for their care. In fact, shortly after we first contacted
Mrs. Lake at the State mental hospital she was precipitously
released. Just as our team members often felt overwhelmed
by Mrs. Lake's incoherence and by the chaos in the family,
so did the other agencies. In addition, their staffs did not have
the support system that was available to our workers: most
notably, a team approach, supervision, and periodic case conferences to review progress in work. It was understandable,
then, that other agencies were anxious to withdraw from the
family interaction and let someone else take over.

Recognizing that this multifactor high-risk family would
tax the resources of any one agency, we felt it was important
that all the agencies continue their involvement, but do so in
a more structured and coordinated manner with specific areas
of responsibility assigned to each agency. Our efforts to coordinate services and improve lines of communications among
agencies were hampered by the fact that for ten weeks Mrs.
Lake refused to sign release forms giving us permission to
contact other agencies. She also appeared to play off one
agency against the other by distorting what each agency was
doing for her. For example, she spoke to us of her persecution
by the Department of Social Services (DSS), while she (as we
discovered later) complained to DSS of the pressures we were
putting on her. The clinician dealt with this impasse by encouraging Mrs. Lake to verbalize her fears about interagency
communication and by patiently reassuring her that the in-

formation would be used to make things as good as possible for her baby, her family, and herself. But many weeks elapsed without our being able to coordinate or even to comprehend fully the efforts of the community agencies on behalf of the family.

Focus on the Unborn Baby: The Infant Specialist's Involvement

The infant specialist was introduced to Mrs. Lake in the seventh month of her pregnancy, after she had been meeting with the clinician for six weeks. The infant specialist's role was to provide an additional source of emotional support and developmental guidance with specific focus on the unborn infant, and to monitor and maintain Mrs. Lake's health and physical well-being. The infant specialist saw Mrs. Lake six times prior to the delivery, twice at home and four times at the office. Mrs. Lake's loose, tangential thinking during these visits made it difficult to obtain even elementary information. For example, when the infant specialist inquired about her last prenatal visit, Mrs. Lake began a long, involved account of a shopping trip with her sister, purchases made for the children, and baby-sitting arrangements for the toddler during her outing. During a subsequent visit the infant specialist learned that Mrs. Lake's sister took her to the hospital clinic for prenatal visits and began to understand Mrs. Lake's earlier associations.

There are no records of prenatal care during the first two trimesters of the pregnancy, which included Mrs. Lake's psychiatric hospitalization. She did attend the prenatal clinic at the local hospital after her discharge and prior to delivery. It was unclear whether she continued taking her usual psychotropic medication (Mellaril) during her pregnancy. The hospital records said she did; Mrs. Lake said she did not. We were inclined to believe Mrs. Lake, who said she discontinued medication during pregnancies for fear that the drug would harm her baby. Furthermore, we learned over time that even when she was not pregnant her intake of medication was at best erratic.

Mrs. Lake did not take particularly good care of herself during this pregnancy. She smoked a pack of cigarettes a day, drank coffee continually, and by her own report ate very poorly, although it was nearly impossible to get concrete answers to our questions about the details of her diet. She never was seen to eat when the clinician or infant specialist was present.

The infant specialist structured her visits to help Mrs. Lake organize her thinking and prepare for labor and delivery through prenatal exercises designed to relieve whatever physical discomfort she was currently experiencing. This structure seemed to facilitate the development of rapport and Mrs. Lake quickly began to relate to her infant specialist as a nurse and to use her as a medical authority. Yet Mrs. Lake did little to follow through on the infant specialist's advice to cut down on her intake of cigarettes and coffee and to improve her eating habits and diet.

Mrs. Lake Delivers

Mrs. Lake was never sure of her exact due date and did not contact us when she delivered. When her clinician returned from a two-week vacation, Mrs. Lake seemed pleased to see her and said that she had something to show her. Mrs. Lake then left the room and returned with a covered bundle, which turned out to be her newborn infant, Betty, then 5 days old. The primary clinician in no way suspected that this bundle was an infant because Mrs. Lake carried it as if it were a package. But she was much more coherent and oriented during this visit than in the past and said she was pleased to have had a girl.

The labor and delivery had been uncomplicated: a spontaneous vaginal delivery with local anesthesia after 10 hours of labor. Betty was small for gestational age (37 weeks); her birth weight was 6 pounds 3¼ ounces, her length 19 inches,

and her head circumference 33 centimeters. Apgar scores
were 9/9. Her hospitalization as a newborn was uneventful,
and mother and child were discharged three days after delivery.

The Brazelton Neonatal Assessment Scale was first administered when Betty was 7 days old and had been at home
for four days. Betty was a sallow, scrawny infant who seemed
to prefer to be left alone so that she could continue sleeping.
When stimulation was used to bring her to an alert state, she
responded with irritability at being disturbed and attempted
to return to sleep. Her alert states were very brief, and she
needed a great deal of stimulation to reach an alert state for
even a few seconds. As a result, her capacity to interact was
quite limited. Tracking of both human faces and inanimate
objects was fleeting as Betty quickly lost the visual stimulus
and returned to a sleepy state. Attending to auditory stimuli,
both human and inanimate, was likewise confined to a momentary brightening, with no effort to locate the source of
sound. But Betty molded well when held, was successful in
quieting herself, and could tolerate mild stress (being un-
dressed, being pulled to sit) well.

The infant specialist's overall impression of Betty was that
of a frail, passive infant with very poor "sending power" who
preferred to be left alone. These characteristics, in conjunction with Mrs. Lake's poor reality testing and her preference
for an undemanding infant, made us worry that Mrs. Lake
might take no initiative in attending to her baby's physical
needs and that Betty might not protest when she had not
been fed or changed. We feared that Betty might be neglected
by her mother and would starve without anybody being aware
of it.

When Betty was 13 days old, a slight improvement in
her performance on the second Brazelton Assessment encouraged the infant specialist. (Generally we administer that
scale at 3 days and 30 days, but Betty's poor performance on
the Brazelton at 7 days was so worrisome that we scheduled

an additional assessment.) Betty was now able to maintain an alert state for a slightly longer period of time than had been the case a week earlier, and the quality of her responses to inanimate objects and to the infant specialist's face and voice were somewhat improved. She showed a preference for inanimate stimuli and responded more to the bell, rattle, and red ball used in the assessment than to the infant specialist's face and voice. She continued to calm herself easily when left alone. Her coloring was still sallow; she lacked a healthy, rosy glow.

Throughout the examination, Mrs. Lake sat passively; although normally quite loquacious, she made only two comments during the 30 minutes of the exam. Both comments referred to her perception of the baby's performance. However there were also indications that Mrs. Lake did have some positive thoughts about Betty. For example, on the Broussard Caretaker Perception Profile Mrs. Lake indicated her belief that Betty would cry less and have less difficulty with some movements than the average baby.

The Initial Concerns Crystallize

After Betty's birth, Mrs. Lake agreed to have the clinician visit twice instead of once a week. In addition, she began to attend the program's Infant Center weekly, and during those visits she continued her contacts with the infant specialist.

In spite of this intensive intervention, the family deteriorated. This decline in functioning was soon mirrored in Betty's condition. Mrs. Lake, who, as mentioned earlier, had discontinued her medication, was showing a very precarious link with reality. The clinician often found the baby on the outside porch of the family house unsupervised while Mrs. Lake seemed absorbed in her hallucinations. During the clinician's visits, Mrs. Lake often carried on a running "conversation" with "the Voice," an activity that seemed to give her some pleasure because the talk was punctuated by laughter. Mrs. Lake could reengage with her environment when the clinician encouraged her to do so. However, she spoke in a mechanical manner of caring for Betty, as if reciting a text rather than describing real-life occurrences between herself and her baby.

The situations of the other family members seemed no better. Mr. Lake complained bitterly about the behavior of the three older children. The oldest daughter, Monica, had started to stay away from home at night; her truancy at school also escalated. Mr. Lake felt that she had become unmanageable and that the 14- and 12-year-old sons were beginning to imitate her behavior.

Although we were becoming alarmed about the quality of Betty's daily experience, we were unable to direct the parents' attention to their baby's well-being. They believed that Betty was not a problem and focused on the older children as their most immediate concern. As a result, we again scheduled office visits with the entire family in order to explore what was happening and to encourage the family to speak to one another. In the initial visits, the older children expressed intense anger at their father for his failure to provide for the family. Mrs. Lake joined in the children's criticism and accused her husband of spending money on alcohol and cigarettes while the family's needs remained unmet. Mr. Lake responded by telling his wife that she was "crazy" and by declaring, both verbally and nonverbally, that he would not work with her. The children became increasingly anxious at the overt display of anger between the parents and finally refused to continue coming in for family sessions.

Mrs. Lake responded to this painful reality by taking flight from it. She became less available for rational, coherent conversations and reported that "the Voice" was taking increasing control of the family's actions. Mr. Lake began to stay away from home for several days at a time. He was working at a large church doing minor repairs in exchange for food and other household necessities. He declined to be paid in cash for fear that his Social Security disability grant would be reduced, and began extending his working day until it was so long that the trip home was futile. He then began spending his nights at the church, sending home the food with someone else.

Betty's Situation: 6-Week Assessment

The effect of this stress on Betty was evident when the infant specialist administered the third Brazelton Assessment at the age of 6 weeks. The slight improvement noted at 2 weeks was no longer apparent. Betty had a great deal of difficulty maintaining a quiet alert state. She reached an agitated crying state after the administration of each item and fairly extensive periods of consoling were needed to bring her back to a calm state for even brief intervals. She was irritable even during feeding. That Betty's interest in the world was only minimal was indicated by poor tracking of such auditory and visual stimuli as the bell, the human voice and face, and the bright red ball used in the exam. Her responses to both animate and inanimate stimuli were confined to brightening and brief eye movements. In addition to Betty's poor performance, her physical appearance was worrisome. She was emaciated and pale and looked like a "war-baby." The infant specialist's concerns were further heightened when she observed that Mrs. Lake was feeding the baby skim milk. When the infant specialist asked about this, Mrs. Lake reported that Betty was fed Similac concentrate diluted in half with water. It was apparent that Mrs. Lake did not realize what she was feeding the baby.

Rescue Efforts

Given the situation, we realized that we had to do more to help Betty: her very survival might be at stake. The infant specialist called the Public Health Department to discuss her growing concerns and consulted with the public health nurse already involved with the family. Both professionals were in daily contact for the next several days, with one or both of them making home visits daily. The primary goal of these visits was to make sure that Betty was being fed adequately. The nurse and infant specialist observed that Mrs. Lake fed Betty every four hours. Betty would suck for a few minutes and then stop to rest. At that point, the mother would give the bottle to her 3-year-old son, who would often finish it off. In the meantime, Betty would drift off to a sleepy state. The infant specialist asked Mrs. Lake to persist in giving Betty the bottle in spite of the baby's apparent disinterest. We also reviewed the process of formula preparation with Mrs. Lake in an attempt to make sure Betty was getting the nutrients she needed for adequate development.

Despite the professionals' daily visits to evaluate and supervise the feedings, Betty was clearly losing weight. She was hospitalized at the age of 6 weeks, 3 days for dehydration and failure to thrive. Since birth she had gained only 13 ounces. During her 7-day hospitalization, she gained 8 ounces.

The Rescue Efforts Increase: Interagency Network

The decline in Betty's birth weight and her hospitalization made it dramatically clear that even our close monitoring of the family, in conjunction with the public health nurse, had not been effective in helping this mother to negotiate the first developmental task of the mother–infant dyad, the promotion of the baby's physical growth, basic comfort, and patterns of eating and elimination.

The next step was to review the role of each agency involved with the family (the Health Department, the Department of Social Services, Protective Service, the Department of Education, and the Clinical Infant Development Program) to assess areas of effectiveness as well as difficulties in meeting the family's needs. We hoped that this self-scrutiny would lead to the identification of areas where care could be improved and interagency cooperation increased. We therefore took the initiative in calling for and coordinating weekly meetings which included both the on-line worker and the supervisor from each of these agencies. These meetings took place for 8 months beginning with Betty's hospitalization.

During the initial meetings both the on-line workers and the supervisors from each agency indicated they felt at a loss about finding ways of helping the family. An overriding feeling of helplessness and frustration revealed itself in extreme defensiveness on the part of each agency's representatives about the possibility that others might think they were not doing enough for the family. We also observed a pervasive fear of Mrs. Lake's "craziness" and frustration with Mr. Lake's deafness and refusal to "cooperate" with agency personnel.

The workers reflected their desire to escape from this frustrating case in two conflicting requests; they wanted us either to take over and make all decisions involving the family, or to have Betty removed from the family and placed in foster care.

The first alternative was unfeasible because the needs of this family clearly were too diverse and too pervasive for any one agency to meet. The second alternative seemed to us premature: the family had not yet received the kind of coordinated interagency care that we thought would make it possible for them to give Betty an adequate opportunity for development. We thought that removal would be inappropriate until the agencies had succeeded in offering high-quality, coordinated care, and the family had proved that it was unable to benefit from such service. Furthermore, since neither parent expressed any desire for voluntary termination of parental rights, we knew that Betty's forcible removal would be likely to entail a succession of temporary foster home placements, a possibility which was potentially more deleterious to her adequate long-term development than a closely monitored residence at home.

Following this reasoning, we undertook the task of attempting to set up an interagency network through which the worker from each agency would have quick access to the workers from other agencies for sharing and updating information.

The first step in this process was to decrease the overall anxiety and defensiveness of the group and to foster an atmosphere of mutual trust and a sense of common goals. The CIDP clinician pointed out to the group that in many different ways the conflicts evident during the meeting were a reflection of the splitting and conflict within the family. She also addressed the general feeling of helplessness aroused by the failure of the agencies' well-meaning efforts to help the family; she sympathized with the underlying desire to give up. In essence, the CIDP team took on the role of a support system for the community agency workers. This intervention resulted in a drastic decrease in their defensiveness, a diminution of the on-line workers' desire to have the supervisors present, and an increase in the cohesiveness and trust within the group.

The next step was to set up a working plan for the family. An intensive intervention program was adopted. Following Betty's discharge, Mrs. Lake would start coming to the CIDP Infant Center three times a week with her infant and her toddler. A parent aide from the Department of Social Service would visit the family once a week, and a public health nurse would visit the remaining weekday. This meant that 5 days a week Mrs. Lake would have a supportive presence in her efforts to care for Betty. The workers involved agreed to cooperate fully with each other. They planned regular phone calls to exchange information and to coordinate the details of providing structure and help to Mrs. Lake. This initial plan was intentionally time-limited; we needed to ascertain its effectiveness before planning further intervention.

The primary focus of all the workers at this time would be on feeding. Mrs. Lake would be shown how to read Betty's rather low-keyed hunger cues, how to pace the feedings, how to tell whether Betty had sufficient milk, and how to burp her. Multisensory involvement of Mrs. Lake with her daughter would also be encouraged through modeling and reassurance. We hoped that with this support, Mrs. Lake would begin to talk, sing, smile, and hold Betty; would learn to observe which behaviors seemed most pleasurable to her daughter; and would be encouraged to report those interventions that felt most mutually satisfying.

Betty Is Placed in Foster Care

The interim plan outlined above was followed rigorously for 1 week after Betty's hospital discharge. During this time there was a noticeable increase in Mrs. Lake's ability to organize herself around Betty's care, and she seemed to derive a sense of control from the structure we were giving her. She became more attentive and responsive to hunger cues and spent time involved in social exchanges with her baby daughter and her toddler; the episodes of sitting alone staring into space diminished, and there were fewer references to "the Voice."

Betty also was sustaining the small but noticeable gains in social responses that she had made during her stay at the hospital. She was alert for longer periods of time and was now more active in tracking faces and inanimate objects and in turning her head to the source of sounds.

This modest but promising beginning was abruptly interrupted a week after it began. A medical follow-up in the health clinic revealed that Betty had lost 3 ounces since discharge. There were definite questions in our minds about the origin of this weight loss. What was Betty's clothing at the time of the two weighings? Had she been weighed on the same scale both times? Betty's pediatrician was alarmed and did not explore these possibilities. Without notifying us, he called Child Protective Services (CPS) and asked for the child's placement in foster care.

This action led to a breakdown in the carefully nurtured communication and consultation network among the agencies. The CPS worker responded unquestioningly to the physician's recommendation. By the time we were notified, the CPS worker was preparing to go to the family's home, accompanied by a police officer. There had been no discussion with the family; they had not even been notified of the impending removal.

Caught in the rapid unfolding of events, the CIDP clinician attempted to minimize the disruption to the family. She managed to phone Mrs. Lake's sister to alert the family of the impending removal of Betty and to expect to be present to give Mrs. Lake emotional support. The clinician also decided to join the CPS worker for the process of removing Betty from home. She reasoned that she could then help defuse antagonism between the CPS worker and Mrs. Lake by establishing some possibility of dialogue between them.

This, unfortunately, was not possible. Mrs. Lake was not at home when the CPS worker, police officer, and the CIDP therapist arrived. A neighbor informed them that Mrs. Lake's sister had come over and that both of them had left with the baby. The group then proceeded to go to Mrs. Lake's sister's house. When they arrived, Mrs. Lake's sister refused to open the door. From a balcony, she screamed that Mrs. Lake was not there and that she would sue the group for trespassing if they attempted to enter. The police officer then threatened to charge her with obstruction of justice if she did not open the door. At that point, Mrs. Lake emerged at the door, screaming "Take the baby then, if that's what *you* want." Her face was red and her whole body was shaking as she seemed to thrust the baby into the CPS worker's arms.

The CIDP clinician's attempts to intercede were futile. Mrs. Lake clearly identified her as being in league with the CPS worker and refused to listen to her. The CPS worker took the baby and left, accompanied by the CIDP clinician. We later discovered that the weight loss used as the criterion for Betty's removal might have been erroneous. Two different scales had been used in the two weighings, a fact that could well have accounted for the 3-ounce difference between the beginning and end of the week. It is true, however, that Betty might not have *gained* weight as would be expected in the course of a week.

The Aftermath: Interagency Planning for Betty's Return Home

After Betty's removal from her parents' home, the CIDP clinician called an interagency meeting to review what had happened and to make plans for the future. This meeting yielded a list which reflected consensus among the different workers about the reasons that had led to Betty's removal from home, the criteria which should determine whether Betty should be kept with her parents once she was returned, and recommendations to facilitate the attainment of homeostasis and the formation of an attachment between Betty and her parents. This list is presented in Table 4-1.

The members of the interagency team met with the parents to discuss formulations outlined in the list. The parents denied the validity of the criteria used for Betty's removal, especially the weight loss, pointing out that Betty had been weighed on two different scales at two different medical facilities (i.e., the hospital and the public health clinic) and that this accounted for the decline in weight. Nevertheless, they agreed to the reactivation of the plan originally formulated to help them prior to Betty's removal. Betty would be brought from her foster home to the Infant Center for three mornings a week, where she would spend about 4 hours with her parents and her brother Andrew. In addition, the clinician would continue to meet with the family to focus on their communication problems. The importance of Mrs. Lake's compliance in taking her medication would be stressed at appropriate moments during these meetings. The other agencies would also continue their therapeutic involvement: the parent aide and a public health nurse would each continue to visit the family weekly to discuss child care issues.

Family Sessions: CIDP Prepares the Family for Betty's Return

Two cotherapists were used in the family sessions: the regular clinician (Mrs. T.) and a male psychiatrist who was the supervisor of the case.

TABLE 4-1

Interagency Conference on Betty Lake and Her Parents

Criteria for Removal to a Foster Home
I.   Infant
    A.   Weght
    B.   Lethargy
    C.   Lack of response to stimuli
    D.   Inadequate hygiene (diaper rash)

II.   Parents
    A.   Absence of mother/infant interaction
    B.   Father out of home much of the time

Criteria for Betty to Remain with Family Once She Is Returned
    A.   Continued progress of infant physically, including height and weight gain and adequate hygiene.
    B.   Continued progress emotionally, including attachment of mother and child, and mutual capacity of parents as a unit to care and be responsible for Betty.
    C.   Mother to demonstrate minimal knowledge of adequate care of infant and to be able to tell professionals about her care giving.
    D.   Mother to be actively involved in taking Betty to scheduled medical appointments and to participate in her care.

Recommendations
    A.   Parents to participate in a program that facilitates physical and emotional development of mother infant, and family.
    B.   Parents to continue to be provided with assistance to care for Betty as long as necessary (WIC, DSS, CIDP, PGHD).
    C.   Mrs. Lake should consider regular use of psychotropic medication.
    D.   Mr. and Mrs. Lake should be in counseling with someone who can sign. It is felt that Mr,. Lake is capable and intelligent and, with support of therapy and the other agencies, could be responsible for Mrs. Lake's taking her medicine.
    E.   Mr. and Mrs. Lake learn sign together.

After Betty's removal, the focus of the family sessions shifted dramatically. Mr. and Mrs. Lake were for the first time willing to talk about the youngest children. We used Betty's return home as the focus for their discussion. Initially, Mrs. Lake had difficulty focusing on anything but her rage toward the clinician for her participation in Betty's removal. Mrs. Lake saw the primary clinician as the one who had taken her child. As Mrs. Lake for the first time explicitly revealed and discussed her feelings about the clinician, the clinician found it at times not only difficult but frightening to sit in the room and be the object of Mrs. Lake's rage. It was as if both Mrs. Lake and the clinician were reliving the episode of Betty's removal, with Mrs. Lake exhibiting the physical shaking and screaming that she had shown when the incident occurred. Her remembrance of the episode was distorted by her delusion that this was all part of a master plan and that she had no responsibility for or control over what happened. Adding to the tension was the clinician's uncertainty about Mrs. Lake's ability to control herself and refrain from physical attack on the clinician.

At these times the clinician pointed out to Mrs. Lake her distortions in thinking and described what actually had happened, including the role of the parents' neglect in precipitating Betty's removal. The parents, however, expressed feelings that the baby's removal had been out of their control. Mrs. Lake now tended to turn toward her husband spontaneously in the sessions, whereas previously she had resisted the clinician's effort to encourage her to look at or reach out to him. Mr. Lake, on the other hand, continued to resist working with his wife and repeatedly complained that she was "too crazy" for him to interact with her comfortably.

It is important to note that at the time these family sessions began, Mrs. Lake had been given 300 milligrams of Mellaril daily. This dosage was gradually increased to 700 milligrams in the course of 3 weeks. This amount was noticeably effective in curtailing Mrs. Lake's delusions and helping her organize her thinking and behavior. It was noteworthy to us that Mr. Lake was unable to acknowledge or respond to his wife's improvement, and continued to insist that she was "too crazy" to be taken seriously.

CIDP Prepares the Family for Betty's Return: Infant Center Visits

Initially, the parents' feelings during the Infant Center visits while Betty was in foster care were angry and hostile, reflected by the "performancelike" quality of their interactions with Betty. We surmised that their hostility masked great anxiety as to whether their child would ever be returned to them. The interactions were excessively demonstrative, and often out of synchrony with the infant's capacity to respond at a particular time. We thought that their involvement was dictated in part by their understanding that this was the way they could hasten Betty's return and prove to the agencies involved that Betty's removal had been a mistake.

After 2 or 3 weeks of daily visits to the Infant Center, the parents relaxed and became somewhat more cooperative. Much emphasis was placed on helping the parents read Betty's cues and think of possible meanings for her behavior. (If she fussed, could she be hungry, sleepy, or bored?) Another important thrust of the work with the parents was to model for them appropriate ways of interacting with Betty, showing them, for example, how first to bring her to an alert state through animated verbal stimulation and postural changes, and then proceed to use additional channels of sensorimotor stimulation (such as smiling, making expressive faces, caressing, jiggling the limbs, gently tickling) to help Betty integrate her responses to multisensory stimulation.

Mrs. Lake was much more receptive and learned much more quickly than her husband, who was hampered by his deafness. Mr. Lake also seemed unable to moderate his stance that he had nothing to learn because he was already fully competent in caring for his children. He also persisted in his accusation that any parental incompetence was that of his wife.

Betty's Foster Care Experience

Betty's foster placement lasted 3½ months, and involved two different foster homes.

The first foster mother was a registered nurse who had two biological children and helped Betty become regulated in feeding and elimination patterns through a routine that was at the same time predictable and responsive to the infant's cues. This foster mother was also sensitive to the feelings of Betty's biological parents, and at our request she wrote notes to Mr. and Mrs. Lake several times a week describing Betty's afternoons and evenings after returning from her mornings at the Infant Center with her parents.

This sensitive care, coupled with our own intensive intervention, soon yielded dramatic results. Betty gained weight rapidly, acquired a healthy, rosy, glowing skin, and became socially more demanding and more persistent in the expression of her needs. Paradoxically, Betty's improvement was more than her foster mother could cope with. She was willing to lavish love and attention on a lethargic, undemanding infant who was content to be left alone for long periods. She was not willing to be equally available to an infant who was learning that she could expect good care and prompt attention to her needs and was now able to demand them assertively rather than accept them passively. After 2 months, the foster mother asked the Department of Social Services to place Betty with someone else.

For the following 6 weeks, Betty was placed with a foster mother who was already caring for five preschool children. Betty was then 4 months old.

During the first 2 weeks of this second foster placement, we became increasingly concerned about the quality of physical care Betty was now receiving. Our concerns were based on the unclean condition of Betty's clothing and our observation of increasingly frequent diaper rash. We also learned from the driver who transported Betty from the foster home to the Infant Center that occasionally the foster mother was not at home to receive Betty and that Betty and the other young children were sometimes supervised only by 5- and 6-year-olds.

By this time Mrs. Lake was stabilized psychologically, taking her medication regularly, and functioning in a more organized and responsive manner. She, too, noticed the change in Betty's appearance and challenged our support of the foster care placement. Mrs. Lake pointed out to us that Betty had not been so dirty and had not had so many diaper rashes when she was caring for her, and yet Betty had been removed from her care. We had to agree.

Betty at 4 Months: Developmental Assessment

The Bayley Scales were administered when Betty was 4 months, 3 days. Two facts about this testing stand out. First, Betty had just been transferred from her first to her second foster home a few days before. Second, she was brought in to the session by her father because her mother had fallen asleep after taking her Mellaril and could not be awakened. Betty's father had as a rule been less involved with her than her mother. The circumstances surrounding testing must be taken into account in understanding Betty's performance. Excerpts from the testing report follow.

> Betty is a chubby 4-month-old with an almost impassive facial expression, slow to react, and with few body movements. The mother was absent during the test session because she had just taken her antipsychotic medicine and had been unable to wake up. Betty was very unresponsive in her father's arms and the examiner's lap throughout the session. There was no apparent differential response to the father and to the examiner.

While Betty's Mental Development Index (MDI) placed her at age level, the examiner had to be very persistent to elicit a response.

This baby has a lethargic quality that made testing her hard, one-sided work rather than a pleasant mutual experience. The baby's affect is very muted. She smiled fleetingly at the examiner only once. She chuckled briefly on two occasions after the examiner had attempted to engage her in frolic play for 10 minutes. She persistently avoided social eye contact and looked at toys rather briefly and without apparent enjoyment. She passed the items almost peripherally, showing none of the gusto in mouthing, reaching, or cooing that is expected in babies this age. She uttered almost no sound, and took a very long time to respond to a bell ringing loudly near her ear. This is particularly noteworthy because her father is deaf, and although he can speak, he communicates with the mother mostly through sign language. One wonders to how much sound, particularly human sound, this baby is exposed.

There are signs that the baby is motivated to respond to various test materials. She moved her fingers slightly when presented with the cube, suggesting she might want to reach for it. She made hand contact with the rabbit, and moved her arms when presented with the dangling ring. These behaviors emerged slowly, after repeated presentations. During the early part of the test Betty showed no initiative and her fingers did not even mold around an object put in her hand.

A striking aspect of her overall motor development is the floppy way she holds herself, in the typical sack of potatoes manner, without either molding to the person holding her or seeming to hold her own weight.

The improvement in performance as the test proceeded, and the fact that Betty finally chuckled after a long time spent by the examiner playing with her, suggested that this baby will need patient, sustained social and physical stimulation to encourage a more ready responsiveness to objects and to people.

It is striking that Betty's performance in the assessment failed to show the noticeable improvements we had observed during her first foster home placement and in the course of our own Infant Center intervention. This suggested that Betty was responding with intense withdrawal to the change in primary caregivers, and it further supported our suspicions that she was receiving much poorer care in the second foster home.

Infant Intervention: Encouragement of Body Control and Emotional Responsivity

Following the 4-month assessment the infant specialist concentrated on facilitating social-emotional interactions between mother and infant. Mrs. Lake was encouraged to hold her infant closely in an *en face* position, to talk to Betty in a highly animated way that included a wide range of voice pitches and rhythms and different facial expressions, to imitate the baby's cooing, and to repeat whatever exchanges provided Betty pleasure. The infant specialist used modeling and verbal encouragement to exhibit these behaviors to Mrs. Lake. Since the mother still seemed inhibited (although willing) in her play with Betty, the infant specialist's own interactions with the baby were very elaborate and emotionally animated in an attempt to have Mrs. Lake imitate at least some of the expressiveness Betty needed. The baby only responded to social exchanges that involved a great deal of exuberance and multimodal input on the part of the adult.

To facilitate Betty's body control, the infant specialist began using some baby exercises involving rolls and large balls for balancing exercises. Betty fussed when placed on the floor and encouraged to use her large muscles. The protest was dealt with by talking and smiling to the baby, by curtailing the activity if Betty continued to fuss, and by increasing only very gradually the amount of time the baby spent on the floor. After a couple of weeks, the infant specialist observed that Betty's body control was developing along with an increase in her tolerance for and pleasure in floor explorations.

In the process, Mrs. Lake was able to imitate the infant specialist's modeling, but she expressed puzzlement about the need for such intensive interaction with Betty. "Don't babies do just as well if left to their own devices?" she asked. The infant specialist addressed this and similar questions by speaking about the pleasure that a baby derives from being loved, attended to, and cared for, and how this pleasure becomes a feeling of well-being that gives the baby motivation and impetus to explore and learn about people and objects. Mrs. Lake listened and agreed, but, predictably, continued to show limitations in her capacity to interact spontaneously with her baby and to derive unselfconscious pleasure from her. As in most areas of her functioning, she continued to demonstrate a rigid repertoire of responses.

For example, if she were asked to show Betty how a rattle sounded, she might go about this task for a full 15 minutes or so, long after Betty had exhausted whatever initial pleasure she had derived from the experience and was ready to explore something else. Similarly, if the infant specialist commented that it would be nice to encourage Betty to crawl by placing an attractive object a little beyond her reach, Mrs. Lake would obligingly do so and continue to do so for weeks after Betty had mastered crawling and was crawling spontaneously with no need for special incentives. The infant specialist attempted to cope with this problem by suggesting a variety of possibilities for interaction to Mrs. Lake. However, Mrs. Lake's concrete thinking and inability to adjust her behavior to the social cues of her baby continued to be serious stumbling blocks in providing Betty with an affectively rich and emotionally responsive primary relationship. This is where the role of the Infant Center staff became most vividly highlighted, since they were able to provide Betty with a variety and flexibility of social exchange that she could not engage in with her mother.

Plan for Betty's Reentry into Her Home

When Betty was 4 months, 3 weeks old, we raised the issue of an early reentry plan for Betty at the interagency meeting. Our reasons for recommending early reentry were (1) the poor quality of physical and emotional care Betty was receiving in her foster care placement; (2) the mother's increased capacity to care for Betty; and (3) the desirability of a stable primary caregiver as Betty approached the age at which we normally see the consolidation of focused attachments and the onset of separation anxiety.

The reentry plan from foster care routinely recommended by Protective Services lasts 6 months. Using the reasons outlined above we urged the interagency team to consider a revision of this plan that would accelerate the reentry process and complete it within 6 weeks.

These plans were formed against a background of active legal efforts on the part of the Lakes to obtain custody of their baby immediately through the court. During the first weeks of Betty's foster care placement, the parents had secured the services of a private attorney, Mrs. Jones, to represent them in this endeavor. From the manner in which Mrs. Jones represented the Lakes, it was apparent that she had not familiarized herself with the case. She did not know that the Lakes had other children, that the family was involved with our program, and that Betty's failure to gain weight was the stated reason for Betty's placement in foster care. After the first court ordered evaluation (when Betty was 2½ months old), the Lakes became dissatisfied with Mrs. Jones and terminated her services. Their new attorney, Mrs. Gilbert, initially saw herself as defending a loving but helpless family that she perceived as arbitrarily abused by the bureaucracy of the community and government agencies. She was committed to representing the family effectively and in the process of doing so she learned the facts that the family had been unable to disclose to her. As she discovered the reasons for Betty's foster home placement, Mrs. Gilbert became an auxiliary member of the interagency team. She was instrumental in helping the family understand the supportive nature of the team, explaining the meaning of its assessments. Mrs. Gilbert urged the

Lakes to agree to the revised reentry plan instead of insisting on Betty's immediate return, which had already been denied twice by the court. The Lakes followed her advice. When the revised reentry plan was presented in court, all the inter-agency team members and the family supported, and the court authorized, the plan. An emotionally and financially costly legal battle was averted.

Betty Returns Home

When Betty returned home after 3½ months of foster care placement, she was 6 months old. Her normally subdued affect became more pronounced during the first days she spent at home. However, she continued to show the capacity to respond with pleasure to social interaction if she were per-sistently wooed.

The infant specialist worked to encourage Betty to be-come more assertive and motorically active as well as more engaged with her mother. Games of peek-a-boo, for example, were encouraged in which the infant specialist could sit behind Mrs. Lake, facing Betty. After first gaining the baby's attention she would invite Mrs. Lake to do the same while expressing surprise and delight in the baby's response. Mother was also urged to talk to Betty *en face* and in the mirror. When Betty would roll from side to side or be passed from one adult to another she would remain passive. The infant specialist would model certain motor exercises to mother, for example rolling Betty forward on a ball on the floor or from side to side with her arms extended.

Mrs. Lake was able to imitate the infant specialist's mod-eling although she verbalized little understanding of the need for such involvement with Betty. The infant specialist found it necessary to draw the mother's attention in explicit detail to the progress of Betty's development. For example, she worked hard to move the mother's attention from encouraging Betty's visual attention to tracking to include reaching, grasp-ing, and turning, gradually incorporating as many of the senses in body movements as Betty would respond to. To compensate for Mrs. Lake's continuing tendency to be rigid and to perseverate, the infant specialist would encourage Mrs. Lake to move along to the next level of interaction, using praise for the mother and her affection for Betty as reinforcement. For example, after Betty would respond positively to a doll, with a smile and a grasp, the infant specialist would encourage the mother to hand the doll to her daughter so that the baby could have the added pleasures of mouthing and feeling and exploring the doll. This served to interrupt Mrs. Lake's more fixated pattern of squeezing the doll and holding it at arm's reach for her daughter.

The increasing pleasure Betty took in the simultaneous interaction with inanimate objects and her mother became additional positive reinforcement to Mrs. Lake for the value of the complexity of the interaction between herself and her daughter. She would express genuine pleasure and excitement in her capacity to stimulate and animate her daughter and was increasingly comfortable in the floor play so long as the infant specialist was involved with her and her daughter. We had the feeling that her capacity to regress in the service of play with her daughter was simultaneously enhanced by the presence of the infant specialist, with her suggestions and encouragement, and the positive feedback she got from her daughter in the pleasure of the interaction.

Continuing Work with the Family

One of the recommendations made at the court hearing on Betty's return home was that a therapist who could use sign language be incorporated into the family's treatment. The reasoning was that such a therapist would help Mr. Lake become more invested in treatment. Following this recommendation, we engaged a social worker trained in family therapy who specialized in sign language and communication with the deaf. With Mr. and Mrs. Lake's concurrence, this clinician took the place of the psychiatrist in the family therapy sessions.

The new presence triggered a realignment in the therapeutic relationship. Mr. Lake welcomed the new cotherapist warmly. He seemed to feel that he now had an ally, someone who could really understand him. He initially tried to have private conversations with this cotherapist, excluding both Mrs. Lake and the primary clinician. Mrs. Lake, for her part, treated the new person as an "interpreter." She stopped facing her husband and signing directly to him, and instead asked the new therapist to sign to her husband what she wanted. Mrs. Lake's continued effort to convey information to her husband was in striking contrast to his attempt to have the new therapist "all to himself."

Mrs. Lake and the Clinician Become Pregnant: A New Therapeutic Alliance

Even before Betty's return home, we had begun to suspect that Mrs. Lake was pregnant again. Since the primary clinician was pregnant, the question of how to address this topic was a delicate therapeutic issue. It was decided that the clinician would first announce her own pregnancy; in the weeks that followed she would inquire about Mrs. Lake's own state.

Mrs. Lake responded to the news of the clinician's pregnancy with hearty congratulations. As her own possible pregnancy was addressed, however, she responded with vehement denials and with the suggestion that the clinician, too, was now imagining things and hearing voices. Two weeks later, Mrs. Lake acknowledged being 2 months pregnant. Betty was 7 months old and had just returned home.

Mrs. Lake seemed to derive a feeling of comradeship with the clinician from the idea that they were both pregnant. She inquired about the clinician's health and gave her advice about where to buy maternity clothes. She asked the clinician about her dietary habits and compared them to her own poor habits. The rage at the clinician for her perceived role in Betty's removal diminished dramatically. Yet Mrs. Lake would not discuss her pregnancy directly, and could not bring herself to discuss the impending separation caused by the clinician's anticipated maternity leave. When the clinician explained that the infant specialist would take her place during her absence, Mr. and Mrs. Lake sat passively and made no comment. They showed little interest in making plans to care for what would soon be three young children.

Soon after acknowledging her pregnancy, Mrs. Lake stopped taking her Mellaril. We had known that Mrs. Lake only took medication because she felt pressured to do so by the different professionals and agencies with whom she was involved. As soon as she found an acceptable reason, she discontinued the medication. Almost immediately she suffered a severe regression, including frequent breaks from reality during her visits to the Infant Center, which she continued to attend three mornings a week. At those times, Mrs. Lake could be observed sitting alone in an isolated corner of the room, holding a monologue frequently punctuated by laughter. She could be brought to reality and respond appropriately when a staff member brought her attention to some current need of either Andrew or Betty, such as feeding or changing. But the fact that external intervention was necessary for Mrs. Lake to interrupt her hallucinations raised serious questions about her children's well-being away from the Infant Center.

The infant specialist, therefore, recommended that Mrs. Lake and the children attend the Infant Center five mornings a week. Mrs. Lake agreed, but not quite for the same reasons that prompted the infant specialist's suggestion. Rather, Mrs. Lake liked the idea of not having to prepare food for herself and the children (food was still scarce in the Lake household) and she also liked the thought of having transportation readily available if she went into labor at the infant room. (This did happen, and we took her to the hospital when she went into labor.)

Developmental Assessment: Betty at 8 Months

A developmental assessment conducted at 8 months, 26 days (2 months after Betty returned home) showed marked improvements in sociability, affective range, and cognitive performance. Betty was engrossed in the test items and explored them enthusiastically with her hands and mouth. She engaged in reciprocal games with the examiner, had good eye contact and a quick smile, and took the initiative often in establishing social interaction with her mother and the examiner by smiling, vocalizing briefly, and offering a toy. Most striking was Betty's purposiveness in establishing social contact and in exploring inanimate objects. She was likewise persistent in her efforts to master particular tasks that were slightly above her level. Her cognitive performance placed her 2 months above her chronological age.

Although Betty initiated interaction both with her mother and with the examiner, the quality of these exchanges was different. Mrs. Lake tended to respond briefly and in a mechanical, repetitive fashion. When Betty was engaged in vigorous manipulation of toys and turned to her mother with a gleeful smile, Mrs. Lake would smile in return but would not pursue Betty's clear invitation to join her in play. Similarly, when Betty was tired and leaned against her mother, Mrs. Lake did not respond at all. Several times Betty sought eye contact by turning to her mother and looking at her, but Mrs. Lake seemed detached, looking away, and no eye contact was established. In contrast, Betty found in the examiner a willing social partner, and there was a striking difference between the long reciprocal exchanges between them and the brief, abortive attempts Betty made to engage her mother. Mrs. Lake smiled with apparent pleasure while observing Betty and the examiner, but made no attempt to join in their play. Interestingly, Betty kept visual tabs on her mother, turning her head repeatedly in Mrs. Lake's direction even while interacting with the examiner.

A Second Baby: Phil Is Born

Betty was 11 months old when Phil was born. During the last month of Mrs. Lake's pregnancy, the infant specialist had assumed primary responsibility for the case because the primary clinician remained on maternity leave.

At birth, Phil weighed 6 pounds, 14 ounces and was 20 inches long. His Apgar scores were 7/9. He was 37 weeks gestational age. The neonatal course while at the hospital was uncomplicated.

The Brazelton Neonatal Assessment Scale was first administered when Phil was 3 days old. He responded with alert interest to the examiner's face and voice, following the face with his eyes as it moved across his field of vision, and turning his eyes in the direction of the examiner's voice. He also oriented well to the inanimate visual and auditory stimuli—the ball and the bell. He molded well when held and was very efficient at self-quieting through mouthing his hand. He seemed like a baby quite capable of organized responses to stimulation, even of an aversive nature: he responded with directed swipes to having his face covered by a cloth. He also had a high threshold for irritability: he fussed and cried only in response to the more intrusive procedures and quieted spontaneously upon termination. His reflexes were normal.

Mrs. Lake's response to the assessment was discouraging. After watching for a few minutes, she fell asleep. Throughout her hospitalization she complained of having a headache, and repeatedly declined to have contact with Phil. She asked the nurses to feed him, held him loosely without supporting his head (or not at all), and either averted her gaze from the baby or looked at him quizzically, as if puzzled by his appearance. Efforts by the infant specialist and the hospital staff to encourage Mrs. Lake to interact with her new baby proved futile. Mrs. Lake persistently argued that her headache prevented her from paying attention to anything else.

Before the mother's and baby's discharge, the infant specialist and the cotherapist who knew sign language visited the home to ascertain how Mr. Lake was preparing for their return. Upon arrival, they found 4-year-old Andrew, and Betty, 11 months, in the care of the three teenage children who had proved so unreliable in the past. Mr. Lake was at the Deaf Club, where he had spent most of his time toward the end of his wife's pregnancy. The infant specialist and cotherapist visited him there, and told him about their concern for the infant's well-being. Would there be food, clothes, diapers? At first Mr. Lake could only repeat in a monotone that he wanted the baby to come home; only much later was he able to say that there was no food for the baby and that he had no means to acquire it in the next few days. He requested that Phil be kept in the hospital over the weekend (this was a Friday), and said that he would try to get a loan to buy food on Monday. The infant specialist relayed this message to the neonatologist, who agreed to the request. Mrs. Lake, bewildered by the fact that Phil was staying at the hospital, was discharged that day. She could neither understand nor agree with her husband's request to keep Phil hospitalized over the weekend.

On Monday, a social worker from the Child Protective Services, apprised of the infant specialist's visit 3 days earlier, made a home visit to evaluate the family situation prior to Phil's arrival. She found the home even more chaotic than it had been 3 days earlier. There was no food for Phil; supplies for the rest of the family were meager. Both Mr. and Mrs. Lake perceived the Child Protective Service social worker as their protector and provider and gave her a guided tour of their home in which they enumerated its many deficits, as if they expected to be the recipients of the services of the Department of Social Services. The worker acknowledged the genuine needs of the family but also determined that because of the grave physical deficits (such as lack of food and an appropriate place for the baby to sleep), the mother's withdrawal from Phil, and the father's literal inability to hear his son's cry, the infant should be placed in foster care. There was a perfunctory and short-lived outcry of protest by the parents, followed by a quick recovery and a realistic request that Phil be placed with his maternal aunt, who had agreed to be his foster mother until the family could assume his care.

The Protective Service worker, who knew the aunt, agreed. Phil was discharged from the hospital at 8 days of age to the care of his aunt, who lived a few blocks from his parents and had taken in Betty and Mrs. Lake earlier.

When Phil was 14 days old, Mrs. Lake, Andrew, and Betty resumed their Infant Center visits four mornings a week. Phil was picked up from his aunt's home and joined his mother and siblings for these sessions. Once a week the family was accompanied by Mr. Lake, who came in for the family therapy sessions which were conducted by the co-therapist who knew sign language while the primary clinician was still on maternity leave.

On the first office visit after Phil's birth, Mrs. Lake ignored Phil completely, except for one 10-minute episode during which she fed Phil after a staff member had inquired about the baby's feeding schedule. For the remainder of that visit, Mrs. Lake concentrated all her attention on Andrew and Betty. During their visit the next day, the infant specialist isolated the mother and Phil in another room to model for Mrs. Lake how she might be involved with Phil. Mrs. Lake's initial response was a defiant refusal to acknowledge any need to be involved with him. She said that she knew that the infant specialist did not approve of her ignoring the infant, but she, as a mother, was not going to "spoil the infant just to please the program staff." We felt she was fearful of allowing herself to feel too attached to this child out of concern that Phil, like Betty, would be removed from her care. Our view was based on her expressed feeling that Betty was removed because of agency prejudice rather than because of her own lack of attention to her daughter's needs, and that the same experience would be repeated with Phil. Despite Mrs. Lake's initial response, the infant specialist persevered in her modeling of interaction with Phil, explaining her behavior and pointing to the baby's positive responses to being held, cuddled, and talked to. After several minutes, the infant specialist placed Phil in his mother's arms and encouraged her involvement with the infant by talking to her "through" the baby. Mrs. Lake responded by touching and examining the infant's body for the first time (something most parents do spontaneously in the first hours after birth) and was rewarded with Phil's obvious enjoyment of the intimate contact. Mrs. Lake spent the rest of her visit "getting acquainted" with her infant by caressing, cuddling, talking, and crooning to him. This was the beginning of a bonding process which proceeded positively for the next 2 weeks.

When Phil was 30 days old the Brazelton Scale was administered again. He showed a marked improvement in his ability to use stimulation, especially the infant specialist's voice, to maintain an alert state which enabled him to complete the task at hand. Phil's performance on this assessment was altogether encouraging. He was developing promising coping skills. His mother was available to him physically and making strides toward emotional availability. Mrs. Lake was no longer blatantly refusing to interact with Phil as she had on their first office visit 2 weeks earlier. On the contrary, she was beginning to show some spontaneity and pleasure in holding and talking to the infant, who was in turn responsive to her.

At about this time a court hearing took place to evaluate Phil's foster care placement. In spite of the positive developments, the family was still unprepared to assume primary responsibility for Phil's care, and it was decided that foster care would continue for at least another month. That a crib had not yet been acquired, that the deaf father was waiting for a signal light that would flicker when the infant cried, and that Mrs. Lake had not yet resumed taking her antipsychotic medication and was functioning less competently outside the structure of the Infant Center were factors leading to this outcome.

It was apparent to the interagency team that Mrs. Lake functioned more adequately when she was taking antipsychotic medication. This observation was conveyed to the staff of the mental health clinic where Mrs. Lake received her medication. Shortly thereafter, Mrs. Lake agreed to begin receiving Prolixin injections. Following her second injection in a 2-week period, she developed Parkinsonianlike symptoms, severe enough to render her dysfunctional in terms of caring for her three small children. This state lasted 2 weeks, during which Mrs. Lake asked us whether she and her children could come to our Infant Center for 5 hours, 5 days a week so that our staff could care for her children. We agreed.

After Mrs. Lake had been on an anti-Parkinson agent for 2 weeks and her physical symptoms had decreased considerably, it became apparent that the tenuous, emerging bond between her and Phil had deteriorated. The spontaneity and pleasure Mrs. Lake had shown in her interactions with Phil 2 weeks earlier had disappeared; she now sat passively in the room while we cared for the children. At one point Mrs. Lake began asking others to attend to Phil when he cried; since this occurred after the severity of her Parkinsonianlike symptoms has subsided, her reluctance to engage herself with her new baby could not be attributed by her to a physical disability. The infant specialist asked the staff to decrease gradually their caretaking responsibility for the children, especially Phil, in order to facilitate Mrs. Lake's reinvolvement. Rather than feed Phil or Betty ourselves, as we had been doing while she suffered from the medication's side effects, we would actively encourage Mrs. Lake to take over the feeding, diapering, and attending to other physical needs of the children as well as playing with them in the crib and on the floor. She readily responded to this encouragement and resumed her active involvement with them. After the staff had spent a few weeks pulling back and verbally prompting Mrs. Lake to be more involved, she began to respond to Phil's cries of discomfort spontaneously and would take the initiative in feeding or changing him. We then renewed the previous schedule of Infant Center visits—3 hours daily for 4 days a week.

Betty at 12 Months: Developmental Assessment

Betty's 12-month assessment revealed a cognitively and socially competent toddler. Two assessment instruments were administered in two separate sessions which took place 2 weeks apart: the Bayley Scales and the Uzgiris-Hunt Ordinal Scales. In both assessments, Betty became quickly interested in all the items and was persistent in attempting to master even the more difficult tasks. She showed age-appropriate fine and gross motor coordination. In tasks involving causality, object permanence was consistent in the higher levels of stage 5 in sensorimotor development—certainly adequate for a child her age. For example, in the means–ends tasks she was able to gather the necklace to put it in the box, she also used a stick to obtain an object that was out of reach. In tasks that assessed object perseverance, Betty's most mature response was to find the object after two successive visible displacements. Her purposefulness here was striking: she persisted in her efforts to locate the object for a full eight trials after an invisible displacement! But it was the causality tasks that held Betty's interest the longest. She was able to release a toy in order to activate it and also handed the object to the examiner when she was unable to activate it herself.

The only area of concern was Betty's language development. She made a few spontaneous vocalizations while manipulating objects, but social vocalizations were minimal. There was no gibberish with conventional inflections, and she did not imitate words. Although her expressive language was approximately 5 months below age level, her receptive language was better developed. She listened selectively to familiar words and responded correctly to verbal requests.

The change in Mrs. Lake's behavior was noticeable during these assessments. She was attentive to Betty's performance and gave frequent interpretations of her daughter's behaviors—justifying an occasional failure or explaining why Betty might be less interested in a particular object. Her comments were sensitive and reasonable, and she showed much pleasure in her daughter. Nevertheless, during the free play session Mrs. Lake tended to be stereotypic and repetitive in her interactions with Betty. She seemed to find it easier to enjoy her daughter through observation rather than through direct interaction. She often missed Betty's glances in her direction and Betty's attempts to interact with her at a distance by showing her a toy or turning to her. When this happened, Betty quickly returned her attention to the inanimate environment. Predictably, Betty also responded with more animation to her exchanges with the examiner than to her exchanges with her mother.

Phil Is Returned Home: The Entire Family Is Together

Phil was returned home when he was 10 weeks old. Betty was then 14 months. Mrs. Lake responded with pleasure and pride to Phil's return, and was able to work cooperatively with the infant specialist. She joked about the latter's tendency to "spoil" babies by holding them and talking to them, but she herself held Phil with obvious pleasure and engaged in long exchanges with him. Most strikingly, Mrs. Lake seemed able to take care of her three small children quite adequately—she was often seen holding all three together, looking quite content. Her faithful adherence to Prolixin injections no doubt contributed to her improved functioning.

Summary and Discussion

This case illustrates work with a multirisk factor family at many levels—work which involved addressing concrete needs, providing an ongoing therapeutic relationship, devising specific clinical techniques to foster the development of infants with particular vulnerabilities, and, perhaps most important, integrating effectively the efforts of elements in the existing community service system. While the Lakes will almost certainly need continuing support as they rear their children, avoiding the all too familiar cycle of foster care placements for two infants was no small achievement.

Several aspects of our work with the Lakes raise questions worthy of further consideration. One such dimension concerns the shift in Mrs. Lake's attachment to the treatment team. As we have noted, Mrs. Lake was able to develop an ongoing, although vulnerable, relationship with the treatment team, particularly the primary clinician, until Betty was 5½ months old. At that point she pulled away, and the degree of relatedness was never the same again. Trying to understand this pattern, we first associated Mrs. Lake's withdrawal with her ambivalent feelings toward us for being involved in the foster care placement and the impact on Mrs. Lake of the primary clinician's pregnancy. Another possibility is that distant relationships may constitute a more generally comfortable adaptation for Mrs. Lake; we may have engaged her initially during a special "open" phase, related to the pregnancy and birth, which ended during Betty's sixth month and for some reason did not recur with Mrs. Lake's subsequent pregnancy.

The family therapy, instituted to facilitate more open and reasoned communications between Mr. and Mrs. Lake and their children, presented special challenges. Initially Mrs. Lake was the only person who could communicate with her husband except by writing. She often withheld information or distorted it, and Mr. Lake, for his part, refused to pay attention and insisted that his wife was "too crazy" to be taken seriously. Although the pattern of communication between Mr. Lake and the family became more direct when the social worker with training in working with the deaf joined the team, Mr. Lake remained unable to acknowledge changes in Mrs. Lake which followed her resumption of psychotropic medication. Despite efforts of the family treatment team, the entire family continued to isolate Mrs. Lake, often treating her as an alien.

If Mr. and Mrs. Lake were each isolated within the family unit, so was the family isolated from the community and their relatives. The Lakes barely knew their neighbors, were reluctant to call on their own families, and were suspicious of anyone offering "help." When the Lakes did get involved with some outside source of assistance they tended to present a distorted picture of themselves and their situation (which ended by alienating potential helpers) or used services in a way which undermined, rather than fostered, family coping. Thus the Lakes' contacts with lawyers around Betty's placement had the potential for exacerbating rather than resolving the situation, and the family's inappropriate responses to the Child Protective Services social worker during her home visit just after Phil's birth resulted in placement rather than the hoped for material assistance. Mr. Lake used the Deaf Club and church to meet his own needs, but did so in ways which removed him from family life and possibly helped him rationalize his avoidance of family responsibilities.

Achieving a coordinated, comprehensive community interagency approach to the treatment of this family represented the key to a successful intervention strategy. The formulation of a reentry plan following Betty's precipitous foster placement became a mode of negotiation and collaboration among the family, the CIDP staff, the agencies which had already been involved with the Lakes, and even a new element in the system, the Lakes' attorney. This approach, in which each element of the system took on an appropriate share of responsibility and in which ongoing communication was maintained and found rewarding, was eventually successful in heading off a possible series of foster care placements for Betty and in organizing a sustained support system for her and her new brother.

An additional feature of this case—not often addressed in intensive intervention with hard-to-reach families, particularly when one or both parents are psychotic—concerns the feelings experienced by the CIDP staff toward the Lakes. Frustration, anger, confusion, overidentification with the children, and withdrawal were all feelings we came to recognize in ourselves. We recognized, too, that addressing our own feelings—particularly the negative ones—toward such a family was a necessary prerequisite to establishing a trusting relationship with the parents and to sustaining the work over many months. The CIDP experience taught us if staff members were not *aware* of their own emotions, they were more likely to *act* on them. For example, we observed staff members, frustrated and angry at a program participant who missed sessions and then "has the nerve" to criticize, become aloof and controlling rather than empathetic and supportive. The participant might then leave the program, feeling rejected. If, on the other hand, staff members could become aware of their feelings in discussion groups and individual supervision, they were less likely to act them out and better able to understand the unexpressed thoughts and feelings of participants. For example, a rejecting participant might be shunning the staff member because she herself expected to be rejected. Recognizing the feelings generated by the participant's behavior enabled the staff member to anticipate and deal with the participant's emotional reaction to the intervention approach.

5
Magical Thinking and Destructiveness:
Mrs. M. and Amy

Euthymia D. Hibbs, Ph.D.
Patricia Findikoglu, M.A.
Alicia F. Lieberman, Ph.D.
Reginald S. Lourie, M.D.
Robert A. Nover, M.D.
Serena Wieder, Ph.D.
Stanley I. Greenspan, M.D.

Introduction

In an earlier volume of Clinical Infant Reports (*Infants and Parents: Clinical Case Reports*, edited by Sally Provence), we reported on our work with Amy and her mother, Christine M. Their cases illustrate a difficult but all too common clinical occurrence: a situation where no one therapeutic course of action was in itself sufficient to maximize the infant's chance for normal development. The potential gains that could be derived from one approach, parent–infant psychotherapy, were preempted by the mother's narcissistic absorption in herself, and her persistent inability to establish affective connections between her own experiences as a child and the experiences that, as a mother, she now gave to her children. A second approach, individual psychotherapy with the mother, was begun and continued but did not immediately result in an improvement in maternal caregiving. Still a third alternative, family therapy, was hardly a realistic possibility for a family where the only adult was a drug-abusing mother engaged in a self-defeating search for an ideal father figure for herself and her children. Finally, direct intervention with the infant, although implemented from the beginning of the treatment, was often interrupted by the mother's periodic unavailability and by the unstable arrangements for the child's daily care, which often made Amy difficult to find, as she was unpredictably switched from one baby-sitter's home to another. Our search for optimal treatment under far from optimal circumstances did produce significant benefits for this family during the more than three years that we worked with the Marlowes. Using an eclectic approach, we moved simultaneously in different areas treating the mother, treating the infant, making an appropriate referral for Amy's older brother Harold and monitoring its implementation, and establishing contact with Mrs. M.'s parents and with her boyfriend when appropriate or necessary. From an infant whose deterioration in functioning during her first months of life alarmed our intervention team Amy grew to an intelligent, likeable 3-year-old making a fine adjustment to nursery school. The early intervention of an infant specialist, the use of our Infant Center as a home away from home providing daily routine and constancy in human relationships, and therapeutic play sessions with the infant specialist helped Amy cope with her mother's erratic life and sporadic unavailability. Amy's older brother Harold acquired age-appropriate cognitive and social skills after functioning at a level of moderate developmental retardation for much of his young life. A younger brother, Danny, born to Mrs. M. toward the end of the treatment period, was born healthy and robust; unlike Amy, he was welcomed by a mother who was sensitive to his cues, delighted in his abilities, and could be realistic in her planning and expectations. The psychological growth achieved by Mrs. M. and demonstrated in her relationship with Danny seemed, even if unstable and subject to regression, all but unattainable during the early stages of our work.

Our earlier account of work with the Marlowe family presented a detailed report of direct intervention with Amy and summarized the work with Mrs. M. This chapter, in contrast, will focus on Mrs. M. and the magical thinking and destructiveness which so severely impaired her ability to mother and her chances for the serene life she dreamed about.

Initial Impressions

When Mrs. M. joined the program, she was 23 years old, had a 2-year-old son, Harold, and was 6 months pregnant with her second child. Mrs. M. was potentially beautiful, with long blond hair and delicate features, but her appearance was marred by deep circles under her eyes and by a sad facial expression which sometimes changed to anger and suspiciousness. She was usually dressed casually in blue jeans and flat shoes. On the first meeting with the clinician, Mrs. M. was reserved but had good eye contact and was receptive to joining the program, saying that she wanted to know more about children and that she could foresee some "minor" problems with her son Harold after the birth of the baby. She anticipated that Harold who, in her words, had "all her love and attention," would feel neglected, jealous, and abandoned when the new baby came.

At first glance, Mrs. M. seemed articulate and well organized in her thinking. She used a large vocabulary and was able to elaborate on various topics and to make coherent shifts from one topic to another. She appeared able to distinguish between fantasy and reality. She had some difficulty expressing emotions, however, and her affect was flat when she spoke about emotionally charged events, such as an abortion she had had before her present pregnancy. Mrs. M. reported that this event had been very painful for her and that her intense anxiety had triggered an attack of hyperventilation. Yet as she described the experience she seemed remote and impersonal, as if speaking about someone else.

Mrs. M. soon demonstrated her capacity to distort reality and to act impulsively on the basis of these distortions. For example, while verbally assuring the clinician of her love for Harold and the personal sacrifices she made to guarantee his well-being, Mrs. M. in fact demonstrated both physical and emotional neglect of her son. Later, when Amy was less than 6 months old, Mrs. M. suddenly accepted a job as a "housekeeper" for a man she barely knew and his two children. The job was in the country and Mrs. M. fantasized a wholesome rural life and eventual marriage. In reality the job was far away from any friends or services, involved working under primitive conditions with unrealistic duties and virtually no salary, and ended in threats of violence when she finally wanted to leave.

When Mrs. M. first presented herself to the outside world she was able to keep out of sight the deep dependency needs which inevitably emerged later in the relationship. She had an impressive ability to find jobs on the strength of a positive first impression, but she could not sustain these jobs once she became better known to her employers. During some periods of several months' duration Mrs. M. might change jobs as often as once a week.

Mrs. M.'s History

Mrs. M. was the oldest of four children; she had two brothers and a half-sister. Her parents were divorced when Mrs. M. was 5 years old. She was then sent to live with her maternal grandparents while her younger siblings stayed with her mother. This situation continued until Mrs. M. was 12 years old.

Mrs. M. revealed having angry feelings toward her siblings. She said that she was angry at her half-sister because she was treated better than Mrs. M. She was angry at her brothers because when she lived with her grandparents her mother took them on a trip to Florida but did not take Mrs. M. along. This was one of the few events she remembered between the ages of 5 and 12.

In general, Mrs. M. could not recall any events from her childhood. She did not remember specific details of her stay with her grandparents, but said in a flat tone of voice that her grandparents were "good to her" and that her grandfather "was a father" to her. She remembered that he took her shopping and that he warmed her feet in a blanket during cold nights. She also recalled that the grandparents used to say that Mrs. M. was "their fourth daughter."

Mrs. M. was proud to say that her grandparents took her to visit several big cities where her mother and her younger siblings had not been. She reported little interaction with her grandmother, but she considered her grandfather to be a very smart man whom she loved and admired. His death, when she was 12, was a very traumatic event for Mrs. M. Although her affect was flat, Mrs. M. repeatedly described feeling anger at this man who had "abandoned" her through death. Characteristically, she denied deeper feelings of grief or mourning until, later in our work, she was able to experience underlying feelings and could cry for her grandfather's death.

After her grandfather died, Mrs. M. returned to live with her mother, stepfather, and three siblings. She described herself as being the Cinderella who did all the hard domestic jobs while her sister was treated like a princess. There were violent physical fights between herself and her stepfather whom she disliked, and she felt very hurt when her mother commented that if she had to choose between her daughter and her husband, she would choose the latter. The physical fights with her stepfather seemed to have been sexualized in Mrs. M.'s mind. She found it appalling for a "big man like him" to spank a 16-year-old on the buttocks, pull her hair, and hit her with "his hands all over (her) body." Mrs. M. associated the fights with an incident of molestation by an uncle in a swimming pool when she was 5 years old. She said that she remembered that event vividly: the scene was charged with fear, which later reemerged as a variety of psychosomatic preoccupations and symptoms, including abdominal pains and attacks of hyperventilation.

Mrs. M. reported sexual exploration with one of her brothers when she was 12. This consisted of touching the genital area and breasts. This time she said she was "ashamed to feel like that, but liked it and enjoyed it."

Mrs. M. had few friends during latency and early adolescence, and could not remember having any close friends. She played with some children at school but the relationship stopped there. She began to have some peer involvement at midadolescence, but these relationships seemed to revolve around the use of drugs: as she graphically put it, by the age of 16 she had experimented with "all the drugs that were on the market." Several times she had drug-related hallucinations which consisted of men entering through a window to harm her. Every time she had these hallucinations, she called her mother, who told her that nobody could enter through the window. Her mother did not suspect drug abuse.

Mrs. M. initially reported that she was 16 at the onset of her menses. The theme was never raised again until later, when in an outburst of anger against her mother she revealed that she first menstruated at 18. She said that she heard her friends talking about "having their period" but she could not understand what "period" meant. She blamed her mother for not talking to her about menstruation and had sensed that her mother was anxious about her being "late." She recalled that when she first menstruated, her mother was happy and excited, but she herself was frightened. This description of troubling issues surrounding the onset of menses gave us one of the first signs of Mrs. M.'s lack of confidence in her own body. She tried to deal with this uncertainty through suppression, attempting to keep her feelings out of conscious awareness until a crisis heightened her sense of body inadequacy or damage. As will be described, a number of such crises occurred during our work with Mrs. M.

At the age of 18, Mrs. M. met her future husband, a young man who depended on his mother to accomplish even minor tasks and make the smallest decisions. Mrs. M. married

Philip soon after they met in order, in her words, "to escape my mother's house." She first had sexual intercourse on the second night of her honeymoon; the first night, she reported, her husband was not able to achieve an erection. Mrs. M. felt very disappointed at this failure and found intercourse itself was a disappointing experience, since Philip was "not very good" and unable to "turn her on." The couple divorced 3 years later.

Mrs. M. reported that during her marriage she continued to be interested in her old group of friends, the drug providers, although her husband did not participate in that milieu. Mrs. M. found Philip boring and "too straight" for her and left him. Much later, after several unfortunate experiences with other men, Mrs. M. began to appreciate Philip's ability to be "straight" and "honest." During her marriage, however, she was, in her words, "too high" to understand her husband.

In the drug milieu, Mrs. M. met Robert, a young man with whom she "fell in love at first sight."

Mrs. M.'s Relationship with Robert, the Father of Her Children

Mrs. M. moved in with Robert immediately after leaving her husband and was soon pregnant with Harold. She was then 21 years old.

Mrs. M.'s relationship with Robert was stormy, including daily use of drugs and alcohol, and physical abuse. Mrs. M. reported that Robert had hit her several times, but she insisted that he never hit Harold. However, life must have been chaotic for the infant. Both parents were involved in delinquent activities involving drugs and driving stolen cars. Drunken driving and driving with suspended licenses led to dealings with the police, although not to imprisonment.

According to Mrs. M., Robert was a carpenter and an artist, but he stopped working as soon as they moved in together. Robert was not able to fulfill Mrs. M.'s basic dependency needs; she complained about his failure to take care of her and about their fights and drug consumption. The situation deteriorated. One day while Robert was out, Mrs. M. took a friend's van, emptied the apartment of all the furniture and moved in with Chris, a man who had been her lover while she was still married to Mr. M.

The new living situation did not work out and Mrs. M. and her baby moved out after 3 weeks. She begged Robert to "start all over again" but he refused. She rented a room for herself and her child and continued to see Robert, mainly to go to parties. Occasionally they had sexual intercourse. Mrs. M. then became pregnant with her second child. Soon after she discovered this pregnancy, Mrs. M. found an apartment where she hoped Robert would join her. Robert did not, limiting himself to occasional visits and to giving Mrs. M. about $10 a week for Harold's support. In spite of this behavior, Mrs. M. believed that Robert was in love with her and that one day he would marry her. She spoke of Robert's pride in his son Harold, of how moved she was when he sent her flowers in the hospital when Harold was born, and of the many clothes and gifts he bought for his son. She considered herself married to him, she said, because they had lived together as husband and wife for two years. But it was apparent that it was Mrs. M. who initiated contacts with Robert and that his visits to Harold occurred because of her insistence rather than his devotion.

When Mrs. M. was in the eighth month of her second pregnancy, Robert informed her that he was living with another woman and was planning to marry her in 3 months. Mrs. M. flatly denied that this could be true. She insisted that Robert was in love with her and with nobody else and that he could never marry anyone else. This denial was of such proportions that it involved serious distortions of reality. Mrs. M. said that Robert could not marry his girl friend because they had nothing in common. As evidence, she argued that the girl was "straight" and Robert was not, that the girl was a churchgoer and Robert was not.

Robert had denied that he was the father of Mrs. M.'s second baby. Yet as if to underscore her magical thinking and distortions of reality, Mrs. M. fantasized that the day she gave birth, Robert would see his child and come back to marry her and have a family with her and their children. As the clinician tried to help her prepare for the new baby, Mrs. M. refused to discuss any contingency plans to allow for the possibility that Robert would in fact marry his new girl friend. She could only think of different ways in which she would announce the birth of their new child to him.

In spite of these hopes, Mrs. M.'s ambivalence toward Robert was apparent in her complaints that he was not a good father to Harold because he did not buy him toys or take him out for picnics. The clinician felt that Mrs. M. was also voicing her disappointment in Robert as a provider for herself, as the "good father" she had never had and whom she sought, without success, in all the men in her life. Mrs. M. did not reject that interpretation.

Meeting with Mrs. M.'s Family

Meeting with a participant's family of origin, when appropriate, was part of our project's protocol, helping us to find out about childhood events and to make a firsthand assessment of the family. When the clinician raised this issue with Mrs. M., she was reluctant to approach her mother with our request. The clinician explained to Mrs. M. that she wanted to learn more about her early years since it was apparent that she had forgotten much about her childhood. Mrs. M. liked the idea, and said that she too would like to hear about her childhood. But she cautioned the clinician that her mother was "a cold and mean person."

A family meeting took place at Mrs. M.'s house. Mrs. M.'s mother came half an hour late, and explained that she had been delayed because she was searching for Mrs. M.'s baby book.

Mrs. M.'s mother, Mrs. Snow, was a tall, thin, big-boned

but attractive woman. We could see a close physical resemblance between mother and daughter. Mrs. Snow's shoulders were stooped and she held one hand in the other for almost the entire visit. She seemed very anxious initially, but slowly she began to relax when she realized that the conversation and the questions of the clinician were not threatening, as she had feared they would be.

Mrs. Snow reported that she had not planned her pregnancy with Mrs. M. She had never planned any of her children, she reported with a touch of pride. It had been a good pregnancy, she said; Mrs. M. had been a "good baby." She liked to be held and cuddled, she was quiet and slept a lot, but she did not eat well. She kept food in her mouth and did not swallow it. When she swallowed solid food she often vomited afterwards. Yet, in spite of these feeding problems, Mrs. Snow described her daughter as a fat baby.

The developmental milestones were delayed. Mrs. M. walked at 16 months and said her first words at around 2 to 2½ years of age. She talked more fluently at 4.

When the clinician asked Mrs. M.'s mother to reconstruct the years when Mrs. M. lived away from home, the mother used the very same words that had been used by Mrs. M. to describe the separation: Mrs. M.'s grandparents "were like parents to her"; "They considered her to be their fourth daughter." Mrs. M. was "happy to go live with her grandparents." Her grandparents "took her to many cities" and "bought her the most beautiful dresses" while Mrs. Snow "did not have the money to take her two boys for a haircut."

Mrs. Snow described her daughter as an "excellent girl" during her teen years. She didn't study very much, but she managed not to repeat any year in school. She did not "run around with boys, did not date even as a teenager." But suddenly, at 18, she married.

Mrs. M.'s stepfather joined us in the middle of the session. He was a neatly dressed man who held a clerical job with the city government. He gave a similar account of Mrs.

M.'s adolescence. She was a "good girl." When the clinician inquired about their arguments and disagreements, he said that he did not remember but that if they had some disputes, it had been because Mrs. M. was lazy. She did not want to do housework and help her mother. But in general, he said, he was proud of all "his" children. While other parents complained of their children's problems with the law, he explained, his children had not given him problems of that kind and he was proud of that fact.

Both parents criticized Mrs. M. for not being married, for having two children out of wedlock, and for being a welfare recipient, "a parasite of society." (Mrs. Snow herself had worked as a secretary all her life.)

After the meeting was over, Mrs. M. reported that her mother had had a boyfriend on the side during her entire married life. Whenever things did not go well with her husband, she threatened to leave him for the boyfriend. Sometimes, on weekends, she lied to her family and said that she had to go shopping but went to see her boyfriend. Currently, according to Mrs. M., Mrs. Snow was seeing her boyfriend during her lunch hour.

Both Mrs. Snow and her husband were clearly endeavoring in this meeting to present themselves as an ordinary family with uneventful lives and close family ties, hard working and proud of their children. Although their ambivalence toward Mrs. M. was apparent in their overt criticism of her life-style, they seemed unaware of it: contradictory statements were made without any evident consciousness of inconsistency. Thus, Mrs. M. was described as a fat baby but also as one who ate little and vomited often; the Snows were "proud of their children" but condemned Mrs. M. as a "parasite" for being on welfare. It seemed as if unpalatable facts had to be subordinated to acceptable general statements that served to fend off anger, anxiety, and self-blame. In this pattern we recognized the origins of the dichotomy that had puzzled us in Mrs. M.'s behavior: her repeated statements that she loved her son and made many sacrifices for him, and the abrupt, harsh, primitive manner in which she interacted with him. She, like her parents, constructed with words a satisfying illusion that bore little resemblance to her actual feelings.

Mrs. M. was reluctant to talk about her biological father and said that "she did not want to think that he existed." Although he lived only 2 hours away, she had no contact with him and knew little about him. She had last seen him 3 years before. On several occasions Mrs. M. said, "as far as I'm concerned, my father is dead," adding that her "real" father was her grandfather. But on other occasions she identified with her father, saying that she could understand him because "no one in his right mind could live with that bitchy woman" (her mother). These statements appeared to illustrate a painful underlying ambivalence in which Mrs. M. expressed negative affect through the primitive mechanism of "making somebody dead."

Late Pregnancy and Delivery

The last months of Mrs. M.'s pregnancy were marked by quasi-delusional magical thinking involving Robert. In her fantasies, he would be there for his child's birth and, upon looking at the newborn, would realize how deeply he loved the child's mother, Mrs. M., and their story would have a "happy ending." If the clinician attempted to help her deal with reality, Mrs. M. said that she, and not the clinician, was the one who had lived for two years with Robert and knew him.

Fantasy somehow helped Mrs. M. to endure the unpleasant realities of her situation as a single parent, pregnant with a second child, in financial difficulties, isolated from family and friends, and rejected by Robert. The fantasy wish for Robert's return symbolized her wish for reunion with all the important figures she had lost, especially now that she was pregnant and her need for regression, for being taken care of, was strong. The clinician decided to work with Mrs. M. by addressing urgent and concrete issues, such as who would care for Harold while Mrs. M. was in the hospital, where the baby would sleep after coming home, and what agency support systems were available.

Some of Mrs. M.'s magical thinking might have been drug induced. Although she claimed that she had stopped using drugs during her pregnancy, a few weeks before delivery she called the clinician at 2 A.M to report that "men were coming through the window to steal the car." This was a recurrent visual hallucination Mrs. M. had experienced since she was a teenager whenever she was on drugs. It is possible that in this area too there was a dichotomy between reality and what Mrs. M. wished was real: between her actual continued use of drugs during pregnancy and her wish to believe (and to make believe) that she had stopped using drugs for the sake of her unborn baby. In the face of Mrs. M.'s denial that she used drugs while pregnant, this possibility remains an open question. It is certain, however, that the hallucinations represented a breakdown of her wishful thinking about a reconciliation with Robert and the onslaught of severe anxiety regarding her bodily integrity as she was bearing a child.

As the delivery date approached, Mrs. M. started talking about the sex of the new baby. At first she said that she wanted another boy because she wanted Harold to have a brother. Only gradually did she acknowledge that she actually feared having a girl; she said she feared being as "overprotective" with a daughter as her mother had been to her. At the same time, Mrs. M. was convinced that she would, in fact, deliver a girl, because she found her present pregnancy different, and much harder than her previous one.

Two things were striking in Mrs. M.'s perceptions. One was the magnitude of the protective distortion in her perception of her abandoning, neglecting mother as "overprotective." The second was her equation of womanhood with pain: her feeling that carrying a daughter was "harder" and more burdensome than carrying a son. Interestingly, this theme

was elaborated during labor. Mrs. M. spoke to the clinician,
who was present through labor and delivery, about her worries
regarding how to handle a daughter. Between contractions
she spoke about her mother slapping her hands when she
touched her genitals as a child. She went on to say that she
could feel close to a baby daughter but would not know how
to be the mother of an older girl. The clinician felt that Mrs.
M. was giving voice here, in this most womanly of experiences, to her unresolved conflicts about being a woman and
to her fears of her own sexuality.

The delivery was fast and thoroughly normal, and, indeed, Mrs. M. gave birth to a girl. Mrs. M., who had not
received any sedatives, immediately asked to see and hold
her baby. Her first comment was that the baby looked like
Robert. She then asked that the clinician call her mother to
tell her about her new granddaughter. Upon hearing the
news, Mrs. M.'s mother asked for the baby's name and then
said she was in a hurry to hang up because she was going
away for the weekend. It was chilling to witness the grandmother's matter-of-factness as she pursued her weekend plans
without a thought of changing them to welcome her granddaughter and to be available to her daughter in this time of
need.

During her 3-day stay at the hospital the clinician was
Mrs. M.'s only visitor. Mrs. M. called her friends, but everyone was too busy to visit. She made excuses to the clinician,
giving reasons for the failure of friends and relatives to visit
her. But on the third day she broke down and said, between
tears, that she felt lonely and abandoned. She was holding
her baby, and began breast-feeding as she promised Amy that
she would be a good mother, unlike her own mother.

Amy's First Month of Life

While Mrs. M. was able to impress hospital personnel
with her apparent involvement with Amy, the clinician noted
that Mrs. M. spoke of Amy even from the first as "a poor little

thing" who was lonely, with no father to care for and love her. In addition Mrs. M. was disappointed that Amy had failed in her mission to bring Robert to her mother's bedside. As the clinician began to address these issues, Mrs. M. retreated from the pain of reality into a fantasy that Robert need only see his daughter to return to the family.

But Robert did not come back. Mrs. M. called him continually and Robert told her again and again that he was planning to marry in 2 months. Mrs. M. did not believe him. She maintained that Robert could not marry another woman because he loved her and she loved him. She continued to make plans about their getting together again. She fantasized that Robert would come to visit while she was nursing Amy. She would put the baby in the crib and cover her with many blankets so Robert would be unable to see her. Robert could see the baby only if he begged to. Mrs. M. associated this fantasy with a "worry" she had. She felt Robert wanted Amy dead. She worried that because of Robert's wish, something might happen to Amy and she might die. Upon questioning, she said that Robert never expressed such feelings but she knew it "deep inside." In speaking of this, she began crying and said that she was afraid Robert's wish would come true. Her own ambivalence about Amy was projected onto Robert and expressed in the worry that Amy would become sick and die.

As if to counteract that ambivalence through close bodily contact, Mrs. M. devoted an undue amount of time to nursing Amy, who spent most of her waking time at her mother's breast. Sometimes Mrs. M. woke Amy up in order to nurse. It seemed as if Mrs. M. was attempting to protect Amy from her death wishes by intensifying the symbiotic tie between them, literally making Amy a part of her body. The clinician used developmental guidance to deal with this issue, speaking about the diversity of physical and emotional needs of the baby and the different forms of interaction that were important between mother and baby. Mrs. M. listened carefully but could only relate the information to herself, accusing her mother for not having given her that kind of care.

Mrs. M. returned frequently to the theme of her own deprivation of maternal care. The clinician sympathized with her but also pointed out that she was not her mother and could undo with her own daughter what had been done to her. Although Mrs. M. spoke of her efforts to give Amy the kind of mothering she had not had, her words were very seldom translated into concrete examples of emotional nurturing. Indeed, the interaction of Mrs. M. with Amy was pathetic. Mrs. M. looked like a deprived little girl who had received her first doll and did not know what to do with it. Amy was often unclean and smelled strongly of urine. Mrs. M. held her in a detached manner looking blank and preoccupied. She did not look at the baby's eyes, smile, or talk to the baby. She never sang to Amy, and did not cuddle her or rock her. She placed Amy on her lap or her breast as if the baby were an inanimate object. The only overt sign of affection was the kiss she routinely gave to the baby before handing her over to the clinician while saying in a flat voice, "I love my baby." Predictably, Amy also began to be very apathetic in social interactions. It took the clinician a long period of warm-up before Amy responded to her playing, but the clinician eventually succeeded in eliciting gazes and smiles from the baby.

The deterioration in Amy's performance in the course of her first month was extremely worrisome. One expects a baby to become increasingly more alert and able to sustain social interaction in the first weeks of life, but Amy showed a reversal of this process—a decline in her ability to sustain eye contact, to track a moving face, and to orient to the examiner's voice. It was clear that her deterioration was due to the poor quality of Mrs. M.'s mothering, to the chaotic home environment, and to the absence of a substitute caregiver who could provide Amy with the sensitive care Mrs. M. could not give.

Mrs. M. was unable as yet to make use of the clinician's

suggestions for care of her children. She could use the clinician only for her own needs: to talk about her unhappy childhood and her anger at her mother, to daydream about a happy future, and to rely on as a resource if she needed concrete help, like calling an agency on her behalf. But the clinician's intervention as an educator concerning the baby, who demonstrated patterns of child care, and encouraged Mrs. M. to learn them, met with limited success. Although the clinician taught Mrs. M. how and when to change diapers, how to bathe Amy, how to hold, play, and talk with the infant, and Mrs. M. performed well in the clinician's presence, by her own admission she "kind of forgot" the rest of the week.

This pattern was reminiscent of the dichotomy between Mrs. A.'s ability to impress others by speaking of her devotion to her children and her inability to follow through on her words through concrete instances of responsiveness to her children's needs. As long as she had an audience, she could motivate herself to "show off" in order to gain love and approval. But when she was alone with her children her depletion of inner resources was unmitigated by the desire to please, and she had nothing to give.

At that time the Clinical Infant Development Program (CIDP) was growing and more people were hired. We decided then to modify the therapeutic plan and involve an infant specialist in addition to the clinician. The infant specialist would focus on offering concrete developmental guidance and work directly with Amy in providing age-appropriate stimulation. This plan acknowledged Mrs. M.'s inability to "share" the clinician (the good, available mother figure) with her children. The clinician's attempts to focus on the children had been meeting with a defensive withdrawal from Mrs. M., who regarded her children as rivals for the care and attention of the clinician. Also, she often seemed ashamed of speaking with the clinician about her shortcomings as a mother and her ambivalence toward her children; any comment that might indicate that she was less than a perfect, all-loving mother was immediately followed by repeated statements about her love for her children and the sacrifices she made for them. Tentative efforts to interpret these patterns were unsuccessful, and it was concluded that Mrs. M.'s ego organization might well be too primitive to use psychodynamic interpretations without an initial period of ego-strengthening work. We based our new treatment plan on the hypothesis that if the clinician could meet Mrs. M.'s dependency needs by being understanding, available, and dealing with the issues that were of importance to her, Mrs. M. might in turn become gradually more aware of and responsive to her children's needs. We hoped that until this occurred, the infant specialist's direct intervention would help Amy attain competence in cognitive and socioaffective development.

Mrs. M. and Her Family: Amy's First 4 Months

During this period, the plan of using a team approach involving both a clinician and an infant specialist was put into effect. The general plan was explained to Mrs. M. simply and directly: the clinician would help her with her feelings about herself and about her children whereas the infant specialist would work directly with Amy and would show Mrs. M. ways of caring for the baby and encouraging her development.

However, initially both the clinician and the infant specialist felt "confused" and occasionally competitive and possessive, since there was an overlap in their respective therapeutic domains. Probably this confusion was transferred to Mrs. M., who used the two professionals indiscriminately. This pattern was initially a repeat of Mrs. M.'s childhood and adult adaptation: obtain what you need from whomever is available. Although a differentiation of the professionals' roles occurred over time, even after the roles were defined, the clinician continued to offer caregiving suggestions and the infant specialist responded to comments by Mrs. M. about her feelings toward Amy. That Mrs. M. clearly differentiated each interviewer was demonstrated by the distinct level of therapeutic relationship she was able to achieve with each one. As the work of the clinician and infant specialist became progressively more integrated, the value of this dual approach became increasingly apparent.

Mrs. M.'s problems were deeply rooted and this short-term intervention, even though intensive, could not reverse her basic maladaptive functioning. Her physical and emotional neglect of both Harold and Amy was so pervasive that foster care was a topic of frequent staff discussions as a measure to sustain Amy's development. We decided, however, to intensify our intervention program.

While the infant specialist provided direct intervention for the baby and modeling of child care patterns for the mother, the clinician tried to help Mrs. M. sort out reality from the wishful thinking in which she continued to indulge. Robert was a central topic in all the sessions, which took place weekly.

Gradually Mrs. M. realized that Robert was not coming back. Through mutual friends she learned that he was in fact planning to get married. She then began weaving a new fantasy in which, when spring came, she would dress herself and her children beautifully and would go out to the park to meet "the man of her life." This "ideal" man whom she would meet and then marry would be handsome and "straight." However, she said, she would settle for someone like her, someone who had experimented with drugs and alcohol but was now off them, as she was.

In order to meet a new man, Mrs. M. decided to start going out, and did so about once a week. She went with friends to bars where she usually became very drunk and very loud, cursing and using profane language. On one such occasion she lost her pocketbook, with all her papers and four dollars. Mrs. M. became very angry at the bartender and began yelling and insulting the customers. The management had to call the police to intervene. The police finally found her pocketbook in the men's room. All her papers were intact, but her four dollars were missing. We noticed a striking similarity between this event and her core fantasy of having her belongings stolen by an intruder.

While searching for a new man, Mrs. M. continued to seek contact with Robert by attempting to persuade him to visit the children. She phoned him regularly to tell him about Harold's repeated colds, and on occasion described the child as "gravely sick" when the child had 101-degree fever. Robert remained unimpressed. He refused to visit and in addition blamed Mrs. M. for Harold's poor health. He showed no interest in meeting his daughter.

Mrs. M.'s interest in her children at this time seemed predicated largely on their ability to secure Robert's presence. As it became clear that they would not bring Robert back, Mrs. M. began speaking openly of her need to take care of her own life first, which for her meant finding a man who would give her love, acceptance, and financial security.

As a result, Mrs. M. was unable to follow through suggestions concerning her children. She was absorbed in herself. She day-dreamed of her reunion with Robert, talked about wanting to meet another man, and criticized the men she did meet in bars for being "good-for-nothing drunks." At this time, the clinician tried to bring her back to the immediate reality of the children, but she could not sustain appropriate awareness of the children's needs for any consistent length of time. Daily demonstration and encouragement were necessary. Mrs. M. responded with transitory efforts to establish appropriate routines for feeding, sleeping, and hygiene. But she soon reverted to lackadaisical care patterns as she again became preoccupied with magical solutions for the narcissistic hurt that Robert's rejection had produced.

George

At about this time, a friend introduced Mrs. M. to a car mechanic who would fix her broken car. George was 33 years old and divorced. His wife had left him and their two children several years before. Mrs. M. reported that, according to their mutual friend, George had formerly used heroin and "acid" and partied a lot, but was not on heavy drugs anymore. Mrs. M.'s girl friend praised George, saying that he was a loner who was searching for "someone to settle down with." This gave great hope to Mrs. M. She asked George to fix her car. George failed several times to have the car ready and repeatedly asked for extra money for parts. The situation was made worse by the fact that George lived 60 miles away and did not have a telephone. Mrs. M. became angry at George because she needed her car to go shopping and to function as the head of the household, but she also found many excuses for him, attributing the repeated delays to the distance. At other times she felt sad that "George didn't have it all together" because she hoped that she could have a "close relationship" with him. However, the fact that George "didn't have it all together" did not stop Mrs. M. from daydreaming. She said that she would like first to be good friends with George and later to become his lover. He would be the "ideal" man who would marry her and love her children. She contrasted Robert's "immaturity" with George's maturity, adding that the latter was a "real man." These descriptions were made on the basis of the briefest of contacts with George and in the face of Mrs. M.'s actual experiences with George's unreliability and monetary exploitiveness.

As Mrs. M. wove her imagined romance, the children deteriorated. Amy was now showing pronounced gaze avoidance in social interactions. Harold's speech was increasingly delayed, and he constantly sustained minor injuries. The aggressive quality in Mrs. M.'s play with Amy during the child's 4-month assessment made us wonder whether Mrs. M.'s emotional distance from Amy was a form of protection against a powerful urge to hurt the baby. The neglecting mother might become an aggressive one.

As a result of this assessment, intervention with mother and baby was intensified. The clinician saw Mrs. M. twice a week, while the infant specialist visited the home weekly. The immediate goal of the psychotherapy with Mrs. M. was to help her become aware of her ambivalence toward her children. As a first step, the clinician would try to bring some flexibility to Mrs. M.'s rigid defenses against anger, enabling her to make some progress toward object constancy by diminishing the primitiveness of her splitting mechanisms.

This intensified intervention seemed to have little immediate effect. Mrs. M. denied any ambivalence toward her children, spoke at length of her love for them, continued neglecting them both physically and psychologically, and saw no contradiction between her words and her actions. Then something happened that made possible some positive change.

The Ambivalence Emerges

At the beginning of one session, Mrs. M. announced to the clinician in a flat tone that a few days ago she had sent Harold out in the street to play and he had not come back. She searched for a long time but she could not find him. She began running around the housing project calling his name, but there was no answer. She then saw a cruising police car. A policeman got out and asked Mrs. M. if she had lost a small boy. Mrs. M. saw Harold sitting in the back of the car and described him as looking frightened. Before the clinician had time to comment on the event, Mrs. M. said that she thought it was normal for a 2½-year-old boy to run away. She had a girl friend, she said, who had a son who also ran away at Harold's age. She went on to say that a month ago, Harold was wandering around in the project when a woman found him and took him into her apartment. After many hours of searching, she said, she asked the manager to call the tenants of the project to inquire about Harold. They finally found him in the lady's apartment. Mrs. M. then reported a third incident that had taken place recently. She had left Harold in the house sleeping while she drove one of the children for whom she baby-sat to school. When she came back Harold was not there. After half an hour he was found walking toward the school. Mrs. M. thought that Harold "was very smart to do so because he knew where his mother would be."

The fact that Mrs. M. had earlier concealed events was significant. There had been two weekly sessions with the clinician plus several telephone conversations during the week in which the incident occurred.

Acting on the new information, the clinician first worked with the transference issue, speaking to Mrs. M.'s wish to please the clinician and to her fear that unless she was a good "mother," the clinician would become angry and abandon her. Mrs. M. could agree with feeling to this interpretation. The clinician was able to use the affect now available to provide an entrée into the way Mrs. M. dealt with aggressive feelings and to relate them to her earlier reactions to being abandoned. When the clinician linked these experiences to Mrs. M.'s present feelings toward her children, she commented that "sometimes parents feel that they will do much better if they did not have any children." Mrs. M. then took a deep breath and said, "Sometimes I wish I was free and without children to be able to do what I want." But, "at the same time," she added, "I have so much love to give them and when I am down or depressed it feels so good to have Harold or Amy around."

This was the first time Mrs. M. expressed some ambivalence in her feelings about her children. It was the first breakdown in her splitting mechanisms, and the first hopeful sign of therapeutic progress, after 7 months of intensive intervention.

The Department of Social Services Child Protective Services became involved with Mrs. M. as a result of Harold's running away. Mrs. M. became very "upset" with the agency for considering her a "bad" mother. Being "upset" was her way of expressing her anxiety. She was afraid that her children might be taken away, a projection of her own ambivalence and also possibly a reliving of the feelings of herself having been taken away as a child and separated from her mother.

She protested Protective Services involvement, saying that she was a good mother while her mother had been bad toward her. As the clinician reminded her of her own recently acknowledged ambivalence toward her children, Mrs. M. recalled how "upset" she had been several times because she heard her mother "talking through her mouth." She then described a dream she had when she was 7 years old: "A big ugly fish ate both her mother and father." As she spoke of this dream, Mrs. M. could remember for the first time her intense anger at feeling abandoned by them. She then said: "My mother told you once that we are a close family, but I never felt close to my mother," adding that she could never ask her mother for help in case of need. She then promised to be a better mother for her daughter: "I am sure that I would never hurt my daughter as much as my mother hurt me." We felt that she was struggling with her wishes to overcome her past and be a "good" mother for Amy and her parallel fears that she would be unable to do so.

Mrs. M.'s Father Becomes Real

During the same period, Mrs. M. talked often about her father, expressing the wish to meet and get to know him better. She also said she feared that she might not be her father's daughter, but rather the product of any one of the affairs that her mother had had. As she elaborated the theme of illegitimacy, Mrs. M. found herself wondering whether her uncle might also be her father because of the physical resemblance she found between herself and him. At about the same time, a male cousin of Mrs. M.'s began searching for his father and suggesting that Mrs. M.'s biological father might also be his own because of the physical resemblance between the cousins. A family search for fathers began. Mrs. M. joked that she came from an incestuous family. The clinician encouraged Mrs. M. to find and get to know her father. Mrs. M. sent him a letter to let him know that she wanted to see him. He answered by phoning her. She was "shocked" that he actually answered her. Although moved by the fact that her father had called her, she could not talk during this first phone call. She pretended that she had something urgent to do and asked him to call back in half an hour. She was astonished when her father did call back. Her idea of her father, she explained later, was that he was a "bullshitter" because years ago he had not answered a letter she sent him. Looking back, she now believed that her mother might have received the father's reply and had not given it to her. "After all," she said, "my mother told me that he was a bullshitter." Mrs. M.'s splitting mechanisms were again apparent here: she now needed to believe that her father was all good and had to blame her mother for the disappointment he had caused her.

Mrs. M. was very interested in her father's love life, which had been described to her in detail by her mother. While he was married to Mrs. M.'s mother, one of his girl friends had a child by him. At the time of the delivery, the girl friend registered at the hospital under the name of Mrs. M.'s mother, for insurance purposes. The baby was premature and a social worker went to visit Mrs. M.'s mother to inquire about the child's health. This is the way Mrs. M.'s mother discovered the relationship.

Mrs. M. met her father 3 weeks after his phone call. She learned that he had married five times. He was married to his first wife twice, to Mrs. M.'s mother once, and to his third wife twice. He had nine children from all the marriages.

Mrs. M. told her father that she had been married twice and divorced twice, counting her relationship with Robert as a marriage. She explained that she did so because "all fathers want their daughters successfully married, if possible married to millionaires, to have children and live happily ever after." As she tried to find a reason for the separation from her father when she was 4 years old, she said that she had always had the impression that her mother wanted to punish her because her father loved Mrs. M. so very much. She believed that this was the reason her mother "gave her away," did not take her on weekends with the rest of the family and, especially painful, did not take her to Florida with her brothers, despite Mrs. M.'s tearful appeals. She also remembered her mother telling her that her father did not love her because one day when he was driving into the driveway he smashed her tricycle instead of stopping in time and moving it out of the way. According to her mother, Mrs. M. cried for a long time when this happened and it was very difficult to console her. Mrs. M.'s mother also told her that her father did not love her because he did not buy her clothes and shoes. Mrs. M. associated this with a dream she had while she was living with Robert. She dreamed that Robert did not want to buy shoes for Harold and she slapped him. Robert woke up with a start at the sudden slap she had actually given him in her sleep.

With the clinician's help, Mrs. M. was able to acknowledge her deeply rooted anger and her feeling of being rejected by her father as a child and to remember many events about her childhood which she had forgotten. She now looked forward to a better relationship with her father, with whom she had promised to keep in touch. She no longer doubted that she was his daughter.

The hope was that a real-life relationship with her father would help to resolve some of the splitting that occurred in Mrs. M.'s early life, when her grandfather was idealized as being all-good and her father was seen as bad and ungiving. And in addition, the hope was that the renewed relationship with her father would lead to a healthier relationship to men and an enhanced capacity to care for her children. But this was not to occur right away.

Flight to the Countryside: The Clinician's First Vacation

Soon after the meeting with her father, Mrs. M. made a rather abrupt decision: she accepted a housekeeper's position with George, the mechanic, who lived in the country with his two children. Since George had no telephone and seldom came to the city, a mutual friend acted as the broker.

Mrs. M. went to live at George's house with no direct agreement between the two of them regarding salary, work hours, duties, and other work conditions. Although Mrs. M. did have some misgivings about George (she thought he was "peculiar" because he had been very slow to fix her car and also spoke very little), her ability to assess the situation realistically was quickly overpowered by her fantasies: she would live in the country, run in the meadows, and go horseback riding. The children would eat fresh vegetables, eggs, and milk. At the beginning she would be the housekeeper and baby-sitter for George's children, but she hoped the relationship with George would change and that they could marry and form a family.

In retrospect, Mrs. M.'s decision was multidetermined. One unconscious factor might have been the need to flee from the incestous wishes awakened by her recent reunion with her father. The wish to have a man of her own was, as usual, very strong, and George was the only man available to her now that Robert seemed determined to marry someone else. Finally, and at a more immediate level, the clinician had just announced her plans to take a month's vacation.

Mrs. M. reacted to the news of the clinician's departure with a barely concealed sense of rejection. She likened the clinician to her mother, who had gone to Florida without taking her. She said she would go to Florida by herself someday, and hinted she could do it right away because she would inherit some money from her grandmother, who had recently died. But instead of Florida, she decided to move to the countryside.

Preparations for the Move: Amy's Weight Loss

As Mrs. M. prepared to move, the situation in her home became chaotic. She was anxious about the lack of any concrete arrangements with George. She also was anxious about the clinician's impending departure. She responded by fighting with her landlord and with every neighbor, by asking the infant program to "stay off her back" for a month (the month that coincided with the clinician's vacation), and by taking only marginal care of the children, although she assured the clinician and the infant specialist that her child-care practices would improve after her move. The clinician's efforts to point out the realities of the situation went unheeded. Mrs. M. could not wait to move to the country in pursuit of the ideal life of which she dreamed.

The move took place. During her first week as a house-keeper, George gave Mrs. M. $20 for food for two adults and four children. The following week when she asked for more money for shopping, George became very angry and said, "I gave you $20 last week." Mrs. M. then realized she could not rely on George's common sense to help her manage his house. She was upset, but she insisted that although things would be harder than she expected, her dream would come true. Efforts to help her assess her situation more realistically and deal with issues like salary and money for food purchases were unsuccessful. Mrs. M. became very angry at the clinician and told her that she did not understand Mrs. M.'s aspirations. The clinician left on vacation on this note. The infant specialist spent many hours establishing a network of community agency workers who would become involved.

It is important to point out that the infant specialist's main efforts on behalf of the children were undermined by Mrs. M.'s negative transference toward the absent clinician. This negative transference was expressed in an even more pronounced than usual neglect of the children: once again Mrs. M. was repeating her past in the present by "abandoning" her children (through physical and psychological neglect) when she felt abandoned by the clinician. Nevertheless, the importance of a teamwork approach in a case like this cannot be overemphasized. Had a second intervenor not been involved, even the limited protection provided for the children during this period would have been unavailable, and their deterioration may have been even more pronounced.

The concern about Amy's welfare increased enough during this period that many members of the Infant Program (among them the pediatrician and the psychologist in charge of Amy's developmental assessments) urged the involvement of Children's Protective Services (CPS) in the case, or at least a serious conversation with Mrs. M. in which our concerns were clearly outlined and the possibility of CPS involvement, unless conditions improved, was raised. Finally, the decision was made to continue the efforts to coordinate the intervention of local social agencies and to await the clinician's return.

The Clinician Returns: Flight Back to Safety

As soon as the clinician returned from her vacation, she found an infuriated staff: "Amy is in bad shape"; "Mrs. M. is doing worse"; "Such an intensive intervention without results!" "You must make a contract with Mrs. M." The staff was probably voicing Mrs. M.'s anger toward the clinician who had abandoned her. The clinician and the infant specialist visited Mrs. M. and her children the next day. They found a very thin, dishevelled, distraught Mrs. M., and thin, sick-looking unkempt children.

Oblivious to the children, Mrs. M. was only eager to confide her woes to the clinician now that she had her to herself again. While the infant specialist worked with the children, Mrs. M. took the clinician to her room and told her that as soon as she received the message of the clinician's return, she had told George that she would be leaving in 2 weeks. She complained that George was a tyrant. Both of them spent every night "doing drugs," yet he expected her to have breakfast ready by 8 A.M. and became impatient at the briefest delay. Once he threw the dishes against the wall, smearing it with pancake batter, and expected Mrs. M. to clean up the mess. Mrs. M. was puzzled by the difference between their morning and their evening relationship, since they felt close to each other while on drugs, although they had no sexual involvement. They evidently could sustain a semblance of intimacy while on drugs, but the shallowness of their object relations became apparent during the day when they were faced with the realities of work and the children.

Mrs. M. then outlined her plans for the future. She would go to a small town nearby where there was a Navy yard and a friend in the area who promised to find a suitable apartment for her and the children. She hoped she would find "a Navy man." In order to prevent another devastating experience, the clinician suggested that she return to her former surroundings, where the infant program could be more directly helpful to her and her children. As if she were hoping for the suggestion, Mrs. M. immediately agreed to "come home." She then started to call the clinician "mother," explaining that the clinician was her "good mother" who "could take care of her" and "could listen." Mrs. M. expressed relief that the end of her countryside adventure was at hand.

But getting away from George proved to be less than easy. Mrs. M. needed to look for an apartment in the city before moving out, but she had no money and George became furious if she left his house to search for a new home. Violent fights ensued, and one day George threw Mrs. M. and the children out. He kept their belongings—furniture, a stereo—as the price, he said, of their destroying his house and bringing in roaches. When Mrs. M. wanted to pick up some clothes, George held her and the children at gunpoint and would not allow them into the house. Mrs. M.'s mother then became involved and agreed to pay George $215 to ransom her daughter's belongings.

From George's house Mrs. M. and her children first went to spend a few days in her mother's trailer house near the beach. They then returned to the city, but it was difficult to find housing with no money. They moved in with two male friends of Mrs. M.'s who had a big but condemned house. The two young men belonged to Mrs. M.'s old drug milieu and were still using drugs and alcohol heavily.

Intensive work took place in the month that followed.

Mrs. M. was able to contact the welfare and housing emergency agencies by herself and to have them work to her advantage. But she took no better care of the children than before. She continued to use marijuana and alcohol daily. The children were coming to the program office without shoes or with only one shoe, without shirts, or without underwear. It was apparent that Mrs. M. could not cope with the demands of getting housing and food and at the same time attend to the children's needs. It was decided to provide intensive intervention outside the home for the two children. After much searching, a therapeutic nursery school was located, and the administrative procedures that would allow Harold to attend on a subsidized fee were completed. The plans for Amy involved daily visits to the program's playroom for 2 to 3 hours.

This plan was, of course, an acknowledged "second best." We would have preferred to help Mrs. M. provide for her children the kind of relationship the program was endeavoring to give them. But Mrs. M. continued to be immersed in herself and her needs, unable to extend her glimmerings of self-understanding to her children. Mrs. M. enthusiastically accepted the playroom arrangement, which gave her a chance to look for an apartment without having to worry about baby-sitting and also allowed her to meet alone with the clinician.

The clinician continued to spend as many as 10 or 12 hours a week with Mrs. M. during these weeks of crisis. Mrs. M. spoke of her shattered dreams about George and her disappointment in Robert and her own family. For the first time she seemed interested in understanding herself and why "those things" were happening to her. The clinician made the connection between Mrs. M.'s early experiences and their influence on her current behavior and pointed out the parallels between her mother's proposed child-rearing practices and her own. She had ways to reverse the cycle so that her children would not suffer as she had. In addition, the clinician had to deal with reality issues: the need to find housing appropriate for the children and the need for Mrs. M. to take better physical care of herself and of the children.

At her 8-month developmental assessment, Amy showed many of the symptoms of an institutionalized child: object hunger, promiscuous interpersonal ties, shallow affect. But it was felt that the child retained enough interest in the world to profit from further therapeutic approaches. On the other hand, the intervention with Mrs. M. had showed little progress. Although Mrs. M. seemed a little more able to withstand and explore feelings of ambivalence, this emerging capacity was not being translated into any tangible improvement in her relationship with her children. The intervention staff continued to see a most worrisome pattern in the relationship between mother and children, and seemed unable to modify it soon enough to help Amy. Mrs. M. continued to get drunk and use drugs every night. During the day she often looked dazed and disoriented. She offered Amy her breast for the slightest fuss, but if the phone rang she abruptly removed the baby from her breast to answer it. She still did not keep the children's medical appointments.

In an attempt to convey to Mrs. M. the seriousness of the situation, the clinician raised the possibility of foster care for the children until Mrs. M. found a house, got herself organized, and was better able to take care of the children. Mrs. M. rejected the idea violently. She berated the clinician for joining the "others" who thought she was a bad mother, and protested that she cared for her children and would not give them up. But, at the same time, she called Robert and told him that she would put Harold in a foster home while waiting for adoption. Robert told her plainly that she was crazy. Mrs. M. then retreated and asked him for money to rent an apartment and to buy food for Harold. Robert responded that he was going to Florida but that he would give her money on his return if he had any left. Mrs. M. was very upset. Someone else was now going to Florida without her. The search for an apartment continued.

Given Mrs. M.'s violent reaction to the suggestion of foster care, the clinician sought another solution. She proposed making a homemaker available to help Mrs. M. with the children and to work directly with the children under the supervision of the infant specialist. Mrs. M. liked this idea, and it was agreed that a homemaker start working with the family as soon as Mrs. M. found housing.

When Mrs. M. finally found a three-bedroom house with some garden space on a side street in a low-income housing project, the long crisis of flight to the country and return was over. In a pattern we now recognized, Mrs. M. was exhausted but ready for a new start. The first week after moving to the new house, she worked hard to fix everything nicely. She decreased her intake of drugs and alcohol, renewed her search for the "straight" man who would rescue her and her children, and promised to be more careful of herself and her children in the future.

The "new start" lasted only briefly. Over the period of the ensuing 5 months, the following events took place in quick succession:

1. Mrs. M.'s cousin Sally, her boyfriend, and his child moved in. Sally and her boyfriend were drug pushers who were out all night and slept during the day. They slept in the living room, and were the first sight one encountered on visiting the M.'s. Several weeks passed before the rental office found out about these guests and threw them out.

2. Robert got married. This was very hard for Mrs. M. to accept. She coped with the news by continuing to insist that Robert loved her and would divorce soon to marry her. Soon afterwards she started to pick up men. She invited them to her apartment and smoked marijuana with them, but asked them to leave when she found out they were married or concluded that they were not the "straight" men she was seeking. She did not engage in sexual intercourse with them.

3. When Amy was 11 months old, Mrs. M. developed an abscess on her breast and abruptly discontinued breast

feeding. Amy made the transition to the bottle fairly easily, since the bottle had been gradually introduced over the previous 3 months. Mrs. M.'s abscess spread to the rest of her body. One of the boils on the breast became so big that an operation was needed. Mrs. M. had to be hospitalized but there was nobody to take care of the children. Her mother refused; her cousin Sally also refused because she was angry at having been told to leave Mrs. M.'s apartment by the management. Due to the lack of child care, Mrs. M. had to undergo the operation on an outpatient basis even though hospitalization had been recommended. She felt abandoned and alone. She also said she missed the closeness with Amy she had had through breast-feeding. At the same time, she blamed the breast-feeding, and hence Amy, for the onset of the boils.

During Mrs. M.'s illness, the homemaker reported that many times there was no food in the house. There was nothing to feed the children, and the homemaker often spent her own money to give the children something to eat. Amy's weight was again a source of worry. At 11½ months, she was in the 5th percentile for weight and the 40th percentile for length.

Mrs. M. emerged from her illness physically, psychologically, and financially drained. She used the approaching Christmas season to rally herself to action. She insisted that she had to work to supplement her Aid to Families with Dependent Children (AFDC) income in order to give her children a "good Christmas"—one with lots of toys. Mrs. M. told the clinician that giving the children many toys was her way of compensating them for not having a father. The clinician pointed out that a "good Christmas" has many meanings, and that being available to her children was more important to their well-being than having many toys. Mrs. M. agreed perfunctorily but remained determined to find a job. It is very likely that she was seeking an escape from her depression and also pursuing her mythical search for a man. The clinician became frustrated at her inability to prevent the next foreseeable crisis and thought that "at times like this Mrs. M. seems like a car without brakes—nothing, short of emotional disaster, can stop her."

Mrs. M. threw herself completely into the task of looking for a job. She found one, but in the ensuing 2 months she changed jobs on an average of once a week. Sometimes she stayed at a job for 1 week, sometimes for 1 day. She worked as a waitress, a job that Mrs. M. liked because it gave her the opportunity to meet men, and was gone from home between 12 and 18 hours a day. During this period, the children changed baby-sitters as frequently as Mrs. M. changed jobs. To introduce some predictability in their environment, we arranged for both Harold and Amy to spend half of every day in our therapeutic nursery. With Mrs. M. virtually never at home, it made little sense either practically or therapeutically for the homemaker to continue going to the home and keeping house for Mrs. M. It was decided instead that the homemaker would continue seeing Amy at the Infant Center in order to provide some continuity in caregiving. Mrs. M. followed through only periodically on these plans. At Amy's 1-year assessment, which took place about 2 weeks after the beginning of this arrangement, Mrs. M. seemed to be defending against separation anxiety by withdrawing interest in the world.

Therapeutic Issues in the Work with Mrs. M. during this Period

Mrs. M.'s work as a waitress and her search for a new man provided an important therapeutic entrée into Mrs. M.'s conflicts around mothering. While working as a waitress, Mrs. M. met a barman with whom she soon was smoking marijuana during work breaks and lunch hours. When he attempted to have sex with her, she rebuked him angrily. This episode served as a starting point for an exploration of Mrs. M.'s sexuality and her use of drugs. Although this exploration was incomplete because of Mrs. M.'s inability for sustained introspection, some interesting clues emerged. Mrs. M. equated sex with closeness and protection; she said that she did not care about sexual intercourse in itself. It seemed likely, in light of these comments, that she was nonorgasmic and might fear the physical closeness involved in intercourse. This possibility was given added weight by the many instances in which she rejected sexual advances and the vague allusions to sexual dissatisfaction in her marriage. Mrs. M. also spoke, often in quick sequence, of her greater sexual satisfaction with Robert and of the violent fights they had with each other. This suggested that aggression and sexuality were so deeply fused for Mrs. M. that she could only become sexually aroused in the context of a sadomasochistic relationship.

Mrs. M.'s drug use became a simultaneous area of inquiry. She acknowledged that smoking marijuana helped her feel "full" and "high" when she was having feelings of "emptiness." The sexual imagery she used suggested to us that drug "highs" were being used as substitutes for the sexual satisfaction she could not attain in her relationship with men. Mrs. M. never spent her own money on drugs but procured them from her friends (usually men) who were well supplied and generous. Smoking marijuana with them was an avenue for the intimate sharing that was closed to Mrs. M. in everyday life. The clinician spent a great amount of time in drug-related counseling and Mrs. M. was able to stay off drugs for periods of as long as 2 months.

As Mrs. M. began tentatively to explore the issues in her relationship to men, she was able to acknowledge how difficult it was for her to feel close to people. She was also able to see how this difficulty manifested itself in her relationship with her children. As she could tolerate an increasing awareness of her own ambivalence, the tendency to use splitting as a defense became considerably attenuated. At one point she was able to say: "I sometimes feel that I would be better off without any children but they are there and I love them."

Never before had she been so able to acknowledge her negative feelings toward her children.

Mrs. M. Meets a New Man

Perhaps as a result of the therapeutic work, Mrs. M. was soon able to feel physically attracted to a new man, Harry. She had met him at a party, and although they spoke very little Mrs. M. quickly started fantasizing about him. From then on, Mrs. M. focused all her energy on trying to find him again. After a search of several weeks, she located a mutual friend through whom she sent Harry a message that she was interested in him. Harry responded by inviting her to dinner. Mrs. M. was fascinated by his manners. He opened the car door for her. He was very polite at the restaurant, always asking her first what she wanted. When they finished dinner he drove her home, took the key from her hand, and opened the door. She invited him in, they had some beer, smoked some marijuana, and talked. When he was leaving he tried to kiss Mrs. M. and she pushed him away violently. He left angry. This time, instead of Mrs. M. becoming angry, in return, she became distressed over her behavior and wondered why, since she liked Harry and wanted to feel close to him, she had responded abruptly by pushing him away. Mrs. M. wanted to call him and tell him how much she had been hurt in her life by men. She wanted to explain the reason for her pushing him away. She was ready to tell him her life story. At the clinician's suggestion, however, she did not pour herself out to him but did call Harry, handling the situation appropriately. He responded to her approach and they began seeing each other steadily.

Harry was a carpenter. He had a good job and was well paid. He was also attending school to expand his skills as a construction carpenter. Mrs. M. described Harry as very shy and rather quiet. She learned through friends that he had lived with a girl friend for 6 months. She also learned that Harry drank a lot. His own father had been a heavy drinker but had finally joined Alcoholics Anonymous. His mother was a nurse. Harry was living with his family. He had been thrown out of his apartment several months earlier because he did not pay the rent. He could not save enough money to rent an apartment by himself.

Mrs. M. hoped that she could attract Harry through her children. She always had her children with her whenever she met with Harry. When one of them climbed on Harry, asking for attention, Mrs. M. concluded that they loved him.

Mrs. M. seemed to have an immediate need to fuse with Harry, to depend on him entirely, and to have him be both her father and the father of her children. When the clinician pointed out this pattern to her, Mrs. M. accepted this interpretation at an intellectual level but could not postpone her need to have the relationship with Harry move very fast. She was afraid to lose him and wanted to become completely dependent on him. This desire was expressed in several ways. Whenever her car stalled on the cold winter mornings she wanted to call Harry to fix it. She wanted Harry to take her shopping. She wanted to ask him to baby-sit for her children while she was working in the evenings. She wanted Harry to change Amy's diapers and bottle feed her. One day the clinician asked her to talk about her fantasy regarding her future with Harry. Predictably, she answered that she daydreamed that she and Harry would love each other, move in together, marry, and live happily all their lives. But she preceded this fantasy with a telling remark: "Yes, Harry drinks a lot, but I'm sure he is not going to beat me up." Only then did she proceed to talk about her fantasy. Her sasomasochistic wishes were very close to the surface.

During this period, Mrs. M. became openly aggressive toward Harold, saying that all her problems originated in him. She accused her son of being emotionally disturbed and very demanding. It seemed that she was displacing onto Harold her aggression toward men in general and Harry in particular. She felt jealous of her own children for the relationship with the father figure that she craved to have exclusively for herself.

As the clinician touched on these issues, Mrs. M. began to express her feelings toward her children more openly. She saw Amy as the poor, abandoned baby that represented the empty, lonely part of herself. She could recall her own feelings of deprivation as she grew up, and said that she saw herself as the "poor Amy" who had "lost her father," and whose father had never accepted her as his daughter. She overtly expressed her anger against Harold, who probably embodied the primitive, dangerous, aggressive part of herself. On some levels, this work had a stabilizing effect on Mrs. M.: she found a job sorting mail in a mailroom, and was able to keep the job for many months to come. But the relationship with Harry kept her uncertain about herself, and the children were still receiving the brunt of her anxiety and her anger.

Unfolding Relationship with Harry

After dating Harry for 3 months, Mrs. M. still had not had sexual intercourse with him. She reported that Harry had "confessed" to her that he had difficulties "making love to girls" because he had been "hurt many times by girls." He tried unsuccessfully to have sexual intercourse with Mrs. M. and one night became very upset and belligerent toward Mrs. M. and left. Mrs. M. then became Harry's "therapist," trying to help him talk about his problem, to understand him and to guide him. As a rule, Harry drank heavily or used drugs before attempting to have intercourse, and several times he fell asleep in the process. Although Mrs. M. continued to be kind and understanding toward Harry, she continued to displace her anger onto Harold.

One night when Mrs. M. went out to a bar with Harry she lost her billfold, just as she had during the same month the previous year. Panicky, Mrs. M. began yelling at the customers, accusing them of stealing the billfold. She was upset with the manager and the waiter. After 2 days, Harry called her and said she had left her billfold in his car.

The lost billfold seemed to have a deep symbolic meaning

for Mrs. M. Now that her femininity was acutely threatened by Harry's sexual inadequacy, old fears of loss and castration were being symbolically enacted again, as they had been the previous year when Mrs. M. was in the process of mourning the loss of Robert. The symbolism was linked with her adolescent drug fantasy that a man would come in through the window to take away her belongings. As the links between Mrs. M.'s sexuality, fear of body damage and loss, and paranoia began to emerge, the clinician began to understand an important component in Mrs. M.'s relationship with her children, namely, their role in reassuring Mrs. M. that she was complete, that her body was not inadequate as she feared. This connection helped to explain why Mrs. M. hoped to attract men—first Robert and now Harry—through her children and through her role as a mother. By herself, without the children as a concrete reminder of her womanhood, she felt unable to attract and keep a man.

Whatever symbolic meaning motherhood may have had for Mrs. M., there were no signs that the emerging insights about herself she was painstakingly gaining through her therapeutic work were having any positive effect on her actual mothering. Harold's therapeutic nursery school placement was helping him make remarkable improvement, but Amy continued to deteriorate. Since there seemed little prospect that Mrs. M. could improve soon enough to help Amy with the developmental tasks she needed to master, we instituted a full-fledged therapeutic regime designed to meet Amy's specific developmental needs. We now had available for the 17-month-old Amy a therapeutic Infant Center, an expansion of the earlier infant playroom. Here Amy came for the whole day, 5 days a week.

When she first started her attendance, Amy's large gray eyes, fragile frame, eczemalike rashes, and ill-fitting clothing presented a sad picture to the Infant Center staff. Her vocabulary consisted of two or three words, her affect was flat and somber, and her whininess wearied even the Center staff.

Yet during the next 7 months, the Infant Center and office became a "home away from home" for Amy, where two caregivers and other friendly adults and children offered Amy an opportunity to establish genuine and rich human attachments in the context of a predictable daily routine. Most importantly, there was also an opportunity for regular individual sessions, described in detail in *Infants and Parents*, where Amy could initially play out and then talk about her concerns with aggression, separation, loss, body damage, and eventually shift into age-expected interests in the control of aggression, pleasure, curiosity about the human body, and the satisfying aspects of dependency. We continued to hope that as Mrs. M.'s therapy progressed, she herself might come to offer developmentally facilitating experiences to her children.

"Pregnancy"

Mrs. M. and Harry were finally able to have sexual intercourse. Things seemed stable: Mrs. M. was in an excellent mood and she was more available to both children. But about 3 weeks after the first intercourse, she declared that she was pregnant. Mrs. M. began experiencing typical symptoms of pregnancy, including morning nausea and fatigue. She also said that she felt her stomach growing. When the clinician inquired about dates, Mrs. M. became very upset. The first intercourse had taken place during the last day of Mrs. M.'s menstruation, and she insisted that this was a woman's fertile time. Believing herself pregnant, she stopped smoking marijuana and drinking alcohol. She believed that as soon as she announced her pregnancy to Harry, he would ask her to marry him. When a pregnancy test produced negative results, Mrs. M. declared that the doctors were "quacks" who knew nothing about her and her body. Mrs. M. did not want to hear any suggestions that she might not be pregnant. Approximately 28 days after the presumed conception, Mrs. M.'s cousin Sally came to visit, bringing cocaine. They all "did some cocaine," and the next day Mrs. M. "hemorrhaged." (It was her menstruation.) She said she had strong pains and declared that this was a miscarriage possibly caused by the cocaine. She went to the emergency room in the hospital and was told that this was not a miscarriage but a normal menstruation. Again Mrs. M. did not believe "those quacks" and continued to be sick and experience pain. She went to another emergency room of another hospital, where she again was told that her bleeding was not a miscarriage. She went to yet another hospital, and then to private doctors, all of whom confirmed the original evaluation. Mrs. M. became more and more angry, insisting that no one knew her or her body.

As the clinician inquired about Mrs. M.'s ideas regarding conception, she discovered that Mrs. M. believed pregnancy occurred anytime during the menstrual cycle: "Any time you make love you have a baby, unless you are on the pill." The clinician sought to straighten out this misconception and spent some time talking to Mrs. M. about the functioning of a woman's body. She then suggested that Mrs. M. might not have been pregnant because intercourse had taken place on the last day of her period. Mrs. M. became very upset and asked the clinician to leave her house, calling her by some ugly epithets. This was the first time Mrs. M. was able to express her anger directly at the clinician. She usually displaced the anger she felt toward the clinician onto her mother, baby-sitter, or doctors, needing to be "the good girl" for the clinician and afraid to "disappoint" her with her behavior. Her discovery that her directly expressed anger did not kill the clinician helped Mrs. M. diminish her need to use the primitive "splitting" defense mechanism.

Mrs. M.'s desire for pregnancy was remarkable in its intensity and resistance to reality-testing. Pregnancy represented a way to keep Harry close at a time when the relationship was vulnerable to the couple's increasing familiarity and the subsequent decrease in their idealization of each other. The pregnancy was also used to control the relationship, to force Harry into making the decision to marry Mrs. M. At a deeper level, the pregnancy represented for Mrs. M. what her earlier pregnancies had also represented—a way to be a "good" person, to start a "good" life, to "fill up" her emptiness and to incorporate some part of the man she was currently idealizing.

Soon after the crisis of the fantasized pregnancy and the emergence of anger at the clinician, the clinician announced plans for a vacation. Mrs. M. replied: "I knew it was coming." When the clinician suggested that Mrs. M. might be angry at her for going away, she said: "I am used to that, my mother used to leave me and go away also . . . go to Florida," adding that she promised herself that one day she would go to Florida. Anyway, she added in an off-hand manner, she now had Harry to lean on, and she did not need the clinician as much as before. But the month preceding the clinician's vacation was tumultuous, as Mrs. M. developed somatic symptoms. She maintained that her relationship with Harry was good but that drug use had "destroyed" her body. She believed also that part of the baby she had supposedly miscarried was still inside her. The miscarriage was not complete, she said, and this was giving her stomach pains. "I am carrying a dead part of my baby inside me." Again we saw a manifestation of Mrs. M.'s perception of her womanhood as dangerous and destructive.

Harry himself did not know a lot about how a woman's body functions. He became very worried about Mrs. M.'s sickness, and he felt responsible. However, this did not mean that they stopped fighting. The fights usually started between Harry and Mrs. M., but both of them ended up by blaming Harold as the cause of their discord.

A few days prior to the clinician's departure on vacation, Mrs. M. finally found a doctor who was willing to admit her in the hospital for laporoscopy and D and C. She now told the clinician that it would be stupid for her to go away now that she had to go into the hospital. She said that she might have cancer, since cancer ran in her family, along with heart attacks and diabetes. She said that the clinician was like her mother, who was never there during the critical periods in her life. She added that she was happy that Harry was available to depend on, but immediately after that remark she started raging against her mother, in a displacement of the anger she felt toward the clinician. The clinician was able to point out that such displacements were not helping her in dealing with her physical complaints and that the main issues were her anger and separation feelings.

This sequence shows the onset of anaclitic and symbiotic separation themes with the clinician, which marked the beginning of a higher level of object relations than the preobject narcissistic level at which Mrs. M. had functioned earlier. It is interesting to speculate here that the pregnancy delusion and psychosomatic symptoms might represent a developmental step in the resolution of some of Mrs. M.'s primitive ambivalence. In this intrapsychic developmental schema, the steps would be: (1) people regarded as nonhuman objects; (2) people conceived of as split objects, either idealized as completely good or primitively rejected as completely bad; (3) a breakdown of the splitting mechanism and the emergence of integrating psychological structures; (4) the attainment of a primitive level of integration in object relations involving psychosomatic symptoms derived from conflicts, experienced at the somatic level, over the emergence of aggression; (5) representational conflicts. The basic idea in this scheme is that psychosomatic symptoms represent a developmentally higher form of functioning than magical splitting, and that Mrs. M.'s painstaking move from one level to the other represents a form of psychological growth.

Harry Plans to Move in

Harry and Mrs. M. began discussing the possibility of living together. During the month preceding the clinician's vacation, Harry was actually moving into Mrs. M.'s house in a piecemeal fashion, bringing a box here, a suitcase there, whenever he visited her. This represented a source of acute anxiety for Mrs. M. She wanted desperately to be with Harry, but at the same time she was very scared, feeling insecure about her capacity to keep a man and manage to have a balanced relationship with both Harry and her children. Her anxiety was expressed in an increased consumption of alcohol and marijuana. It was also expressed in an attack of hyperventilation that occurred at work and was so severe that the management called an ambulance and sent Mrs. M. to the hospital emergency room. In attempting to find a reason for the attack, Mrs. M. recalled the earlier episode of hyperventilation which had occurred when Robert and her mother "forced" her to have an abortion. She went on to explain that the present episode was a reaction to her recent "miscarriage" and the loss of the infant, but was able to acknowledge that she was also very anxious about Harry moving in with her. She complained that his inability to make a decision about moving in kept her "on a limb." She then promised herself a baby as soon as possible to replace the one she had just lost. On this worrisome note, the clinician left on her vacation. At this time, 19-month-old Amy had been attending the Infant Center for 2 months.

Mrs. M.'s Relationship to the Infant Center During the Clinician's Absence and after her Return

The interaction between Mrs. M. and the Infant Center took a long time to become relatively stable. Initially, communications between the mother and the infant specialist took place through the clinician. This plan had been designed in order to ensure that all the interviewers knew what was happening and that Mrs. M. knew that the clinician and the infant specialist worked together as a team on behalf of herself and her child. In practice, the plan suffered from repeated mix-ups regarding picking up arrangements and who said what to whom. It was strongly suspected that Mrs. M. sometimes played the clinician off against the infant specialist or vice versa in order to protect herself when she did not follow up on her word.

Communication problems worsened when the clinician went away on vacation during the second month of Amy's attendance at the Infant Center. The separation was obviously difficult for Mrs. M., and she displaced her anger at the clinician on the infant specialist and other Infant Center staff members. She caused several mix-ups by failing to notify the staff of changes in her plans to pick up Amy in the afternoon. She failed to have Amy ready in the morning and lashed out verbally at staff members over the phone.

When the clinician returned, she found herself in the middle of a growing conflict between Mrs. M. and the Infant Center. Both Mrs. M. and the staff were angry at her. Mrs. M. rebuked her for going away and leaving her in the hospital, while the staff, possibly giving voice to Mrs. M.'s deeper feeling, expressed dismay that so much therapeutic intervention had not yet proven useful in helping Mrs. M. become a better mother.

It is quite possible that the Infant Center staff and the clinician were acting out some of the splits of Mrs. M.'s personality, the staff reacting to the hostile, provocative, narcissistic side of Mrs. M. and the clinician taking a protective stance toward the sad and empty little girl who asked for help. Most important, however, Mrs. M. was showing, by her own and the staff's anger, that she was learning to protest.

Mrs. M. was indignant to find that the clinician had been told of the mix-ups and the conflicts that occurred during the latter's vacation. She had to be reminded that there were no secrets in the program: everybody worked together. It was also decided that all communications involving Amy and the Infant Center would now be handled directly between the infant specialist and Mrs. M. This diminished the chances for manipulation in playing staff members against each other. The infant specialist also made clear to Mrs. M. her responsibility in having Amy attend the Infant Center.

Mrs. M. responded well to her responsibilities as a mother when these could be stated as simple directives, but when her own problems overwhelmed Mrs. M., Amy's needs continued to come second.

There were moments when Mrs. M. radiated as a mother. She brightened up on being told of a newly acquired skill by Amy. The difference between Amy and Harold when he was Amy's age was readily apparent to her, and she commented on it frequently. When asked to what she attributed the difference, she reminisced about the "mess" her life was in when Harold was a baby, and spoke of how much better she was doing now. Inevitably the conversation turned to her own childhood. Her anger toward her mother was vivid.

On the other hand, it seemed that we could never be a good enough mother to Mrs. M. She was not popular with the other mothers because she remained aloof from them. She had also managed to alienate herself from most of the support staff by being rather abrupt or lashing out at them on the phone. Although the infant specialist had never displayed any anger toward Mrs. M., she often began phone conversations by saying "You might be angry at what I'm going to tell you but . . ." It was as if she anticipated the anger within herself also to be in others. She would be ready by attacking first.

Mrs. M. continued to be only sporadically available to the children, and was still prone to jump from sweetness to vituperative anger. Yet she did have more strength to build upon: guilt and the desire to be a good mother were there. She wanted to do what was right: she borrowed library books, read to the children, got them toothbrushes, asked for conferences. Between Harold's therapeutic nursery school and the infant program she had been inundated with good modeling. She understood that there were a variety of ways to interact with children. She proved to have some observational skills and was now interested in and able to talk about child development and child rearing. Although her ability to follow through after these discussions was questionable, moments of quality in Mrs. M.'s interactions with her children occurred more often than ever before.

Harry Moves In

Three months after Amy began attending the Infant Center on a full-time basis, Harry finally moved in with Mrs. M. From the beginning the situation was far from optimal. There were many fights, most of which centered around Harold. Harry drank heavily during the day and smoked marijuana at night. He was "high" most of the time. He was belligerent with Mrs. M. and harshly punitive toward the children, particularly Harold. Harry accused Mrs. M. of being "high" all the time herself, and of being unable to keep a clean house. Probably sensing Mrs. M.'s dread of separation he constantly threatened to leave her. Mrs. M. responded to this threat by hyperventilating frequently.

Tensions were compounded by the fact that soon after Harry moved in, Mrs. M. had to find a new job. She very much liked the mailing house job she was doing and had received a small promotion that made her feel valued. But company rules required that once Mrs. M. had worked 1,000 hours for the company, she had to leave and wait for 3 months before she could be rehired.

Shortly before Christmas, Mrs. M. had an experience that forced her to come to grips with feelings of aggression. Mrs. M. was out shopping with Harold when she saw Robert. She became very excited and approached him to say "hello" and to have Harold greet his father. But Robert looked past her and walked on to join his wife, who, according to Mrs. M., "looked pregnant." It was a very painful experience for Mrs. M. She identified with Harold, who had an unloving father who walked away from him. She felt pity for Harold and bought him extra toys for Christmas. During the weeks that followed, Mrs. M. began to fantasize that when Harold was old enough she would bring him to his father's door and would have Robert close the door on his son's face. Then Harold would understand who his father was, and understand the fact that his father never loved him. She planned to tell Harold "you see, your father doesn't want you, doesn't love you." (This is similar to what Mrs. M.'s mother had done to her, much to Mrs. M.'s anger.) She fantasized that the house Robert and his wife were living in would burn down with his wife inside. Robert would be outside so he could feel the pain of his loss. This fantasy was developed a little in the days that followed, as Mrs. M. said that she might be the one to set the house on fire.

A New Family Crisis: Harry Moves Out

Five months after first moving in with the M. family, Harry moved out. Mrs. M. then decided (yet again) that she could no longer tolerate alcohol or drug abusers; once more, her dream was to find someone who had once abused drugs or alcohol but was now "straight," as she considered herself to be. She criticized Harry constantly for his drinking, his immaturity, and his belligerence. Sometimes she admitted that she was often frightened by the unpredictable behavior he exhibited when drunk. Yet despite these criticisms, Mrs. M. asked Harry to remain good friends. Harry in turn promised to give her some financial support for a couple of months.

After Harry left, Mrs. M. began feeling a need to be pregnant and to have Harry's child. She wanted intensely to replace the "baby" she fantasized she miscarried and believed that if Harry learned that she was pregnant, he would come back to her and become an ideal father to their child. As the clinician pointed out to Mrs. M., she was repeating her pattern with Robert. An initial infatuation was followed by the need to live together in order to be "inseparable." Small disagreements were then followed by violent arguments. When separation became imminent, Mrs. M. then either became pregnant, fantasized that she was pregnant, or wished for a pregnancy as a means to hold onto the relationship, to retain "part of the person inside her."

While perfunctorily agreeing with this interpretation, Mrs. M. began planning once again how to find a new man. She began the familiar sequence of going to bars, drinking, and meeting men whom she disparaged as "bums."

Two months after Harry moved out, Mrs. M. started seeing him again. They dated once or twice a week and occasionally had sexual intercourse. Harry continued to drink heavily, and shortly after renewing the relationship with Mrs. M. he had a serious accident, hitting a parked car and demolishing both it and his own automobile. He called Mrs. M. immediately to help him out. Harry had to spend one night in the police station for drunken driving; there Mrs. M. took the role of the protective mother who was taking care of another baby. She forbade him to drink and made him promise, just as the probation officer did, to join Alcoholics Anonymous and to see an alcohol counselor. During a "honeymoon" which followed this incident, Harry and Mrs. M. talked about getting married in 2 or 3 months. Harry had his own apartment, but they met several evenings during the week and Harry often stayed at Mrs. M.'s house, especially on the weekends. He had, of course, lost his car and depended on Mrs. M. to drive him back and forth to work. Mrs. M. arose at 5:00 A.M., drove him to work, returned home, and started getting herself and the children ready for the day.

Ostensibly the relationship with Harry was stable and satisfying, but Mrs. M. increasingly expressed conflict through somatic complaints. She felt that her body was very weak. She repeatedly went to doctors for all kinds of examinations. One doctor told her that she might have a vitamin B_{12} deficiency and prescribed injections. Mrs. M. felt that this was the answer to her problem. She did not miss one clinic appointment to have her shot.

The honeymoon period with Harry lasted only 1 month, to be replaced by the old pattern of fighting, but with one variation: the fights took place on Friday night. Harry then would not come over for the weekend, and on Monday evening Mrs. M. would go to his house to "make up." This pattern was repeated again and again.

As this pattern was unfolding, a new crisis occurred. Mrs. M. came to see the clinician at the office and forgot her purse in the Infant Center next door. While she was talking to the clinician, her purse was lost. The crisis over the lost purse lasted almost a full 2 months. Whenever something unpleasant or inconvenient occurred to her from then on, Mrs. M. attributed it to the loss of her purse. She became angry with the Center and angry at the clinician for not canceling the rest of her appointments that day to help her find her purse. She decided that the purse had been stolen by some teenage boys who were visiting the Center that day. She planned to put announcements all over the Center offering rewards to the person who returned her purse, while secretly confiding to the clinician that she did not plan to give a reward.

This was the third consecutive spring in which Mrs. M. had lost her purse. We still did not completely understand the symbolism involved nor the connection between symbolism and season. Given the affective context of separation and romantic turmoil in which the loss always occurred, we guessed that her fear of closeness and intimacy was connected with the "purse being stolen." Her sexual body parts, both male (as in her long-held wish to be a mailman) and female (symbolized in the inner space of the purse) were perceived as endangered. At one level the danger might involve castration; at a more fundamental level, it involved her sense of identity, perhaps through a loss of gender, or perhaps through the loss of that part of herself that deserved and received the good things in life.

The sense of loss and the defensive use of anger revealed themselves in numerous interesting situations in the Infant Center. Mrs. M. accused the Center of losing articles of clothing even though the Center had, in fact, given numerous bags of clothing to Mrs. M. and items she borrowed (diapers, etc.) were often not returned. She accused other mothers of "taking her stuff." Many times she said, "you don't know how much I have lost in my life." The actual theft of her purse while in the Infant Center was a traumatic event that caused her to threaten again and again to take Amy out of the program

because "of what you let happen there." Her anger was intense, lasted many weeks, and was very resistant to therapeutic exploration.

It was at this time that Mrs. M. decided to follow through
on a long-standing invitation that the clinician had extended
to Harry to discuss the children together. Mrs. M. had all
along maintained that Harry did not like "nosy psychologists"
digging in his past; the clinician repeatedly emphasized that
she was interested not in Harry's past but in the children's
development, and that if Harry understood the children better
he might become a better caregiver for them. Now Mrs. M.
suddenly found this rationale very appealing and initiated an
appointment for a Saturday morning, when Harry did not
usually work. She told the clinician that she would call to
reconfirm the appointment because there was a chance that
Harry might have to work that particular Saturday. Mrs. M.
did not call and hence the clinician did not make a home visit.

That afternoon Mrs. M. called the clinician at home in
a fit of anger. She accused the clinician of breaking an appointment, of letting her down, and of not being there when
Mrs. M. needed her. She warned the clinician that Harry
would never want to set up a future appointment. A few hours
after this phone call, Mrs. M. called again and spoke warmly
to the clinician as if the first call had never taken place.

Coming on the heels of the loss of the purse and her
anger at the clinician for allowing it, this episode underscored
for us Mrs. M.'s pattern of setting up a situation where the
important other (clinician, lover, child) would fail her, hurt
her, or in other ways victimize her. It was a repetition com-
pulsion based on her early and overwhelming experiences of
parental abandonment and neglect, which she now sought to
reenact with the clinician. Patiently and repeatedly the clinician explored these issues with Mrs. M. As before, therapeutic progress fluctuated with the external events and many
crises of Mrs. M.'s life.

On the Road to Recovery

As time went by one could observe some improvement and growth in Mrs. M. The crises, for instance, were of less intensity. She became more aware of her internal conflicts and of her behavior. She began to develop a self-observing capacity. Although she was not able as yet to be in total control of her impulses, when possible she called the clinician when she felt she was ready to provoke a crisis.

An example of this improvement was demonstrated during the Christmas season. As usual, the urge for more money to buy toys for her children was strong: Mrs. M. talked many times during the therapy session of this strong need and always ended the conversation by saying, "I remember you told me that the children need me more than toys." We saw that (1) it was possible for her to talk about an impulse instead of acting it out, and (2) she could use the clinician as a partially internalized source of her self in order to "reason" about her children's needs.

The clinician helped Mrs. M. to learn to find more acceptable solutions, such as satisfying part of her need by working a few hours a day when the children were at school.

Harold's school needed a bus aide at that time—Mrs. M. applied for the position and got it. She was very happy because part of the job consisted of helping in the classrooms and helping in the kitchen to prepare snacks and lunch for the children. In addition, she said, this job enabled her to be close to her son, talk to his teachers, and witness his progress on a first-hand basis. The school staff was also happy with her work.

Mrs. M. expressed the wish "to be a teacher or something like that." The clinician talked to the school counselor and arranged for Mrs. M. to take a 6-week course on child development. This course was offered by the county for school aides. The classes were on weekends and Mrs. M.'s mother (Mrs. Snow) baby-sat for the children. Mrs. M. became more accepting of her mother, commenting, "I know she was not a good mother to me, but, as you say, she is not going to change. I have to learn to deal with her and change myself." Mrs. M.'s mother, it should be noted, remained very provocative and antagonistic toward her daughter. Her ambivalent feelings were seen on many occasions: when Mrs. M. was in a bad financial situation Mrs. Snow would intervene to help her but berate her as inadequate, good for nothing, and as "a parasite on the society." When things were going well with Mrs. M. her mother would interfere somehow to disturb the peace.

Now that Mrs. M. was more content with herself and showed progress and emotional growth it was Mrs. Snow who provoked the crises.

Mrs. Snow came to her daughter's house and literally stole the night table which had stood next to Mrs. M.'s bed during the 8 years (4–12) she had lived with her grandparents. Mrs. M.'s grandmother had given it to Mrs. M. when she returned to live in her mother's house. Since then Mrs. M. had never parted with this night table. One day, Mrs. Snow visited her daughter, took the table and left, disregarding Mrs. M.'s protests. Mrs. Snow said that this was her mother's and that she wanted it. We now understood Mrs. Snow's antagonism and rivalry. The fact that Mrs. Snow's parents loved Mrs. M. "as their own daughter" probably had been a threat to her. Now that Mrs. Snow's parents were dead she came to claim what belonged to her. To Mrs. M., her mother's behavior at this point felt like "sabotage" of the calm and feeling of contentment she was experiencing. Yet we observed Mrs. M. repeating the same pattern with her children: she wanted the Infant Center staff, the clinician, and Harry to love and care for her children "as their own." But, when interest in and care for her children were demonstrated, Mrs. M. did sabotage the situation.

This family pattern of relationships was described to Mrs. M. She closed her eyes as if trying to avoid pain and said, "How true! What can I do? My mother is a sick woman!" She continued of course to excuse herself by enumerating the mishaps of her life.

Amy's 24- and 30-Month Assessments

The periodic evaluations that were part of the CIDP documented the progress Amy was making from being a pathetic, inward child to an even-tempered little girl who experienced such satisfaction in interacting with trusted adults that she had endeared herself to the entire program staff. Her weekly routine at the Infant Center included two therapeutic play sessions, whose content is described in our earlier report, *Infants and Parents*. Given the security and availability of a few warm adults, Amy replaced her promiscuity with cautiousness in human relations, began to explore and take initiative, and increased her language development, range of affect, and ability to express warmth toward others. At Amy's 30-month assessment, examiners were impressed by her precocious language and representational capacities, tools which she used to deal with current and past conflicts.

Harry Moves In (Reprise)

Mrs. M. had been free from any drugs and alcohol intake for many months now. Harry also stopped drinking after his accident, encouraged by his affiliation with AA. He did, however, smoke marijuana, occasionally. Mrs. M. maintained her abstinence because she wanted to be a "good girl" in the eyes of the person she would like to marry. (The clinician had once told her that men who indulge in drugs do not usually marry women who are also on drugs because they remind them of the bad and destructive part of themselves. This impressed Mrs. M., who immediately recalled Robert's choice of a "straight church-going girl" to marry.) Since she wanted to marry Harry, she made a real effort to give up drugs, and she succeeded.

Mrs. M.'s relationship with Harry was relatively good. She played mother to him by making sure he attended the

AA meetings. She played therapist to him by helping him to communicate better. Harry in turn was a good provider and a "good father" to Mrs. M.'s children. This did not mean that they had no arguments. When she discussed the nature of their disagreements Mrs. M. always added, "If I could only be in control of my mouth, things could be better if I first think and then talk." Fights usually started when Harry was irritable because of the alcohol withdrawal. Mrs. M. could not tolerate his irritability or anger. She was afraid that they meant he did not love her and that at any moment he would announce that he was leaving her. To avoid hearing that he would leave, she began screaming and threatening to leave him.

The clinician saw the couple once every 2 weeks. Meetings usually began by discussing child development but soon turned to the couple's relationship. They were able to air some of their anger and complaints about each other and another point of view was offered by the clinician.

One day Mrs. M. announced to the clinician that after discussing the situation, she and Harry had decided to live together. This announcement gave a chill to the clinician who, in trying to explore how the decision was made, always received the same answer, "We love each other; and it is normal to want to be together, and we will marry in 2 months."

Immediately the search for a house began. They did find a spacious one in a middle-class neighborhood, where Amy and Harold could each have their own bedroom.

The move took place the day before Christmas. The first thing to be put in place was a large Christmas tree. On Christmas morning the family and Harry had breakfast together and opened their gifts. For lunch Mrs. M. and her children went to Mrs. Snow's house and Harry visited his parents in the early evening. Harry also visited Mrs. M.'s family and they all went back to their new home. Mrs. M. was very happy. "This was the best Christmas in my life," she said, "although we did not have many gifts."

Mrs. M.'s Pregnancy

Life continued in this fashion for a couple of months. Mrs. M. worked at the school, Harry at his carpentry jobs. They had arguments, but also family outings on Sundays.

Harry, however, did not mention marriage and Mrs. M. became restless. She made great efforts to please him but a marriage proposal was not forthcoming. One day she dared to bring up the subject and Harry answered, "We do not have money, and I am not sure I would like to spend my life with you and your bastards."

In spite of such comments, Harry was rather good with Harold and Amy, playing with them and buying them clothes. He confessed to the clinician that the most difficult times for him with the children were when he returned from work in the evening. The two children, starved for affection, immediately would jump on him, asking to play. He could not resist them but became irritable. Meanwhile, oblivious to Harry's needs and feelings, Mrs. M. would be proudly admiring the warm family scene from the kitchen window.

The fact that Harry did not want to marry her and called her children bastards challenged Mrs. M. and her wish to give Harry a "nonbastard" became stronger. She talked a lot in the therapy sessions and one day she mentioned it to Harry. His answer was again "No way! The world is full of hungry bastards and you have two of them."

The clinician tried to explore Mrs. M.'s need to be pregnant again and have a baby with Harry. Mrs. M. numbered her (conscious) reasons: (1) to replace the alleged miscarriage; (2) to have a baby growing in her; (3) to have Harry interested in her through the baby; (4) to feel like a woman again, with Harry witnessing her womanhood; (5) to have a new start with a man she loved; (6) to be a better mother to this baby, because she felt she had failed the other two; and (7) through the baby, to convince Harry to marry her.

While still working on those issues in therapy Mrs. M. announced that she was "2 weeks pregnant." The pregnancy was confirmed shortly thereafter. While Mrs. M. was elated and happy and feeling "very pregnant" in the third week of pregnancy, gaining weight, and experiencing morning nausea, Harry was suggesting an abortion.

Not surprisingly, some disruption occurred in their relatively calm relationship. More arguments, threats by Harry to leave, crises of hyperventilation, and somatic complaints such as general weakness, back problems, followed by doctor's appointments. At the same time Mrs. M. became very angry at her mother and the clinician because she felt, she said, that neither of them wanted her to have a baby. Mrs. M.'s intuition was correct, but at the same time she was projecting her own ambivalent feelings about her pregnancy. When Mrs. M. stopped coming to therapy sessions the clinician would call her at her usual therapy hour and discuss her anger, having already learned Mrs. M.'s ability to discern the clinician's anger on the phone better than in person. Every angry phone call would be followed by another from Mrs. M. which was polite and apologetic; it seemed as if Mrs. M. wanted to make sure that the clinician was still not hurt by the anger and/or available to prevent disaster.

The turmoil around Mrs. M.'s pregnancy subsided as soon as Harry accepted the pregnancy and began treating Mrs. M. "as a pregnant woman who carried his baby." Now we saw a change in Mrs. M.'s attitude. She regressed, became dependent and needy, and absorbed Harry's love and care like a sponge. Harry took care of everything from the finances to housecleaning and the children. But Mrs. M. wanted more; she had an insatiable need for care. When the clinician indicated what was happening, she answered, "I carry his baby; he must take care of his baby." By baby she meant the fetus but also probably the baby in herself.

She left her job. "Being on a bus for 2 hours everyday, I breathe the gasoline fumes," she said, "and this may hurt the baby." The most important thing, she added, was to take care of the baby inside her: for that she had to eat well and get plenty of rest. She gained a great deal of weight during the first trimester of the pregnancy as if she were taking in what had been due her all her life.

Around the fourth month of pregnancy, Harry became exhausted. He complained that he was too tired to work during the day if during the evenings he had to take care of the house and the "people in it." Immediately Mrs. M. began "feeling sick." "This baby is not like the others, it makes me more sick than the other two," she complained. She began again, going from one doctor to another but "no quack doctor" understood her pain.

While these events were taking place, the clinician announced that she was planning to take her vacation, the third vacation during the work with Mrs. M., which left four weeks before her departure in which to work through the separation and expected anger. Mrs. M. reacted abruptly: "I was expecting that this would happen, you always leave when I am in trouble." She stopped for a few seconds and lashed out angrily. "After all, why should I care? You are not Harry, you are not my mother, why should I care if you go on vacation?" Soon afterwards she began quarreling with her mother and stepfather, calling them "inadequate parents." But by the time the clinician was to leave, Mrs. M. said, "I suppose you are right, I do feel upset that you are leaving and I will miss you. But, I still think you are leaving at a bad moment."

Harold

The reports from Harold's nursery school at this time indicated that he continued to do well. His language skills were age appropriate and his learning abilities were advanced enough that he was mainstreamed into a regular kindergarten in the public school system. His teachers had much praise for him both cognitively and behaviorally, and said that he interacted well both with adults and with other children. During his visits to the Infant Center one could see that Harold was struggling with anger at his mother and jealousy of his sister.

(Mrs. M. often saw her son as a personification of primitive and frightening impulses within herself.) But it was satisfying to know that these struggles were not interfering with Harold's cognitive and social development.

Amy

After three years of intense involvement, the work with Amy was not yet finished. CIDP staff continued to think of her as vulnerable, partly because there were still areas in which her progress remained limited and partly because environmental disruptions were likely to continue affecting Amy. Mrs. M. was still unable to work with her daughter around issues of intimacy, body concerns, sexuality, and aggression. As for Amy, her difficulty in expressing aggression was still not fully resolved. She resorted on occasion to self-victimizing, and the tendency to somatization remained a possibility. Her cautiousness continued to interfere with her ability to get the most out of a situation involving social or cognitive expectations. She also seemed to hold back affectively: although her range of affect was wide, the depth of its expression was narrow. We wished that she could free herself to laugh harder or to cry louder.

Yet Amy now possessed many strengths. She was an intelligent child, tuned in to the wonders of the world. Although limiting in some ways, her cautiousness paid off in others: she had a good eye for detail, a long attention span, and a love for books and music. Cooperative and receptive to adult attention, she was well liked by almost all who interacted with her. Her comfortable use of language helped her in her relationships: she could remind her mother of what she needed for school or "pester" her mother to address her physical needs.

Amy no longer resembled an institutionalized child, as she had at her 8-month assessment. She had a capacity for intimacy, fostered by her therapy and her Infant Center "home away from home." We were impressed and relieved by the resiliency of this child and her wonderful ability to elaborate and reason out her concerns, maintain a warm trusting relationship to key adults and peers, and slowly become more assertive.

At 3 years old, Amy had managed to separate out the two worlds in which she lived and had learned that certain adaptive coping mechanisms employed at home were different from what the outside world asked of her. She had also learned means of dealing successfully with the outside world. We hoped that with ongoing support Amy would eventually be able to integrate these two worlds. Her mother continued to become more adequate in her interactions with Amy as Amy's own adaptive functions became more stable and resilient to stress.

The New Baby

The remainder of Mrs. M.'s pregnancy was almost uneventful with the exception of some arguments with Harry and some somatization. The clinician continued to see the future parents to prepare them for the arrival of the new baby as well as for the possible reactions of Harold and Amy, and, of course, the impact of the birth on their relationship.

At approximately the due date, Harry called the clinician from the hospital one night to announce the birth of a son weighing more than 10 pounds. On the phone he sounded like a very proud father and reported that he assisted in the delivery room. When the clinician visited Mrs. M. at the hospital the next day, Harry was also there. The glow, pride, and happiness on Mrs. M.'s face were very different from what the clinician had witnessed during Mrs. M.'s hospital stay when Amy was delivered.

The baby boy was born healthy and robust with excellent interactive abilities. Most remarkable and even surprising, however, was Mrs. M.'s ability to consolidate her gains in her nurturing of her new child. In the evaluation at 3 days and 1 month, and at 4 months, as well as from general observation,

Mrs. M. attended in the early months to her infant's cues, was very soothing, and helped him orient and alert by varying her voice, facial expression, and gentle movements. By 4 months there was a rich, joyful attachment with warm smiles, loving looks, and most importantly, a joyful, responsive interactive well-coordinated physically beautiful 4-month boy. In contrast to her flat affect when Amy was an infant, Mrs. M. was bubbling with feeling, delighted in her baby's abilities, and most important, realistic in her planning and expectations.

Conclusion

The progress made by Mrs. M. was noteworthy. As this report makes plain, much of the therapeutic work consisted of crisis intervention. The clinician allowed herself to be viewed as the "good mother" who could be relied upon to provide solicitous care. But after each crisis was over, a painstaking process of clarification and working through took place. Through this process, a major shift in Mrs. M.'s functioning occurred, resulting in some resolution of her ambivalence and the emergence of pride and positive feelings toward her children.

Mrs. M.'s progress can be conceptualized as a sequence of developmental steps: (1) When she first joined the program she relied heavily on self-absorption and quasi-delusional magical thinking as part of her use of splitting mechanisms to cope with her rage and disappointment in others. (2) She gradually became able to approach followed by withdrawal whenever the anger threatened to break through. (3) As the clinician proved able to withstand her withdrawal without abandoning her, Mrs. M. was able to establish a constant relationship with the clinician. (4) The constancy in the relationship enabled her to tolerate a certain amount of ambivalence in her feelings toward the clinician. (5) Mrs. M. eventually allowed herself overt expression of aggression, illustrated by her anger when the clinician left on vacation or made unwelcome interpretations. (6) The onset of somatic preoccupations and symptoms (i.e., her worries about kidney dysfunction, her feelings of being "sick to her stomach," her conviction that drugs had "messed up" her body) signaled the build up of psychological structures to replace the primitive splitting mechanisms used to deal with conflict. (7) An increase in constancy and availability took place: Mrs. M. started to bring Amy to the Infant Center regularly and was able to tolerate and follow through on suggestions for appropriate caregiving practices. (8) The beginning of a capacity for self-observation and observation of her children enabled Mrs. M. to begin to identify her patterns of behavior and to exert some control over them; for example, she could look at her obsessive urge to make a lot of money for Christmas at any cost and, eventually, was able to resist this urge. (9) Genuine pride and positive feelings toward her children emerged, Mrs. M. could feel satisfaction at teacher reports on Amy and Harold.

At the conclusion of the CIDP, Mrs. M.'s achievements were still very vulnerable to regression in the face of internal or external stress. But a major shift in personality organization had been made, and we felt new hope for Mrs. M.'s ability to form and sustain enduring human relationships, particularly with her children.

6

Another Baby, Another Chance: Madeline and Anita

Serena Wieder, Ph.D.
Eva L. Hollingsworth, M.S.W., L.C.S.W.
Joan M. Castellan, M.A.
Judy Hubert
Reginald S. Lourie, M.D.

Introduction[1]

The story of Madeline will illustrate the extensive reaching out that was needed to engage a hard-to-reach mother of four children under the age of 4, each of whom exhibited severe developmental and emotional problems. Like other mothers in our study, Madeline was so enmeshed in the daily struggle for survival, often competing with her children for resources, which were all too few, that she could not look beyond her day-to-day existence to seek help for long-term or emerging problems. With Madeline, our initial question could not be whom to treat or when, since she herself acknowledged no need for treatment. She saw no purpose in joining our program except for "wanting a little company

---

[1] A time line is provided at the end of this chapter to help the reader follow the complex unfolding of this case (p. 328).

sometimes." This tiny thread of interest led to the most extensive intervention offered to a participant in our program. In working with Madeline, the usual therapeutic modalities one considers at the onset of treatment became the goal of our efforts rather than the conditions for treatment. Although we could not prevent foster placement of Madeline's first four children, in the four-year course of treatment multiple treatment modalities permitted Madeline another chance to reexperience becoming a parent, this time within the context of a new "family" of intervenors, a new daughter who reached out to her, and the new baby's father, who became Madeline's partner in the first long-term relationship she had ever been able to sustain. The well-known pattern of further deterioration of mother and child with each subsequent baby in the multirisk families reversed in this case. Because an effective pattern of intervention was provided and used, the birth of another child provided a chance for success and mastery rather than further failure.

This case will also illustrate several other critical factors to be considered in clinical intervention:

1. The constitutional and temperamental proclivities of the infant: Madeline's first daughter born during her affiliation with the program was a passive, lethargic infant who could not reach out to her mother. This baby, Susan, became a failure-to-thrive infant by the time she was placed in foster care at 3 months. In contrast, her second daughter, Anita, was an active and responsive infant who reached out to her mother from the start with her bright, alert gaze. Given the complementary care of our program, this baby was able to sustain her engagement with the human world and persisted in reaching out to her mother until Madeline could respond. Anita led the way for her mother's development as she proceeded competently through her own. Indeed, Anita frequently moved ahead of her mother developmentally; we were challenged to help Madeline feel less threatened while

she too developed the capacities she had failed to acquire earlier in her life which would permit her to keep up and grow with Anita.

2. This case will illustrate the need for long-term and multiple intervention efforts. At many points in treatment the intervenors might have given up on Madeline. In the beginning, the work was sometimes so stressful and the situation so unyielding that it was only the team's mutual support and commitment to a long-term effort that permitted them to persist and pursue Madeline, whose flight derived both from an inability to organize her life and from resistance to therapy. Later, she and Anita appeared to be doing so well it was tempting to reduce our efforts. We knew, however, that it would take a long time for Madeline to consolidate change and that the intervention would have to last through the early years of development so critical for her daughter. We also needed enough time to implement the multiple integrated therapeutic programs from which we believed Madeline, like other high-risk mothers, would benefit. These went beyond the use of any single traditional treatment modality, such as individual, group, or family treatment. Over the four-year course of intervention, we used every treatment modality we had available, including careful assessments of Anita's individual differences; special patterns of care to help her and her mother maximize their potential for growth; daily participation in the programs at the therapeutic infant center; individual and group psychotherapy; developmental guidance; joint home sessions with the mother and father; a high-school equivalency class; a work skills training program; and various educational and health workshops. Madeline needed all of them in different ways at different times.

3. This case illustrates not only that work with fathers often cannot move forward until a trusting therapeutic relationship has been established with the mother and she has developed the capacity to sustain a human relationship, but also that work with fathers who are often considered unavail-

able and uncooperative *is* possible in the course of an overall treatment program and should not be ruled out prematurely. Madeline had never been able to depend on or even sustain contact with the various fathers of her children. We believe that her learning to allow dependency in her relationship with us enabled her to sustain the relationship with the father of her last child. Although he agreed to her participation in our program, their daughter was 2 years old before we could start working with both parents.

4. This case will demonstrate how we worked with the foster mothers of Madeline's four children to interrupt the typical cycle of temporary foster care placements. The intervenors also served as a bridge between Madeline and her children in foster care. Later, the use of assessments, consultation, and personal assessment helped support the foster mothers' efforts with their difficult charges. Both foster mothers eventually adopted the children.

It is important to remember that only in the process of pursuing Madeline and trying different therapeutic approaches did we come to understand her. Initially, she would not speak and could not tell us anything about her experience of life or what it was like to be a mother. She seemed totally unaware of her children's problems and had not formed firm attachments to them or anyone else. She appeared so passive and depressed that we wondered whether she was psychotic or retarded. Her all-encompassing fears and distrust were hidden behind a defensive suit of aggressive armor which put off everyone. However, Madeline's great neediness and dependency made her intermittently available to help. Although she pulled away again and again, she finally responded to our pursuit and reaching out to her.

The story of Madeline will be told as it unfolded over a 4 year period. Describing in detail our reaching out and specific interventions makes the case very lengthy, but in this way we hope to demonstrate *how* we worked with Madeline and her family. Unable to use traditional psychotherapeutic approaches, we harnessed the unfolding process of the baby's developmental tasks to help Madeline experience and learn what she missed in her early life. The work with the foster mothers and her first daughter's development will be described separately so that this story will not disrupt the flow of our primary narrative. (See page 328 for a summary.)

Madeline

INITIAL REFERRAL AND RECRUITMENT

Madeline, a young black woman, was referred to the Clinical Infant Development Program (CIDP) by Joan Castellan, a public health nurse who had recently heard of our program and interest in recruiting hard-to-reach, multiple-risk mothers. At 20, Madeline was the mother of three sons and was pregnant with her fourth child. Joan had seen Madeline with her children in the local well-baby clinic on several occasions. Joan also knew of the intervention efforts begun over a year earlier by another public health nurse at her clinic following a protective service referral. Madeline's second child, David, had been brought to the local hospital emergency room intoxicated. The investigation determined that the drinking had been accidental. On the nurse's home visits, Madeline was often found sitting with her coat on in her cold, primitive quarters. Repeatedly, the nurse emphasized the use of birth control, but did not detect Madeline's third pregnancy until the last month. Madeline had ignored the fact that she was pregnant. The fourth pregnancy was similarly ignored until the ninth month when Madeline's first and last prenatal visit was occasioned by a trip to the clinic for her children. At that time, staff observed she was pregnant and urged her to seek prenatal care. She had complained of intermittent headaches and was found to be anemic. More significantly, she appeared totally unconcerned about and uninvolved in her pregnancy. These facts prompted Joan to recruit her into our program.

Joan referred the case to Eva, our primary clinician, and

they decided on a joint home visit to introduce Eva to Madeline and to discuss the new program. Shortly thereafter, Joan joined the staff of the CIDP as an infant specialist and was assigned to work with Madeline.

A steep, deeply rutted road led to Madeline's grandmother's house, located in a previously rural section which was now surrounded by new developments. The two- or three-room house had a dug-out basement which served as Madeline's quarters. It reminded Eva and Joan of a "dungeon" and lacked electricity, toilet, sink, and running water. On the dirt floor stood three single beds, a little table, and a few chairs. A small wood-burning stove and some clothes and utensils were piled in a corner. This cramped, dark, cold, and dirty basement was the home Madeline shared with her three children, her mother, and four younger siblings. She invited Joan and Eva upstairs to her grandmother's house, apparently embarrassed to bring them into her own place. When Eva voiced concern that she left the children downstairs unattended, Madeline replied that she need not worry because Danny, her 4-year-old eldest son, could take care of them. As they walked up the stairs Eva and Joan both noticed how the tiny house spilled over into the outdoors; clothes, tires, and old cars were dispersed around the yard and the outside bathroom.

Following this first meeting with Eva and Joan, Eva reported the following:

> Madeline is a young, shy, childlike girl. She looked no more than 16, and though surrounded by her three children she did not look like a mother. Nor did she look pregnant, she was so small. Madeline avoided eye contact when I spoke and the few words she uttered were whispered in a low flat tone which I could hardly hear. When we described the program she just stared sullenly past us and it was not clear whether she heard or understood. She asked no questions when we asked if she wanted to

know anything more about us. When I offered help with the children she simply said she had no difficulties and could take care of them, especially since Danny, the eldest, helped her with the little ones. Finally, she said she might join if we could help her with some housing, but most of all indicated, "You could come back sometimes because I need a little company."

Madeline delivered one week later and there was no opportunity to offer her "a little company sometimes."

FIRST IMPRESSIONS

Following this first visit, Eva, Joan, and other members of the team met to discuss their impressions. Was Madeline depressed, retarded, suspicious, or all of these? She had avoided eye contact, her voice was flat and low, and her manner was detached and distant. She was passive, withdrawn, barely able to respond, and whispered monosyllables. There was some uncertainty about whether she understood what was said to her or whether she was too depressed to show any interest. She could not elaborate on anything asked of her and most of her responses, as well as her passive/hostile manner left others feeling that they must figure out what was going on and they would have to proceed carefully. From our few observations we surmised Madeline represented the second or third generation of a family with little or no ability to cope with their life circumstances. Her mother and grandmother were both living in extremely distressful and impoverished circumstances. The massive depression which engulfed Madeline seemed more significant than possible retardation. Madeline's apparent denial of her situation and the lack of concern for herself or her children, coupled with the poor relatedness to her environment and to us, made us question her reality testing and judgment. We did not, however, have enough information to evaluate this further. Madeline left a vacuum to be filled by the observers, who assumed feelings, thoughts, and concerns for her as they tried to guess what was happening within her. Nevertheless, the appeal of this helpless, waiflike child shimmered through the depression and drew us toward her.

ONE WEEK LATER: SUSAN'S BIRTH

Less than a week after our visit to the "dungeon" and almost 1 month before her supposed date of delivery, Madeline gave birth to her first daughter, Susan. Labor began spontaneously and was uneventful except for the use of Demerol and Vistaril for analgesia. Her membranes were ruptured artificially and delivery was accomplished vaginally without any problems. Madeline only complained that hospital staff did not "put her out" as she had requested, and the 4 hours of labor she experienced were difficult. Excessive bleeding following delivery prolonged hospitalization for 4 days.

Immediately on receiving a call from Joan that Madeline had delivered a baby girl, Eva went to visit her in the hospital. When she walked in, Madeline called out with some excitement, "Did you see the baby yet?" She sent Eva to see the baby although she could not accompany her because of her own discomfort. When Eva returned, Madeline was smiling and extremely proud. This was not conveyed in words but she lifted her head and beamed, in marked contrast to her behavior during their first meeting. She not only appeared less depressed but also was pleased with Eva's visit. Eva noted that the bright, cheery hospital room provided a different environment in which Madeline seemed far better. Eva, in fact, felt far better as well. The new baby, Susan, was very cute, and had a full head of hair. She gave Eva and Madeline something to focus on and this became a basis for some exchange. Eva noted that she too was very proud of Susan, who was the first baby born in the program.

Susan was born after a 40-week gestation and weighed 7 pounds. Her Apgar scores were 8/9. The perinatal course was unremarkable. When the Brazelton Neonatal Assessment (BNA) was performed at 1 week, Susan was found to be a low-keyed, guarded, and passive infant. She was most responsive to animate visual and auditory stimuli, which she could use to comfort herself along with hand-to-mouth activity. When her own efforts to console herself did not succeed, she quieted readily with minimal intervention. However, there appeared to be a watchful, vulnerable quality to this baby, who withstood the most aversive maneuvers without loud crying. Though she was capable of smooth body movements, there was very little spontaneous activity and she appeared to be a baby who would be considered "good" by her mother, content to sleep, eat, and watch quietly while alert.

During the hospital visit Eva discovered that Madeline had made no plans for herself or her daughter. She did not know how she would leave the hospital nor had she prepared a bassinet or baby clothing. She did not know where she would get food, nor had anyone in her family offered any help or visited. All she could say was she thought her mother would take care of them, although her mother had not said she would. She did not appear worried or concerned and acted as if she expected someone to take care of her.

This impression, that Madeline would let herself be taken care of, was the first clue we had as to how to help Madeline. By meeting some of her many concrete needs we hoped she would accept our interest and tolerate our contacts. We realized Madeline would not be able to verbalize her feelings or fears, or tell us anything about her history or why she did things. She proceeded from day to day with little underpinning or awareness of how dependent she was and of how quickly she pushed others away if they threatened her fragile self-esteem.

THE FIRST SIX WEEKS

The next contact with Madeline following the Brazelton assessment was Joan's visit to check on a vaginal discharge reported earlier. When she arrived the two older boys stared at her silently and suspiciously, unable to return her greeting them by name. Inside Madeline was preoccupied with her daughter. Joan used the time to show Madeline how to clean the perineal area and to support Madeline's caretaking. Susan appeared alert and vigilant. Madeline seemed delighted with her first daughter, smiling and talking softly for brief moments. She held Susan intently, even caressing and soothing her. Susan was quiet, watchful, made few demands, and allowed her mother to do with her as she wished. Madeline's preoccupation with Susan resulted in Madeline totally ignoring her three young sons. She gruffly shook off her 14-month-old toddler when he climbed on the bed and clawed at her back for attention. Joan's attempts to reflect the feelings of the other children were met with a distant stare and agitated restlessness. Madeline could not attend to anyone but herself and her daughter, and she seemed to see Susan only as an extension of herself, to be cared for when Madeline pleased.

As Madeline let us continue to visit, we saw her sons become increasingly sad and sullen. Danny, the 4-year-old, was an attractive boy but he was dressed shabbily in clothes far too big for him. He did not speak at all but his eyes conveyed fear and sadness. As the oldest, he cared for his younger brothers. Danny appeared burdened by the weight of the family and had the sad, wizened expression of an old man. David, the 2-year-old, was more active, sometimes running around, but at other times much more passive, staring sullenly and silently. He appeared less saddened and depressed than Danny, perhaps because he had been deprived a shorter time. Antonio, the 1-year-old, still reached out and begged to be picked up and caressed. He was the fighter who demanded attention and whined and grabbed whatever he could get until something was forthcoming. He was unable to fathom, as his brothers had, that he had already lost his mother's attention. They appeared to have stopped protesting or expecting very much from Madeline long ago. Madeline, however, continued to be as oblivious to Antonio as to the others, and our words did not appear to have any impact on her. Her orders and commands were delivered in a gruff and angry voice. We did not see them getting very much from her, yet they occasionally reached out for something that she had to give. There was a clear preference for her and no attempts to get away from her. Their reactions to us were more distant and anxious, as they did not come forth to interact with us for a very long time. Slowly they became more comfortable, smiled, and seemed less tense.

Madeline continued to be preoccupied with herself. She had developed pelvic inflammatory disease related to the birth complication and complained of the pain but gave no thought to seeking medical attention. We saw this as an opportunity to offer her something. She allowed us to take her to the clinic. During the next month she also permitted us to visit briefly to fulfill some concrete needs. We never came by without some formula, food, diapers, or clothing, which she would accept passively. Madeline continued to appear depressed and overwhelmed, but had little to say. We soon learned how unrealistic our expectations had been regarding helping her explore her feelings or accepting offers of developmental guidance. Hours would pass during which Madeline would only occasionally utter a yes or a no. Yet she agreed to our coming back and seemed pleased that we cared to visit her and brought her the things she needed. These seemed to be the crucial elements in maintaining contact with her; that is, she tolerated and in her own way enjoyed our presence and accepted help with concrete needs. However, having observed her limited capacity to take care of her children and herself in even basic ways, we were now even more concerned about Madeline. Her children were objects around her whom she attended to when she could muster herself beyond her passivity and depression. The children suffered terribly from her neglect. Our increased visits did not lead to any of the traditional vehicles for treatment. While she let us into her home, our worries escalated as we could not penetrate the barriers of her concreteness, unrelatedness, and depression.

SIX WEEKS TO THREE MONTHS: FROM DOORSTEPS TO THE STREET

When Susan was 6 weeks old, Joan stopped for a visit. Madeline was crying fiercely as she and her four children struggled down the steep road which led from the tiny house. She was unable to tell Joan what had happened and asked Joan to call Eva. Apparently, Madeline's trust in Joan was still inhibited by her association with protective services and the public health system. To Eva she finally reported that her grandmother, coming after her with a broom, had thrown her and the children out. Madeline would not say what had made her grandmother angry. Her older sister took her in temporarily and she asked us to help her locate an apartment.

Now the intervention shifted from the "dungeon" to Eva's car. Each day she and Madeline drove around the county searching for an apartment while the children came to our offices. When her sister refused to house Madeline any longer, the Department of Social Service (DSS) moved her to a motel on an emergency basis. They also warned her that unless she found a place to live and provided a stable home for the children, the children would be placed in foster care. As time began to run out, Madeline displayed the same lack of concern or anxiety we had observed after Susan's birth. Eva noted:

It seems the more frantic I became looking for an apartment, filing applications, calling the DSS, or helping her move to the motel, the more passive and dependent Madeline became, sitting silently by my side. She did not seem eager to locate an apartment, but appeared to tag along with me and my plan for her. It was as if she were helping me to find an apartment. She stated she wanted to take care of her children on her own, but did not initiate anything to reflect this and I did not get the feeling that her words, feelings, or behavior had anything to do with each other. Nevertheless, she voiced strong, angry feelings that she did not want the children to go into foster care. She saw this as the children's being taken away from her, rather than being a result of her inability to provide for them.

Every day Madeline brought her starving children to our offices. She then departed with Eva, neither mindful of what would happen to them all day nor concerned about the separation. Madeline's children did not know how to play or interact with others. Danny, the oldest, was hyperactive when he first encountered the array of toys available. He moved from one toy to another, ignoring adults until they placed their hands on him to get his attention and talked to him to calm him down. In order to introduce and familiarize each child with games and activities of reciprocation, such as playing ball, we had to assign one adult to engage each child. Gradually Danny was able to listen to stories and to learn. At first, for example, he threw toy people and toy animals into a box helter-skelter. After learning the nursery rhyme of "The Old Woman in the Shoe," he started to separate the two, putting the people in a shoe and placing the animals in a toy barn. After a few days at the center Danny began to say, "Me no go home." Gradually this gave way to, "I don't want to go home," as he anticipated the arrival of his mother late in the afternoon. This chant started about 1:30 in the afternoon. Danny also approached interested adults rather than waiting for them to approach him. This seemed to indicate either a lingering resiliency which allowed him to initiate contact or the knowledge that unless he demanded whatever he could, he would get nothing. By the time Eva and Madeline returned late in the afternoon, after an almost day-long separation, the children were extremely demanding. Madeline would be tired, angry, and disappointed. Her few resources were even more depleted than before. She responded harshly when the children asked for something. If she ordered them to stop they listened, seemingly afraid of her. As her anger and her hostility escalated moment by moment, she issued commands prohibiting their every move. "Put that chart down! Come here, Danny! Don't do that, Antonio! Stop, David!" The boys cowered in fear. Madeline could not comfort or reassure them, seeming to have fewer emotional resources than they did. Only toward Susan did she appear somewhat more gentle and affectionate. She was willing to hold her again.

The staff began to absorb the impact of working with mothers like Madeline as we reached out to her as the first of our multiple-risk mothers. We were uncertain of what we would be able to do. Would it be possible to sustain this family? Already everyone felt depleted and overwhelmed by the challenge. Eva verbalized another feeling which also emerged about Madeline, "I felt a need to rescue this family. There is a likeable quality about Madeline which draws me to her and I want her to like me in return." Again a shimmer of relatedness observed earlier came through and we continued our efforts to keep this mother and her children together.

A "FOSTER HOME" FOR MADELINE AND HER CHILDREN

The work with Madeline and the children entailed close collaboration with many community agencies who were first enlisted to help locate housing. We soon recognized we would not be able to obtain an apartment because DSS and housing laws required her to have three bedrooms to accommodate children of two sexes and no more than two children were permitted in one room. The cost of such an apartment far exceeded her welfare grant. We then looked for a home where she might rent some space. Our community contacts supplied the name of Mrs. C., a black woman who was active in community affairs and willing to respond to the plight of this family. She agreed to take them into her home in exchange for Madeline's total Aid to Families with Dependent Families (AFDC) check of $285 per month. She was also determined to "change" Madeline into a responsive and responsible mother. She demanded that Madeline be involved in the routine care of the children and find a job while she cared for the children at home. Because there was no alternative Madeline reluctantly agreed to move, but she resented Mrs. C.'s authority and expectations. She also resented Eva for putting her in this situation, but when Eva attempted to explore these feelings, Madeline glared silently. Instead, her interaction with the children became more negative and the children got more and more out of control. Moving into an organized household with rules and expectations was a sudden jolt for them. Their running around and doing what they liked in this home was destructive, while before there had been nothing to destroy. The more confined and restricted they were, the more unsocialized and wild they appeared. Madeline tried to control them. She yelled, threatened, and inevitably whipped them.

Madeline seemed to experience Mrs. C. as an overseer, someone from whom she could not hide, someone who watched her day in and day out. She would sulk and be sullen, walk with a defiant gate, and refuse to respond directly to any of Mrs. C.'s efforts. Mrs. C. was alternately angry and helpful. She responded at first to Madeline's plight by trying again and again to help, but then began to see her as lazy. Although the children did begin to respond favorably to the structure, consistent care, and interest Mrs. C. offered them, Madeline could not tolerate this replacement maternal figure. Not only was Mrs. C. taking better care of her children than she had, she was also like Madeline's grandmother, demanding that Madeline act like a mother and make commitments to her children. This triggered tremendous rage in Madeline.

Eva sometimes found Madeline sitting on the porch, dirty and unkempt, staring ahead catatonically as if Eva were not there, warding off all her attempts to make contact. During this time Madeline's physical condition seemed to deteriorate as well. The pelvic inflammatory disease persisted, she ate poorly, and was losing weight. She could not tolerate being fed by Mrs. C. and it was unclear how much food she could accept from others. She declined to discuss the issue and refused our offers of medical help.

On several occasions Madeline left the children unattended while she went to visit someone. This behavior seemed to stem partly from Mrs. C.'s refusal to allow company in the house and partly from Madeline's need simply to run away from stress. She never identified her friends and denied having a boyfriend at the time. As we imagined it, Madeline wandered around needing to be by herself, or just wanting to meet anyone who might briefly respond to her alone, isolated from her problems and inadequacies. After Madeline stayed away overnight, Mrs. C. no longer wanted her and the children in her home. Madeline also no longer wanted to live with Mrs. C. This arrangement had lasted about 1 month.

Madeline then went to stay with her sister until a fight with her sister's roommate resulted again in her being asked to leave. This time she went to live with her father. They, too, had a confrontation and Madeline was forced to leave after 2 weeks. For a few days she found refuge with friends. During this time we had little contact with her. Madeline would not let us know where she was, and never revealed what the fights were about. Feeling that she was constantly running behind Madeline as she went from relative to relative, Eva pursued her. When Eva could find Madeline, she was met with ambivalence and anger because she could not solve Madeline's housing problem. When asked if she were angry, Madeline denied it, but Eva could feel her rage. Madeline's face would be bloated and her body was tense, or she would lower her head. She seemed to be only a minute away from exploding.

A pattern emerged: Madeline, in desperate straits, turned to family members for help only when no alternative remained. She did so in a way that gave others no alternative but to help her since no one wanted to turn her away with four children. After "dumping" herself on them, she would become more depressed, passive, and helpless, abdicating all responsibility and merging with her children's dependency in a hostile and resentful way. Her helplessness, however, was not only reactive to the immediate situation but appeared to serve partially as a defense against her angry and aggressive impulses. These surfaced in the form of very provocative behavior, which precipitated fights and resulted in her being rejected and cast out again.

A NIGHT IN THE STREET WITH THE CHILDREN: FOSTER PLACEMENT

When Susan was 3 months old Madeline called us for the first time. When Eva asked where she was, she responded, "In the street. Last night we were all in the street." The kids were with her. She asked to come to the office to talk and Eva arranged for her transportation. When she arrived she looked tired and depressed, barely holding onto Susan. The three boys tagged in after her, dirty and hungry. We got food for them and Madeline asked for help in putting the children in foster care until she could find an apartment. Eva suggested that she make the call to request foster care and offered to help her in any way possible. At first Madeline seemed distressed and anxious about whether the children would be placed that day. Eva, however, had recognized the dimensions of the crisis and had already alerted the social worker after Madeline's first call. As the hours passed, Madeline's primary reaction seemed one of relief. Her only comment was that no one in her family had ever given up their children before. She refused, however, to share her plans with her family when we suggested she call to see if they might still be able to help her. She showed less and less emotion and did not appear upset that her children would be separated from her. When approached again, all she could say was, "I have no place for them." It was 10:30 at night, and the children, who had eaten and were playing, were now beginning to fall asleep. Eva asked Madeline what she could do for her. Did she need transportation? Madeline said no. Although it was late, she insisted on walking, revealing neither her plans nor her destination. Eva's questions seemed to precipitate Madeline's departure. Without saying a word to the children, she walked down the hall as if she were going out only momentarily. She seemed detached and unconcerned—again, not unlike the way we had seen her in the past. The two older children saw her leave but did not ask for her. Just as passively and compliantly, they accompanied the social worker who came to get them shortly afterwards.

Having no alternatives for Madeline at this time, we could only help the social worker find appropriate placements. It was impossible to locate a home that would accommodate all four children, so the older and younger ones were divided. The older children were placed in a temporary home for 3 weeks and then transferred to a permanent home. Joan contacted Mrs. A., a foster mother she had known for several years from the clinic who had a good reputation for caring for handicapped infants. Since she was at a neighbor's house painting and could not be reached by phone, Joan rushed down that night to talk with her. She had one vacancy but expected another shortly; after hearing about the crisis she said, "Sure, by all means, bring them over." Joan then returned to the office to get Susan and Antonio. By the time they got to the foster home it was 11:30 at night. Susan did not appear to react to the sudden move to a strange place. She fell asleep in Joan's arms while being driven to Mrs. A.'s and was immediately placed in a crib. We had noticed that she was sleeping a great deal recently, almost never fussing or crying. Antonio was awake and upset. At that late hour, Mrs. A. gave him a warm bath and something to eat to comfort him. When placed, Susan weighed under 10 pounds, having gained less than 3 pounds in 3 months. She was wary and withdrawn, uninterested in relating to others. When she fussed, she would usually fall asleep before anyone could get to her, seemingly expecting little intervention or help. In Mrs. A.'s care she quickly gained weight and reached her expected weight within a few weeks.

Not unexpectedly, Madeline withdrew from us again. She neither called, left an address, nor asked for the children. Eva and Joan again began to pursue her, returning to the various places she had been before only to discover that Madeline was again wandering from doorstep to doorstep. When we found her she would not respond to our efforts to talk about the separation and loss. We still could not tell if she felt guilty, sad, or perhaps just relieved. Since we could not help by discussing feelings, we hoped that our persistence in keeping in touch with her would impress on her the importance of keeping in contact with the children. We told her where they were and offered to accompany her or to provide transportation if she wanted to go alone, but she only followed through a few times. After this, she said she would visit but never did.

OUR REACTIONS

Everyone in the program was shocked and concerned about Madeline's lack of expression of emotion as she left her children. Had we already failed with one of our first cases? Eva and Joan were bewildered by Madeline. She walked out alone late at night without seeming to be frightened, sad, or angry. She showed no feeling, but must have felt *something*, if only to blame us for having to give up the children just as we felt she blamed us for her situation at Mrs. C.'s. Since Madeline did not express her feelings, they could only be surmised by observing the feelings of those who interacted with her. We saw the depression in her children, the anger in her family, and we felt the fear, as well as our own guilt for not rescuing her, for not preventing the separation. It was as if we had failed to prove to Madeline that we were different from all the others who had tried to help her and failed to prove that we really cared for her. Recognizing these feelings increased our determination to keep working with Madeline and her children at all costs. We wanted her to trust us and to take another chance.

IN THE INTERIM: MADELINE'S HISTORY

We had little contact with Madeline during the weeks following the placement of her children. We struggled to piece together the little history she had shared. So far it had been impossible to interview her specifically about her family, but her story had emerged little by little during the first few months.

Madeline was the fourth of 12 children, who ranged in age at this time between 27 and 11 years. Her parents married after the birth of their fifth child, but they never lived together for long. Her mother remained tied to the grandmother in whose home she continued to reside. Madeline reported that she and her mother were not very close. She said that her mother gave her little attention because there were so many children to take care of, but that she still was "real nice." Her younger sister, Madeline jealously implied, was subjected to fewer demands for work and received more lenient treatment. On the other hand she felt proud that she was the one on whom the mother could depend, even though the younger sister was preferred. Madeline, however, never felt that she could depend on her mother to do things for her, such as coming to school for special occasions. She shared little about her relationship with her father except to become very angry when she said she could not depend on him. She remembered waiting for him to pick her up in his car and his never showing up. She also felt that her father prevented her mother from doing many things for her.

As a young child, Madeline ran away from home on several occasions. The first time was at age 7 when, according to Madeline, her mother was angry because she would not wash the dishes and was going to beat her. She ran away and her mother and her sister chased her, whereupon she ran to her grandmother's and spent the night. The following day her mother came and brought her home. She left home again at the age of 15 when she was angry at her mother for not letting her go out with her friends. Her sisters, she felt, were treated more leniently. This time she went to live with her boyfriend and his family. Her mother did not come to look for her and did not want to bring her home. Madeline did not ask permission from the boy's parents to move in but just kind of "eased in" in a way we saw her do many times later.

She had little to say about her school experience except that she liked school in the elementary grades. She changed schools frequently because she went to live with various relatives and the family also moved. She denied any behavioral learning problems in school and said her grades were average. However, she lost interest in school in the eighth grade, started truanting and dropped out in the ninth grade when she moved in with her boyfriend.

We also knew very little about Madeline's sexual experiences. She did reveal that she was 13 at the time of her first sexual contact, with a boy of 16 whom she met while walking down the street and who followed her home and visited her on several occasions. She said that "He was nice to me, he gave me money and anything I wanted." Later on he went into the service. At this time she met and moved in with the boyfriend, Dale, noted above, who became the father of her eldest child. She described him as "nice, a little bit gentle, and mean sometimes with a bad temper." Madeline indicated that she could deal with his temper because she also had a bad one. Although her stomach kept getting "bigger and bigger" she claimed she was unaware of being pregnant. When her pregnancy was confirmed Dale and his family were happy and she received attention that she never received in her own family. She said she was "treated like a baby." She received special care and was not expected to do things around the home. She seemed to have gained a certain kind of status once she became pregnant and relished this. Two weeks prior to the baby's birth, however, Madeline returned to her mother's home because of a conflict with Dale's mother. Madeline accused the mother of "telling lies on her" and of saying that Madeline was "messing around with another guy," and that her son was not the father of the baby. Madeline felt Dale sided with his mother and this made her extremely angry with him. She then decided to go home. When she went into labor, her mother dropped her off at the hospital and Madeline remembered feeling scared and alone. During the delivery she received no support and although he visited her in the hospital, Dale abandoned her after the birth of the baby. She gave the impression that her boyfriend could not handle the responsibility of being a father once the child became a reality.

Nevertheless, her first child had given Madeline entry back into her mother's home, where she rejoined the two generations of women who had reared her. Again, we knew nothing about her early experiences with her first infant except that the care of Danny was shared by her mother and other family members.

The only more recent information we had about Madeline was that she had become pregnant by another man and delivered her second son at the age of 18, when her first son was 21 months of age. Her third child was conceived with the father of her first child; she delivered this baby at the age of 19.

This was all we knew about Madeline at this point, and it was little enough. It was not possible to question her about her family during the early months of our contact. The survival needs of her children were too pressing to allow us to pursue her past. Also, Madeline was extremely resistant and guarded; when questioned usually she would not answer. The information we obtained seemed to slip out in the course of car trips or other activities, but when she became aware that she had revealed something about herself, she usually withdrew and refused to say anything more. She looked at us as if we had manipulatively extracted information from her that she did not intend us to know. Three more years elapsed before additional details about Madeline's past were to emerge in the course of treatment. The more complete history will follow at that point in our narrative.

Whenever she spoke of her mother, grandmother, or father, Madeline's face appeared distorted with fury and intensity of emotion, but she could neither articulate her feelings further nor acknowledge them when we reflected upon her appearance. Clearly she had learned not to expect positive things from her mother or anyone else in her family. Instead, she seemed to adapt a pattern of rejecting and disappointing others before they rejected or disappointed her, thus avoiding feeling hurt. Madeline's anger reached its peak when she referred to the incident of being put out by her grandmother, but she refused to elaborate on her feelings about her grandmother or what had caused her to take this action.

Madeline spoke about individuals in a way that suggested contact with them had no lasting value, as if the people with whom one was involved in life merely came and went, and as if relationships held no future. It seemed clear that she did not trust anyone, and while her own needs pressed her into involvements, these were based on impulsivity, desperation, or anger. For example, the precipitous fight with her first boyfriend's mother seemed related to the pattern of projecting onto others the responsibility for hurting her, causing fights, or throwing her out.

The most striking aspect of Madeline's behavior was the way she used repeated childbearing to meet her own unfulfilled dependency needs. Her childhood dependency had been experienced in such a hostile, rageful manner that she was essentially arrested at this phase of development. She now appeared to be forcing her children to reenact this drama with her. It also appeared as if Madeline and her four children existed in total isolation from each other. This lack of connection and relatedness alarmed us greatly because these traits also characterized our experiences with her and seemed likely to jeopardize our efforts to help.

REEVALUATION: COULD WE HELP MADELINE?

We reviewed our impressions of Madeline and the impact she had on us. Madeline's inability to communicate her thoughts and feelings in words combined with her passivity, led Eva and Joan to make some assumptions and implement interventions without really knowing what her goals were. One could, however, feel her rage at everyone who did not assume responsibility and meet her dependency needs. Madeline projected onto others evil intentions toward herself. She was also terrified of the magical power she imagined in those upon whom she depended, which caused her to flee or provoke a fight to render them powerless. When she resorted to magical thinking, Madeline feared her own powers, although such thinking defended her temporarily from her fears and painful reality. She lived trapped in neediness, seeming to function as if there were no past and no future. Madeline could not see any cause-and-effect relationship in what was happening to her or her children. She was sometimes irrational, functioned on the most concrete and somatic levels, was unable to differentiate between self and others, and was unable to plan ahead and unable to delay gratification. When she felt frustrated and angry she vacillated between impulsive and self-destructive acting out, and withdrawal and negativism. Her primitive personality organization was further severely compromised by chronic depression. She did not present any psychotic manifestations but it was impossible to ascertain what her capacities were.

These impressions were not encouraging. Could we really help someone like Madeline? She appealed to us but could not trust us. She treated us at most as a source of goods, but often rejected what we offered. Madeline's dilemma was most evident when Eva tried to feed her. Although she was very hungry, Madeline would not accept the food. Characteristically, when finally pressed to accept she complained and was never pleased by what she ate or where she consumed it.

We recognized that this was the point most agencies would give up on clients like Madeline. Her children had been placed in foster homes and it did not appear that Madeline had the internal or external resources required to retrieve her children and offer them a home. Even if we knew she could find an apartment, we would be plagued with doubts about her capacity to mother. It was also highly likely that she would get pregnant again. But more than anything, she appeared to need a mother; it was on this basic level she appealed to us and motivated us to try again. Our feelings and reactions to her would have to be the clues to the next steps to take.

CONTINUED FLIGHTS AND DEMANDS

After Madeline's children were placed in foster care, we attempted to arrange for her to visit them. Madeline, however, fled them as well as us. We had no contact with her. We felt abandoned, unneeded, and helpless, especially when she stopped seeing the children, who were our link to her and to our hopes to reunite them. After more than a month, Madeline called Eva to say that she was "living in the street." A man's voice could be heard in the background telling her what to say. She stated that she was once more with Susan's father, Mr. S., and that he was going to help her get the children from foster care. She said no one else was really interested in helping her get the children back. Meanwhile he shouted that they were going to the Department of Social Services (DSS) to demand housing, food, and emergency assistance. Madeline repeated his phrases like a puppet, but her voice also conveyed anger and fear. Eva offered her food if they would come by the next day. They showed up, but Mr. S. told Madeline to be very quiet and that he would do all the talking. He was agitated and verbally abusive, demanding the children as well as going on about having served in Vietnam and being entitled to benefits for his child. He raved on about Madeline's being depressed and sick because her children had been taken away. Also, he was angry at Eva because she did not provide the particular foods he wanted. Although Madeline followed his lead, she appeared embarrassed to respond this way to Eva. Mr. S. also claimed that he and Madeline had been married. Later he changed that and stated he told DSS officials they were married, but was telling Eva the truth.

His behavior was not a total surprise. Mr. S. had acted similarly when he and Madeline had gone to see Mrs. A., the foster mother, to pick up the children on a Friday evening for a weekend visit. He accused Mrs. A. of not caring for his children and threatened to report her to the authorities. The visit was short-lived and the children were returned by 8:30 A.M. on Saturday morning. Mr. S. claimed Antonio "wanted to go back where he gets what he wants." Eva recognized Mr. S. as a hostile, agitated, and potentially destructive man driven by his needs for concrete goods. His motivation for obtaining help for Madeline was based on his desire to share her benefits and to be taken care of himself. By remaining calm and being responsive to his underlying desire for concrete goods, Eva was able to mollify his agitated behavior. He agreed to keep in touch and have Madeline call when they found a place to live.

Madeline and her boyfriend went to DSS where they presented themselves as a married couple in need of emergency housing and food. They were given financial assistance and the location of a residence where they could rent a room. Mr. S. instructed Madeline to call and let Eva know where they were living. Eva visited them on one occasion. While she was there, Mr. S. was again agitated. He impulsively began a fight with the man from whom he was renting the room. Mr. S. had obviously serious difficulties, including poor impulse control, and Eva left as soon as she could. Eva felt that Madeline was frightened also, although completely dominated by Mr. S. About a month later, Madeline "ran away from him" when he became physically abusive and started beating her after he had been drinking. Madeline escaped to the home of her father who agreed to take her in as protection from her boyfriend, against whom she subsequently pressed charges. It was only much later that Madeline was able to share her fear of Mr. S. and state that he drank excessively and beat her whenever he wished.

REESTABLISHING A RELATIONSHIP WITH EVA AND JOAN

A turning point in the relationship with Eva occurred after Madeline left Mr. S. She called Eva to accept her invitations to come into the agency. She exhibited less hostility and responded to Eva's expressions of concern and empathy. The relationship which had developed during the earlier crises appeared rekindled. Eva was delighted that Madeline called and accepted her presence "unconditionally." Madeline seemed to make use of the face-to-face contact even though she did not talk about what she was feeling or what had happened. Madeline had no means of financial support and Eva urged her to call her DSS worker to arrange for enrollment in a job training program. Once this was accomplished, Eva and Joan suggested she reestablish contact with her children. Madeline agreed and accompanied Joan, the infant specialist, on visits to Mrs. A.'s home. Joan urged Madeline to play games with the children but the baby, Susan, did not feel comfortable with her natural mother. She maneuvered to get on the floor, where she would become involved with the toys. Even then Susan would periodically seek out Mrs. A.'s presence and scoot away from Madeline. As soon as she spotted Mrs. A., she would return to her toys but not to her natural mother. Shortly afterwards, Madeline remembered Susan's first birthday and made arrangements with DSS to visit Mrs. A.'s home that day. Joan also spent several hours in the foster home that day to support Mrs. A., who was worried that Susan's father, Mr. S., might come by and "make trouble" but wanted to permit as long a visit as possible between Madeline and her children.

Madeline would not say anything about these painful visits to the children. Instead she focused on what she had to attain for herself. She obtained a part-time stock-girl position in a leading department store through the job training program. This was her first job and she seemed excited about it. She liked working and indicated that she was treated nicely by the people there. Her newfound success was quickly evident. Madeline's self-image began to improve and she took pride in her appearance. She came into the agency on her day off and spent most of the day there. She blossomed in response to the praise and support from the staff. On occasion she talked about wanting to get her children back. We helped her work out a plan whereby she went to the foster home, helped dress her two younger children, brought them into the center, and spent a period of 4 or 5 hours with them on her day off. We felt that Madeline needed the opportunity to get to know her children, who had progressed developmentally. The children needed to spend some time with her to get to know her again. The foster mother was also pleased with this arrangement because she was considering closing her home and she wanted the children to be reunited with Madeline.

Although Madeline had entered into a more stable relationship with Eva and Joan and contacts with her were more predictable, it was still very difficult to get close to her. She could only tolerate the here-and-now connection and only on the most superficial level. Although her social adeptness suggested she might be able to explore some feelings or thoughts, she still would not talk about anything which made her anxious. At this point Eva reported:

> I tried to involve her in planning for the future. She said she wanted to get an apartment and get her children back, but she could not elaborate on this. I tried to elicit her feelings about perhaps being relieved at not having to care for her four small children, but she denied this and could not expand. I tried to get her to talk about the

pain she probably felt at being separated from the children, but she could only say that she missed them and wanted them back. There was sadness on her face, but she was unable to articulate any feelings. Although she talked minimally about wanting to get her children back, I sensed that she was relieved to know that they were doing well in the foster homes. She was most concerned about her own needs. She gave little indication of planning ahead or talking about what it would be like when she had the children again. Instead I tried to focus on birth control issues with her, reluctantly anticipating she would become pregnant to replace her lost children.

MADELINE'S DEPRESSION APPEARS TO LIFT

Before long, Madeline met another man while walking to the beauty shop. He seemed stable, was employed, and was considerate toward her. She continued in the training program and also started to gain some control over her life, and she thrived. As her depression lifted, her face was smiling and happy; she held her head up, looking at Eva as she talked. Her self-image improved and she seemed to be gaining more confidence in herself. Around the office, she was more outgoing and talkative with the support staff.

The support and encouragement Madeline received each time we saw her was further reflected in her appearance and manner. She absorbed the compliments and praise shyly but was eager for more. The therapeutic efforts proceeded slowly because it remained difficult to engage Madeline on a level at which she could talk about feelings or reflect on events.

But the relationship with her therapist deepened as her depression lifted. A major breakthrough occurred during which Madeline was able to accept food from Eva. For more than a year she had always refused to accept anything to eat from Eva when she came to the office. As she became more comfortable, she would accept a cup of hot chocolate or some juice or a soda. On several occasions she and Eva went out for lunch and she seemed to enjoy this. Gradually she was willing to accept food from the other staff members. Sometimes when she came into the office, she volunteered to get lunch for us. She also volunteered to help with addressing envelopes when we were planning an open house at the agency. Eva recognized that Madeline had become "her girl," like a daughter she wanted to nurture, reward, and keep encouraging to grow. Madeline acknowledged Eva's importance when she visited the center, letting others know Eva was her "mom" and the special person she came to see.

MADELINE GETS PREGNANT AGAIN

It was only after her weight gain was very obvious that Eva confronted Madeline about her pregnancy. In her adolescent manner Madeline had also denied the pregnancy to herself and had "discovered" it only after going to the emergency room several days before because of cramps. They diagnosed the pregnancy at 6 months. Though Eva had expected the pregnancy, she was shocked and disappointed.

Madeline seemed sad and disappointed that she was pregnant again just when she was trying to "get myself together," but Eva felt that there was a part of her which was pleased because her boyfriend, Thomas, wanted a baby, his first, and was happy that she was pregnant.

We began investing in her pregnancy. Joan arranged for prenatal care and Madeline followed through. At first she appeared to relate to this pregnancy as we engaged her in questions about what she wanted, how she felt, what she wore, how she slept, and so forth. By our interest and concerns we tried to bridge the distance between herself and her fetus, remembering how she had ignored her previous pregnancy. Neither the relationship with us nor with her boyfriend, Thomas, could forestall the impending depression which appeared shortly afterwards. She began to feel unwell during her seventh month and quit her job. No physical problems could be diagnosed. She appeared increasingly depressed and helpless, showing more resistance to talking to Eva. Her affect was flat and her face looked sad, but she kept denying sadness and worry. Her energy level kept slipping and her gait was much slower. She began to look like the Madeline we had first met: passive and dependent, unable to anticipate the birth or plan ahead, pulling away from everyone yet expecting others to take care of her. There was little we could do to keep her from slipping back.

Again we found ourselves struggling to understand Madeline. She appeared to need a baby to mediate between herself and the world, herself and her boyfriend, and herself and us, the "baby program." Another baby could mean another chance. Our task was to redefine the experience of being a mother for Madeline. Madeline gave us "another chance" as well, but this time we had a better sense of where to meet her.

THE THIRD TRIMESTER

As she approached the end of the pregnancy, Madeline's depression persisted. She was emotionally inaccessible and appeared more withdrawn each week. Our attempts to get her to reflect on her depressed state were met with empty stares and denials. She did, however, continue to come into the center weekly and she participated in Susan's 18-month assessment. In this assessment and free play she was totally unavailable to her little girl, who made some attempts to involve her mother. When Susan's efforts failed, the baby would wander around aimlessly and slide onto the floor and suck her fingers for comfort. We observed this painful scene, cringing again at the evidence of failures in attachment and chronic depression which had impaired Madeline's capacities to relate to any of her children.

We continued to infuse her and the pregnancy with greater nurturance and attention. We focused on what she ate, how she looked, whether she wanted a boy or a girl, and her plans for the birth. These issues seemed of little significance or utility to Madeline. She barely responded to our intensified investment in her and the pregnancy or our efforts to meet her boyfriend and his sister. However, she did accept our encouragement to pursue prenatal care. During her last trimester she went for six prenatal visits and gained 8 pounds. She took multivitamins with iron but during the last visit she was still found to be anemic and folic acid was prescribed.

Projective tests—Rorschach, TAT, and figure drawings—were administered three weeks prior to her delivery. These were part of the routine protocol carried out prenatally with all mothers participating in our program. We also hoped they would help us understand Madeline better as we saw depression overtake her. The test results indicated Madeline was arrested at an infantile level at which she could be unconditionally dependent so long as she was not pushed to give in return. If she felt pushed, she pushed back harder and more determinedly, presenting impenetrable barriers.

Her depression was deeply rooted in unresponsive parental figures who might die, be killed, or otherwise abandon her. As a result she had to be in control and pushed away anything and anyone moving in on her, in order to contain both her aggression and fears of annihilation. Pervasive primitive defenses severely limited her experiences and engagement with the world. While reality testing was usually adequate, structural weaknesses and boundary fluidity interfered with self–object differentiation and impulse control. Further, she was bound to bodily preoccupations and fears at the cost of all other affects and relationships. This only in part related to her pregnancy. She functioned entirely on a concrete and somatic level because she had failed to develop representational capacities to help her process her experiences and feelings.

Intervention would therefore have to be geared toward meeting her basic dependency needs without placing demands on her, and be geared also toward developing trust and opportunities for success to help raise her self-esteem and alleviate her depression. A more complete picture of her past eventually helped us understand the sources of her psychopathology.

MADELINE: THE PAST—A FULLER PICTURE

Madeline could never "tell" the story of her life or her family for several reasons. At first she did not trust us enough to reveal her past. She withdrew suspiciously if we asked. Bits and pieces slipped out, however, during our contacts with her. As the fragments emerged it became more evident that Madeline's memories were scattered and unrelated. She did not convey feelings or awareness of how her experiences had affected her. It was more as if "life happened to you" and there was little to be done but to block it out. Because Madeline's experiences were never captured in words or reflections of feelings, they could not be shared with us. Her history was stored in various compartments, a series of episodes, which had never come together to offer her some understanding of who she was or what directed her life, her existence seemed to consist of a crushing pressure to survive and have her needs met at any cost. The utility of words and communication only became apparent to Madeline after years of treatment which fostered the development of some symbolic and representational capacities. Her willingness to "tell more" came only after she had developed a trusting and successful relationship with her therapists and the program and was reinforced by her experiences in group therapy where she heard others examine the past. This development also coincided with Anita reaching the stages of symbolic and representational thinking.

When, after three years of working with Eva, Madeline was asked about the past, she still reluctantly asked, "Do I have to? I block it out." This contrasted with her earlier silence and blank staring when questions about her earlier life were raised. Madeline now agreed to talk, so long as it was clear that she would not have to talk about certain things, "secrets" that were hers alone. Although her story still had missing pieces and a paucity of details, what Madeline was finally able to tell us, combined with the history presented earlier and our observations and material from therapy sessions over the years, gave us a much better sense of Madeline's life.

Madeline's grandmother inherited her home and land from her father, who had worked for a farmer. The house was on 7 acres fronting a cemetery in an area which was very rural until 15 years ago when low- and middle-income housing and commercial development intruded into the neighborhood. The small house, without electricity or running water, was built about 50 years before. A great uncle and aunt resided in a trailer behind the house. The land was no longer farmed and foreclosure had been threatened a few years ago for failure to pay taxes. Madeline's sister helped pay the taxes with insurance money she was paid following a car accident. Although the surroundings had changed, the family remained insulated and isolated from the rest of the community. Madeline's grandmother had never gone beyond a 5-mile radius of her small home and all her children and grandchildren had stayed nearby. Both she and her brother, Madeline's great uncle, refused to have contact with our staff.

The grandmother gave birth to 11 children, the first at 12 years of age. That she never married, strongly influenced her granddaughter, Madeline. Madeline's mother, born in 1934, was her third child. The grandmother was clearly the matriarch of the family, whose members feared her disapproval and rejection. A very religious Catholic, the grandmother attended church every day and exacted high, although inconsistent, moral standards of her granddaughters. Thus Melissa, Madeline's sister, was thrown out of her home when she became pregnant at 15, but Madeline was accepted.

Madeline's mother finished the 11th grade and had her first child at 17. She delivered 12 children, 11 of whom survived. The father of the first two was unknown to Madeline. She was the second child, and first daughter, of the liaison between her parents; that is, the fourth child overall. It is not clear for how long or at what points Madeline's parents actually lived together. They married when Madeline was 1 year old and began separating when she was 2 or 3 and finally separated when she was 12. Her mother did not leave the grandmother's home except for intermittent stays with her husband and other relatives. Her parents have continued their 29-year relationship to the present, spending time together but not living together in the same home. Madeline was unaware her father had other women—one of whom wanted to raise her older brother and herself, but her mother refused to send her. She also reported her mother had other men and that her two youngest siblings had a different father, although they all carried her father's name.

Madeline's father was the youngest of three children. He was born in 1932 in the same area. He had an elementary education and was 24 when Madeline was born. He was steadily employed over the years, and at the age of 45, when we first met Madeline, he was a warehouse truckloader and boarded with a family. He presented as a warm, related, and friendly man, but was very passive. When problems occurred he would say, "We'll see, we'll see," but offered no help.

Of all of Madeline's siblings, only her eldest sister succeeded in graduating from high school and in developing some autonomy. She worked and had her first child only after she was more established, during her early twenties. She also maintained a relationship with one man who also fathered her next two children. Little else is known about the other siblings except for the legal and drug entanglements of the two older sons.

Madeline's memories of her early life were sparse and difficult to elicit. She was called "Pinky" because she was quite pink and red when she was born. She claimed to look just like her father, but also her maternal grandmother. This was a no-win situation: her mother and grandmother treated her badly because she looked like her father, and her father treated her badly because he hated her grandmother. Made-

line's reports were a series of irreconcilable contradictions
reflecting her confusion and ambivalence about her family
attachments. For example, when asked to describe her father's
personality, Madeline said, "It's good. Sometimes he's not all
that great. Not that bad a person. Friendly, but sometimes
not so friendly." She added, "I'm the spitting image of him.
He's short, light skinned, and small build. Now, I'm taller
than him." Her mother told her that her father used to favor
her, buy her things, and take her everywhere when she was
small. At first Madeline's own recollections did not confirm
this. She said, "I didn't know who the man was." In fact, she
remembered avoiding him until she was old enough to realize
that he was her father, but she could not say when that was.
Later she remembered his friends called her "Little Max"
because she looked so much like him. She also thought he
treated her as special because she was his first daughter, revealing for the first time that her eldest and two next youngest
siblings were fathered by someone else. Later recollections
of her relationship with her father became more intense and
she would not give details, only saying, "It was rough as a
teenager." Madeline angrily reported that he smacked her
when she was 17 and she still had not forgiven him. Even
later when he rescued her during her wanderings, he demanded $100 and hit her when she refused to give it to him,
"even though I was grown up." Although her resentment
toward her father continues, she enjoys his visits with her
mother on weekends when he sometimes takes the two
women shopping. Madeline always gives him money for gas.
She also thinks that because her father wants to leave shortly
after Thomas arrives, he does not like Thomas, but she does
not know why.

Madeline's experience and perception of her parents' relationship could probably best be summarized by her adamant
refusal to get married. She says, "If you're not married, you
can't get hurt. It doesn't matter what you do because you are
not married." This position conveys her distrust of depen-

dency and attachments and defends her against the loss and rage which in turn keep her from believing a relationship can have permanent value and be trusted. This distrust pertains to the mother–child relationship as well as to men and women. At 12 she was sent to live with an elderly woman, "loaned out" to help her for 18 months, until her mother retrieved her. Later, her sister's children were taken away after being sexually abused by a boyfriend. Madeline went from boyfriend to boyfriend until three different men had fathered the four children she ultimately relinquished.

The quality of Madeline's relationships with her family were most clearly conveyed through our observations of her and her sister, Melissa, who joined the program shortly after Madeline. For the most part, they acted as if they were two unrelated participants in the program. Neither conveyed concern and affection, or rivalry and anger toward the other. At first, even when Madeline was aware Melissa was having terrible difficulties, she did not convey empathy or offer to help. They appeared distant and detached despite their great stress and neediness. Each was struggling for her own survival. Even after Madeline's life had stabilized in her relationships with Thomas and Anita, it took several years before she appeared to be able to offer minimal help or express concern regarding Melissa or her troubled son. As far as the other family members were concerned, it was "okay" if they came to see Madeline but she would not reach out or visit them. They existed in her mind, like her children, and thinking about them seemed to be enough. Real contact probably meant further hurt and disappointments. The strongest affect Madeline ever experienced was jealousy toward her younger adolescent sister, whom she thought was "too smart" because she always got her way and could connive Madeline out of clothes or money. Occasionally she revealed something about her brothers, one of whom was in jail for breaking and entering and another who took dope. However, she provided only isolated fragments of information which could not be connected or understood.

THE FATHERS OF MADELINE'S CHILDREN

Whenever Eva had tried to explore Madeline's experiences with the fathers of her children, Madeline had made it clear that she "blanked out" all of them as if to say that if she did not think about them, they did not exist. In later years she finally responded to questions but some of the details varied from her initial reports.

Madeline met Dale, the father of her first child, on a blind date. She was with her oldest sister and her sister's boyfriend in Annapolis. They all visited at someone's house and then they went to the movies. Dale lived nearby and he began to visit regularly. She described him as being "real nice" and said he brought her flowers. Madeline was not too impressed with the flowers, but the next time he brought her an outfit of clothes and she was delighted. He had saved for several months to be able to get this for her. Dale was 19 years old, the third of six siblings (four girls and two boys). He was a light-skinned, attractive black man. He lived with his mother, his father lived uptown, and Dale had quit school in the 11th grade. Madeline said he was very intelligent and worked very hard in some manual job for the local school board. She described him as being "free-hearted," and she enjoyed shopping with him because he would get her expensive things. As she talked, she indicated she had really loved him then, but not now. After she became pregnant she eased into his home, and his family accepted her. As reported earlier, during the pregnancy she was happy to be with this new family who treated her well, "spoiled" her, and allowed her to regress without making too many demands. But before long Dale's mother "turned on her." Madeline believed his mother told Dale lies about her and caused him to "turn on her" as well. She was very unprepared for this. They had talked about getting married and had planned to get married during Christmas. She changed her mind and by Christmas she had returned home. At that time Madeline learned that Dale could be very nice until he took some "dope pills" that "sent him crazy." She thought he had a bad temper, but she did not mind because she had a bad temper too. After her first son, Danny, was born, Dale came to the hospital and later would visit every day. He showed interest in her and bought diapers and milk for the baby. His mother, however, did not want anything to do with his child. When his mother inquired about the baby 2 years later, Madeline would not tell her anything about the baby. Later, Madeline felt things might have worked out better if Dale had not gotten into drugs. She did not have much contact with Dale after Danny's birth until a brief liaison 2 years later that left her pregnant with Antonio.

Madeline lived in her grandmother's home with her first son, her mother, and her siblings. About a year later, she met Will, the father of her second baby, David. Will was 28, she was 18. They met on a Sunday in front of a supermarket when Madeline was coming home from church. They talked and he walked her halfway to her house. She liked him immediately because he was "quick," like she was, and he did not like "a lot of noise." He was the "fun type" and they started to go to movies and clubs together. Will was described as a friendly, easy to get along with person. "He wasn't bad." He did not use any drugs, did not smoke, and only drank an occasional beer. He said that he had finished high school, and he was a truck driver. Will's parents were divorced and he had one older brother. Madeline never met his mother, who lived out of state, but she did meet his father and she did not like him because his voice scared her. When Madeline became pregnant, Will did not want anything to do with her pregnancy. Madeline was very shocked and could not believe this at first. In time, he became more interested in her having his child and came to visit her in the hospital every day after she delivered David. He asked to marry her but she refused. However, she said that she loved him more than anyone else. Will was also good with Danny, her first son, and he tried to befriend him. He took him to the store, and tried to make him talk. They never lived together, but continued to see each other for about another year until Will moved away. She remembers going with the baby to visit, and being very disappointed when he moved, and missing him afterward. She kept remembering he was "nice and all," and his going "tripped me out," but she said that she got over missing him very quickly. She did this by getting drunk when the relationship first broke up in order to relax her mind and put him out of her thoughts. She has had no contact with him since.

Meanwhile, she met Dale again, got pregnant again, and delivered another little boy, Antonio, one year after her second son's birthday. By then Madeline was 19 years of age and had three sons.

The next man she met was Mr. S., whom we met after Madeline joined our program. They met one hot day while Madeline was taking her children to the clinic. He offered her a ride; she accepted and was very surprised when he came back to the clinic to take her home. Three days later they went to the movies. She said he was nice when they first met, and she did not know "what got into him" later. Madeline also knew that he was the second oldest in a family of five and had three sisters and one brother. He lived in the same area as Madeline so she had a chance to meet his whole family including his mother and father. She thinks he finished the 10th grade, but when he was 16 or 17 years of age he went into the service and then into the reserves. He took drugs and wanted Madeline to be involved, but she refused. When he was high he would be alternately silly and violent. He was good with the children until one day Danny did something of which he did not approve and he whipped him mercilessly. When Madeline tried to intervene he tried to hit her and she said she would kill him.

When Madeline met Mr. S., he was living with another woman whom he put out. Madeline moved in. This was the first time she had left home after having children. Madeline realized she might have some trouble with Mr. S. but it was so crowded at her grandmother's house that she took the

chance, moved in, and gave him her money. They lived together for about 3 months until he lost the apartment. She
again returned to her grandmother's house. Madeline then
got an apartment through a public housing program, and let
Mr. S. move in with her. Before long she discovered that he
was a heavy drug user, and demanded money from her to
supplement his wages as a mechanic fixing buses for the school
board. Within a short time Madeline became pregnant again.
Mr. S. was a little "surprised," but could not wait until his
baby was born. He had a daughter who was 4 years old from
another relationship.

After Susan was born, Mr. S. came to the hospital to hold
her, was proud of her, and enjoyed having a daughter, but
he gave Madeline no support. By then he was not working.
Madeline would say she thought she loved him at the time,
and wanted the relationship to work, but a moment later, she
said she hated him because he tried to control her. Mr. S.
also did not like her boys because they were not his.

Although he had offered no support he "went crazy" when
he found out that the children, including his daughter, were
placed in foster care. Although Mr. S. was with Madeline
during the early months of our contact, when she was pregnant, and then gave birth to his child Susan, she never let us
know until she turned up with him after a month's absence
following the placing of her children in foster care. (It also
seems that it was his presence that precipitated her grandmother's throwing her out. Madeline finally described how
her grandmother came down to the basement with a broom
and "swept her out," yelling and screaming that she had better
get away.) The fights between Madeline and Mr. S. increased
and he became more and more abusive toward Madeline. His
frequent beatings frightened her. Finally one night she made
up her mind to leave and ran to some neighbors, scared and
cold and crying. She then fled to her father's house and told
him what was happening. He was very upset and said that he
would shoot Mr. S. but agreed to take her in and protect her

from him. Mr. S. never came around again. He was later jailed for several months and she has had no contact with him since.

Madeline met Thomas about 9 months after the children were placed in foster care. She was walking to the store, he came up, and she "couldn't get rid of him." She said that she really did not want to be bothered and was waiting for her mother to get out of the beauty shop. He followed her and waited until she came out at 4 o'clock in the afternoon. She tried to get rid of him and avoided his questions, but he was persistent. They went to the movies that night and talked a lot. She remembered how unusual it was because she had never talked to anybody for 4 hours. She was impressed that "he was different from the rest of them, that he was altogether different, and a nice person." The following Sunday she went to a barbecue and found that while she did not want to think about him, she was thinking about him, and that there was something very different about him. He had given her his telephone number but she did not use it. He knew where she lived and persisted in coming for her. They went out again and she enjoyed their second date, although she complained that people were staring at them "like they're crazy." About 6 weeks later the aunt with whom she was living said she could not have any more company in the house. One night Madeline went out and when she came home she was locked out. When Thomas came by the next day, she told him that she wanted to leave her aunt's house and Thomas invited her to come live with him. At first Madeline said "no," but he took her things to his apartment. However, when they got there, after seeing some woman's shoes on the floor and asking whose they were, she discovered he lived with his sister.

Thomas was born and grew up in North Carolina. He reported he was one of 14 children, with one brother and four sisters living, and 8 sisters who had died. He was 28 years old, and his father had died about 15 years earlier. He stayed in touch with both his mother and his 99-year-old grandmother. He grew up in a closely knit farm family. He was born prematurely when his mother was in the barn and was taken to a hospital where he stayed for 6 months. Madeline did not know whether he had gone to school, but she did not think so. Thomas could read but not write properly. His childhood had been full of hard work and difficult family circumstances, including seeing one of his sisters die in a fire. He had moved to Madeline's area 6 years before he met her, to join the older sister with whom he was living when he met Madeline. Madeline described Thomas as a friendly man who was quick tempered, who liked to fight, but only if he had to, who talked a lot, and who was sometimes moody. She claimed they did not have sex until 2 months after they met, even though they were living together by that time. When she got pregnant, he was very happy, "jumped for joy," and wanted to have a girl. Madeline, however, did not feel good about being pregnant. Somehow she did not expect to get pregnant even if she did not use birth control. She said, "I didn't think I could, it had been so long." Anita was born 9 months after they met, at 40 weeks gestational age. Madeline's first four children remained in foster care.

Another Baby

ANITA IS BORN

Madeline's expected date of delivery was unclear: exams suggested early March, although Madeline's information suggested mid-February. In fact, she went into labor on January 29, at 5:30 A.M., when her membranes ruptured. She was admitted into the hospital at 9 A.M. Thomas accompanied her and stayed through delivery. Pitocin was started at 11:55 A.M. and an internal monitor inserted at 12:10 P.M. The final stage of labor was intense and painful but she delivered by 1:36 P.M. Despite her repeated requests, Madeline received no medication during labor with the exception of local anesthesia at the end.

The baby weighed 7 pounds, 9 ounces and attained Apgar

scores of 9/10. Fair-skinned, with thick black hair, she appeared to be very sturdy and alert. Thomas was elated and Madeline, though in pain, was pleased.

Madeline called Eva and Joan immediately after the birth and she was pleased when they came to visit, urging them to go see the baby although she was too uncomfortable to walk with them. She chose the name Anita because she liked it. She also was proud that Thomas was by her side the entire time. Madeline did not compare this birth with her others.

While visiting Madeline at the hospital, Eva also had the chance finally to meet Jane, Thomas's sister, whom she drew aside to talk with privately in the lobby. Jane appeared eager to ventilate her angry feelings about Madeline and Thomas; a stream of criticisms followed. Jane felt Thomas and Madeline had been irresponsible in not preparing for the baby or having things ready for discharge. They expected her to be responsible. Her brother had never even asked if Madeline could live at her place and he did not pay his rent regularly. Madeline had four children in foster care. She did not believe Thomas was the father of this baby but felt that was his problem. She also questioned how Madeline's mother could approve of the way she was living. Jane was very angry and felt they were taking advantage of her. Eva listened patiently while noting that Jane was a very controlling woman who, though only a few years older than Thomas, had assumed a dominating maternal role toward him. Jane reminded Eva of Madeline's grandmother, who would demand that she perform and have little patience with Madeline's hostile dependent patterns, although she wanted to be helpful.

Her anger notwithstanding, Jane said she would permit Thomas, Madeline, and their baby to live with her because she knew they had nowhere to go. She said she would try to help them, but they would have to assume responsibility for providing for the baby. Eva asked permission for our homemaker to visit to help Madeline, and Jane consented, saying she knew Madeline would need a lot of help.

The situation was all too familiar, and we wondered how long it would take before Madeline and Jane would have a fight and Madeline would be thrown out and/or get fed up and leave on her own. We braced ourselves for another crisis, hoping our connection with Madeline and the use of a home-maker would at least give us some time to promote an attachment between mother and baby during the initial months.

ANITA'S 3-DAY BRAZELTON NEONATAL BEHAVIORAL ASSESSMENT SCALES

Before leaving the hospital, Joan performed the Brazelton assessment. Anita presented as a sturdy, alert infant who was extremely responsive to the human face and voice, who followed eagerly, and for long periods. She was also interested in the inanimate world, locking in quickly to visual and auditory stimuli. Motor maturity was exhibited by wide smooth arm movements and good tone. Reflexes were good and the few tremors and startles observed were quickly controlled by the use of visual stimuli and postural changes. Anita could also quiet herself readily by hand-to-mouth sucking and needed minimal intervention.

Madeline observed the Brazelton, watching her new daughter with a mixture of curiosity and admiration. When Anita quickly responded to Joan's face and voice, she said she knew Anita was "a nosey baby" because right after the birth she was already "nosing around right on the delivery table." Madeline laughed when she observed Anita "walking, crawling, and placing." Joan used this opportunity to help Madeline learn about her new baby. Joan particularly wanted to show her how slow and gentle handling would reduce the baby's tremors and startles. She encouraged Madeline to talk softly while looking at Anita's face. Madeline nodded her head and smiled slightly.

The contrast between this baby and Susan was striking. Anita was an infant who had "sending power." She would be able to invite her mother to her. Susan had been more passive and harder to engage after birth. Anita was also sturdy and active, able to take care of and comfort herself as well as seek out the world and respond to various stimuli. Susan had merely withdrawn into sleep, ignoring even hunger. Susan had slipped away when her mother could not respond, but Anita looked as if she would be a fighter. We were delighted, and realized we had a new person on our intervention team.

MADELINE RETURNS TO JANE'S HOME

After 4 days in the hospital, Madeline and Anita returned to Jane's home. We immediately arranged for Judy, our home-maker, to visit every day to help Madeline organize the baby's care, including making formula and doing her laundry, as well as manage some household chores and prepare meals. This assistance was designed to help Madeline carry out respon-sibilities expected by Jane as well as to take care of Anita physically so Madeline could have more time just to be with the baby. We also hoped the arrangement would help dimin-ish the escalating tensions with Jane, who was enraged at Madeline's irresponsibility. Although the plan appeared to work at first, Madeline soon shifted back to her old posture. Now she expected Judy to do things for her when she came rather than organize or carry through herself. She became as dependent on Judy as she was on everyone else. Judy con-tinued to help her, doing whatever she could, and Eva and Joan visited frequently, but the situation continued to dete-riorate as Madeline was again unable to meet the demands and expectations of others. Anita, however, was able to hold her own by using whatever Madeline could give her as well as engaging the many other adults in her environment.

THE ONE-MONTH BRAZELTON

At 1 month Anita surpassed her earlier performance on the Brazelton. Her responsive orientation to animate stimuli, such as the human voice and face, persisted. Her response to inanimate stimuli was very adequate, although she did not reach the same level she had reached with human stimuli. Her motor maturity and reflexes were excellent. Again she demonstrated strong capacities to comfort herself by sucking her fist or latching onto some visual stimuli, like Joan's face, to calm down. This latter capacity enabled Anita to draw others into her world. She persisted in looking at and following one until she got a response.

When she became hungry after the assessment, Anita also demonstrated other strengths. Her whimpering and irritability conveyed she wanted to be fed. Madeline could read her clear signals and gave her a bottle, which she sucked vigorously and quickly. After drinking 2 ounces, her hunger abated, she then sucked more quietly as she divided her attention between looking and listening to the activities around her. Anita could take care of herself and get what she needed. Even Madeline seemed pleased, saying, "She's not like an ordinary baby," and "She is fast."

A physical exam was given by our program pediatrician, who used the opportunity to reinforce Madeline's positive perceptions of her daughter as well as to demonstrate how responsive Anita was to her mother's voice and face. The videotape of Madeline and Anita when they were left alone following this exam shows Madeline intermittently drifting into her own world as she gave Anita a bottle, responding only when Anita choked from drinking too fast. This happened three times before Madeline took more active measures of positioning her more upright and beginning to rock and talk to the infant as she fed. Anita responded with smiles and embracing looks and then drifted off to sleep contentedly.

During a home visit a few days later, Eva found Madeline very depressed again. She appeared alternately sad and angry, holding her head down and talking in whispered tones. She tried to attend to the baby but had difficulty responding and was totally out of synchrony with her little girl. She only complained of being bored and said that the baby turned away from her. She could not articulate her feelings but said she wanted to move away from Jane. She threatened she might just pick up and leave, but when asked where she would go, she did not know. Eva tried to convince her to wait until she had worked out some plans. To make things more concrete, she pointed out that it was extremely cold outside and Madeline would want to protect her baby.

At this point Jane returned home and immediately began to ventilate her anger and frustration about Madeline. She was furious that Madeline did not even clean up after herself and the baby, and she wanted her out of the house. While she went on, insensitive to Madeline's needs or presence, Madeline just held her head down and made no effort to say anything. Shortly afterwards Thomas came home from work and a heated argument ensued between him and his sister. At that point, Madeline absented herself by going upstairs to her room to avoid the conflict. Jane was angry that Madeline had said nothing, "Madeline never said anything and didn't do anything." Thomas answered that Madeline was not supposed to spend most of her time cleaning and that her job was to take care of the baby.

Eva's impression was that Thomas was supportive of Madeline and he seemed especially proud of his little girl. She also got the feeling that part of Jane's anger was related to Thomas's siding with Madeline rather than siding with her. It appeared that their relationship had changed since Madeline had come into Thomas's life and Jane seemed to resent this. Finally, a few nights later, Jane closed her door to Madeline, Thomas, and Anita. They sought refuge in a delapidated old boarding house across the street.

Madeline did not call to let us know she had been evicted again. Eva and Joan discovered her move 2 days later when they went to see her. Jane said she had "had it" and was still furious that Thomas had brought Madeline into her home to begin with. She thought Madeline would never be able to take care of this baby and that she should be placed in foster care like the others. We cringed, listening to her words. We wondered if Madeline could make it and feared she could not, although now there was only one baby and Thomas was with her.

Joan and Eva immediately went across the street and found Madeline and Anita in a squalid room which was dark, cold, and depressing. Madeline was sitting with her head in her hands, oblivious of the dirty diapers and unwashed bottles which littered the room. She again appeared extremely depressed and withdrawn. Unless we could intervene dramatically and forcefully, we might not be able to prevent her having to give up this child like the others. We decided to invite her to our recently opened Infant Center, which included facilities for laundry and cooking. We asked Madeline to come every day. To our great relief, she accepted. Madeline would now be able to receive continuous support in mobilizing her energies around the care of Anita. Despite the fact that this was Madeline's fifth child, it was as if she had never had the opportunity to learn how to care for an infant. In the Center, she would not only be helped but could observe appropriate behavior modeled by others and perhaps be able to integrate these behaviors into her interactions with her baby.

OUR NEW PLAN

By this time it was very clear to us that the only intervention which would work for Madeline required a total restructuring of her daily life and experience of others.

We decided our new environment would have to offer Madeline the basic dependency relationships and life experiences she had missed in her own family. Reexperiencing multiple roles and feelings might permit Madeline to work out her numerous difficulties. Madeline had never had a home or family she trusted and could not have one or provide one for her daughter until she could change. She did not know how to mother or sustain a relationship with a man and could not assume these responsibilities until she, too, was mothered and related to in a way that would give her an alternative to the intense passive-aggressive patterns she had developed. Our goal was to help Madeline mother Anita and to grow with the baby while we facilitated the development of both. To do so, we became Madeline's family and brought her in daily to eat, play, work, and interact with everyone in our program. We helped her go to school, gave her a job, provided a setting for peers and friends, and, most importantly, helped her parent and enjoy Anita. Our approach was stable, organized, and planned every day. Madeline had individual sessions with Eva and Joan twice a week; a daily day-treatment program in the infant room with Judy, Pat, and other mothers and babies; and a chance to participate in all of our structured programs, including group therapy, high-school equivalency courses, and various health and educational workshops. Very importantly, our approach included contact with Thomas, who supported her participation in our program. We hoped Madeline's participation in our program would reduce the dependency on him and so prevent the relationship from being destroyed.

Madeline's willingness to come to the Center was the one initial factor which allowed our work to move forward and which reflected the impact of all our earlier pursuits and efforts. It is not certain we would have been able to face starting all over again without having established the Infant Center as an alternative home for our participants and a place which could support our efforts. Had we been able to provide an intensive and comprehensive program earlier, Madeline might still have refused to come or been unable to tolerate being with us all day. Two things contributed to her response at this time. First, her core dependency yearned to be met and her depression and passivity permitted others to take over at least initially. Second, almost 2 years of pursuit and concern established some element of trust and connection between us. This tie would now be tested.

MADELINE IN THE THERAPEUTIC INFANT CENTER

We decided to personalize all aspects of our intervention with Madeline, including bringing her in and taking her home.

Judy, our homemaker and infant room assistant, was assigned to pick up Madeline and Anita on her way to work and to take them home after work. Madeline had appeared comfortable with Judy during earlier contacts and we hoped she could establish a close relationship with this warm, maternal, and understanding woman who might in time be perceived as a peer and friend. This relationship in fact developed quickly.

Judy was attracted to Madeline, who reminded her of another quiet, sad young woman she knew and liked. She noted that Madeline was both very pretty and very withdrawn. Since Madeline did not talk, Judy did, sharing information about her own family, particularly her children. Madeline always listened with great curiosity. Judy also asked her continuously about Anita, granting a new importance to every detail of her daughter's life which Madeline had never experienced. Suddenly, it was important to note what time Anita arose, how many ounces she ate, when she was bathed, and what she wore. Soon Judy extended her questions to what Anita liked to look at and to which sounds she responded. Day by day she expanded the repertoire of Madeline's observations as they rode to work, did the wash, prepared the formula, and went through the basic routine care Madeline still needed to learn to establish. That Judy shared her own car rather than a taxi or the program station wagon meant something special to Madeline. The car provided a protective environment in which the women could talk coming and going between the center and home.

Judy soon became the first person to find out what was happening with Madeline, who shared details about her life with Thomas and talked about birth control long before she could discuss these issues with Eva or Joan. For example, when Anita was about 2 months old, Madeline asked Judy about having her tubes tied. After talking about it, Judy asked, "How about if I go with you?"

Judy went with Madeline to the hospital to sign papers but Madeline never contacted the hospital again for an appointment. Before long Madeline was calling Judy "ma" and Judy noted that she could say things to Madeline without her being angered. Madeline also used Judy to influence Thomas by letting him know what Judy said or by asking Judy to talk to him. Judy also answered his personal questions and was the only one to talk about herself, being much more of a "real" person to Madeline than her therapist and her infant specialist could be.

MADELINE RESPONDS

Madeline responded almost immediately to coming to the Infant Center daily. Life suddenly seemed to have a new meaning, with possibilities she had never imagined. Judy's warmth set the tone and Madeline would greet everyone, checking to see who on the staff was there each day. She held Anita proudly in front of her for everyone to admire. Others would ask Madeline how she, Thomas, and Anita were or what they had done the evening before. For the first time, Madeline had to account for herself and her family; no one had ever cared before. Details became significant: did Anita eat well, did they play something new, was she bathed, did she sleep through the night, were they planning to shop or visit? These questions reinforced Madeline's importance as a mother as well as reinforcing the structure and organization of mothering which we were helping her internalize. After these greetings, Madeline would get something to eat and greet other mothers and babies coming in, as Anita looked wide-eyed at all the activity around her. Some days Madeline brought in her laundry and helped make lunch. Each day had a program, and she spent time with various people for various purposes. Anita was always with her. When Anita was napping Madeline sometimes went out to lunch or to shop but she returned promptly, anxious lest Anita awaken in her absence. When they left, Madeline and Anita would again pass down the hall saying good-bye to everyone and waving before getting into Judy's car. There the morning's conversation would be resumed.

WORK WITH ANITA AND MADELINE

Although Anita thrived, Joan assumed nothing and proceeded to work with Madeline at the most fundamental levels. During these individual sessions they would work in one of the infant rooms or in Joan's office. Joan would hold Anita in front of her face and talk with her while maintaining eye contact and moving her rhythmically. Madeline would watch and try again and again, working hard to put together the multiple modalities of looking, talking, and moving. Doing these all at once was a big leap to make, but she was so delighted with Anita's response she worked hard. Joan first helped her hold Anita up so that her face was in direct line with her mother's; then she suggested some things to say such as "Hi, Anita, hi, my baby." Then she asked her to nod her head and move Anita in concert with her. These were obvious, simple interactions, but ones Madeline did not know and had to develop, adding one modality after another. Before long Madeline was trying these on her own when Anita would wake up or to show off to someone else. Needless to say, Madeline always had an audience.

In addition, Joan provided some toys to take home and to share with Thomas. Madeline did not have any idea of how to use toys with a tiny baby. As far as she was concerned, toys were for kids to play with by themselves; the parent just had to be sure they did not put them in their mouths. Again, Joan started at the most elementary levels to show Madeline how Anita responded to definite colors, shapes, and sounds when presented with various rattles, small toys, or mobiles. Madeline learned that Anita could watch and follow objects, turn to definite sounds, and even prefer some things over others. Madeline was impressed and could be seen practicing day after day. Before long she was recommending some objects to other mothers while indicating Anita did not like others as much.

Joan also helped Madeline learn to observe how Anita responded to being fed, changed, or bathed. Routine care now took on a language in which others were interested, a language which could be shared. This was a step-by-step process. At first Joan simply described what Anita was doing. "Look, Anita likes this soft bunny." Then, at other times she described what Madeline was doing, "Oh, Madeline, you did that so well. You really know how to get her attention." Soon the observations were internalized. Then, Madeline would be addressed as her baby's expert. She would be asked rather than told what to do. "What do you think Anita will do now?" "Do you think we should do this or that?" All these steps were further reinforced by Pat and Judy on a daily basis.

Joan also helped Madeline with specific caregiving techniques such as bathing. Initially Anita had fussed and squirmed when her mother placed her in the bathwater. Madeline was tense and awkward when she handled Anita even though this was her fifth child. Joan demonstrated how to prepare the bath and towels, how to hold and bend, and how to wash the baby as she talked and soothed her with her voice and small motions. While Madeline was learning these steps, Joan would keep up a steady stream of talking to Anita which had a calming effect on the baby and gave Madeline more confidence as she went through each of these motions. After a few of these sessions Madeline was able to move smoothly on her own and relax enough to start imitating Joan in talking to her infant. Bath time became a particular activity mother and daughter enjoyed together with Anita soon splashing gleefully and Madeline laughing with pleasure.

ANITA ESTABLISHES HOMEOSTASIS AND ATTACHMENT

Within 2 months after the start of our daily intervention program, Anita was seen giving her biggest and most frequent smiles to her mother. She had clearly developed a differential pattern of response to her mother which contrasted with her response to Joan, Judy, and others in the infant program. The special attachment and bonding we had hoped for had become established. Madeline was learning to care for her baby and enjoy it. Anita had established homeostasis, as evidenced by her smooth and predictable patterns of sleeping and feeding, her interest in the world, and her preference for her mother, to whom she was growing increasingly attached.

Madeline could not acknowledge this special attachment when asked directly how she felt about Anita or whether Anita related differently to her. As far as she was concerned, Anita was still the same as all the others except, "a little faster." She claimed caring for Anita was just something she had to do because Anita needed her. Madeline rejected the notion that anything she did for her baby was going to influence her later development. She also denied Anita was ever fussy or ever spit up even though these observations had been made with her on various occasions. It was as if Madeline had to maintain the posture that she did not affect Anita and Anita did not affect her. At one point she switched from using Similac to evaporated milk and Anita started to spit up. Madeline rejected our advice to return to Similac for more iron or to add more water and Karo syrup to the evaporated milk. Rather than confront this opposition directly, we enlisted the help of the Public Health Clinic's pediatrician, who asked her to change. She complied with her request but still refused to stop feeding Anita cereal at 2 months. Fortunately, further difficulties were minimized because of Anita's adaptiveness and clear and unequivocal cues, which elicited Madeline's responses. That Anita's needs were also very stable and predictable permitted Madeline to follow a daily routine of care which fit the baby's needs but did not depend on Madeline's reading of cues.

MADELINE ENLARGES HER RELATIONSHIP POTENTIAL: WORK WITH EVA

Since Madeline and Anita were attending the Infant Center on a daily basis, Eva had the opportunity to have daily contact with her on some level. Soon, Eva suggested that she and Madeline meet twice weekly alone to talk, but added that if she wanted to talk at any other time, all she had to do was let her know. The sessions that followed were the first meetings with Madeline that did not focus on concrete needs. Initially, Eva had to seek Madeline at the designated times and accompany her back to her office. Madeline would sit with her head down and say very little. Her affect was flat, she appeared depressed, and the old angry look would appear. If Eva asked questions, she would answer minimally. If Eva wondered how she felt or expressed how Madeline made her feel, she would deny it or stare silently. There were no spontaneous productions and her few responses were extremely constricted and concrete. Usually she just said, "I ain't got no problems," or "I don't feel that way." She was unwilling to talk about herself although it was not clear why. She appeared so limited and primitive in her personality development that she could not process experiences and feelings. Words and symbols conveyed nothing meaningful to her. She needed to develop some symbolic and representational capacities.

The contrast between Madeline's behavior in the Infant Room and her behavior when alone with Eva indicated that it would be more useful to talk about Anita than herself. Madeline responded to this approach: she would describe her day-to-day interactions, and just "practicing" some kind of verbal exchange seemed useful. Soon Madeline started to talk about Thomas, not in terms of an issue or their relationship, but as concrete facts. Madeline would report not cooking for Thomas or refusing to have sex with him. At first she said it was because she did not want to, but soon she would identify some grievance she had against him. Her conversations with Judy were critical here: she would first report these incidents to Judy, who would be the first both to accept and examine with Madeline what happened, often saying, "Oh, Madeline why did you do that?" It is unlikely anyone had ever asked Madeline to reflect on her behavior before. She had grown up in a world of quick retribution and retaliation rather than understanding. Madeline would then be able to tell Eva some of these things but exploration was still very limited.

Eva proceeded as Madeline permitted. While Eva could see her patterns of withholding, avoiding, and retreating from Thomas when she was angry or disappointed Madeline could still see none of this. Meanwhile, the quality of her social relationships with other mothers in the program began to improve, as did her self-image. Madeline claimed the Infant Center, as if she were establishing her territory. After all, she came every day and knew more about it than anyone else. She began to engage others who came and appeared warm and amusing when she was not under stress. She often acted as a guide to others. This was a remarkable contrast to the earlier hostile and reticent Madeline, who turned others off rather promptly. As her relationships with the staff, other mothers, Thomas, and Anita continued to develop, Madeline was more able to talk about these relationships with Eva. The words only became meaningful following her present experiences. For example, she said that she enjoyed living with her boyfriend but she certainly would never want to get married. Eva could not explore the feelings about her parents and their marriage because Madeline was still not able to link past events to her present state. But they could focus on how pleased Madeline was to be able to sustain a close, satisfying relationship with a man.

By building upon her here-and-now experiences, Eva was able to help Madeline develop another sense of herself which she could accept and value. On this basis they went on to think about the future and then the past. This became evident when Madeline began to talk about how she wanted to send Anita to a Catholic school where she would get a really good education and the teachers were strict. She also wished Anita was old enough so Madeline could have parties for her, buy her things, and be close with her. Eva would gently ask what it had been like for Madeline with her mother when she was a child. Madeline would then report that her mother never seemed to expect much of her although her older sister finished high school. She said her mother never had a party for her and had little time for her, but she wanted Anita to be able to talk to her about problems.

Eva would thus try to go back and forth, gently exploring her past and the fears of closeness she had developed. It was apparent that Madeline must have suffered far greater deprivation than we had realized but could only relate the less painful experiences. Past events did not really feel distant or past to Madeline; she was always on guard lest they recur and lest she be hurt again. Similarly, her rage was also ever-present, defended against by mechanisms of avoidance, denial, and projection. When an issue was raised in one session, it was often avoided during the next few. Eva would then reinforce the ego strength Madeline was developing in her day-to-day life in our program.

Madeline could not yet initiate anything in her sessions. Eva would gently begin by friendly chitchat, asking Madeline how she was or about a specific event that had taken place. This basic exercise in socialization provided Madeline with a model to imitate. An attempt was made to maintain the structure of scheduled time and days so that these therapeutic sessions had consistent and safe boundaries. Eva sometimes wondered what was the use of meeting because so little seemed to take place, but she persisted, encouraged by Madeline's steady progress in the Infant Center and Anita's thriving development. In fact, it was Anita who became Madeline's most progressive therapeutic agent by presenting her mother with new tasks in development they could master together.

ANITA'S 4-MONTH ASSESSMENT

At 4 months Anita was given the Bayley Scales of Mental Development. She was precociously wary of the examiner and gazed at her so intensely it was difficult to disengage her in order to get involved in the test items. Once she got started she frequently turned around to look at her mother, and Madeline was able to return her to the test items. Anita performed in the middle of the average range. Her behavior with the examiner and her mother, especially the impressive range and frequency of vocalizations she used in her interactions, made it clear that she was most interested in the human world.

After the assessment Madeline and Anita were left alone for a 10-minute free play period. In contrast to her availability during the structured test sessions, Madeline appeared to drift away into her own thoughts and feelings for a few minutes at a time. She then spontaneously came out of her reverie and tried to engage Anita. Anita persisted in watching her mother as if she were ready and able to interact with her as soon as Madeline was available again. Madeline softly asked her daughter, "What do you want to talk about?" and then got her to laugh by moving her face toward and away from Anita in a playful interactive way. Anita laughed gleefully each time she came close. She continued to laugh so hard that she got the hiccups and her laughter became less gleeful and more distressed. But Madeline did not appear to notice the impact of her constant stimulation and Anita's signals to slow down. Madeline had difficulty modulating her efforts in response to Anita's signals. Nevertheless, for the first time, she was interacting with her baby on her own initiative and had been able to show remarkable interest and support during her test performance.

MADELINE SURRENDERS HER TWO OLDEST CHILDREN

For three more months, Madeline and Anita enjoyed coming to the Center. Madeline kept her appointments conscientiously and practiced what she learned. Unexpectedly, she hinted that she might not come anymore because she was looking for a job. This appeared to coincide with her DSS worker raising the issue of permanent placement of her two older children. Their foster mother was prepared to adopt them if Madeline would give them up voluntarily. Madeline was upset and angry. We observed her pulling back from Anita. We first noticed this when she began to hold the baby across her knees rather than close to her bosom as she had before. Joan decided to speak for Anita, lending her voice and feelings to concretize to Madeline what Anita's experience must be like. She said for her, "Are you angry with me Mommy?" "Why do you hold me so far away?" Joan also put her arm around Madeline, letting her feel the comfort she too needed. Soon Madeline could again pick up Anita and hold her tightly.

Eva and Joan initiated a meeting with Madeline to talk about her children in foster care, a subject both Madeline and her therapist had thus far avoided but which the DSS now raised because legal time factors required that some decision be made. Whenever Eva attempted to explore Madeline's feelings about her older children, Madeline would say she did not want to talk about them. She said she thought about them and that was enough. Eva did not feel that Madeline was preserving some wish that she reunite with them or that they would be there when she was ready for them. Instead, "thinking about them" was her way of feeling connected with them and blocked the reality that she had placed them and had not seen them in close to 2 years. Madeline told Eva she did not talk about the children to anyone, with the rare exception of her boyfriend. Further, the children were a "secret" in the Infant Room. Although the other mothers knew every participant had to have at least one other child to be eligible to join the program, no one dared ask Madeline if she had other children when they saw her alone with Anita. There was something about Madeline's style and manner which made it clear to all that questions were not to be asked.

Madeline slowly became more willing to talk to Eva about the children after Eva persistently reminded her that the children were not a "secret" between them because of all they had been through together. Eva would attempt to contrast Madeline's current maternal capacities and caregiving with Anita to her earlier experiences. For example, when Anita became ill with bronchitis, Madeline rushed to the emergency room. She recognized how frightened she had been watching

Anita's difficult breathing. In the past Madeline had rarely even kept clinic appointments. While supporting her new successful experiences with Anita, Eva would also ask Madeline what she thought it would be like if she had to care for five children. Madeline would shrug and say, "The same (as caring for Anita)." As the Easter holidays approached Madeline appeared excited about celebrating with Anita and Thomas. Eva tried to explore how she felt by commenting on her observations of her excitement and plans to dress up Anita. As Eva attached feelings to actions and persisted in identifying the feelings, Madeline was finally able to say she was happy with Anita and Thomas but sad about her other children. Expressing this feeling was always followed by her recognizing that they were in good homes where they were cared for and loved.

Eva persisted in exploring Madeline's feelings about the boys in anticipation of a meeting with the DSS worker to discuss permanent plans. Madeline became angry at the social worker and said she did not want to talk about plans, that she would think about them. But behind the anger was hurt, fear, and a sense of relief that some decision would have to be made soon. Eva then approached the issue more concretely over several weeks. What did Madeline want? Did she want to care for the children? Did she have a place for them? Had she discussed her concerns with Thomas? Did she feel she could adequately care for them? Did she realize what their special needs would mean since both were attending a special school for learning and emotionally disabled children?

Three months after these discussions began, Madeline finally indicated that she wanted to visit Danny and David. Eva made arrangements with the foster mother. Madeline brought Anita, and the boys were happy to see their mother. Madeline was pleased to see how well the boys were developing. Madeline then suggested they all have a picnic soon and the foster mother agreed to have it at her home and to prepare the food. Unbeknownst to Madeline, the boys later asked their foster mother when Madeline would take them back because she now had a home for their little sister.

As long as Madeline had no contact with her children, she held onto the fantasy that she would provide a home for them. The first visit after 2 years of separation made the boys a reality again, and this experience helped Madeline decide that she could not care for them. It also helped her know they were well taken care of and could stay with their foster mother. She was relieved when the foster mother agreed to let her have contact with the boys after the surrender; she did not have to give them up entirely. Following the visit, Madeline signed the papers to surrender Danny and David for adoption. She did not tell us she was about to do this but one day returned to the center relieved and proud that she had signed. However, she could not tell anyone else, including Thomas or her mother. Eva praised Madeline for having felt enough concern about the boys to be able to give them the kind of home they needed. Madeline continued to talk about them and followed through on the picnic she had planned earlier, although the two younger children could not come. She also planned another picnic at the center with Antonio and Susan, which took place after the summer.

Madeline's surrender of the children was supported by us, albeit indirectly, because we feared that adding the two difficult boys to Madeline's existing responsibilities—given the fragility of her emerging maternal abilities—would overwhelm her and make her retreat again from all her children. Further, Thomas was not interested in her other children and wanted Madeline to devote herself entirely to Anita.

THE INFANT SPECIALIST WORKS WITH MADELINE BETWEEN 4–8 MONTHS

After the 4-month assessment when Anita had focused almost exclusively on the examiner's face, Joan suggested ways to distract Anita from her rigid interest in the human face in order to promote interest in other objects. Madeline was encouraged to hold Anita in her lap while she dangled toys in front of her line of vision and to encourage Anita to reach for the object. She was also taught to animate inanimate objects by giving them movement and sound which Anita could track. However, when Anita did begin to reach out and play, we noticed that she became less expressive and vocal and appeared more somber, with dampened affect. Madeline also observed this change and explained that Anita was "inspecting everyone," a phrase she had heard us use before. There appeared to be some meaning in this observation because Anita actively looked and searched visually with a weary and reserved expression when it was an unfamiliar object, analogous to a "stranger anxiety with objects." This seemed precocious for her age, but as new objects became more familiar and joined her existing repertoire of interactions with Madeline, who was encouraged to let her explore, Anita became more comfortable and accepting of unfamiliar objects.

Madeline also continued to grow. She cared for Anita during her waking hours and when Anita slept she planned activities for herself. Though there were many others around, Madeline was expected to be the full-time caregiver for Anita and others would fill in only momentarily when needed. Anita developed a very predictable schedule which made it easy to plan for her and Madeline was observed playing with her daughter more and more frequently. She would wait for her to awaken and spontaneously talk with her while she changed and fed her. Madeline was also encouraged to get down on the floor with Anita and roll from side to side or present toys to her while prone.

Madeline indeed internalized new maternal behaviors in response to our intensive efforts. But there were times when the old gruff, abrupt manner broke through. One day she was heard telling Anita in a very angry tone to get her fist out of her mouth, even though Madeline was aware of the importance of her daughter's mouthing at this point. During a subsequent session with Joan, she again told her to get her thumb out of her mouth. Joan again explained how babies often put things in their mouths to learn how they are shaped and how they feel; that is, it was a way of discovering something just like inspecting objects with their eyes. Repeated explanations and demonstrations were offered with Joan even urging Madeline to try mouthing, but Madeline would only listen warily. Joan also pointed out that Anita was using her thumb to console herself, that this was natural, and that babies could even do this before they were born. When asked about this on another day, Madeline seemed to have forgotten but then giggled and repeated the "right answer" about self-consoling. This was something that did not register easily with her.

Joan then attempted another approach in which she described the individual differences and needs of every baby. To make this more concrete Joan would invent story upon story of families and babies she knew who did different things. One would suck a pacifier, one would suck her thumb, one would suck any object he could reach, and they all stopped at different points as well. Joan also assured Madeline that when Anita was satisfied with sucking, she would be more active and talkative. This indeed happened and Madeline could be seen becoming less and less controlling of Anita's behavior.

We wondered how her discomfort and objections to Anita's mouthing related to Madeline's own oral conflicts. We remembered how she had refused to take in our food, and her fights with everyone who had fed her in the past. These themes, however, could not yet be discussed with Madeline.

In some instances, intervention focused on Anita modified Madeline's own impulses and old patterns, in other instances it introduced new ideas about development she had never entertained, let alone used in caring for her other children. For example, when Madeline was pushing Anita to walk, standing her up to walk around the room, she was urged to give the child more time to sit and crawl and was able to do so. Again and again Joan showed Madeline things Anita enjoyed; Madeline would then imitate Joan, eager to enjoy the activity with Anita. She learned, for example, to play object permanence games with Anita: she would drop a toy out of the child's line of vision to see if she followed the objects; the first time Anita turned around and searched for the toy, Madeline was delighted and repeated the game, as everyone watched.

When Anita was 6 months old, Joan again helped Madeline watch for Anita's signals and cues to figure out what she wanted. She introduced the idea that Anita would signal her desire for many different things, not just "to fuss or get her way." This notion was very new for Madeline. In the past her interactions with her children had been limited to controlling and intrusive directions, prohibitions, or withdrawing from the children completely. Now, she was learning to follow her daughter's lead by looking at what Anita found to be enjoyable. For example, during one visit Anita had been placed in an infant seat so that we could dangle toys in front of her to get her to practice reaching. When Anita started to become a little irritable, Joan suggested to Madeline that she might be ready to come out of the seat and go on the floor. Madeline removed her from the infant seat and placed her on the floor. Madeline then put a chain with colored disks out of reach for Anita and started to rattle them to encourage Anita to come after them. Instead Anita turned away and returned to the infant seat out of which she had just been taken. Joan then suggested, "Let's see what she'll do now, Madeline." Rather than continue rattling the toy disks to attract attention, they both sat back and watched Anita, who spent the next 5 minutes exploring the straps on the infant seat, fingering the tag, fingering the plastic seat itself, and putting the stainless steel rings in her mouth. This gave Joan an opportunity to point out and marvel at the exploratory powers that Anita was demonstrating. After a number of similar experiences with Joan and many chances to watch similar behavior, Madeline learned to sit back and observe what was of interest to her daughter, without insisting that Anita follow what she had in mind for her.

Step by step and day by day, Madeline learned new things not only about Anita but about her own capacities to mother. In addition to her individual sessions and watching others in the Infant Center, Madeline was given prescription sheets which described the specific activities she had practiced in the Center and could repeat at home. These prescriptions also helped to include Thomas in play sessions with his daughter; Madeline could use them to teach him what she had learned. In contrast to many of the fathers in the program, Thomas was very interested in his daughter's progress and learned from Madeline. She benefited, too, from being the "teacher" and pointing out how important she was to Anita.

ANTICIPATING NEW STEPS

Madeline came to the Center every day, and we used every hour she was there to help her learn about Anita and herself. Joan spent large blocks of time preparing Madeline for Anita's next steps in development, anticipating what Anita would be doing next, and relating it to what she was doing now. Sometimes Anita was especially cooperative during these sessions and would demonstrate exactly what Joan was saying. For example, when Anita was 7 months old Joan was noting how Anita would soon be crawling all around the room, but would seek Madeline out periodically as a "fueling stop," and come back to check on her. Just then, Anita, who was playing across the room with the infant seat, came scooting across the room and pulled on Madeline's skirt to be lifted.

By 8 months of age, Anita's development was progressing well. Her strong attachment to Madeline was demonstrated each time her mother left the room and she began to scream. Anita was very mobile and coordinated, pulling to stand, crawling, and feeding herself. She noticed new objects, was eager to inspect and manipulate them, and was alert and responsive to people around her. Madeline had also greatly increased her psychological availability and capacity to mother. She was meeting the basic needs of her daughter in a consistent and responsive manner and developing a differentiated view of her and Anita's experiences. When some of the old abrupt manner crept in at times, Joan would look for a positive behavior Madeline had demonstrated and point out this alternative approach to Madeline as a way of modifying the more abrupt and inappropriate behavior. With positive reinforcement and encouragement, this behavior-shaping technique worked well. Madeline became so involved in her sessions that she would make sure Joan gave her an alternate hour if for some reason Joan was unable to keep her appointment.

THE 8-MONTH ASSESSMENT

At the 8-month Bayley Assessment Anita had an upper-respiratory infection which made her fussy and irritable. Nonetheless, she could be sufficiently engaged and distracted to cause her performance to move into the superior level of mental functioning. She was now very interested in the various test items and she frequently objected to their removal. She was continuing her active vocalizations and particularly enjoyed the peekaboo game as well as other tests of object constancy. Fine and gross motor functioning were good and she was already attempting to scribble.

Madeline's appearance and performance were at least as impressive as Anita's. She dressed up and looked very attractive. She was also available to support, comfort, and help Anita reengage in the test when she became too irritable to respond to the items or the examiner. Anita would then turn to her mother who could appropriately console her.

Although Madeline worked hard to perform during the free play, the interaction with Anita varied in quality. When Madeline relaxed, she could respond contingently to Anita's cues and have tender and extended rhythmic and affectionate exchanges, such as facing Anita on her lap while she sang and rocked her. At other times, during a peekaboo game, she would start out playfully, with Anita responding with glee, but become so overstimulating and driven by her own excitement that she seemed unaware when Anita's glee turned to screeching. Only when Anita finally started to hiccup could Madeline shift gears. All in all Madeline's persistence and pleasure in interacting with Anita were very impressive. While she was overstimulating and still showed little variation in her play, she was no longer retreating from the expectations that she "perform" and she enjoyed Anita's responsiveness and accomplishments.

ANITA MOVES AHEAD AND MADELINE FEELS THREATENED

Madeline began to appear restless following Anita's 8-month assessment. She started to talk again about wanting to go to work or to study for her high-school equivalency. This push to move away seemed related to Anita's new stage of mobility. Anita was crawling and standing, pursued her own interests, could go after things she wanted, and related to other people in the world. While it was clear to us that Anita based these new developments on her secure relationship with her mother, to whom she always turned as she was beginning to move about, it appeared to Madeline that her daughter was moving away from her. Madeline's reaction was to pull away from Anita first. Eva wondered if Madeline felt that Anita needed her less now. Madeline recognized this immediately and nodded. Eva then could reflect both the sense of loss and the threat Madeline experienced with Anita's new mobility, as if it meant Anita would no longer need her and was becoming too independent. By presenting simply stated reflections of what she thought Madeline was experiencing, Eva gave her the opportunity to consider what was said. At times she nodded in agreement or disagreement, at other times she repeated Eva's words. This was very much like talking to a preverbal child who could understand what was being said and could be made to feel less anxious by a comforting and responsive parent, but whose experiences were still global, diffuse, and impossible to describe in words.

In our intervention program Madeline's intense dependency needs had been met along with Anita's. This nurturing enabled her to meet Anita's needs as long as Madeline could identify and experience them with the infant. Now that Anita was ready to move forward but Madeline was not, Madeline's impulse was to pull away from her daughter. It became more apparent to us that because of the unresolved issues and unfulfilled needs in her own development, Madeline might not be able to keep up with her daughter's growth. Madeline's need for a dependent infant in her arms related to internal pressure to keep her own dependency alive, and may have led to her repeated pregnancies. We decided to focus on Madeline's need for a "replacement infant," while trying to help her foster Anita's development without feeling too threatened or abandoned. Meeting the needs of mother and daughter when they coincided had required all our resourcefulness; now our task was to meet the needs of mother, daughter, and the parent–infant couple at a time when these might diverge or even conflict.

During subsequent sessions with Madeline, Eva tried to relate the issue of feeling needed to having another baby. Madeline denied wanting any more children soon, although she felt some pressure from Thomas to have another baby. Eva wondered what else Madeline might want and what other needs she might have which were not related to motherhood. Madeline quickly stated she wanted to get into a high-school equivalency program or get a job for herself. Eva introduced the idea of doing this while she continued to work with Anita. Madeline's interest led us to explore the possibility of starting a high-school equivalency class at our program. Arrangements were made with the Board of Education which permitted Madeline to attend classes several times a week just down the hall from Anita's infant room. Anita gained positive experience from the separations and reunions and continued to feel her mother's availability when needed.

Madeline's relationship with Judy continued to grow both during their daily rides and at the Center. When Madeline complained about Thomas spending too much time at his sister's place, Judy would suggest that she offer him something better to do. Madeline responded by suggesting to Thomas that they go to a movie or meet friends. The relationship was even more enhanced by Madeline's visits to Judy's home. Judy's children loved Anita and Madeline received in Judy's home the love and excitement she could not get from her own family. She reciprocated, buying Judy a necklace, and later a scarf for Christmas when she visited her home. In time, Madeline's relationship to Judy shifted from "mother," to "sister," to "friend."

ANITA'S 12-MONTH ASSESSMENT

Both the Bayley and Uzgiris-Hunt scales were administered at 12 months. Anita presented as a very vocal, smiling, and responsive child with a remarkable sense of humor. She laughed continuously, taking great pleasure in herself and in the examiner's imitation. She was also attentive and persistent even with tasks which went beyond her abilities. She frequently turned to Madeline to show her items or seek her support. Madeline was responsive to her daughter and delighted by her progress. Anita maintained her superior functioning; language, fine, and gross motor development were proceeding evenly. On the Uzgiris-Hunt she also responded at or above age level on all scales, including means, imitation, object permanence, and causality. Her most mature responses were in object permanence.

The free-play session started with Anita squirming to get down from her mother's lap, walking around the room, looking in the mirror and picking up a book. She did not respond to Madeline's various comments designed to get her attention. Madeline finally went over to her and yanked her by the arm over to the couch. She then tried to read a book to Anita, who was not really interested. When Madeline put the book down,

Anita climbed into her lap to get the book, then started to point to the pictures herself. Madeline was able to join her, and their interaction was responsive and contingent, with Madeline imitating Anita's vocalizations and Anita responding in turn. Anita then crawled onto her mother again and they engaged in some frolic play, much to each other's delight, before resuming their looking at the book while snuggled comfortably near each other.

The way Anita initiated and asserted her wishes in this session confirmed to us her "executive powers" and her attachment to her mother. She engaged in affectionate and reciprocal interactions and recovered easily when her mother handled her gruffly. Madeline yanked her daughter inappropriately in the same manner we had seen her use with her other children, but this brief behavior was outweighed by her new ability to follow and respond to Anita in reciprocal ways. She also read to her daughter, something she had never done before.

The Second Year: New Challenges

Evidence of the remarkable progress made by Madeline and Anita during Anita's first year of life might have led some intervention programs to reduce their efforts, particularly if their efforts had been as intensive and extensive as ours were with Madeline. We realized, however, that different challenges would have to be faced during Anita's second year, when she would have to develop symbolic and representational capacities through the use of language and play. These were capacities her mother had failed to develop; therefore, our interventions would continue to be critical. There were early signs that Madeline was becoming increasingly threatened by Anita's spurts of development which seemed to surpass her own, but she could not express this in words. Although a firm attachment had been formed and reciprocal interactions were now possible, much more work was needed. Our efforts were intensified to help Madeline so she could allow Anita to continue to thrive without being jeopardized by having her mother defensively withdraw from her.

THE ENSUING MONTHS

Following Anita's first birthday we noticed that Madeline brought Anita to the Infant Center in the morning and then left Anita in the care of the staff while she sought her own satisfaction either by getting food or going out to have a cigarette. She had to be urged constantly to come back and care for Anita. We recognized that she was reacting to her daughter's increased motoric confidence and ability to initiate independent moves which at times led her away from Madeline. For Madeline such beginning independence seemed to mean that Anita was no longer a baby and did not need her mother as much, a feeling we had reflected several months earlier. Joan pointed out again and again that Anita's early moves were only possible because of the stable and secure relationship she had with Madeline. Joan also emphasized that, in fact, Madeline was responsible for Anita's being able to take off on her own to explore the world, in this case the infant room. Joan attempted to reinforce this view by helping Madeline observe the different places Anita went and wondering with her what might have been of interest there. Madeline found it hard to understand what Joan was saying. She attempted to absorb these new ideas, but she needed increasing encouragement and support because she persisted in seeing exploratory behavior as Anita's moving away from and perhaps ahead of her. Joan observed Madeline walking ahead of Anita, who was struggling to keep up; she tried to point out how Anita might feel, struggling behind her mother unable to tell her mother that she wanted to walk along with her. It was evident that this had not occurred to Madeline. She had not realized that she would have to pace herself to her daughter's pace but rather had assumed that once her daughter could walk on her own, she could "do it all" on her own.

We also noticed at this time that Anita was not developing

distinct syllables in her vocalizations. A high-pitched squeal had replaced her early babbling. Contrary to our own expectations, based on Anita's early and expressive babbling, the child's speech was not emerging as clearly and as effortlessly as we anticipated. Joan encouraged Madeline to continue reading to Anita and to urge her to imitate simple words such as *mama* and *dada*. Madeline was also shown how to label various familiar objects. Although Madeline already did this with Anita at home, we doubted she was doing so very frequently, given the paucity of Madeline's spontaneous use of language in other situations and the fact that Madeline had become increasingly preoccupied with the upcoming decision concerning the placement of the older two children. Madeline's old patterns appeared to be reasserting themselves at this time. We wondered if she would pull away from Anita before the child could move away from her. Madeline seemed to have lost the interest and enthusiasm she had shown toward Anita when she was a more dependent infant during the first year of life.

THE RELATIONSHIP WITH EVA GROWS

The first 6 months of Anita's second year were characterized by Madeline's persistence in wanting to meet with Eva even though she was unable to talk once they met. Eva recalled feeling that Madeline was very much like a child who would pass her in the hall and indicate, "Where are you? Do you still have time for me?" When they met, at their appointed times, Madeline would sit down eagerly, face Eva, and ask, "What are we going to talk about?" She waited passively for Eva to introduce different topics or issues. If Eva asked her what she wanted to talk about or if she had any problems or concerns, Madeline quickly answered, "I ain't got no problems." As a result, Eva had to initiate a situation on which Madeline could work. This permitted Madeline to make some limited response, and then Eva would have to take over again. Eva persisted in shaping the sessions because she felt Madeline could be pushed only so far and needed to have someone else organize and articulate her experiences a while longer. Eva tried to focus on what was happening in the here and now to help Madeline express or describe what she was experiencing in her current life. During this phase Madeline reached the stage in a therapeutic relationship of "talking" with someone and recognized Eva as a special person with whom she could tolerate one-to-one contact. Her life was no longer a crisis-ridden scramble for survival services. More important, she had formed a strong attachment with Eva which was reflected in her eager pursuit of Eva for their sessions, her willingness to share her "secrets," and, finally, her admission of Eva into her home to meet with Thomas.

MADELINE SURRENDERS SUSAN AND ANTONIO

One month after Anita's first birthday Madeline was again approached by DSS regarding her plans for the younger children in foster care. This time Madeline immediately indicated that she could not provide a home for them and hoped there would be no further delay in finding a good permanent placement. She signed the papers releasing Susan and Antonio on her own without telling Eva, Joan, Thomas, or her family. (The DSS worker had, however, told Eva and Joan.) When Madeline returned to the Infant Center after signing the papers, she looked relieved and carefree. The absence of sadness or loss suggested that Madeline had emotionally surrendered the children long before the formal signing. She had in fact not seen them for 2 years. Perhaps Madeline's experience of the surrender was attenuated by the quality of her earlier attachments, which had been severely compromised and undeveloped.

Eva tried to discuss with Madeline how she felt about giving up the children. Madeline did not express her feelings but finally asked whether Eva thought she had done the right thing. Again, Eva reviewed with her how she had made this decision and what the care of the children would have meant.

Madeline could then say that she did not think she could take care of them and that Thomas did not want her to have them anyway because he wanted her to take care of Anita. This led to discussion of whether she would tell Thomas or her family, particularly her mother, what she had done. Again Madeline said, "No," because no one in her family had ever voluntarily done such a thing. She was also afraid that Thomas might think she would sign Anita away and therefore did not want him to know. Eva attempted to help Madeline see some alternative ways for sharing news of her decision with the significant people in her life. For example, Madeline could help Thomas see that she was now committed to their new life together and that what she had done earlier was part of the "old Madeline." Madeline could not make such differentiations. She also withdrew from Eva in their sessions. When Eva persisted in trying to elicit her feelings about giving up the children, Madeline said she did not think about it and would not talk about it anymore. Even though she could not discuss anything related to what was happening or her feelings, she still sought Eva's proximity and acceptance and persisted in their sessions.

Meanwhile, Madeline gave up thoughts of going to work and made plans for a large family christening for Anita. Eva again refocused her work through Anita and followed Madeline's excitement and plans for christening her daughter. This was the first time she had christened any of her children. When Eva asked whether Madeline felt any difference between the way she related to Anita and the way she had earlier related to the other children, her answer was no. Though her behavior was changing, Madeline could neither examine nor see any conceptual differences in her treatment of the children. Denial, inadequate differentiation, and poor representational capacities did not allow her to discern the numerous qualitative differences we observed. She still thought that what she provided for Anita was only physical care, which she believed she had given all her children.

THE NEXT STEPS

Eva decided to try another approach saying, "Let's look at what happens between us. Now I am going to sit back and you decide what you want us to talk about." Madeline was very taken aback and surprised when Eva next indicated that the difficulty Madeline had in raising issues had to do with her difficulty in trusting Eva. Madeline had never thought of this in terms of trust. Eva pointed out that Madeline never really gave her a full picture of anything that happened in her life, providing only bits and pieces from which Eva might be able to put together a picture. When Eva indicated that she could not help Madeline as much as she might unless Madeline became more active and tried to think about the things she wanted to learn, Madeline said she would try. With this Eva again pursued Madeline's keeping the adoption of the children a secret from Thomas. Madeline persisted in saying that she did not know what he would think of her if he knew but could not see how these feelings would affect any other part of their relationship. As far as she was concerned, if she did not talk about an issue, it did not exist.

Given this level of concreteness, Eva proceeded to help Madeline learn how to think more about her relationship with Thomas. She explored what they did together, what they did not do together, and what Madeline did and did not expect of him. It became apparent that Madeline and Thomas had some difficulties in their sexual relationship, but Madeline would only say that at times she refused to have sex with him: she told him to just turn over and go to sleep. She would not elaborate. We wondered if she were withdrawing from Thomas sexually. If sex had been a way for Madeline to achieve closeness and meet dependency needs that were now being met by our program, might she now feel she no longer needed sex? If this were so, it would lead to some serious consequences. If her refusal continued, Thomas might move away from her. On the other hand, we knew that her relationship with Thomas had begun around sex even though she indicated in the beginning that they did not have sex for two months after they'd started living together. We wondered whether we could help Madeline see that sex could be enjoyable and that potential relationships did not have to be rejected. However, she refused to talk further and again retreated.

Each small step forward seemed to be followed by a small retreat until a reformulation could be offered and explored again. This was usually based on some external event. The next time it had to do with Madeline's fears of moving into a new house. Thomas had decided to rent a big dilapidated house which he hoped to repair in order to rent rooms to boarders. Madeline was very frightened about moving into this large, 13-room house and being alone with Anita. She asked Judy to tell Thomas that the house was in such deplorable condition that it would be too difficult to take care of and that perhaps he should reconsider the situation. We did not know how much thought Thomas had given this move and whether he was doing this impulsively. These plans also coincided with Madeline's mentioning that she had some difficulties with her menstrual cycle and the birth control pills she was taking. She said that Thomas did not want her to take the pill anyway because he would like her to have another child, but she denied that she wanted any more children at this time.

To facilitate our focus on Madeline's relationship with Thomas, we decided to implement home visits which might include Thomas. Eva suggested that she and Joan would each visit weekly in the late afternoon after Thomas had come home from work and that it would be nice to talk with them together in their own home. Madeline complied without saying very much but seemed to welcome Eva's and Joan's interest. When Eva met Thomas, she found him to be a warm person who related easily and seemed proud of his "woman" and daughter, but he presented a mixed picture. He expressed strong supportive and protective feelings for Madeline and Anita, while on the other hand indicating that he might move to Delaware

to work. When Madeline announced that she would not go
with him, he teased by saying that he would take Anita. It
appeared that Madeline was going to face a test of attachments. Was she going to follow Thomas? Would she speak up
and exert pressure on Thomas to stay rather than withdraw
sexually and indicate that she just did not care what he did
but would not follow him? Although little else was discussed,
Thomas decided to stay.

In addition to the weekly home visits, Eva continued to
see Madeline once a week in her office. Madeline continued
to maintain that she did not have any problems saying, "I
don't let things get me down. I try not to think about it."
When Eva attempted to comment on her nonverbal behavior
or her facial expression, she simply denied the interpretation.

Madeline again became agitated and restless in the Center and indicated that she was "bored" and did not want to
come every day. Center activities did not seem to fill the
loneliness and emptiness she appeared to be feeling. These
feelings were heightened by the big, empty house to which
she returned each day. Madeline had also reached out to her
mother several times but did not get the hoped-for response.
She may have been feeling disappointed and abandoned again.
Eva and Joan became very concerned that to fill some of the
emptiness she was feeling, Madeline might conceive. The
home visits became more focused on identifying activities that
Madeline and Anita might do at home and with other people
in their neighborhood.

The weekly home visits continued for several months but
were not very productive. Madeline appeared more depressed and unresponsive in the empty and sterile surroundings of her home. Eva also found it harder to keep their
discussions going in that environment without the activities
at the Infant Center which had lent so much life and substance
to Madeline and supported their efforts. Nor was Madeline
making much headway in reaching out to people in her neighborhood, although she finally began to take some walks with

Anita and visited some girl friends. Eva also noted that Thomas was unavailable. He would come home when she was there but then slip out to take care of his car.

Thomas and Madeline's relationship became more worrisome. There was evidence that Thomas was entertaining other women and Madeline was angry when they called him at home. Somewhat later it also became apparent to us that Madeline was seeking out other men and was having an affair. She started to dress up at the center, spent long periods on the phone, and left for dates while Anita was sleeping. We thought she was frightened by the next steps she would have to take in the relationship with Thomas.

ANITA REACTS

Not unexpectedly we began to observe changes in Anita's behavior. She had always been an infant with clear cues and was becoming a toddler who knew what she wanted. But the earlier contentment and pleasure so readily expressed were now accompanied by increasing signs of anger, hostility, and frustration. She was reacting to changes in her environment and her mother's more limited capacities to support her development during the second year of life. Joan continued to reinforce the importance of Madeline's role as a mother and the notion that Madeline could now serve as a base for her daughter's explorations. She also demonstrated how to use more distal modes of communication with Anita, particularly talking or smiling across the room. These modes would require Madeline to move beyond the more physical and proximal modes she had developed during the first year. Madeline, however, had difficulty using language and other distal modes which were not familiar to her.

In her individual sessions with Madeline and Anita, Joan also pursued ways to deal with Anita's negativism. She demonstrated ways to distract Anita from doing things to which Madeline objected. Madeline was helped by Joan putting Anita's actions into words to develop some sense of what Anita felt and what her behavior meant, and what her goals were. Joan might say, "Look Mommy, this is something new and interesting, give me a minute to look at it," or, "Let me do it my way, I can do it myself," or "I can't stop it, help me stop it." In this way Joan provided Madeline with an alternative way of perceiving Anita's behavior than automatically identifying with the negativism or aggression and reacting to it by gruffly telling her daughter to "stop it, don't do that girl!" or threatening her with a switch. Slowly Madeline became more aware of her reactions. We attributed this to the individual work as well as the examples of consistent and appropriate limit setting done by the Infant Center staff day after day. As Madeline witnessed Anita's response to their approaches, the alternative behaviors began to sink in. She noticed how differently Anita responded when an adult was in charge or when it was better to follow Anita's lead.

It was becoming evident, however, that the difficulties Anita was experiencing went beyond her mother's response to her; they involved her father as well. Leaving her small cozy apartment had left Madeline feeling hollow and empty in the strange open space of the large house they now inhabited. Madeline responded by withdrawing from Anita, letting her run around the big space or ride her "big wheel." Madeline was unable to set boundaries she did not feel herself. In fact, Madeline was afraid of the space that Anita freely roamed and used Anita to escort her around the house. In addition, there were the indications reported earlier that she and Thomas were pulling further away from each other and, inadvertently, from Anita. Anita reacted: She expressed anger and frustration in early temper tantrums and negativism and began to manipulate, playing Madeline off against Thomas.

FURTHER WORK WITH FATHER

During one of the first home visits with Thomas, Anita had a temper tantrum because Madeline and Thomas responded differently to something she wanted. She threw herself on the floor, screaming and out of control, and hit her head hard enough to cause a laceration. Madeline and Thomas became very frightened and angrily blamed each other for the outburst. Because Joan was present, she was able to piece together what happened. When Madeline told Anita she could not have something, Anita immediately sought out her father. He, as he proudly told Joan, could never refuse his daughter anything. Joan used this incident to explain how their different responses confused Anita. She was old enough to sense the "split" between her parents and to try to use this by going from one to the other. This tactic would not be useful to her, however, because Anita became anxious and frightened by her manipulative and angry impulses. Step by step, Joan went over the meaning of Anita's behavior and the impact of their responses. In the course of examining what had taken place, Joan also provided guidelines for decision making. For example, Anita needed room to explore and exercise her growing autonomy, but she also needed two adults who were in charge and could establish firm limits when needed. Joan reviewed the "Three D's" as guidelines for when to limit Anita's actions, that is, only when something became Dangerous, Disturbing, or Destructive. At other times, they could follow her lead and admire her initiative. With constant support and repetition, Madeline and Thomas gradually learned to deal with Anita's negativism more appropriately.

The visits also permitted a better view of how Madeline functioned at home. We observed her pulling back into one small crowded room, as if she were trying to recreate life in the small, cramped basement of her grandmother's house. She could not make use of the space in the new house and initially inhibited Anita's use of the space as well. Whenever she felt frightened about going to another part of the house, Madeline took Anita with her. Anita could, in fact, lead the way for her mother with confidence and curiosity. Joan helped Madeline define new areas for play where Anita might use her bicycle for exercise. She also had Anita show her the rituals of going to bed. An elaborate game of "nighty-night," covering, uncovering, sleeping, snoring, awakening, and finally getting up and dressing ensued. Madeline at first watched the drama from a distance and finally got down on the floor to "play" with Anita and Joan. As we saw Madeline learn to play from Anita, we hoped that the little girl would lead her mother up the developmental ladder.

In the Infant Center Joan engaged Madeline in various activities which required her to name or label objects. The objective was to teach Madeline concepts of colors, shapes, or classifications of objects which she then could use with Anita. Joan would name items or ask Madeline certain questions and then have Madeline repeat the same items. Teaching Madeline these "scripts" was essential in helping her go beyond the concrete and limited verbal level on which she functioned; Anita was already beginning to use ideas and needed someone to join her in her exploration of the world and the development of ideas and fantasy. Madeline would then teach these "scripts" to Thomas. Joan supported their efforts at home and in the Center.

As we reviewed our efforts, we realized how Anita benefited from having two parents, two interested adults, to play off against each other. This experience would be adaptive in the development of her relating capacities, particularly in contrast to relating to the withdrawn and sadistic parent we had known Madeline to be when we first met her. With two parents Anita certainly had a different experience from her siblings. She was going to learn that she could be "in charge" too, able to let her feelings be known, and able to influence and negotiate with her parents. We also recognized again how crucial it was going to be to help Madeline deal with the anger likely to be triggered by Anita's new development. Under stress, Madeline had always resorted to projective identification and flight. Both of these defense patterns would have to be modified quickly for Anita's benefit: Anita was already acting out her anger in tantrums and Madeline was beginning to take flight and pull away from both Anita and Thomas.

THE 18-MONTH ASSESSMENT

At the 18th-month assessment Anita's negativism was prominent. She was difficult to engage, and changing tasks was hard because she insisted on holding onto various items and screeched in protest until she got her way. Her negativism was also reflected in frequent refusals, throwing items at the examiner, hoarding toys, and otherwise trying to control the situation. Since she was also able to use her persistence to complete items, Anita completed the assessment despite her negativism, seemed pleased with her successes, and continued to show off as well as seek support from her mother. On the Bayley, her Mental Development Index (MDI) declined 7 points (the standard error of measurement being 5 points) but was still in the bright–average range. This small decline was due, in part, to her negativism. Of greater concern was her poor performance on the language items, particularly expressive items. The few words Anita did articulate were unclear, and the shrill, piercing vocalizations heard earlier had intensified. On the Uzgiris-Hunt she performed adequately although her negativism interfered with reaching higher stages. Here, too, she ignored items or only played selectively.

During these assessments Madeline was available although not as responsive as she had been in the past. She did try to help Anita complete test items. During the free play Madeline's distance became more apparent. At first Madeline was able to follow Anita's interest in a puppet or the toy phones. Each time Anita moved on, she followed and tried to engage Anita in a phone conversation but Anita was more interested in just dialing. Recognizing this, Madeline did not interfere and then offered her a doll, which Anita examined at length while Madeline named its parts. When Anita returned to the phone but did not "talk" to her mother, Madeline appeared to retreat into her own thoughts while Anita wandered aimlessly. The interactions were mostly brief and at the end Madeline told the examiner that, "Anita was very bored."

This assessment reflected some of the same concerns the clinical team had noted in their day-to-day observations of Anita's negativism and aggression. It also focused on the minimal progress Anita was making in the area of language development.

MADELINE MEETS REGULARLY WITH EVA: 18–24 MONTHS

Madeline continued to seek out Eva, pursuing her in the hallway, and meeting regularly. With cues still not coming from Madeline, Eva continued to initiate and guide the therapy session. At times she wished to trigger some anxiety which might give her some therapeutic leverage, but none was forthcoming. Eva had to keep guessing what Madeline might be feeling or thinking. Sometimes Madeline would finally say she was "bored," a signal to Eva to back off. While Eva at times felt pressured or discouraged by these meetings, she needed only to observe the changes in Madeline's behavior in the Infant Center to realize the progress Madeline was making. She related more to the staff and to other mothers. She offered greetings, listened, and even commented occasionally: there was no doubt she wanted to belong. She was also becoming more of a "mother," and this role suggested the avenue for further work.

Eva encouraged Madeline to describe Anita's recent development. When Eva compared Anita to her siblings, Madeline now noted differences. When asked, Madeline also said she thought about them all the time and wondered how they looked or how they were growing up, but she would not pursue these thoughts with Eva and did not call or visit her children. If Eva asked whether she would like to, Madeline still appeared overwhelmed by the prospect of having to give them anything, holding onto what she had in the present as if this might be in jeopardy. Although Madeline never asked about the children and never initiated any discussion regarding them, she was interested in the bits of news Eva would convey from time to time.

Eva also periodically pursued Madeline's feelings about having another baby, especially after she indicated she was bored or noted that Anita was growing up. Madeline denied wanting any more children, but the periodic questioning exerted both a certain amount of pressure and an expectation for Madeline not to get pregnant without a conscious decision and planning. These discussions usually followed our observations of Madeline's retreats from Anita. Eve initiated joint sessions with Joan and Madeline. These sessions served several purposes: they provided concrete situations to observe and discuss; they showed Madeline how adults could talk openly, express different opinions, and clarify misunderstandings. Madeline appeared to follow Joan and Eva closely and soon began to participate. She would take sides or offer a third view. While the joint sessions stayed focused on concrete observations and interventions, they also helped Madeline to move toward more symbolic and differentiated levels in the process of identifying more and more with other adults. The joint sessions also helped the interviewers, who could use each other to bridge the connection to Madeline.

Madeline once more slipped into a pattern of daily attendance at the Center. She was eager to participate in the various programs offered and in her individual sessions with Eva and Joan. The daily contact permitted us to detect changes in her environment or moods quickly and address them. For example, around Thanksgiving Madeline appeared more depressed. She called Judy over the weekend to tell her that she was angry and hurt that Thomas blamed her for Anita's falling and getting hurt. She also complained that Anita was having more temper tantrums. Eva reflected her depression and finally clarified that Madeline felt jealous and anxious because Anita was "getting her way" with Thomas and because father and daughter related so well together. Eva renewed her efforts to focus on the relationship with Thomas, and to help Madeline clarify what she was feeling, so that he would understand her. She also urged Madeline to talk with Thomas about Anita's tantrums and plan together how they would respond. Although Madeline's mood did not appear to change very much she did not withdraw from the center but continued to attend every day. She finally reported that Anita had gone four days without a tantrum and that she and Thomas were working things out. As Christmas approached, Madeline again appeared subdued and withdrawn. Eva wondered if it had anything to do with the holidays and her other children. Madeline acknowledged she did not know what to do about gifts and Eva elicited more of her ambivalent feelings and pointed out alternative actions she might take. Madeline finally could admit she did not want to see the children and was relieved when Eva offered to deliver some gifts for her. Again and again Eva would review the connections between Madeline's moods, feelings, and behavior, hoping Madeline would begin to explore these on her own. Again, the frequent contact permitted the team to ascertain what was going on in Madeline's life and bring it into the sessions until Madeline could do so on her own.

ANITA'S 2-YEAR ASSESSMENT

At 2 years Anita presented as a warm, bubbly, and busy toddler. She was clearly in charge, choosing to respond to various items and rejecting others. When she wanted to perform, she persisted in her efforts, vocalized frequently, and showed great pleasure in her accomplishments. She was quick to imitate, worked quickly, and was very goal directed. Anita excelled in perceptual-motor integration and enjoyed these tasks the most. As her excitement heightened, she screeched and began to leave the table. Negativistic and oppositional behavior followed, interspersed with cooperativeness on symbolic tasks such as feeding the doll. She moved about, responding unpredictably to the examiner, but she did respond to some limit setting by her mother. Despite her negativistic behavior, Anita still achieved a score in the average range, although her expressive language indicated a four-month delay.

During the free play Anita demonstrated initiative by taking the box of toys to her mother and inviting her to a tea party. Madeline joined this symbolic play and mother and daughter enjoyed themselves greatly, talking as they sipped their "tea." When Madeline did not understand Anita's intentions, Anita persisted in conveying her wants, including throwing objects, but they could then clean up together. The symbolic play and persistence indicated that the long months of intervention had yielded impressive gains in Anita's development.

THE THIRD YEAR: FURTHER GROWTH

Intervention continued into the third year of Anita's life. Madeline's attachment to her therapists and the clinical staff deepened, so much so that we sometimes forgot that Madeline was a participant rather than a staff member. She responded to everything that was offered, actively participated, and encouraged other mothers to do the same. As in the past, Madeline's needs prompted us to added job training and outside activities as intervention modalities to prepare her for the real world. We saw these as part of the next crucial steps to support and sustain the progress she had made in our protective, nurturing environment.

Anita continued to thrive. Intervention now focused on the issues pertaining to development in the third year of life such as training, aggression, and control. Again the decision was made not to reduce the level of intervention, so that we could support Madeline's and Anita's reach toward higher levels of functioning related to symbolic and representational modes than Madeline and her other children had attained. We also knew that it was still necessary to witness Madeline and Anita's day-to-day life in order to assess how they were doing, what needed to be reinforced, and to offer the concrete repetition and the range of new experiences needed for growth and change. Since Madeline could not yet observe and describe her actions very well, promoting these ego functions required intensive and frequent work.

MADELINE AND ANITA CONTINUE THEIR WORK WITH JOAN

Joan continued her work with Madeline and Anita in weekly or twice weekly sessions to which Madeline always came eagerly. The work covered a wider range of areas than it had earlier addressed. During the first part of the year Joan continued to help Madeline deal with Anita's temper tantrums. In addition to anticipating, distracting, or ignoring certain behaviors, Joan helped Madeline to think of ways she could help Anita pull herself together when she became so disorganized that she would have a tantrum. Giving her this objective distracted Madeline from getting locked into a head-on battle with her daughter; she proudly came in one day saying that when Anita had a tantrum she picked her up and danced with her (Joan applauded this). This seemed to be an extension of one of Joan's suggestions to hold Anita very closely so that Anita would get the idea that her mother was not going to leave her to her more destructive impulses.

Madeline also waited patiently until Anita was 2 years old before she attempted to train her. Madeline had just moved up to a third-floor apartment in the large house where there was a bathroom and this made it easier for Anita to reach the bathroom without having to climb the stairs. Again it was striking that although Anita was her fifth child, Madeline had never really gone through a training process before. Madeline listened intently to Joan's suggestions, which were spelled out step by step, such as suggesting to Anita to go to the toilet, having her go with her mother when she went, not being angry or upset at accidents, and reinforcing successes with a great deal of praise and rewards. Initially, Anita did quite well in training, but she began to have numerous accidents after she came to the infant center in the morning or when she was angry with Madeline. It appeared that Anita felt Madeline withdraw from her when they arrived at the infant center in her eagerness to get involved with the other people who were there and to go to class, and responded with training accidents, even though her mother had just taken her to the toilet shortly before. At other times, accidents occurred when Madeline and Anita were together but while Madeline was doing other things and was not very involved with Anita. This contrasted with the lengthy period Anita could maintain her control when her mother took her walking with her or played with her. Joan suggested a chart where Madeline could put little stars following Anita's successes to reinforce both their efforts, but before she actually implemented this, Anita seemed to improve. Anita was even able to carry her success over to her weekend visits at her Aunt Jane's, where Madeline was leaving her so that she and Thomas could be alone.

These weekend visits were reported inadvertently and were somewhat surprising. Madeline said she liked to have some time for herself, and even though Thomas would go visit Anita and Jane on Saturday mornings, Madeline preferred to stay at home. This seemed to have more to do with her reluctance to be with Jane's and Thomas's old friends than her wanting or not wanting to spend more time with Anita. Madeline also reported that with Anita away she had the opportunity to go out with her mother and father. They would sometimes come by and go shopping together, outings which pleased Madeline a great deal. Joan once commented that she probably felt good being able to do this, and for the first time Madeline spontaneously reported that she felt good being with her mother but not her father because of what he did to her. She then reported that her father had taken $100 from her and "then put her and the kids out." She went on to say that that was "why the kids are where they are today." When Joan reflected how angry she was, she became very agitated and upset, adding, "Yeah, and that's not all, he slapped me across the face when I was 17 for just talking to my mother in the yard for no reason!" When Joan noted how upset she must have been, Madeline became extremely depressed and pulled away. It was her very ability to express some of these angry and painful feelings, of course, that permitted Madeline to have contact with her parents again and to enjoy these visits, as she clearly did. She also began to participate in some gatherings of the extended family and to visit her sisters. As she had more control over herself and her own life, Madeline felt less ashamed and more able to belong to her family as well as to Thomas. She also moved closer to her mother as she was able to transfer the relationship with Judy more directly to this primary figure. She even reported spending a day with her father. He took her to a baseball game and then out to eat. When Joan noted how exciting this must have been, Madeline's enthusiasm suddenly turned to sullen disappointment as she said it would probably never happen again, setting up her defenses against any further expectations or wishes. Despite this reaction, it appeared that Madeline was able to recapture moments of being a child again with her parents now that her parents were offering her some limited nurturance.

During the course of their working together, Joan also discovered that Madeline and Thomas were permitting Anita to sleep with them since she had outgrown her crib. Joan discussed this with Madeline, who was then able to permit Anita to sleep on the sleep sofa in the living room. Interestingly, she could not carry out the initial plans to fix up a room for Anita which would have been no further away than the living room. Madeline was not ready to extend into additional space and the furthest away she could permit Anita to be was in this living area that was already familiar to her.

In addition to dealing with specific areas of behavior, such as tantrums, training, or sleeping arrangements, Joan tried to support Madeline's respect for Anita's growing autonomy and pleasure in the child's new achievements. This was an extension of the earlier theme they had pursued regarding Anita's needing a mother in different ways as she grew older. Madeline was also able to indicate that she felt very proud when she saw Anita dress or undress by herself. Joan used some of Madeline's spontaneous reports to reinforce things they had talked about earlier. For example, Madeline reported that Anita did not want to hold her hand when they crossed the street and that she walked closely behind Anita to be sure that she was safe. Joan used such occasions to ask Madeline which of the three "D's" this instance represented. Madeline could not remember the earlier lesson concerning danger; it took constant repetition of certain concepts for her to internalize and translate them into concrete action.

Another major area of intervention involved helping Madeline provide interesting and stimulating activities for Anita which might encourage her language and speech development. Anita's language continued to be slow and unclear as she entered her third year. The suggestions included special times to read books which Madeline and Anita established each morning after breakfast. They also included putting labels on different objects they used daily and identifying categories of things such as colors and sizes. It was very difficult for Madeline to latch onto these categories; her concreteness seemed to interfere with being able to transfer activities from location to location (for example, naming colors or opposites at the Center and also in the home). Joan then attempted to listen to Madeline's spontaneous comments, point to some characteristic of an object, and move from there to a discussion of a more general category. For example, Madeline noted that when Anita had put her hand on the cold metal of a chair, she had withdrawn it. Madeline noted that Anita was feeling the cold. From this Joan tried to lead Madeline into thinking of different things she might say about cold and its opposite. Although Madeline would nod and show interest in what Joan was saying, Joan felt that she was losing her even as she was talking.

Perhaps the most important area Joan tried to encourage was having Madeline follow Anita's initiatives as Anita moved into imaginative and symbolic play. Anita had no difficulty imitating either her mother or other people at the Infant Center while playing and Madeline needed to be reminded continuously that she did not have to correct or impose reality on Anita when she was involved in imaginative play, but that she might join her in her play. Joan would explain how children like to do things again and again as a way of mastering new behaviors and skills or as a way of getting over things which had frightened them. She also tried to demonstrate how these little activities could be turned into stories. Joan would talk through the activity that was going on as if she were reading a book. She hoped that Madeline would begin to imitate and use language to describe what Anita was doing and encourage further language development. Joan also prepared lists of different activities, such as puzzles, books, and imitative play, and went with Madeline to purchase toys and help her learn why different toys were more useful than others. Madeline enjoyed these excursions, which were her first opportunity to buy her daughter appropriate toys.

Individual sessions were interwoven with small talk about events at the center and other things going on in Madeline's life. Joan hoped to weave the threads of the various lessons into a texture which could be internalized and self-reinforcing. Even after several years, this continued to be hard work, requiring persistence and patience from Joan. She was not always sure what would stick and what would not, but Madeline *could* learn and despite her concreteness and difficulty in keeping up with Anita, she gave examples and reports of Anita's behavior which suggested she was internalizing some of the new behaviors and concepts being taught. This encouraged Joan to persist. Madeline often looked surprised when Joan asked something about a past experience, such as a fight after Thomas had taken her to a cabaret. She would respond, "Oh, I forget." Joan wondered whether Madeline was still living a day at a time without being able to relate to yesterday or anticipate tomorrow. During such moments the prolonged efforts with Madeline were discouraging; at other times it only took a brief glance at Anita to see how far Madeline had come.

Anita had become a delightful toddler. She was squarely

built, appeared very steady on her feet, and moved quickly as she ran from one point to another. She enjoyed being read to, and anticipated stories she knew with excitement. Her speech and language improved tremendously during her third year. She enjoyed practicing new words and new combinations and was almost ready to speak in sentences. She also played with a little boy who attended the Center daily. She got involved in lengthy imaginative sequences for 20 to 30 minutes. For example, Anita elaborated a symbolic sequence of feeding and caring for her "baby," as well as preparing food and serving herself and her little friend. When her friend indicated that he was eating grapes with pits, for example, she mimed the process of spitting the pits out and putting them on the dish between them on the table. Anita was also very competent in hand–eye coordination and completed puzzles quickly and efficiently. To elicit a response from adults around her, she would say "hello" several times until each person responded. Anita's "take charge" quality was further evidenced by her telling her aunt Jane that she wanted to go home to be with her father and mother after a day at Jane's house. Madeline reported this with great pride, as she realized that she was, in fact, the most important person in Anita's life.

ANITA'S 2½-YEAR ASSESSMENT

At this time Anita presented as a vivacious, sociable, easily engaged toddler, who gleefully invited her mother to look on and join her interest in the new items. Her cooperation was interspersed with testing the examiner's limits; she would walk away or not let go of items and screech in protest. She was an assertive little girl who enjoyed her antics and provocative interactions with others. She demonstrated this clearly by laughing and teasing as she tested limits. This also characterized her play with her mother, who could successfully calm her down and redirect her. We also observed Madeline's inability to sustain an activity, such as symbolic play, as long as her daughter. For example, while Madeline initially joined Anita in a drama of eating and serving food, she would interrupt to suggest they read a book even though Anita was still engrossed in elaborating her play. Anita sustained her play and then took her cup to rejoin her mother, who still had a few pages to read. This was followed by a rich range of other activities on the phone, with puppets hugging and laughing, and finally shooting each other with guns. Anita was excited by this aggression and persisted even though Madeline tried to distract her, tried to read, and finally began to put the toys away. At this point Anita gave the gun back, after yelling to her mother "shoot me," prior to resuming play with her dishes.

Cognitively Anita functioned within the average range in all areas of the McCarthy Scales of Abilities. Her performance was remarkably even across the different cognitive and motor areas, and most impressive in her motoric competence and ability to imitate words and gestures. The only area of concern in her performance was a tendency not to persist when items were very difficult, at which point she adeptly changed the subject, left the table, or protested verbally.

More significant was the wide range of emotions and activities available to her. Anita showed great pleasure and delight as well as the protest one expects from children her age. Her play was rich, active, and reflective of the successful negotiation of oral and aggressive impulses. She was clearly in charge but also responsive to her mother's behavior and anxieties, something we had observed from birth. For the most part Madeline could tolerate and contain Anita's aggressive impulses appropriately, even though she still appeared quite uncomfortable with her own. Madeline was also eager to show off both her new skills in interacting and playing with her daughter and Anita's now valued and prized behaviors.

MADELINE IS TESTED AGAIN

Two years following Anita's birth, Madeline, like all the other mothers in the program, was retested by an outside psychologist. The report indicated: "The overall impression was of a young woman who demonstrates some skills to initially cope with situations, mainly by denial, and to recover her defenses, but who was only moderately depressed. . . ." Her depression seemed directly connected to her difficulties with angry feelings, which she feared losing control of and which she tended to turn inward for fear of losing further support from others. The projective tests continued to suggest structural weaknesses in her personality, but these were no longer overwhelming her everyday functioning. Despite some indefiniteness of ego boundaries and fears of physical vulnerabilities, no thought disorder was evident and ego functions appeared to be adequate. The contrast with the earlier psychologicals was remarkable. Thought disorders, fluid boundaries, and poor reality-testing had given way to adequate ego functioning, showing only traces and tendencies. The fact that Madeline appeared only moderately depressed pointed to the impact of the intervention and her new, successful relationships with Anita and Thomas. But further work needed to be done: Madeline still struggled with doubts about her self-worth and her damaged sense of self. She still tended to deny her needs for affection and security with others, as well as denying the impact of others on herself. But she appeared to be in the process of change and gave evidence of increasing emotional depth in her relationships.

FURTHER THERAPEUTIC GAINS

Madeline's therapeutic progress was not always apparent in the biweekly sessions with Eva. These continued to be short, sustained by Eva's questions and structure. Nevertheless, Madeline awaited each session eagerly and began to acknowledge her attachment and affection for Eva. Now late or missed appointments had to be rescheduled and Madeline began to perceive Eva as her therapist for the first time. This was prompted by a discussion in the group sessions about participants being patients. Madeline was shocked. She had never considered herself a patient, and she made it clear that, "No shrink was going to pick my brain." When she could not explain why she was in the program, however, she returned to Eva to clarify the matter. In another instance, the group made her extremely anxious when they responded to her complaints that her eyes hurt. Madeline was surprised by their concern and finally admitted she was afraid to go to the doctor. She became alarmed when other group members started to express their fears of going blind and how they sometimes prepared themselves by walking around with their eyes closed. Madeline fled the group in near panic, rejecting our offers to go with her to the doctor. It was not clear why group members' fears so frightened her, but she was extremely anxious and only Eva could approach her to work it out. Eva sat by her side almost the entire next day at the emergency eye clinic. The long wait gave her the opportunity to put Madeline's feelings into words before denial set in.

As the year progressed Madeline was observed reacting more openly to different events at the Infant Center. Her more visible and audible feelings and reactions provided opportunities to identify these feelings and to use her confusion or bewilderment to explore and clarify emotions and the situations to her. As Madeline was able to experience a wider range of emotions at the Center, Eva could confront and pursue them in their individual sessions. One day Eva asked, "Do you want to work on some of your feelings?" Madeline responded, "Do I have to sign something?" Eva realized that she was thinking of a written contract often signed with social workers at the DSS and asked Madeline to dictate the contract. Madeline indicated the following: "I agree to talk about my feelings and the things that have happened to me."

Another turning point had been reached. Reports of situations and events were now accompanied by some awareness of feelings, which could be examined and tolerated for longer and longer periods as Madeline became aware of her tendency to deny or take flight when feelings were unacceptable or made her uncomfortable. With further work she began to project and externalize less, although she still had difficulty recognizing that she affected others. Even her earlier persistent claim that no one could tell her what to do or affect her began to diminish slowly. Madeline slowly accepted the notion that she was a feeling person with needs and thoughts. Her way of acknowledging her feelings was to act as if they had always been there or that she had already spoken to Eva about them.

Even while she continued to keep her secrets, Madeline was able to deal with her life at the Center and, to some degree, with her life at home. By collaborating with Thomas, she was able to set limits on her family's intrusiveness. She began to recognize the parts of her which did not want to rescue her overcontrolling and unresponsive family. This was linked to her sometimes intrusive and rough behavior with Anita as well as to her defiant and risky behavior with Thomas. While she was examining some of these issues in her individual sessions with Joan and Eva, Madeline moved to another level in the group. She accepted an interpretation that her continuous claims of hunger were for more than food. She could observe that a peer's cramping pains occurred each time she was talking about death. It became apparent to everyone that Madeline no longer had to step backward before she stepped forward again. Her progress was slow but consistent from week to week.

PREPARATION FOR WORK

While Madeline was making these major therapeutic gains, Eva and the team were concerned about how she would function in a less protected environment—the real world. A base for her parenting and family experience had been established. Her capacity to be employed was our next area of concern.

More than a year earlier Madeline had begun GED studies and was making slow but steady progress toward her high-school equivalency degree. She also needed some work experience and identification with success. The old Madeline had been suspicious, provocative, and unable to deal with authority. Could the new Madeline deal with responsibility and supervision?

The program had needed someone at the Center to help shop, prepare meals, and clean up after lunch. Madeline had been helping and had been responsive to the needs of the program as it grew. From time to time she had also mentioned getting a job, but we did not think she could coordinate the demands of working and her child and family. We therefore invented the Food Service program for her. We assigned an independent supervisor who taught her about nutrition, how to plan meals, how to shop economically and utilize available foods, and how to organize and care for the kitchen. Madeline had the opportunity to learn about being responsive to authority, taking orders, initiating and organizing her work, and signing in and out. She was paid a token salary and received a biweekly check along with the other staff which served to reinforce her identification as a valued and competent adult. She thrived in her new role, began to act as though she had been working forever, and soon requested an office for herself. While Madeline's new role introduced some confusion regarding her status in the program, her trips into the community and the GED program served as a transitional step to functioning in the real world. These activities also facilitated her identification as a mature and responsible adult upon whom others could depend and provided her with a sense of success.

Madeline's Participation in Group Therapy

Two years after Madeline joined CIDP, a therapy group for mothers was started and Madeline agreed to participate. There were some doubts about whether she would benefit from a group experience because of her very limited capacity or willingness to talk, but she was invited to participate because we thought the experience might help her learn from others and would force her to deal with the group's reaction to her reticence. When invited, Madeline expressed a "why not?" attitude, denied any interest or anxiety, and said she would come because she "felt like it."

Madeline attended 50 sessions over a 15-month period and became the most consistent and stable member present. Much to our surprise, during her first session she listened with rapt attention, at times agreeing or disagreeing with others, and even reported two significant items. She remembered the baby who had died in her mother's lap and that she had not seen her father very much as a child. We were delighted with this verbal contribution of a few sentences and wondered if we had underestimated Madeline or whether the group would demand she function differently than did her individual therapist. Madeline, however, was not to repeat these behaviors for almost 6 months. Whether she was alarmed by her initial response or whether she sensed we now expected more of her, she chose to be quiet and responded minimally when questioned. Her 15-month participation can be divided into four phases.

During the first phase, Madeline remained silent but stayed in the room. When asked how she felt, she would indicate "fine," but "hungry." The sessions were very intense and she appeared to be listening but would sit in the corner near the window, smoking and looking out the window frequently. She then started a pattern of having to eat just before the group would start. She would come in late and greet everyone as she entered. Sometimes she brought food with her. At other times she just smoked or chewed gum. When other participants got upset, cried, or revealed a secret, Madeline became uncomfortable and would walk out, denying that this had anything to do with the group by saying that she had heard her baby cry or had to go to the bathroom. No one dared to confront her on these disruptions. Interestingly, Madeline would always return after a while, as if she could not stand being away. She maintained her silence, and other participants would protect her right to be quiet if she was pressured to talk.

During the second phase Madeline assumed the role of "reporter." She was now more likely to come on time and report on who had been present or absent during the previous meeting. She spoke less of being hungry and had established her regular seat in the circle. Once or twice she even introduced information about someone else, such as a birthday, which would then get the group going. Once she suddenly commented, "M. would be in trouble if she moved to Oklahoma because she would have to 'fight' if she goes so far away." She then left the room "because she heard her daughter crying" and would not elaborate when she returned. We noted that her single spontaneous comment involved connecting separations with aggression. More often when Madeline was asked something, she would simply say "everything was fine with her" or that "she didn't go through what others went through so she couldn't say anything about it." We continued to observe Madeline's incredible concreteness and lack of verbal capacities to process and relate to any of her experiences or feelings. She depended on denial, projection, and other primitive defenses to stave off the world. During one session when the women were talking about anger at their partners, she finally admitted she threw pots and pans at Thomas when she got angry. The whole group sat up and took notice!

During the third phase, Madeline continued to attend group sessions regularly and to keep the attendance records of others. She now introduced the notion, "I'm bored," and would look away or out the window when approached. She still came late at times and would enter with a grand announcement that she had gone out to eat, but "Now that I'm full, I can talk." She also told her therapist that she wanted to talk but could not. Madeline now began to alternate between silence and talking a little. During this phase she revealed some of her fears and phobias about hitch-hiking or staying alone at night. She also remembered an incident when her brother and sister abandoned her after "scaring her to death" on Halloween. Madeline revealed as well her belief in supernatural powers and considerable magical thinking. She demonstrated her desire to participate in the group by saying that she also got "high" when she felt like it when others spoke of their drug experiences. Although she continued to say, "I didn't go through that, so I wouldn't know," she began to add, "I can't say anything about it, but I have a notion." She also had occasional contacts with another group member outside the Center and began to dress very nicely to attend the group session, perhaps in indirect competition with some of the other attractive women.

During the final phase of her group experience, Madeline began to participate verbally during every session. She remained the reporter and she still came late at times, usually because she took time to eat first. Her late entrances took on a more provocative and anxious quality in contrast to her earlier "I come when I feel like it and I don't care what you think" attitude. Since the group had also become smaller, Madeline and her sister Melissa sometimes met alone with the therapists. She joined Melissa in refusing to answer questions if the therapist did not answer their questions. This defiance clearly brought her pleasure, even though she could not formulate her own questions to ask.

The question-asking procedure became a game to play and evoked further group discussion regarding the purpose of the group and the information that the therapists were a psychiatrist and psychologist. Madeline was "shocked": she did not need anyone to help her understand herself, and she certainly was not going to let anyone "pluck her mind and lock her up." She stormed out of the room (but then stood by the closed door to listen). She would say she would refuse to come any more and then get Eva to "force" her to return. Once she returned she would continue not answering unless the therapist also answered questions, but the discussion now would be accompanied with projections onto the therapist and silent anger so intense that Madeline would stiffen, her face becoming ugly and distorted. She appeared not to have any defense to help her mediate the anger which took such a direct somatic form, and she seemed very scared.

Madeline continued to come to group, and the "I won't tell you, if you don't tell me" exercise became her most overt reciprocal interaction with the therapists. We were now people who could influence her and whom she could influence. A certain barrier had been crossed. As this exercise continued, Madeline could soon tolerate some reflection on what was occurring. She would even laugh when an observation of her behavior was made rather than negate, deny, or pull away as she had in the past. Next, she even called the male therapist some names after he confronted her with her anger and fear after another group member called her a "witch." At first she took being called a witch so concretely that she was very alarmed, as if someone's saying this, made it so. She stormed out. In subsequent sessions she was able to see how she had provoked and insulted her "accuser," and the women were able to talk about the incident and reconcile.

As she was able to recognize and tolerate more the group process, Madeline also talked more. She spoke of feeling like a stepchild in the family because she had always been poorly treated and put upon without knowing why. As a result she had run away from home. She spoke about her youngest sister, who always tried to "con" her. Madeline's ability to continue an issue from week to week and say she had thought about it represented another breakthrough. For several sessions she talked of being fearless and tough in response to the fears of one of the other members. She also talked about being able to stand up better to others who put her down. The intense anger she manifested earlier began to dissipate and she even began to project some idealized notions onto the woman therapist who "must be so happy" and who did not even have a "scratch on her." The latter remark related to a discussion of aggression and hostility between partners.

As the project drew to a close, Madeline still came late to group sessions, flaunting her need to do something for herself first, and then insisting on knowing what she missed. Her silence was replaced by verbalizations, humor, and various reciprocal interactions with other group members and the group therapists. When she said something, she could now hear it, though she appeared to pull back as if surprised she had let something out. She began to communicate verbally, to be curious about others, to prepare to reveal more of herself.

Madeline's participation in the group enabled her to move slowly through developmental stages which she had not negotiated in the past. She started nonverbally but used the consistent availability of the group of peers as she had used other aspects of the program. At first her hunger predominated, she could not relate to or empathize with anyone else, but positioned herself in the familiar pattern of being surrounded by others with whom she had a minimal connection. For a while she needed to go in and out of the meeting room to touch base with the more familiar parts of the program, the familiar others outside the group. Reinforced, she would return. Her first verbalizations were concrete, and her defenses against closeness primitive. Next her negativism intensified. Madeline appeared to have few techniques beyond opposition to use in negotiating with the world. When she was asked about anything that pertained to feelings, she responded with negation and denial. She seemed to lack the most basic symbolic and representational capacities with which to process her experiences.

Frequently, just as we were feeling that Madeline had perhaps reached her limits or been arrested by her aggression and rage, she would move ahead. Her new growth seemed propelled by the pull of the peer group and her desire to belong, as well as by a separation–individuation process from her old self, which had been organized around aggression. Her magical thinking and belief in the powers that others had over her had caused her to feel trapped by their imagined control and kept her both distant and in flight from others. The group, however, added to her experiences, she learned that anger need not be met only by aggression. This realization was followed by more reciprocal interactions with other members and the therapists in the group. We saw evidence of ego development as Madeline became able to tolerate more affect and observe more of her own behavior in the group.

Madeline's participation in the group was paralleled by Anita's moving into the second year of life and learning to relate to others. Through the stages of rapprochement, negativism, and the development of symbolic and representational skills Anita was able to use her mother as a base. She moved from nonverbal to verbal development and through separation–individuation at a faster pace than her mother. Although Madeline had difficulties with these aspects of Anita's growth, tending to respond with control and aggression, she was also pulled to grow along with her daughter. Anita's stages of development and the corresponding group process confronted Madeline with new developmental tasks, and she slowly mastered them. Her work in the group proceeded at a higher level than her individual work with her therapist, in which she could maintain the more regressed and dependent posture she still needed internally while she was pulled and pressured by peers in the group to a higher level of interaction.

As she made slow but steady gains, our initial skepticism about Madeline's participation in group diminished. Interestingly, Madeline was never able to bridge the two treatment modalities in a verbal fashion. The quality of each of her experiences appeared distinct and she had few capacities to integrate these different parts. She appeared to benefit from each, however, and the peers and therapists in the group provided her alternative models.

POST SCRIPT

Madeline and Anita continued in the program until its conclusion. Anita was then more than 4 years old. Before the program ended, Madeline was helped to locate a good day care program for Anita closer to home, began to use public transportation, enrolled in another GED program, and was scheduled to begin job training. She also took advantage of our last workshop on driver education, passed her permit test, and started to take driving lessons. Madeline and Thomas weathered various storms in their relationship and emerged committed and engaged. They also decided not to have any more children so they could give more to Anita and themselves.

Anita continued to thrive and attained a GCI of 99 in her last assessment, maintaining a very stable profile over the years. She had most difficulty on the verbal and memory areas, where she became more restless, controlling, or avoiding. The examiner felt she probably had greater potential but still tended to get into control battles when she was frustrated or she did not get her way. When these battles were with her mother, Anita could still win them. Follow-up assessments later indicated that Anita had higher abilities reflected by a GCI of 108 at 5 years with especially good verbal abilities she could use once past the control issues. At day care she adapted beautifully, becoming an active and energetic member of her class, eager to lead, and cooperative. She was a happy and busy youngster, eager to learn, and enjoying her unique position at home and secure in the world.

Termination appeared less difficult for Madeline than we anticipated. She could express feelings of sadness and know she would miss everyone, but meanwhile transferred readily and assumed new responsibilities during a transitional period. She could look back on the years in the program and speak of how it had changed her life inwardly and outwardly, expressing appreciation to everyone, especially to Eva, Joan, and Judy. And we said "Thank you" in return, for all that we learned growing with Madeline and Anita.

Conclusions

The case of Madeline best demonstrates the step-by-step process involved in change and restructuring of personality.

Madeline's therapeutic gains started first with her acceptance of our concrete presence, our ability to help her survive, and were followed by her coming to accept our human presence, because we cared about her and were available on her terms. From totally unpredictable contacts which occurred whenever we could find her, a stable and reliable connection evolved. The relationship moved into communication, trust, and by the end of treatment, the elaboration of fantasy, thoughts, and feelings, as Madeline became an animated, active, and even overcontrolling person rather than the depressed and passive young woman we first knew. While Madeline may never reach the highest level of using ideas to express and work through feelings, she has made progress beyond any of our expectations.

Our work with Madeline included letting her reexperience the early phases of development on a day-to-day basis over a period of four years. The work was not regressive or reconstructive in the usual sense. Madeline was arrested at an early, primitive level of development, totally dominated by her concrete dependency needs and her mountainous rage at her early lack of nurturing. Meeting her dependency at the most concrete levels and reaching out across her intense distrust and rage were the starting points. Because she was not reexperiencing early trauma but living it, using a day-by-day approach seemed the only way to help her move forward. As a result there were no short cuts or breaks in our work with Madeline. We had to see her daily in order to sustain a human connection and help her form some attachment. Since this continuity had never been available to her, she otherwise could never be able to offer it to her children or partner. She had to be met totally and continuously, very much like an infant. The uniqueness of our intervention was to define and protect her role as a mother and help her function throughout this course of redevelopment.

This case also demonstrates the length and complexity of such a process and the need to offer certain experiences in

direct and concrete form. Madeline needed a "family" of intervenors and a variety of experiences. Each member of the
intervention team and program afforded her a unique relationship to internalize and differentiate over the years. And
the process did take years, a factor which was in part determined by her daughter's developmental course and in part
by the need to offer her an optimal chance to develop the
personality structure and ego capacities that would allow her
to interrupt the inadequate and painful patterns of functioning
which characterized preceding generations of her family. Like
Anita, Madeline had to proceed gradually through these significant years if she were to move to higher levels of functioning. These levels had to be experienced concretely and
repeatedly in order to change her base of experience in life
and move her beyond the dependency and rage she had when
we first met her.

Assessing how much each intervention modality contributed individually to the successful outcome of this case is
impossible. As it unfolded, each element seemed very important and useful. In some ways Madeline served as the pilot
subject with whom we experimented as we tried each new
modality before incorporating it as part of our program for
other participants. She helped us to discover what mothers
like herself needed to experience and learn in order to achieve
the preventive goals we aimed for with their infants. In retrospect, the different "programs" we provided for Madeline
seem less crucial than the fundamental relationships she had
with a small team of people who could support her, Anita,
and Thomas through the critical years of early development.
While more or fewer treatment modalities might have been
used, we do not believe we could have accomplished the same
results in less *time* because of the developmental, sequential,
and restructuring process involved.

Most importantly, Anita progressed through each stage
of development with mastery and competence, supporting
her mother along the way. Because of our preventive inter-

ventions her parents could offer her a rich early attachment
and environment that could support her greater behavioral
organization, initiative and integration of emotional polarities.
With this foundation, Anita could develop capacities to use
symbolic and representational modes. Anita continues to be
in charge and should be able to get what she needs in life.
She is an engaging and resourceful youngster who gets the
most from her mother and father and will in all likelihood do
the same in the world as she grows up.

Our Work with the Foster Mothers

PURPOSE AND GOALS

Following the placement of Madeline's four children, we
decided to work closely with the two foster mothers as an
extension of our work with Madeline. At first our goal was to
facilitate contact between Madeline and her children by me-
diating and supporting the relationship between the foster
mothers and Madeline. Both of the foster mothers were experienced women who had been taking care of foster children
for many years; their initial feelings toward Madeline were
of sympathy and concern. However, we realized that Madeline's unreliable and provocative behavior exacerbated by the
stress of placing her children, was likely to lead to difficulty
in dealing with the foster mothers. We hoped to support these
women's efforts with Madeline's children because we recognized that the children's needs would be great until they were
reunited with their mother (which, initially, we expected
would take place). Further, our involvement would give us
an opportunity to learn more about foster care and how to
utilize this as a resource for other mothers as overwhelmed
and depleted as Madeline, and for helping a mother maintain
attachment with her children until they could be reunited.

Madeline was unable to sustain visitation or other regular
contact with her children. When we realized that she was
unlikely to retrieve her children, our goal shifted to supporting
the foster mothers and helping them retain the children as

long as possible during the critical years of early development. We hoped that long-term placement would prevent the typical course of moving from foster home to foster home. Accordingly, we intensified our efforts to work directly with the foster mothers, particularly the mother who took care of Susan. Both foster mothers permitted us to follow the progress of the children and accepted our intervention during the next 4 years. We learned what it meant for them to be foster mothers and the nature of their attachment to the children. In the case of Mrs. A., who was caring for Susan, ambivalence around working with us was related to ambivalence about keeping Susan and her brother. In order to work with this mother, as will be described in some detail, we had to address other aspects of her life and the conflicts she faced, as well as the more basic motivation which made her a foster mother and how this was expressed in her relationship with Susan. These efforts were primarily carried out by Joan. The intervention with Mrs. J., which will be described briefly, was primarily carried out by Eva. At the time of this writing, both foster mothers have asked to adopt the children that have been in their care for more than 4 years.

IN THE BEGINNING: EARLY EFFORTS WITH MRS. A

Mrs. A. had graciously welcomed Susan and Antonio into her home. Developing a working relationship with the Infant Program was another matter. We expected Mrs. A. to maintain some control over visitation and contacts with Madeline by having them channeled through the DSS. Such procedures are intended to protect the foster mother's privacy and functioning with the children and to help contain the tension related to direct contact with the children's mothers, who are often conflicted and overwhelmed with the guilt of having placed their children in foster care. Nevertheless we hoped that Mrs. A would be responsive to our facilitating the relationship with Madeline and promoting Susan's development, which was at considerable risk when she was placed.

Mrs. A. was a competent woman who expected to be in charge of the children in her care and did not welcome Joan's request to visit on a regular basis. Joan felt like an intruder each time she visited. Mrs. A. expressed her reluctance by indicating she was extremely busy, always prepared with a list of necessary tasks that had to be done that day. Indeed she *was* extremely busy with the care of four or five children under the age of 3. She was also very active in her church community and worked every Saturday and Sunday on family functions. The only help she had was from her elderly husband, who helped her care for the babies. Her two oldest daughters were married with children of their own; two sons, 17 and 13, lived at home. When Joan would call to inquire how she was and to arrange a time to visit, Mrs. A would quickly indicate, "I'm doing fine, my children and husband are fine." She would then elaborate on how much she had to do, making it very clear she preferred not to have Joan visit. When Joan was persistent, she would usually consent but then either convey that Joan had better get out of the way quickly or absent herself entirely, leaving Joan alone with all the children. These responses made it difficult to continue our intervention with Susan on a more intensive basis. We recognized that we would have to reach out to this foster mother in much the same way we reached out to other mothers in our program. Joan felt Mrs. A. purposely kept busy, avoiding even casual chitchat, to prevent any closeness. She maintained a friendly, frivolous front, but the forced quality of her busyness became more apparent and began to suggest to us that Mrs. A. was much more depressed and anxious than she would have us believe. She was a woman who had come to the rescue of others but was uncomfortable when observed in her home, where the facade might be penetrated. There was little alternative but to respect Mrs. A.'s limits as we slowly attempted to engage her around Susan. She was, however, most cooperative with the infant assessments; she perceived these as "tests" and therefore necessary.

Joan attempted to visit Susan and Antonio every week or two during the first few months following placement. She became aware that Susan was spending much of her day in an infant seat, passively looking around and without opportunities to move about. Joan was also concerned that Susan might be experiencing the continuous activity in Mrs. A.'s home as overstimulating and thereby reinforcing of her withdrawn and passive posture. When Joan administered the Denver Developmental Assessment at 5 months, Susan did not reach for any objects or make any effort to go after a toy placed on the floor. She was not able to turn over and seemed reluctant to move at all. She seemed content to be on the floor and look around. She appeared to be depressed, lacking the energy to reach out to toys or humans. Joan shared her concerns with Mrs. A. and indicated the importance of assessing Susan's progress regularly. She hoped this would encourage Mrs. A. to permit her to visit more often. These efforts were only partially successful. We also referred Susan and Antonio to the early identification program run by the county, whose intervenors came to the home to work with the other foster children. They could thus work with Madeline's children without adding to the number of people with whom Mrs. A. had to deal. They accepted Antonio into their program, but despite our recommendations did not feel that Susan was sufficiently delayed to warrant their intervention.

SUSAN AT 6 MONTHS

Our next assessment of Susan took place 6 weeks later. We arranged for Madeline to pick up Susan at Mrs. A.'s house and bring her to the Infant Center. Susan continued to look sober and low keyed. She used only her visual alertness to engage the world. This took the form of long searching inspections before she would react. On the Bayley Assessment it was difficult for her to disengage from the examiner's face to perform an item. In one instance she could not even be enticed to look at the pill on the table. When she looked at the mirror, a hint of a smile finally appeared after prolonged inspection; then she only touched the edge of the mirror clumsily rather than bang or hold it as expected for her age range. Her clumsy, undeveloped fine motor skills also interfered with her performance on other items. For example, she could not pick up the cube but swiped at it, knocking the cube off the table. On the other hand, as the assessment progressed and she became more comfortable with the examiner, her depressed affect lifted and she was able to complete items she had failed earlier. She began to show persistence and interest. For example, she picked up the cup by the handle and manipulated it (5.2 months mean age level). She also uncovered the hidden bunny immediately (8.1 months mean age level). Susan did not vocalize during the entire assessment.

By the end of the lengthy exam Susan was very tired and arched her back away from her unfamiliar mother. During the exam Madeline had held her passively, unable to support or encourage her in any way except on one occasion. This was after the examiner had persisted in encouraging Susan to play with the red ring and she turned around to look at and smile at her mother. Madeline returned the smile briefly, the only appropriate response observed. During the free-play period Madeline attempted to elicit another smile as she faced the mirror with Susan but Susan did not respond; when the examiner moved in to interact with both mother and infant, these efforts did engage Susan, whose eyes followed back and forth between her mother and the examiner.

Susan attained an MDI of 89 at 6 months. Although this was in the low average range, the above observations sustained our serious concerns regarding inadequate social and cognitive stimulation. She also had a bald spot on the back of her head that suggested she might be spending hours lying in her crib or sitting in the infant seat. In view of the lack of a differential response to Madeline, we decided to do future assessments with Mrs. A. whenever possible to see how this would affect Susan's performance.

Joan continued to visit Mrs. A.'s home as frequently as possible. During the busy Christmas season, Mrs. A. was invariably unavailable, extremely busy and hurried. Joan brought toys for Susan and the other children as well, hoping Mrs. A. would be more interested if all the children could be involved. She suggested floor play and putting the toys sufficiently out of reach so that Susan would have to reach for them. Mrs. A. was polite and seemingly enthusiastic about the suggestion but did not carry out any of these ideas during subsequent months.

SUSAN AT 8 MONTHS

We administered the Bayley again at 8 months in Mrs. A.'s home to assess whether Susan would perform more adequately in familiar surroundings with Mrs. A. This assessment, however, confirmed our earlier concern that Susan was deteriorating in the absence of more intensive intervention. The examiner found that Susan did not differentiate between her foster mother and the examiner. She lacked purposeful exploration and was not interested in crawling to explore the world. Her interest in objects was limited to grasping, mouthing, and banging, typical behaviors of a younger infant. Further, and more serious, we observed that Susan's affect was flat and depressed and she seemed to be slipping away from the animate world. This worrisome picture was also reflected by a drop of 15 points on the MDI, and on the Bayley from 89 to 74.

Although Mrs. A. had agreed to work with us during the earlier months, she proved to be too "busy" with so many children in her care. We also wondered if her unavailability was enhanced by the anger that was provoked by Madeline's inability to work out regular contacts which might have given Mrs. A. some relief. Such contacts might also have reinforced her interest in Madeline's daughter. Unfortunately, Susan's basic constitutional patterns did not elicit Mrs. A.'s attention and care in contrast to Antonio's ability to insist and demand more. The assessment clearly indicated that Susan's development had arrested during the early stages of forming human attachments and developing some interests in the animate world. Although she had progressed physically in terms of weight gain, she had withdrawn emotionally. This was probably due to the impact of the tenuous attachment to and separation from her mother, as well as the impact of her new foster home, which was overstimulating to her. She had become difficult to engage and appeared to be at a critical point. We had to find a way to intervene further.

ANOTHER CRISIS FOR SUSAN: MRS. A. COOPERATES

In reevaluating the situation we recognized that Mrs. A. was motivated to take in foster children whom she perceived as handicapped and at great risk. For her the fact that Susan did not present any major handicap other than poor physical development resulted in less interest and attention. We decided to review our concerns with her, this time emphasizing that Susan was in crisis. We now presented Susan as a "damaged" and vulnerable infant who had deteriorated rapidly following her mother's abandonment and who was hypersensitive and needed special care now because of her early emotional and physical deficits. This seemed to alter Mrs. A.'s perception of Susan from a quiet, untroublesome infant who should be fed and held occasionally to a baby in stress who needed her and us in special ways. Thus enlisted as a member of the therapeutic team, Mrs. A. agreed to our more intensive intervention during the new crisis.

Joan began to visit Susan and Mrs. A. on a regular basis. Mrs. A. was encouraged to remain in the room while Joan worked with Susan so she could observe the different interventions Joan employed. This helped her understand Susan's individual characteristics and gave her a model of how she, too, might interact with the child. Joan first had to use nonthreatening techniques to engage Mrs. A. in animate interactions with Joan, then developed an approach to Susan.

Normal attempts to reach out and engage her proved over-stimulating to Susan, who averted her gaze. Such behavior indicated that early difficulties with homeostasis as well as attachment were present. Joan realized that she had to proceed at a slower pace. She would gaze silently at Susan for a minute or so, follow this by low-keyed facial grimacing and soft blowing on Susan's face, and then begin to vocalize quietly. This proved to be the best way to attract and sustain Susan's attention and increase her tolerance. Susan soon began to vocalize herself. As her vocalizations became more reciprocal, she could be engaged in playful animate games such as "there was a little man" and "patty cake." In the beginning, these periods of low-keyed interaction would last only a few minutes before Susan would turn away; after Susan warmed up a bit, Joan could gradually extend the interaction time.

Joan then moved toward activities with inanimate objects. To improve Susan's gross motor development, Joan placed Susan on the floor and put toys just out of reach, where she would have to go after them. To improve fine motor development, Susan was given cubes for grasping, bringing to midline, and transferring from hand to hand. Colorful toys were used to encourage her interest and inspection. A mirror was also introduced to help her react to her own image; this was supplemented by peekaboo and bouncing games to develop a sense of expectation and limitation, with and without a mirror.

These regular sessions with Susan soon showed some impact. She learned to recognize Joan or Eva as they entered the house and to greet them by calling across the room. Her affect became more elevated, and, in sharp contrast to her early indifferent response to people, she seemed to take pleasure in her new interaction with people and her activities with objects. Some of Susan's characteristics remained constant, however. Her sensitivity to overstimulation persisted, and roughhouse games frequently produced cries of fright. As she became more active motorically, however, one could engage her in these games if they were controlled and elevated gradually. By 9 months Susan was beginning to crawl. She made sure, however, never to lose sight of her foster mother, who was now becoming fixed as the primary person in her life. She still demonstrated a tentative approach to inanimate objects. When reaching into a can to pick out a block, for example, Susan would place one hand into the can but pull it out before touching anything. Finally, with a great deal of support she was able to withdraw the block. If there was too much activity going on in the house during sessions with Joan, she would have difficulty keeping engaged and focusing on some of the specific interactions. Joan would then try to find a quiet corner of the house and use these opportunities to point out to Mrs. A. how differently Susan responded to different environments.

SUSAN TURNS AROUND: AT 11 MONTHS

After 3 months of intervention another assessment was administered in order to check on Susan's progress. Susan appeared to be looking well with a full, round face and a heavy crop of hair. Although she was still wary and low keyed at first, once engaged she became more enthusiastic and enjoyed the interactions with the examiner. We could observe a very close bond developing between Mrs. A. and Susan. Mrs. A. held her tenderly, gently swaying her back and forth as she called "darling" or "I love you." Susan frequently turned to Mrs. A. to smile and check on her. She showed a clear preference for her. During free play Mrs. A. initiated games of give and take with a small toy or a piece of cookie and Susan would imitate exaggerated tones of "thank you," as well as "darling" and "I love you." Mrs. A. held Susan on her lap and suddenly let her fall backwards, eliciting gales of laughter. Susan then learned to anticipate these movements and laughed even before she was let go. Both had learned to enjoy games with more elevated affect and movement. By this time

Susan also pulled herself to stand and inspected anything she could get her hands on. Although her movements were slow, a lightness and precision were revealed in her fine motor activity which contrasted greatly to the ponderous, clumsy movements observed at 8 months. She also vocalized more spontaneously, saying "ma ma," "da da," and "eat." Susan surprised and delighted everyone by scoring an MDI of 114, which indicated the degree to which she had recovered from the losses she had evidenced earlier.

Madeline had observed the assessment through the one-way mirror and was then invited into the room to play with Susan when the assessment was over. She went over and picked Susan up from Mrs. A.'s lap. She then sat down on another chair and put Susan on the floor in front of her. Joan suggested that Madeline get on the floor with Susan. Susan looked at her mother this time but continued to munch on her cookie. Madeline then took a cup and saucer from the Bayley kit and placed them in front of her on the floor but did not do anything with them; she seemed at a loss as to how to reach out to her daughter. Susan filled the void by using her mother to pull herself to a standing position. Madeline wiped Susan's runny nose but Susan turned away from her, scooted across the room, rested her head in Mrs. A.'s lap while looking across the space at her mother. Joan then suggested that Madeline hold out her hands and invite Susan to come back to her. Susan responded and put one hand out to Madeline while the other held onto Mrs. A. She then withdrew her hand from Madeline who tried to offer her some of the other toys including the rabbit, the rattle, and the bell. Each was a mild attraction which Susan looked at briefly before scooting back to her foster mother. From this base of support she then could turn again toward her mother and put the objects into her hand or into her mouth with a puzzled expression on her face as she gazed at her mother.

During the interaction described above it was very clear that Susan had become attached to Mrs. A. Madeline never said a word except to call Susan's name. She did not know how to reach out to her little girl, although everyone who was observing felt that she yearned to and felt the pain they imagined Madeline was experiencing as she watched her daughter respond more eagerly to the foster mother than to herself. Madeline could not discuss any of these feelings.

One month later Madeline saw Susan again. She had remembered Susan's first birthday and arranged with the DSS to visit her daughter. Joan accompanied her because Mrs. A. was anxious about having Madeline visit her home and she was concerned that Susan's father, Mr. S., might come by and make trouble as he had done in the past. Again Susan tolerated being held by her mother for a few minutes but then agitated to get on the floor, where she preferred to play with some toys. While playing she would periodically seek out Mrs. A.'s presence and scoot away from Madeline toward the woman she now knew as mother. When she spotted Mrs. A. she would be able to return to her toys and play but she made no moves toward Madeline.

The closeness that Mrs. A. and Susan were achieving was interrupted at the time of Susan's first birthday. Mrs. A. had agreed to accept another foster child, a 5-month-old, severely battered infant in a body cast who required a great deal of physical care and most of Mrs. A.'s energy. Mrs. A. shared with us her observations that Susan and her brother Antonio were jealous of the new baby. She endeavored to provide some extra attention to Madeline's children when we were present, but the reality of her responsibilities toward this new handicapped baby again limited what she would have to offer them.

THE FOSTER MOTHER FACES A PERSONAL CRISIS

When Susan was 14 months old, Mrs. A. faced a difficult crisis in her own life. Her much older husband was dying of cancer. He had apparently been sick before she married him. She expressed a great deal of anger with his family for not informing her of his illness before they married. After his discharge from the hospital, Mrs. A. continued to feel betrayed and refused to receive him back in her home. When we visited Mrs. A. during this period we observed that all the children seemed depressed and Mrs. A. appeared to be more impatient and angry when she interacted with them. Also, with Mr. A. out of the home, there was one less interested adult to interact with the children; she faced the total job herself. This added stress pressed Mrs. A into considering closing her home to foster children.

This period coincided with the period when Madeline had gotten her first training job at the department store, and we were encouraging her to visit the younger children. We devised a plan for Madeline to go on a weekly basis to Mrs. A.'s house to be there early in the morning when the children awoke. Madeline was to help the children dress and have breakfast and then come to our Center for 4 to 5 hours. Mrs. A. was pleased with this plan because she wanted the children reunited with Madeline. However, Madeline was unable to carry out the plan. Mrs. A. continued to care for the children and her husband died shortly afterwards.

When Susan was 15 months old, the mothers on whom she depended or might have depended began simultaneously to withdraw from her. Madeline had met Thomas and was regaining some control over her personal life. Mrs. A. began to seek some satisfaction for her own needs by dating a man she had known for many years. The changes for the two women resulted in an excitement and enthusiasm for their own lives, but compromised their availability to Susan. We again observed that Susan, who had begun to walk, was distancing herself from the adults around her. We wondered if this contributed to Mrs. A.'s ambivalence about keeping the children as she remarked, "the kids are getting spoiled and it's getting time for them to leave." She was interpreting Susan's distancing as a lack of interest in her and using this as justification for pulling away from Susan.

We continued our weekly visits with Susan and Mrs. A. whenever possible to encourage her to work with the child. Eva and Joan complimented her on the improvement Susan had made during the past few months in her home. We brought books for her to use to encourage language development and blocks for Susan to play with, suggesting various games and imitation activities. While Mrs. A. was interested, the number of children in her care and the work this required meant that there was little chance to carry out these activities. This was especially true when a 3-year-old child without lower legs was next brought into her home. She now had five children under the age of 3, two of whom were severely handicapped and required most of her time and energy. Despite the various changes Susan continued to seek close body contact and pursued Mrs. A. both physically and vocally. She was now saying "ma ma," "da da," "bye-bye," and could also identify all the people in Mrs. A.'s home. Other vocalizations mimicked quality and pitch of her foster mother's language.

Susan was not seen for 6 weeks during the summer because of the vacations of Mrs. A. and the staff. Our next observation revealed regression. Although Susan's gross motor competence had developed extremely well, we saw a re-emergence of the tentativeness which she had exhibited at 8 months. For example, when Joan tried to engage her with some new toys and games, she again held back warily, uncertain about touching the objects or Joan. Even when encouraged and held, she could only engage briefly before turning back. Mrs. A.'s redecorating, which had changed Susan's environment radically, may have contributed to her uncertainty. Mrs. A.'s casual, cluttered, comfortable, child-centered home had gradually been transformed into a more elegant abode where the children were more restricted. Mrs. A. again expressed interest in giving up the care of foster children and developing her personal life, particularly the relationship with her new male friend. She repeatedly said, "It's about time they left," appearing to fear her close attachment in light of the uncertainty of her friend's interest in them. As reflected by her redecorating, Mrs. A. was at a stage in which she wanted to reorder and reestablish things for herself. Her need to control her own life better spilled over onto the care of her foster children: she simultaneously initiated both toilet training and weaning with Susan, and a new series of battles for control between this child and her foster mother emerged.

We continued to visit and to observe developments in Mrs. A.'s own life in the hope that she would be able to work things out in a way that would permit her to integrate the care of Susan and Antonio into her new life. However, she continued to say that she was going to close her home to foster children. Establishing a constant, caring adult in Susan's life, in addition to Mrs. A., appeared critical; Madeline again voiced hopes of being able to retrieve her children from foster care at a time when she and her boyfriend Thomas could get an apartment together. This renewed our hopes that Madeline might be able to be reunited with her first daughter and youngest son.

We again suggested that Madeline go to Mrs. A.'s house early in the morning on a weekly basis so that she could assist Antonio and Susan in their rising, bathing, and feeding while Mrs. A. took care of the other children. Madeline would then bring the children to the Center, where she would have the opportunity to become reacquainted with them. In order to help Madeline understand Susan's development since her placement at 3 months and to bridge the time they missed together, we put together a videotape program highlighting different stages of Susan's growth. Madeline showed interest in the videotapes of Susan's early months, which focused on Susan alone. However, when she viewed the 11-month assessment and observed the contrast between Susan's behavior toward her and Mrs. A. (described above), Madeline began to fidget and become restless. Suddenly her interest diminished and she became more anxious. Our attempts to reflect that she was upset or distressed by Susan's response to Mrs. A. were met with denial, avoidance, and a refusal to elaborate on any feelings she might be experiencing. Madeline continued to bring the children to the Center a few more times.

Joan's sessions with Madeline and Susan were often painful and discouraging. Susan could relate to people and play with objects far better than her mother. Joan would read books, label objects, and talk with Susan as she explored her environment and developed language. Before long Susan could be engaged in symbolic play, pretending to cook, eat, or clean up. When Joan urged Susan to reach out to her mother and bring her a toy, Susan complied, but Madeline could not respond. At best she observed her daughter and Joan passively from a distance. She could neither respond nor express her feelings or thoughts. She sat quietly, often appearing bewildered by what Joan was doing. The feelings of depression and futility were overwhelming. We wondered if Madeline felt she could not trust Joan, who might see her inadequacy, judge that she would not be able to care for Susan, and put an end to her chances for retrieving her children. We wondered if Madeline was ambivalent. We also thought it possible that she simply lacked the most basic capacities to read her children's cues and respond reciprocally. Joan began to think it would be impossible to help Madeline learn to parent her children. Eva insisted Madeline must get them back, fearing the fate of the children if they continued in foster placement. Ambivalence and uncertainty polarized the team members.

SUSAN AT 17 MONTHS

When Susan was assessed at 17 months, she dropped 29 scaled points, to 87 on the Bayley Mental Scale. We again saw her extreme vulnerability in response to changes in her environment and the rapid deterioration that set in when she was not being responded to which had been exhibited at the 8-month assessment. The evidence of emotional interference with cognitive processes was now clearer. Susan showed a reluctance to let things go and held onto the last item of tasks; this behavior interfered with her completing tasks and getting credit. For example, Susan would put eight of the nine cubes in a cup or five of the six pegs into the board; because she was unable to let go of the last object, she lost credit for the entire item. In addition to her negativism and numerous refusals which made her look like a precocious, stubborn, independent 2-year old, Susan exhibited a low level of frustration tolerance which also interfered with attaining higher scores. There were, however, some other encouraging aspects to this assessment. Susan continued to show her strong attachment to and affection for Mrs. A., using her appropriately as a base for further exploration in the room. When Mrs. A. teased her by saying "Bye-bye" as Susan roamed around, she became very anxious at the prospect of separation and rushed back to Mrs. A.'s side.

Further observations of Susan in the Center showed that Susan would seek out all the other adults available for comfort and encouragement rather than turn to her mother. When this happened Susan was urged to take toys to "Mama," Madeline was encouraged to accept them and invite her to sit down on the floor and play. When Susan sought body contact with Joan, Joan would respond to her and then gently ask Madeline to hold and cuddle her daughter, pointing out that Susan wanted to be close just then. Madeline could admit that Susan felt different to her now than when she was 3 months old, but could say little else. Mother and daughter were encouraged to play together in whatever ways we could think of. For example, at one point Madeline, Susan, and Joan were sitting on the floor and Susan reached into a tin and presented her mother and Joan with make-believe cookies. Madeline did not recognize what was happening and started to tell Susan that there was nothing in her hand and nothing in the tin. Joan quickly entered into the play by role modeling how to "pretend" and accepted the cookies, indicating they were just delicious. Madeline caught on and became part of the drama. Madeline giggled and enjoyed these moments with her daughter, learning a little about imaginative and symbolic play. In these contacts it became very clear to us that Madeline had never achieved the symbolic and representational capacities that Susan was developing. We recognized that our intervention would have to focus on helping Madeline develop some of these capacities if she were to be able to care for and promote the development of her daughter.

Our plan to have Madeline and Susan meet at our Center and reestablish their attachment and affection continued for about 6 weeks. Then, despite the delight she appeared to be taking in her daughter, Madeline became unreliable in picking up the children at Mrs. A.'s house in the morning. At this time we also observed that Madeline was gaining weight, and she finally admitted to being pregnant. Again, it was Susan's development which was gravely at risk during this rapprochement phase. Madeline's energy turned inward as she reacted to her new pregnancy and began to withdraw from Susan. Mrs. A. was also preoccupied with the physical care of her severely handicapped foster children and her ambivalence about being a foster mother in the face of changes in her own life. As a result, Susan was again abandoned. She lacked a constant, caring adult and our hopes that Madeline would be available to respond to her were aborted. Another plan for reuniting Susan and Madeline had failed. We had to come to grips with this reality and decided to refocus our efforts in our work with Susan and Mrs. A. We hoped that the foster mother might resolve her ambivalence in the direction of keeping Susan for at least a few more years, until the child had established some base for herself which might help with an unknown future.

SUSAN AT 20 MONTHS

Shortly before Madeline's due date, Susan came in for her 20-month assessment. These assessments were now scheduled frequently for two reasons: (1) because of our concerns about Susan; and (2) because the assessments were acceptable to Mrs. A. We hoped they would permit her to view Susan's development in increasingly complex ways and encourage further intervention. We also saw the assessments as an opportunity for Madeline to know her daughter and maintain some thread of attachment. But on this occasion both mother and daughter were unavailable and unresponsive. Madeline sat passively, head down, arms at her side, staring straight ahead as her daughter got on her lap. Susan appeared sober and wary, sucking two fingers constantly and taking long distracted looks at the toys, but only responding intermittently when they were presented. She would hardly look at the examiner during the Bayley and when urged to perform responded with sullen negativism or passively refused item after item. When she did respond, she became easily disorganized. In contrast, when she initiated an activity, like pursuing a ball that she had rolled under the couch, she was much more persistent and goal directed. She displayed the most affect while exploring the hole in the doll's bottom (she was being toilet trained at the time) and crying when the examiner took an item away. When mother and daughter were left alone for free play, Madeline sat in the chair, only occasionally glancing at Susan, who wandered around the room aimlessly and finally sat down on the floor sucking her fingers for comfort. She never turned to her mother. (Later in the infant room she indiscriminately sought consolation from any available adult except Madeline.) Madeline at one point, when Susan was left in the room with other children, broke down and sobbed forlornly.

The MDI of 66 attained during this assessment again reflected not Susan's true potential but rather her great vulnerability to stress and the marked degree to which her functioning could be impaired. It was now painfully clear to us that Madeline's distance from her first daughter was not likely to be bridged again and that she was too depressed to maintain any connection with her child.

Because of Susan's poor performance with her mother, the assessment was repeated 3 weeks later with Mrs. A. This session made clear the particular anxieties Susan was struggling with during this period in which her mother had withdrawn and her caretaker was so ambivalent. As soon as Susan and Mrs. A. arrived, Susan found a book she insisted on keeping with her; she would not let go of it until she was assured she could keep the book on the test table within sight. When shown a card with pictures to name, she held the card closely but would not name the objects. However, she did ask what was in the test kit and only after giving her a new object could the examiner retrieve the card. This procedure was necessary with each item as Susan was reluctant to let go of anything she held. Her intense determination to hold on interfered with actually doing the items. When she could be enticed into doing an item Susan was curious and involved but only for brief periods.

What was more striking than Susan's performance was the change in her behavior and affect from the previous assessment with her mother. Susan smiled and engaged the examiner continuously, showing interest and eye contact. She frequently turned to Mrs. A. and giggled gleefully at her own antics. She took delight in stacking blocks and laughed when they fell or she knocked them over saying, "fall now." She was pleased when she did what she wanted and in this way completed the pegboard and bouncing the ball. But her anxiety rose when objects were hidden and she fussed until she reclaimed the ball and bunny and began to "cook and stir" in the cup. She persevered in stirring the cup when asked to do a series of tasks with the doll and for the first time began to suck her fingers. When she could not find a way of making the task her own, she stirred her cup and could not complete the test. Finally, during the free play, she retrieved her book, climbed into Mrs. A.'s lap and allowed Mrs. A. to show her some pictures for a few moments. Although Susan smiled at Mrs. A.'s overtures to play and played with the ball the examiner offered, she did not become involved in reciprocal exchanges but played by herself. She threw the ball randomly, climbed on the couch and chairs, wandered about the room, and resumed "cooking." In response to Mrs. A.'s encouragement, she was able to put the toys away.

Susan only attained an MDI of 75 on this assessment because of her poor tolerance for disappearing objects and need to control the tasks through negativism and avoidance when she became anxious. Her score, therefore, was only 9 points above the previous worrisome assessment. However, seeing the range of affects and reciprocal interactions she was capable of when not pressured was important. It suggested Susan was still resilient and emotionally available even though so vulnerable and reactive to earlier stress. Susan also reflected her positive attachment to Mrs. A., the wider range of affect available in a supportive environment, and good symbolic capacities. Nevertheless, intervention was indicated. We decided to intensify our efforts to work with Mrs. A., but this again proved very difficult to implement. Mrs. A. refused to set up weekly visits, indicating that she was very busy cooking for church affairs, keeping school appointments with her other children's teachers, shopping, and fixing up her house. Even when appointments were arranged, Mrs. A. would let Joan in and then exit from the room, leaving Joan with all of the foster children, thus making it impossible for her to work with Susan in a more focused way.

Hypothesizing that presenting Mrs. A. with the specific cognitive and emotional areas in which Susan needed help might have been experienced as criticism of her caregiving, we changed our focus. For example, Joan shifted her approach to respond to what Mrs. A. might need in her care not only of Susan, but the other children as well. She sought opportunities to make some suggestions. Mrs. A. could respond to this shift and even began to reach out for help. For example, when she was not able to understand the construction of the Bradford frame for her foster child in the body cast she asked

Joan to help. She appeared uncomfortable, however, when
attention turned to Susan, particularly her increasingly negativistic behavior. A strong contest of wills had developed
between Susan and Mrs. A., who disregarded our recommendations to stop toilet training and to engage Susan in
games which would support object constancy, such as hide-
and-seek. Mrs. A. was determined to have Susan use the potty
despite the child's reluctance to do so. While she was never
physically punitive, she refused to refrain from ridiculing or
shaming Susan into submission. Mrs. A.'s need for order and
control also assumed other forms. After she redecorated her
home, children's toys were no longer in sight. Her dining
room table was removed to make room for new furnishings;
meals were now served on TV trays. Because there was only
one high chair in the home, the children ate in shifts. Susan
was not permitted to attempt to feed herself "because she
might make a mess." Our concerns intensified, but it was
clear that we would be able to go just so far in our efforts with
Mrs. A. who was now letting us know that we were intruding
into her life and that she was going to do things her own way.
We were reminded of Susan's performance on the assessment.

SUSAN AT 2 YEARS

By now it had become apparent to Mrs. A. and to us that
a reunion between Susan and her mother was unlikely, especially now that Madeline had a new infant girl to "replace"
Susan. Mrs. A. continued to resist our efforts to intervene
with Susan on a regular basis and indicated that she was still
planning to close her home to foster children. She reported
that her relationship with her new boyfriend was progressing
very well, and that they were thinking of getting married.
Mrs. A. seemed unable to imagine the possibility of both
developing this relationship and continuing to care for her
foster children. Although she was very concerned about Susan
and Antonio's future and where they might be placed, her
withdrawal resulted in the absence of a committed, available,

unambivalent adult in Susan's life. Fortunately, the bonds of their early attachment and affection were still evident and Mrs. A. continued to provide adequate, basic care for Susan and her brother.

Another assessment was attempted at 2 years because of our continued concerns. The examiner was unable to obtain either a base or ceiling score on this assessment because Susan refused so many items. The items she did perform placed her just below the average range. Mrs. A. also appeared very inconsistent in setting limits to Susan's negativistic behavior, sometimes trying to control her and other times letting her go. For example, she would permit Susan to get up from her lap, but then demanded that she return, confusing Susan. Mrs. A. would also enter an oppositional struggle when it was obvious that Susan would not complete the item she was asked. Object permanence was still poorly developed; Susan continued to fuss when things were hidden. There was also evidence of the poor frustration tolerance seen several months earlier. The only optimistic aspects of the assessment appeared when Susan was left on her own without the demands or stress of a particular task. She then appeared fairly well organized and could initiate symbolic play with both Mrs. A. and the examiner.

MRS. A. PLANS TO RELINQUISH SUSAN AND ANTONIO

Joan found it increasingly difficult to arrange to see Susan, as Mrs. A. continued to be preoccupied with her own life. In the autumn of 1979 she married Mr. T., and appeared very happy and content in her new marriage. She moved ahead with her plans to give up the care of the foster children, and now set the date of March 1, 1980, as an appropriate termination point. Her concern for the welfare of the children was conveyed when she asked whether Madeline had ever thought of signing over her children for adoption. She revealed that she and her new husband had at one point thought they might adopt one of the foster children, but quickly added that they decided against it because they felt that they were too old, since they would be over 65 when the child would be a teenager. This decision appeared to preclude the adoption of Susan and Antonio. We were extremely concerned about their future prospects, knowing we would have to search again for a permanent caretaker.

Once Mrs. A. had announced her "definite" plans to give up Susan and Antonio she began to speak less and less of this decision. Her husband appeared to become more involved with the children, and with time the couple appeared to be less committed to closing their home, adopting a wait and see attitude. In the face of the reality that Madeline would probably not be able to assume care of her children, Mrs. A.'s ambivalence seemed to swing in the other direction, and she began to worry about what would happen to them. Although Mrs. A.'s adjustment to her new marriage compromised her ability to provide an environment which would better support Susan's development, it did leave the door open for the future. We soon learned that the child the couple had considered adopting had been abruptly removed from the home after they decided not to adopt her. This sudden loss of her favorite foster child, an appealing and bright little girl of Susan's age whom she had cared for since birth, shocked Mrs. A. In the past she had described crying when a child left but she had always replaced children quickly, covering her pain and loss. Now she was jolted by the impact of her decision. Perhaps this contributed to a consideration of her feelings about Susan and Antonio.

SUSAN AT 32 MONTHS

The Stanford-Binet and a play interview were conducted when Susan was 32 months old. Good fine-motor coordination resulted in her best performances while poor language skills interfered the most. Although she initiated four- and five-word sentences her language was not always clear and required repeated efforts to understand. While she used lan-

guage to direct others and to play, she would not name specific
items such as parts of the body, and thus failed 2-year items.
But most of all, it was Susan's distractability and poor attention
span on test items that most interfered with her cognitive
performance and resulted in an IQ of 78 (mental age of 24
months). Although she no longer exhibited the intense negativism of the past, when test demands were too difficult she
appeared to avoid them and become distracted by something
else. In contrast, when Susan pursued something she was
interested in she would persist, even threatening to "tell on"
the examiner when she kept asking her to do something else.
During the play interview Susan could not develop any
themes although she engaged in such symbolic play as feeding
a baby for fleeting moments. Instead she moved from toy to
toy in a busy, cheerful but distracted manner. Even when the
interviewer offered her some direction, she found it difficult
to sustain and began to order the interviewer around telling
her to "shut up" or "put it back" in an imitative manner clearly
familiar to her. It was only when reunited with her foster
mother that she showed longer chains of contingent behavior
supported by affectionate hugs, smiles, and laughter, as well
as familiar play.

   We again renewed our efforts to intervene with Mrs. A.
around Susan's development, this time focusing on speech
and language. Because of Mrs. A.'s continued ambivalence
we renewed our referral of Susan to the Early Identification
Program in the county which would have provided her with
small group intervention at their developmental center. Susan
had qualified for this program earlier and we hoped that going
there would offer her more stable consistent intervention. She
was now rejected by the program as not being sufficiently
handicapped; Joan had to depend on Mrs. A. to implement
some special exercises with Susan. To facilitate this Joan
brought books and puzzles to encourage fine-motor and sensory discrimination activities. She urged Mrs. A. to set aside
a quiet time alone with Susan and to play with her dolls and

toys in a symbolic fashion. Mrs. A. would listen to these suggestions, but did not seem interested in carrying them out. She appeared more concerned with maintaining a neat and orderly home. Despite these limitations, Mrs. A. provided a structured and affectionate environment for Susan.

As the adjustment to a new marriage progressed, a more lively interest in Susan and her brother seemed to reemerge and a deepening bond between the children and Mrs. A. and her husband was observed. We were very relieved to see this happening; a change in Susan's caregiver at this stage would have been devastating to her development. Fortunately, Mrs. A.'s targeted date of closing her home came and went. Following this Mrs. A. indicated that she hoped the DSS would be in no hurry to remove the children from her home.

Mrs. A. needed help with some other family concerns and called Joan for help in finding a black therapist for her 13-year-old adopted son. He was having some major problems adjusting to her new husband, a very stern and rigid preacher, studying to be an ordained minister, who moved into the home with strict expectations to which the boy could not adhere. Joan responded immediately to her request. When Mrs. A. called on another occasion to see if we had any information about subsidized housing for her daughter, Joan again responded quickly, hoping that our response to Mrs. A.'s needs would be reciprocated by responsiveness toward Susan and Antonio.

SUSAN AT 3 YEARS

Susan continued to thrive physically, becoming a very pretty and agile little girl. Her negativism had decreased, her language had clearly improved, and she could attend and be engaged for longer periods of time. Nevertheless, her overall cognitive performance on the McCarthy Scales (GCI of 79) was about the same level as the Stanford-Binet 6 months earlier (IQ of 78). She related well and tried harder, retaining a smile on her face, but was unable to follow through on tasks, particularly conceptual tasks such as grouping, sorting, and labeling items. She also had more difficulty manipulating or remembering items visually than remembering lists of numbers of words read to her. As questions became more difficult she would repeat the questions again and again, becoming agitated and less intelligible. It was in the free play with her mother that she and Mrs. A. again demonstrated, with singing and hugging, the strong affectionate bond they shared. Susan responded quickly to familiar exchanges in telephone play and bouncing a ball, while Mrs. A. tried to have her name foods and explore a doctor's kit with less success.

Again Joan urged Mrs. A. to spend some time with Susan alone each day, but most of all to use day-to-day opportunities to label and describe objects, compare opposites, learn colors, etc. Again Mrs. A. listened to these ideas with interest but Joan's impression was that she would continue to be "too busy" to support Susan's cognitive development at this stage or respond to her specific individual needs. Susan would have to fit in with what Mrs. A. had to offer, and appeared to benefit from the affection and busy social life of the family and church.

SUSAN AT 3½ YEARS

At this time Susan was a friendly responsive child, eager to please and able to enjoy what she did. She was very pleasant and cooperated on the next assessment. Her overall performance was consistent with the previous one and did not show any marked changes. She was still performing at the bottom of the dull normal range, making small, but steady gains, and continued to have most difficulty with perceptual-motor integration, concept formation, and language utilization. When items became too difficult for her, she would squirm and walk around, often repeating the examiner's last question but unable to respond. She became confused when she had to integrate two concepts at a time such as selecting the big yellow block. However, she related well to the examiner, continually inviting her to play with the dolls, talking about other children at home, and pursuing her own games with the items presented with pleasure.

During the free play Mrs. A. initiated many interactions which encouraged Susan to name objects or play symbolically. Susan complied on these various tasks, following Mrs. A.'s lead in reading a book, feeding a doll, and talking on the phone. Susan tended to interrupt longer sequences by focusing on a particular comment or object. Because Mrs. A. was so intent on directing her, it remained unclear whether Susan could organize and develop thematic play more on her own. When she did initiate undressing the doll, her foster mother restricted her because her "baby would get cold." Occasionally, Mrs. A. could support Susan's elaborations, such as telling a little story about a picture. Their shared warmth and affection continued to be impressive.

While Mrs. A. was reluctant to have us visit regularly, she did absorb the various suggestions made during the repeated assessments, with which she cooperated fully. Her behavior during the free play appeared to be a demonstration of the various techniques suggested to her although it interfered with her following more of Susan's leads for longer periods. While Susan's cognitive level had not risen, her language was more articulate and elaborate and she had developed into a warm, attractive, and affectionate child.

SUSAN BETWEEN 4 AND 6

Mrs. A. continued to cooperate regarding Susan's assessments during the next two years. Susan was even comfortable coming in alone with Eva or Joan. She was always beautifully dressed, outgoing, and delightful. Susan was also eager to report her experiences at school or at home and spoke expressively, showing a wide range of affect and capacities to relate. The quality of her play also improved as she became more representational and articulate. At 4 years of age her cognitive performance took a dramatic dip which appeared related to her irritability that day and unknown factors in her home, including the continual uncertainty regarding her permanent placement. Within 6 months she just as dramatically recovered to her previous cognitive level and fluctuated between a general cognitive index of 80 and 88, placing her just within the average range during the next 2 years. Susan continued to show a few language and attention difficulties; withdrawing when she felt frustrated. But we felt she was progressing and benefited from structure and direction, attributes which would help her in school.

Most important, Susan's future is now secure because Mrs. A. and her husband decided to adopt Susan and her brother, an event celebrated by all. In retrospect, we probably underestimated the impact we were having on Mrs. A. and Susan, and were sometimes disappointed that she was unwilling to follow through on specific suggestions to stimulate her cognitive development. In fact, Susan made a remarkable recovery, developed very successful relationships with her foster parents and others in their world, and became a trusting and happy child who won a permanent place in her new mother's heart.

Our Work with Mrs. J.

The work with Mrs. J. was carried out primarily by Eva. The initial goal was to sustain contact between Madeline and her two elder sons, Danny and David, until they could be reunited. This goal was not realized, and our objective changed to helping the boys bridge the loss of their mother while they developed their attachment to Mrs. J. Further, the goals now included supporting Mrs. J. in her efforts to meet the special needs of the boys and keeping her and them informed about Madeline over time. This was essential to prevent the uncertainty typical of foster care arrangements in which the resulting suspension of greater commitment and attachment between the foster parent and the foster children impedes more adequate development. Eva's periodic contact continued for more than 4 years.

THE J. HOME

Mrs. J. was a divorced woman in her late forties with grown children and several grandchildren. Her warm and sensitive manner appealed to everyone who met her. She was easy to talk to and very understanding. Many years of experience raising her own, foster, and family day care children lay behind her confident and empathic mothering. She could provide a solid anchor for even the most difficult and distressed child. Many such children came to her home over the years. These qualities were essential for Madeline's boys, who came to Mrs. J. in severely depressed, deprived, and functionally retarded states. At the ages of 4 and 3, Danny and David could not speak, were difficult to control, and had not yet lived in a home with any established routine or predictable response. After wandering for months with Madeline, they were abruptly separated when she walked out of the Infant Center on the night she decided to place them. After 3 weeks in temporary placement, they moved into Mrs. J.'s home. She also cared for a foster girl and several day care children, with the support of her family and a close male friend whom the children called "granddaddy."

Mrs. J. was very responsive to Madeline's difficult plight and willing to relax visitation procedures in order to allow Madeline to visit whenever she wanted to without going through the DSS. All Madeline had to do was work through Eva or call Mrs. J. to arrange the time. Madeline's initial response to Mrs. J. was also positive and she felt more relaxed than with Mrs. A., appearing comfortable when she and Eva would sit together. But she only visited Mrs. J. two or three times with Eva and, while she would periodically say she was going to visit and transportation was made available, Madeline never went on her own. Except for one picnic, which Eva again arranged, and several phone calls, Madeline's contact with her older boys ended.

Eva became Madeline's representative, visiting every few months with gifts or news of Madeline. In this way Madeline did not just disappear out of her sons' lives and they were not merely forgotten by their mother. Eva became the source of continuity for them by her interest and her periodic visits. These visits also committed Eva to develop an alliance with and to support Mrs. J.

BRIDGING THE LOSS

Eva's periodic contact was a crucial factor in the adjustment of Madeline's boys to their new home and alleviated some of the impact of losing their mother. Eva became an object for their transition from a chaotic and starved world to a warm and stable home. Her continuous availability on a long-term basis was especially important while their final disposition remained unclear. This was true for both the boys and Mrs. J. Eva was not only supportive of Mrs. J. but was able to clarify and relate news of Madeline's whereabouts and activities. This awareness permitted Mrs. J. to become more attached and invested in the boys rather than to spend only part of her feelings in the face of the unknown outcome typical of foster children. Because she was not waiting for a sudden call to tell her that the children would be removed, she felt freer to discuss Madeline with the boys, and was able to answer their questions without pushing aside their feelings about their mother. That Eva was also able to acknowledge and give Mrs. J. credit for the very special efforts she made month after month reinforced and rewarded her in ways usually unavailable to foster mothers. When it became apparent that Madeline would not be able to retrieve her children and was willing to relinquish them, Mrs. J. was ready to adopt Danny and David, choosing them from among all the children she had cared for over many years.

DANNY AND DAVID

Danny and David arrived at Mrs. J.'s home understandably distressed by their experiences. Danny was extremely depressed, withdrawn, and mute. David was very destructive;

he ate clothes, sheets, and other inappropriate objects. Both boys were angry, hurt, and frightened, not knowing what would happen to them next. Severe speech and language delays would not permit them to express what they were feeling or to ask questions about what would happen to them.

Mrs. J. provided a stable and warm home. Her extended family, children, and grandchildren became close to the boys. She also immediately implemented our referral to the Early Identification Program because of the children's severe speech and language delays. When it soon became apparent that the boys also needed psychotherapy for severe emotional problems, Mrs. J. took them for treatment. In addition, she persisted in taking them for all their physical, health, and psychological evaluations required to sustain them in year-round special education programs. Most of all, she was able to help the boys work through the process of separation and loss of their mother without having to "forget" her. She helped them accept her distance and permitted them to talk about Madeline whenever they needed to. It was here that Eva's visits were most crucial. They not only permitted Eva to support the many efforts Mrs. J. was making but also reminded the boys of their mother.

THE BOYS TURN AROUND

Given the qualities of Mrs. J. and her home as well as all the special services she was able to implement for them, Danny and David made great gains. They were well mannered, responsive, and more outgoing boys. Danny has emerged from his depression and is speaking, although he remains somewhat shy. He has been able to learn in school and has become more self-confident among peers. He will be mainstreamed into a regular class soon. David remained more immature and continues to need special education programs and treatment, but has become a lively, devilish, and affectionate youngster. The impact of their early years is still evident, but both boys are thriving on the strong emotional bond with Mrs. J. and the security that they will be able to remain with her.

When Eva arrives at the J. home and they see her car coming they run out to her calling her "my lady, my lady." They are eager to show their recent school pictures and projects and tell her of their doings. They also ask about "Pinky," their mother, calling her by the pet name they used to hear when they lived in the dugout of Madeline's grandmother's house where she never became known as "Mama." They ask where she is and how she is, as well as about their little sister Anita. Danny asks if Madeline is married and David wants to know whether she has a house yet. They ask these questions in the presence of Mrs. J. whom they do call "Mama." Their questions seem more related to trying to "fit" Madeline into the concepts of their current world and relationships rather than in their yearning to return to her. Thoughts and comments about Madeline are open and she can be remembered and known. Mrs. J. even asks if they would like to send Madeline their new school pictures. They happily agree but do not ask to see her. It is Eva who has represented Madeline over time and has helped them cross the bridge to their new and secure lives with Mrs. J.

TABLE 6-1
MADELINE: Intervention Time Line

Year 1	Meet Madeline; Delivers one week later	Relinquishes children to foster care 3 months later		Leaves Mr. S. and enrolls in job training	Susan's first birthday
Year 2	Meets Thomas	Gets pregnant again	Gets prenatal care	Gives birth to Anita 20 months after Susan	Begins daily attendance at Infant Center
Year 3	Attends daily	Begins group therapy	Begins GED classes at CIDP	Anita's first birthday	Releases older children to adoption
Year 4	Begin work with father	Continues attending Infant Center		Anita's second birthday	Begins job training on site
Year 5	Continues individual and group treatment and job			Anita's third birthday	
Year 6	Anita begins Day Care	Madeline enrolls in GED classes outside program		Anita's fourth birthday	Program ends

7

Reaching the Unreachable: Measuring Change in Relation to Intervention

Serena Wieder, Ph.D.

The case studies selected for this volume were chosen not only to demonstrate success in working with the hard-to-reach family, but the lengthy and difficult process involved in facilitating emotional growth. As clinicians, we wanted to share how we went about working with our participants, often considered unreachable, in order to help them to change their lives. As clinical researchers we want briefly to share how we quantified and measured some of these changes and report some of the initial results we obtained while we continue to analyze our statistical data which will be reported in greater detail elsewhere. This chapter will discuss the changes in three of the mothers presented in the case studies in order to illustrate the variables we chose to measure, some changes in the entire intervention group, and the relationship of the various measures to program utilization.

The Clinical Ratings

The Clinical Infant Development Program (CIDP) intervention was designed to help the women participating in the program to function more effectively as mothers, as well as individuals, by offering each one therapeutic relationships in a comprehensive home- and center-based program. Each of these aspects, the maternal, the individual, and the treatment, had to be quantified and objective clinical ratings were undertaken to accomplish this. These ratings were done by a team of "blind" clinicians* who were trained and brought to reliability to rate extensive narrative reports and objective outcome interviews in order to measure change. The details regarding the development and reliability of the ratings are presented in Chapter 8 and elsewhere (Greenspan and Wieder, 1984, Wieder, Jasnow, Greenspan, and Strauss, 1984). This chapter will discuss the impact of the program on Madeline, Louise, and Mrs. M. Mrs. Lake is not included because she moved out of state before the outcome studies were conducted. We used visual analogue scales (Folstein and Luria, 1973) which consist of a 100 centimeter line and definitions of each variable at either end (see Appendix 1). The rater marked the point on the line which he/she thought represented each mother; that point is then measured and recoded as the rating. It ranges from 0 to 100, low to high, with the high end being the desired level or behavior.

The ratings were completed at three points: during pregnancy (entry), when the infants were 1 year old, and 6 to 8 months before the program ended (outcome). This report will focus on the results from entry and outcome.

We selected two ratings of basic psychological characteristics in the mothers, by means of which we attempted to capture the relatively enduring aspects of personality which are unlikely to change without intervention. The first rating was concerned with regulation and control of drives, affects, and impulses. This ranged from strong urges usually being acted upon to effective sublimation, awareness, and self-reg-

*The author wishes to thank Christopher Anderson, Ph.D., Griff Doyle, Ph.D., Mahmoud Jahromi, M.D., and Michael Jasnow, Ph.D., for doing the independent clinical ratings of the mothers.

ulation (Bellak, Hurvich, and Gidiron, 1973). This variable was selected because of the frequent acting-out and impulsive nature of our mothers, their struggle with mood and depression, and the difficulties they had relating their behavior to their feelings. The second rating was one of overall developmental level or a developmental diagnosis (Greenspan, 1979). It was concerned with the level of personality and psychosexual functioning ranging from the primitive and concrete to the symbolic and representational. This variable was selected because it is the most basic way of measuring personality structure and was especially important to consider since so many of the CIDP mothers lacked representational capacities in the emotional realms that they ordinarily would have been considered untreatable by psychotherapy in traditional settings.

The next group of ratings were concerned with maternal capacities. These were considered as a separate parameter because of the specific objectives of CIDP to improve maternal capacities and an interest in capturing the maternal component, such as comfort with nurturing, within each woman's personality structure. The specific capacities selected for measurement pertain to the stages of the Greenspan Developmental Structuralist framework and are derived from the functions or tasks each parent must meet in order to support adequately their infant's development. These ratings were not based on direct observation but inferred from clinicians' narratives or interviews given by the mothers reporting their experiences as mothers. The first rating was the capacity for nurturance which reflected the degree to which the mother had worked through issues of nurturance and dependency so that she could attend to the needs of her children in a relatively undistorted and empathic manner. It did not so much measure whether the mother nurtured her child, but the basis for this nurturance; for example, her own neediness or her mature ability to feel enriched by nurturing her child. The second rating was concerned with the mother's capacity for reading and responding to complex affective and behavioral signals.

This ranged from being unable to read because of projection or intrusive and controlling tendencies, to being able to read and follow the baby's lead, helping the infant to organize behavior and feelings. The third rating pertains to the mother's capacity to utilize symbolic and representational forms in interaction with her child. This ranged from the mother who was very concrete and fearful of emerging feelings and impulses to one who could not only read, but encouraged symbolic elaboration across emotional and behavioral domains. The last rating in this group attempted to capture locus of reinforcement; that is, whether the experiences which enhanced the mother's sense of herself as a mother were extrinsic, derived from the expectations or demands of others to be a "mother," or intrinsic, derived from internal gratification.

An additional rating of global risk was included in order to measure the overall risk regarding the mothers' abilities to support their infants' development. Raters were asked to consider the following: psychiatric or psychological disorders, environmental support, adequacy of health care and nutrition, family stress, mother's educational level, substance abuse, historical antecedents, and current maternal functioning.

The last group of ratings were measures of the therapeutic relationship, which we conceptualized in three dimensions: (1) Regularity and stability; that is, the degree to which the participant was able to work with the therapists on a regular basis with minimum or no unplanned disruptions. This dimension was particularly related to the outreach efforts needed and would capture the progress made as participants became more comfortable and committed to regular contact. (2) Attachment or the affective bond which develops as a relationship grows and the participants felt known and accepted by the therapists. This dimension was central to our efforts to help most participants work through their basic distrust of relationships so that they could form less ambivalent attachments to their children. (3) The process observed in the content of meetings with the therapist. This ranged from asking for concrete services to giving information, to reporting behaviors and feelings with others, to making connections between the therapeutic relationship and other key relationships, to repetitive exploration of old patterns and consolidation of new ones. The process dimension can be seen as the outcome of the regularity and attachment which mediate the working through needed for emotional growth (see Chapter 10).

The Mothers: Madeline, Louise, and Mrs. M.

Table 7-1 presents the ratings each mother received at entry and at outcome with the difference or residual score in parentheses. As can be quickly seen, the mothers all changed on every measure and the magnitude of change was often greater for those who started lower. The ratings appear to have accurately captured the level of each mother on the various scales, thus attesting to the clinical skills of the raters to decipher and judge the initial clinical narrative material, and to the skills of the mothers who, by the end of the program, could articulate so much more about themselves to an independent interviewer for the outcome ratings. More important, the ratings were successful in capturing complex psychological processes which are typically bypassed for more behavioral or self-report types of measures because of the difficulty in making inferences about these processes. Because this was a clinical research effort that attempted to change underlying capacities through psychodynamic approaches, it was essential to develop measures of just these capacities, as well as the critical aspects of the treatment process. Each mother will be discussed briefly so that the reader can relate their scores to the case material.

MADELINE

Madeline started out in the lowest range of scores on all the scales. Her maternal capacities were considered very minimal, except for such concrete care as feeding her children

TABLE 7-1

Entry and Outcome Ratings on Three Mothers Who Received Intensive Intervention*

	Madeline			Louise			Mrs. M		
	E	O	D	E	O	D	E	O	D
Regulation of Drives, Affects, and Impulses	22–54		(+32)	33–57		(+24)	31–66		(+35)
Developmental Level	23–59		(+36)	32–54		(+22)	32–63		(+31)
Capacity for Nurturance	35–62		(+27)	40–59		(+19)	28–73		(+45)
Capacity for Reading Complex Affective-Behavioral Signals	17–51		(+34)	38–59		(+21)	28–60		(+32)
Capacity for Symbolic and Representational Thinking	17–51		(+34)	39–62		(+23)	31–56		(+25)
Locus of Maternal Reinforcement	24–63		(+39)	69–73		(+4)	37–63		(+26)
Global Risk	75–36		(−39)	64–29		(−45)	74–44		(−30)
Therapeutic Relationship Scales									
Regularity and Stability	60–78		(+16)	37–74		(+41)	61–83		(+27)
Attachment	50–76		(+26)	39–76		(+37)	48–88		(+40)
Process Level	37–59		(+22)	45–70		(+25)	48–76		(+28)

*E = entry; O = outcome; D = difference between entry and outcome.

(Nurturance = 35, Reading Signals = 17, Symbolic Thinking = 17). Even when she functioned as a mother, it was largely in response to others' demands and pressures (Locus = 24). Madeline's abilities to run her own life were no greater, in part because of depression, and mostly because her personality structure had remained rather primitive, giving her few resources to cope with her strong drives and impulses (Regulation = 22, Developmental Level = 23). The risk she presented at the beginning of the program was extremely high (75) and extremely worrisome.

It is unlikely Madeline would have responded to any intervention, short of the persistent and heroic efforts undertaken by her team. Traditional mental health approaches would surely have designated her as unmotivated, too limited, and nonverbal. Yet, her needs for human contact and successful parenting were no less than those of anyone else. The dramatic change reflected in her scores indicates that much more change was possible than has generally been believed in the past. Madeline's treatment finally brought her into the average range of functioning in most areas. The locus of reinforcement shifted to the intrinsic part of the scale (63), indicating that she may have internalized a great deal. She became quite consistent in her capacity to nurture (62). Even though her reading of complex signals and symbolic thinking was limited by her overall developmental level (59), each of these areas improved threefold. This was very impressive because it is most difficult to move beyond the lower range of functioning. Finally, it appears that the regularity of contact (78) and strength of the attachment (76) helped Madeline better understand and be able to think about her life, her family, and her feelings, by using higher-level reasoning processes in her emotional explorations (process = 59). As a result, her global risk level dropped from 75 to 36.

LOUISE

Louise began with somewhat greater resources than Madeline, particularly in her sense of herself as a mother

(Locus = 69). Perhaps her particularly painful experiences with her adoptive and natural mothers heightened her own identification to an intrinsic locus. But her capacity to translate this important, but often negative, identification into positive maternal functioning was far more limited (Nurturance = 40, Reading Signals = 38, Symbolic Thinking = 39). Louise was also deeply affected by depression and her self-regulation was very poor (33). At entry, her overall development level appeared limited (32) and the risk to her child's development was high (64).

Unlike Madeline, who took whatever she could get, and Mrs. M., who took what she wanted when she wanted it, Louise was ambivalent about her contacts with the program. This is reflected in the very low Regulatory and Attachment scores at entry (35 and 39). Louise was slower to reveal her needs and more guarded about getting close to her clinician. She had to remain in control the longest of all, but her ability to work through her distrust and ambivalence is where she made some of the greatest changes as seen in the outcome scores for Regularity (74) and Attachment (76), which doubled her initial scores. Louise also improved markedly in her maternal capacities (Nurturance = 59, Reading Signals = 59, and Symbolic Thinking = 62). Her parenting was also far more stable and she could support her child's development much more consistently. It is not yet clear from the data whether more successful parenting contributed to more basic psychological change, or improved psychological state improved parenting. However, Louise also showed impressive gains in Regulation, Developmental Level, and Therapeutic Process (gained 24, 22, and 25 points, respectively). It is interesting how parallel these ratings are, considering they were judged separately. Because they are related to the same basic issues, they were very consistent. The improved process rating in this case and in others also suggests that it was the treatment which may have helped the mothers change. Given these improvements, Louise's risk level was also reduced dramatically (−38).

MRS. M.

Mrs. M. made some of the greatest gains in the program, particularly in her ability to experience closeness and trust relationships (Regularity = 83, Attachment = 88). This eventually translated into improved maternal capacities and greater investment in, and gratification from, her children (Nurturance = 73, Reading Signals = 60, Symbolic Thinking = 56, Locus = 63). Through the powerful therapeutic attachment (88), Mrs. M. was able to reach one of the highest process levels amongst the mothers (76). She developed insight and awareness of her feelings and behavior which clearly helped her with regulation (66) and lowered the overall risk (44). By the end of the program, she could work through the difficult separation and learned she could turn to others when she or her children needed more help. She learned to examine her feelings and check her impulses, rather than act out and make everyone else responsible for her unhappiness. Her new trust of dependency also supported the first good relationship with a partner she had ever had. While she remained with certain character limitations reflected by her Developmental Level score (63), she was no longer depressed and had made tremendous improvement in her overall psychological status (gained 31 points).

Changes in the Intervention Group

Madeline, Louise, and Mrs. M. represent the types of changes all of the mothers receiving intensive intervention made. Looking at the intervention group as a whole, all of the changes between the entry and outcome ratings were highly significant. Even the mothers in the less intensive group who received periodic assessments, referrals, and emergency services made significant gains, but not at the same magnitude or with the same consistency as the intensive group (the specific group results will be reported elsewhere). We also learned, when looking at the 12-month ratings, that relatively little change on these psychological ratings occurred during

the first year. Since the objective of the program was to facilitate growth in basic and enduring psychological characteristics, it is not surprising that one year and a few months (the
prenatal phase) would not necessarily affect such changes. The
greatest changes occurred between 1 year and outcome, which
ranged anywhere between 2 and 5 years (depending on when
the mothers joined the program). This very important finding
supports the concept of long-term intervention in order to
help participants internalize and consolidate their gains. It
also speaks to not feeling discouraged when change is not
quickly forthcoming. Intervention efforts are often interrupted when behavioral changes are not readily apparent, and
too few programs work toward internal change. The mothers
in this program taught us to appreciate the process of change
over time, sometimes not seen until they had another chance
with another baby, as 5 of the 27 intensive group mothers
did.

Program Utilization

The trends we discovered as we examined the relationships between the use of the program and other measures are
presented here to enrich the in-depth case studies (Chapters
3–6) which demonstrated how the intervention worked for the
entire intensive group. The use of the program variables included simple descriptive measures, such as time, as well as
several process measures which were determined by the clinical director independent of the analysis of the data and knowledge of specific outcomes. They were added in order to
summarize certain treatment issues, such as treatment compliance, which were not included at the time of the independent clinical ratings. These variables could not have been
readily done independently unless the judges could have rated
the continuous clinical narrative material, which was not always available because of variations in reporting. These variables were considered important to understanding the
intervention process and outcome. They include time in pro-

gram, compliance or resistance to treatment, and rank order of use of program effectiveness; that is, the order in which mothers made most use of what CIDP had to offer. These patterns will be presented only in a brief summary form.

Every intervention program must determine how much intervention to offer; CIDP recorded every contact with each participant and summarized these into an intensity variable for each interval (prenatal, 4, 8, 12 months, and every 6 months thereafter). The results suggest the importance of outreach and persistent pursuit of difficult mothers for long periods. Initially resistant mothers during the entry phase received *more* intensive treatment than initially compliant mothers throughout the duration of the study. This reflects the dauntless efforts the clinicians made to reach the most difficult and hard-to-reach mothers and the continual persistence this required. We also found that intensity was not generally related to compliance during treatment after the birth of the infants. Only at 30–36 months did the cooperative mothers receive more treatment than the resistant ones. These results confirm that the clinicians did not "give up" on mothers who were resistant, even over a period of several years. From 12 months on, there was also a general pattern suggesting that mothers who were in the program longest and who made most effective use of the program received more intensive intervention.

The benefits of time were also evidenced in the maternal and therapeutic relationship ratings and to effective use of the program. Similarly, the longer the mothers were in the program, the better their children did on developmental tests Bayley (1969) and McCarthy (1970). It is interesting too, that mother–child interaction ratings were positively related to effective use of the program only at later stages, particularly at 48 months. Likewise, play interview ratings were somewhat higher for children whose mothers were cooperative at 48 months. Here, too, it appears that the benefits of treatment may not be evident until later ages and require not only long-term treatment, but long-term follow up. These findings may also suggest that children who did better had mothers who stayed in the program longer, perhaps reinforced by their children's success and their growing competence. This, too, speaks to the crucial need to persist with difficult mothers until they can begin to reap the benefits of the intervention, not only for themselves, but for their children.

Finally, it is interesting to note the relationships between the use of the program variables and the antecedent background variables (see Chapter 8). The Index of Misfortune which summarized early traumatic factors in the lives of the mothers was, not surprisingly, negatively related to compliance with treatment; that is, the higher the position on the Index, the more resistant the mothers were throughout the program. Specifically, mothers who were abused in childhood (one of the variables constituting the Index) were significantly more resistant on entry, but *not* during the course of treatment. This confirmed our belief that it was possible to reach and make an alliance with this most difficult subgroup of abused mothers and, contrary to clinical expectations, once engaged, these mothers continued to be engaged in the therapeutic process more than the nonabused mothers. It appears that, once the barrier could be passed, the need for the therapeutic work to be done was stronger, even if it took a resistant form.

Other variables examined included previous psychiatric hospitalization which related to less effective use of the program. Diagnoses which were measured independently by the Diagnostic Interview Schedule (DIS) were also examined. Here, substance abuse predicted shorter postnatal involvement, while depression predicted longer postnatal involvement. There was a trend suggesting that depressed mothers were somewhat more compliant on entry. There was also some indication that outcome socioeconomic status (SES), but not entry SES, was higher among mothers who were cooperative with treatment, suggesting the gains in treatment carried over into better life circumstances and/or increased education. This was consistent with an independent finding that the intensive intervention group was significantly higher at outcome on the Hollingshead Index than the less intensive group.

Conclusion

Studies of the CIDP reflected how intensive preventive intervention works. The intervention approaches developed by the program were able to overcome obstacles long considered impediments to treatment. The CIDP, in fact, often reached what are traditionally considered the unreachable, and found methods to quantify and measure the changes we considered central to maternal functioning and helping mothers support their children's development. While we did not fully reach the fathers as a group, the case studies demonstrate how involved work with the fathers became once our relationships with the mothers was securely established and ambivalences worked through. This has important implications for future work in prevention programs with fathers.

Additional statistical analyses of the program are currently underway and will be reported shortly, together with a more formal report of the patterns described above. Follow-up studies are also underway which will address the most crucial question of all, namely, how will the children of this program do in the long run? Early trends are promising and suggest that they are functioning at least in the average range, surpassing their siblings, and adapting positively to the challenges before them.

Part II: Models for Clinical Programs

8

Antecedent Psychosocial Factors in Mothers in Multirisk Families: Life Histories of the 47 Participants in the Clinical Infant Development Program

Serena Wieder, Ph.D.
Michael Jasnow, Ph.D.
Stanley I. Greenspan, M.D.
Milton Strauss, Ph.D.

Introduction

Although this chapter describes the life histories of the 47 participants in the Clinical Infant Development Program (CIDP) at the time they *entered* the study, the data were acquired over the course of years of clinical work in the program, through conversations and encounters like the ones described in the four preceding case reports. Our families, as we have seen, were often too mistrustful to open the door to a clinician, let alone respond to standard questionnaire or interview techniques. Yet as a result of trust built up gradually over several years, most of the women in the program were able to reveal themselves to an extent that they had never before been able to do. A chronically depressed mother, for example, was able to begin to talk about some aspects of her life history only after several years of work. Women who had been physically or sexually abused as children—and this included a large number of our participants—were often able to reveal information only after they had been able to work through, to some degree, the shame and anger associated with certain life events.

We believe that our method of allowing a working clinical alliance to develop has made possible a more complete and accurate reconstruction of our participants' lives than standard research methods might have revealed. And we are convinced that an awareness of the experiences our participants brought to their own efforts at mothering contributed greatly to our understanding of the personalities of these women and of the impact of maternal character upon the development of children in multirisk families.

Our findings suggest that psychiatric factors and disturbed psychosocial functioning play a large role in the lives of this high-risk population, which represents, we believe, one of the major public health challenges of our time. Working with our families, we discovered a disturbing pattern among study participants. They had been born into families whose social and emotional functioning was seriously compromised. As children, they began to display marked impairment in their own psychosocial development. As adults, they bore children whose functioning seemed already compromised in the earliest years of life.

This chapter does not attempt to unravel the complex web of interrelationships between the various life events it describes. We hope, however, that this picture of what our participants looked like when they joined our program may contribute to a more sophisticated understanding of the problems of multirisk families.

Evaluation of Risk

The CIDP set out to recruit a sample of women presenting significant difficulties in providing adequate mothering for their children. Because "difficulties in mothering" does not constitute a clear and distinct diagnostic category we chose to cast as wide a net as possible and not build in strict inclusion criteria a priori; that is, we chose to think about "difficulties in mothering" as a syndrome rather than as a unitary dimension. In this way we opened our doors to all of those women who for one reason or another the community of health and social service providers viewed as worrisome.

We imposed only three criteria on prospective participants for our program:

1. All had to reside at the time of entry into the program in Prince Georges County, Maryland, a county close to Washington, D.C., which is a mixture of urban, suburban, and rural areas, contains families of many different socioeconomic levels, and is ethnically diverse.
2. All prospective participants had to have at least one child already born so that we could observe and evaluate maternal functioning.
3. All had to be pregnant at the time of referral, preferably no further advanced than the second trimester, and to have decided against obtaining an abortion.

Forty-seven women were eventually recruited into our program and, after evaluation, were considered at significant risk for failure to provide adequate mothering for the child they were carrying at the time of evaluation. An additional group of 14 women was recruited but, after evaluation, was not considered "at risk for difficulties in mothering." This low-risk group does not constitute a true control and will be described separately.

Our evaluation of each prospective participant focused on three major areas:

1. The developmental status of the woman's existing children.
2. The degree to which observed compromises in maternal

functioning would adversely affect the care provided for the unborn child.

3. The mother's status on several dimensions bearing on maternal functioning.

The evaluation was based on clinical interviews with the mother, observations of maternal and child functioning, free-play observations at home and at our office, clinical assessments of existing children, psychological testing of the mother, and the records or reports of other agencies. The evaluation was arrived at through consensus of senior clinicians in the CIDP.

1. *Developmental Status of Existing Children.* In order for us to find the developmental status of the existing child (or children) insufficient, we needed to see evidence of significant impairment on a major line of development. Such lines of development include the ability for appropriate functioning in human relationships, the capacity for reality testing, impulse regulation, focused concentration, learning and overall cognitive functioning.

2. *Status on Maternal Functioning.* Three primary maternal functions were assessed: (a) the mother's capacity to provide physical care and protection for her children; (b) her capacity to maintain an ongoing emotional relationship with the children; (c) the mother's capacity for differentiated awareness of signs of distress and pleasure in her children. Significant impairment in at least one of these three functions was considered evidence of compromised functioning.

We also made clinical judgments of three more highly differentiated areas of maternal functioning: (1) the mother's ability to read the emerging needs of her child (e.g., need for increased autonomy); (2) the capacity to respond in an appropriate and flexible fashion to the needs of her children (e.g., handling phase appropriate aggression or sexuality in an accepting manner); (3) the ability to function with appropriate empathy. If there was no impairment in any of the three primary functions, we considered across-the-board impairment in the more finely differentiated categories as evidence of compromised functioning.

Recruitment Procedures

Two procedures were employed to identify participants: individual referral and open recruitment. In the individual referral procedures, various facilities throughout the county were notified that we were interested in offering periodic developmental assessment and, in selected cases, diagnostic and therapeutic services to expectant mothers. We emphasized that we were especially interested in working with their "most difficult and challenging" women, who had experienced difficulties mothering previous children and who might be expected to have problems with mothering the child they were expecting. We made clear that we were quite willing, in fact eager, to work with families that were considered by traditional health and social service agencies to be hard to reach, and would "go anywhere to see anyone" in the county, including people who had not used the traditional service system easily or with great success. No one would be turned away due to the severity of the presenting problem. This message was conveyed to prenatal clinics, social service agencies, protective services, state mental hospitals, community mental health agencies, and the police.

Soon we were getting calls from prenatal clinics regarding mothers who had missed appointments, appeared confused, and were not adequately following medical guidance, and from protective service workers involved with a family because of neglect of an older child in which the mother was pregnant again and evidencing a lack of interest in her yet unborn new baby.

The second procedure, open recruitment, used two approaches. In the first, a clinician from our program, usually a psychiatric social worker or a nurse, would visit a prenatal clinic and give a talk describing our program. Mothers who expressed interest were then invited for further screening. In the second form of open recruitment, clinicians made regular visits to the county prenatal clinics in hopes of identifying a possible participant. The clinician would approach likely candidates directly, and if they were interested further screening would follow.

We used open recruitment because social agency staff were often too busy to consider a referral, get written consent from the patient, and complete the referral process. Our presence at the clinics saved them time and allowed us to make a direct approach to mothers who would otherwise be suspicious or reluctant to have a stranger contact them. Further, we could be helpful to the agency staff through informal consultations. Regular contacts and visits were maintained with all referring agencies for the duration of the program.

Identifying potential participants was only the first step in the recruitment procedure. In some cases repeated visits and outreach were needed before mothers consented to sign up for the program. In other cases mothers signed consent forms immediately but did not intend to participate and needed to be pursued.

The key to recruitment and forming an alliance with these families was the staff's ability to deal with patterns of avoidance, rejection, anger, illogical and antisocial behavior, and substance abuse. Experienced clinicians were selected, in part, because they were not frightened by such behavior. For example, in the early phases of the work it might be necessary for the primary clinician on a case to make five to six home visits, knock on the door, hear a very suspicious participant behind the door walking around, make a few comments through the door, not get an answer, and then return three days later and continue the pattern until the individual on the other side of the door would feel comfortable enough to open the door and let the primary clinician in. This pattern might repeat itself intermittently for a number of months. Even more difficult were participants who eagerly embraced the offering of services and who then would "flee" by missing three of four appointments, including not calling or returning telephone calls. The continual offering of an interested ear would in most cases eventually meet with success. Sometimes a year would pass, however, before a constant pattern of relatedness would evolve. Meanwhile, the staff had to work hard to resist the tendency to say, "they're not interested in help," "they told us they don't want us," "they're not motivated," "we're being a burden to them," or "we're making them more crazy."

In order to maintain the mothers who had agreed to participate in our program, we needed to develop a regular pattern of services. This included (1) organizing service systems on behalf of survival needs such as food, housing, and medical care; (2) a constant emotional relationship with the family; and (3) most importantly, the offer of highly technical patterns of care geared to the infant's and family's individual vulnerabilities and strengths at crucial times when the infant's development was in jeopardy. For example, a baby with a tactile hypersensitivity, with a hyperactive, suspicious mother who tended to deal with stress by hyperstimulating her baby, would require an approach in which the baby was provided with habituation and sensory integration approaches to overcome his or her special sensitivity. The mother was simultaneously helped through psychological treatment, counseling or guidance (Fantl, 1958), to overcome her own tendency to undermine the baby's development.

Recruitment and Referral of the Sample

The greater part of our sample (64 percent) was referred to us through general medical facilities in the country. In spite of the fact that we wound up with a sample of women, the majority of whom evidenced histories of considerable psychiatric distress, only 17 percent were referred by mental health facilities. The remaining mothers were referred by social service agencies (11 percent), self-referred, or referred by another participant (6.4 percent).

GROUP ASSIGNMENT

After the evaluation procedure and during the prenatal period, participants were classified as either low or high risk for difficulties in mothering. Fourteen mothers were classified as low risk and were assigned to group A. Forty-seven women were evaluated to be at high risk for disorders of mothering. These women were assigned to one of two groups; Group B, the community referral group, or Group C, the comprehensive treatment group. Group B received clinical, developmental, and psychosocial assessments and feedback and were then referred to the community agency or agencies best suited to meet their particular needs. Group C received the same evaluations as the other women but were then offered the intervention resources of the CIDP. The index children of all three groups were systematically assessed at regular intervals with the identical research protocol.

We were only partially successful in our attempt to assign high-risk cases to groups B and C in sequence. No assignments were made to group B until we already had 10 participants because in the early stages of the program it was not yet clear to which agencies the outside referrals could be made. Sequential assignments also broke down in one instance in which the participant evidenced such extreme pathology that it would have been unethical to withhold immediate treatment ourselves. It is for these reasons, in part, that we had 30 participants in the C and only 17 in the B group. In addition to the 47 high-risk mothers and the 14 low-risk mothers, 29 women signed consent forms but refused to participate immediately or soon afterwards. Since all of these dropped out prenatally, we had insufficient information about them to analyze in a meaningful way.

Race

The distribution of race across the two groups was black, 57.4 percent and white, 42.6 percent. There was no significant difference in the distribution of the black and white participants across the B and C groups (chi-square + .203, P = .652).

Age

The median age of our participant at entry was 23.9 years. The mean age was 25.12, sd = 5.0. The range went from 18 to 36 years of age at time of entry into the program.

TABLE 8-1
Religion

Protestant	51.0% (24)
Catholic	17.0% (8)
Adventist/Witness	4.3% (2)
No Preference	27.7% (13)

Education

The level of education varied. More than half of the participants (57.8 percent) had no more than 11th grade education, 28.7 percent graduated from high school, and 13.3 percent had gone beyond high school.

Reproductive History

PARITY

By definition, any woman participating in the program had to have had at least one child prior to the one she was carrying when she entered the program. The median number of children born prior to entry into the program was 2.0 (mean 2.15, sd = 1.3). The range was from 1 to 6.

TABLE 8-2.
Parity: Number of Children Before Entry into Program

1	38.0% (18)
2	29.8% (16)
3	17.0%
4	4.3% (2)
5	6.4% (3)
6	2.1% (1)

INITIATION OF SEXUAL ACTIVITY

The average age of menarche for this group was 12.5, sd = 20; an unexceptional figure. The median age reported for first sexual intercourse was 15.8 with a range of 12 years (ages 9 through 21). There was an interval of almost two years between the median age of first reported intercourse and the median age of first pregnancy. Median age at first pregnancy was 17.36 with a range of 19 years (ages 14 to 33).

ABORTION

Slightly more than one-third (37.8 percent [17]) of these women had chosen to have an elective abortion at some time prior to joining the program, while 62.2 percent (28) did not.

TABLE 8-3
Spontaneous Abortions and Miscarriages

None	1 (8)	2 (2)	3 (1)
75.6%	17.8%	4.4%	2.2%

Status of Relationships

At the time of entry into the program the marital status amongst the participants was as follows: 44.7 percent (21) were single; 34 percent (16) were married; 17 percent were divorced or widowed; 4.3 percent were separated.

The majority of the participants for whom we had such information had known the father of the index child for more than one year by the time they entered the program: 70.3 (26/37).* In almost a third of the cases (31 percent) the participant and the father of the child had been together for more than three years. Almost all of these women reported maintaining ongoing relationships with the fathers of the index children. In 62 percent of the cases the relationship was char-

*All percentages are calculated on the basis of available information. It is for this reason that the denominator is not always 47 and also why we provide the full figure for the reader.

acterized by the participant as one in which the father of the child was consistently present (28/45). In 31 percent of the cases, the father of the child was said to be present only sporadically and not on any stable basis. In 7 percent of these cases, the father of the child was said to be entirely out of the picture.

Sources of Support

The majority of these women depended upon more than a single individual or system to meet their own and their children's needs for food, clothing, shelter, and other necessities.

GOVERNMENT SUPPORT

At the time of entry into the program, slightly more than half (51.5 percent [23/45]) of the participants were receiving Aid to Families with Dependent Children (AFDC). If one also considers other sources of governmental assistance (AID, food stamps, etc.) the percentage of our participants receiving some form of concrete support from a government agency or program increases to 64.4 percent (19/45).

FATHERS OF INDEX CHILDREN

The fathers of index children provided some degree of concrete support in 80 percent of the cases (36/45). This support was described as "consistent" by the participant in 47 percent of the cases and as erratic in 33 percent of the cases. The fathers of the children were described as providing no support at all in 20 percent of the cases (9/45).

FAMILIES OF ORIGIN

The families of origin provided some measure of concrete support in two-thirds (66.6 percent) of the cases (30/45). In about half (46 percent) of these cases the families were described as providing support in a consistent manner: (21/45). In 20 percent of the cases the participant described the support given by her family of origin as inconsistent (9/45). In a third of the cases the participant reported no concrete support at all from her family (15/45).

Almost a quarter (26.8 percent) of the participants described themselves as regularly utilizing nongovernmental sources of support such as Goodwill, the Salvation Army, or various churches (11/45).

At the time of entry into the program only 13 percent (6/45) of our participants were employed. To some degree, this low figure is due to the fact that all of the women were pregnant at the time of entry into the program. In addition, some proportion of the women were full-time homemakers. In part, however, the low rate of employment in this sample would seem to be typical of the general difficulty our participants experienced in meeting successfully the routine demands of living.

The Past: Antecedent Variables

We were very interested in understanding the past lives of our mothers and wanted to identify those antecedent factors which may have contributed to their high-risk status and maternal difficulties. But collecting data and summarizing information regarding our high-risk mothers was no easy matter. We were reaching out to women who, for the most part, had not sought psychiatric services and were often suspicious, scared, or alienated from "helping professionals." We learned early in the program that asking questions was not enough and that research approaches using traditional interview techniques would not yield the information we needed to understand the antecedent variables which contributed to the status of these high-risk mothers. As the mothers saw things, they had only consented to participate in a program for babies; they either did not understand why we were asking so many questions and what these had to do with the baby, or were too depressed and overwhelmed to care to answer our inquiries. Further, few of these mothers saw any use in talking about themselves or their children and had not experienced talking as emotionally meaningful in the past.

In contrast to most research approaches, therefore, we decided to place our initial emphasis on helping our mothers with existing children or the pregnancy rather than trying to uncover past history. We asked these mothers what help they needed and tried to be useful so that they would permit us to visit and observe again. Since so many were struggling with survival, we could always find ways of being helpful through concrete services; these became the vehicle to learning more about the participants as well as evaluating their psychiatric status and mothering capacities. As the mothers became more comfortable with us during the prenatal phase, most could answer more questions, take psychological tests, and be observed behind a one-way mirror. But because many had great difficulty revealing those parts of their past lives which were embedded in secrecy or feelings of shame and pain, information about early abandonment, family mental illness, abuse, or incest often did not emerge until a strong therapeutic relationship had developed. For these reasons we did not attempt to summarize the details from the past until well into our study. Instead, we evaluated each mother through the therapeutic engagement process and only obtained historical information as trust developed.

The antecedent variables described below pertain only to the point at which the mothers entered CIDP, that is, before the birth of the index child. The variables were recorded on a present or absent basis. Unless indicated, there were no significant differences in the incidence between group B (community referral) and group C (CIDP intervention). These variables represent the historical antecedents we considered relevant to maternal experiences and functioning. Even allowing for information which emerged over the course of treatment there were still instances in which the mother either did not know, or did not care to reveal information, or in which we had no opportunity to ascertain specific items because the mother had moved or dropped out of the program. It is therefore probably safe to say that the listed incidence of most of the antecedent variables represents a conservative estimate of reality.

The profile of the typical mother in our study, then, reveals a woman who was born into a family experiencing psychiatric dysfunction, who had difficulties as a child, who continues to experience psychosocial dysfunction as an adult, and, finally, who has children beginning to experience problems early in life. In sum, most of the women we classified as high risk had experienced multiple psychiatric misfortunes before they entered the program. We believe they represent accurately the hard-to-reach, high-risk mothers we set out to recruit and who have never been systematically described before.

Presence of Psychiatric Disorder in Family of Origin

Almost two-thirds of our mothers (64.3 percent, 27/42) came from families with a history of psychiatric disorder, as evidenced by treatment of family member for a specific disorder; evidence of an untreated psychosis; severe character disorder, manifested by substance abuse; or an attempted or successful suicide. While this rate is substantial, because it was based principally on participant's reports, it seems likely that the true incidence of psychiatric disorder in families of origin is even greater.

PSYCHIATRIC HOSPITALIZATION

Slightly more than one-third (34 percent, 16/47) of the participants had experienced at least one hospitalization for psychiatric reasons. Those women who had been hospitalized were significantly more likely to have come from families which had been rated psychiatrically impaired ($\chi^2 = 6.2$, p

= .01). Of the 16 women who had been hospitalized two to four times, four had had four or more episodes. While most were hospitalized during psychotic episodes, others were admitted briefly for acute anxiety states or following rape, assault, or a suicide attempt. There were significantly more participants with histories of psychiatric hospitalization in the C Group than in the B Group (χ^2 = 3.01, p = .10).

Prior Contact with Mental Health Providers

Forty-five percent (21/47) of our participants, including the 34 percent (16/47) who were hospitalized, had had some form of contact with mental health providers. If we remove from consideration the 16 participants who were hospitalized, only 5 of the remaining 31 (61 percent) had any contact with mental health providers. These contacts included participating in the psychiatric evaluation or intake of other family member or child. Only two of these mothers had ever been involved in counseling and none in long-term psychotherapy.

We, however, considered all 31 of these women to be high risk and in need of psychiatric intervention. The ratio of those needing treatment but untreated to those who had some contact was 5 to 1 (26:5). This ratio supports our contention that we succeeded in reaching women who had been served by traditional providers short of hospitalization. We would also emphasize here that hospitalization was in itself no guarantor of continuing quality treatment for these women.

Physical Abuse, Physical Neglect, Sexual Abuse

The incidence of abuse of our participants was sobering. It was also striking that most of this information was revealed only through the longitudinal course of clinical work with our mothers. Years passed before we realized just how many women had experienced some form of abuse. We looked at five categories of abuse, three relating to the participant's life before 18 and two after 18.

DIRECT PHYSICAL ABUSE AND/OR SEVERE NEGLECT OF THE PARTICIPANT BEFORE AGE 18

We included reports of severe and persistent beatings before the age of 18. These beatings need not have been reported to the authorities but must have resulted in marks, scars, or other reportable evidence of abuse. We also included severe neglect (such as deprivation of food, shelter, and the basic needs) which may have resulted in foster or other family placement. Slightly less than half of the participants, 44.7 percent (21/47) fell into this category.

SEXUAL ABUSE OF THE PARTICIPANT BEFORE AGE 18

Thirty-two percent of the women (15/47) reported histories of sexual abuse before age 18. We included reports of sexual abuse, molestation, or incest by family members, boyfriends of mothers, and other persons known to the family, and reports of rape by strangers.

WITNESSING THE ABUSE OF OTHER MEMBERS OF HER FAMILY BY PARTICIPANT BEFORE 18

Thirty-eight percent (18/47) of our mothers were included in this category. The criteria for abuse used here were the same as that used for the first category above, but applied to other family members. Membership in this category does not rule out membership in the other categories but was counted as a separate category because of the clearly traumatic impact on our mothers of witnessing the abuse of others.

PHYSICAL ABUSE OF THE PARTICIPANT AFTER AGE 18

Over half of the women in this sample, 52.2 percent (25/47), reported being subjected to physical abuse during their adult lives. This included beatings and sexual abuse by mates or family members. Although some of the women had sought refuge in shelters for battered women or pressed charges, such action was not a necessary condition for inclusion in this category.

PHYSICAL ABUSES AND/OR NEGLECT OF OWN CHILDREN

Almost half of our mothers (45 percent) were physically abusive and/or neglectful to their own children (21/47). We included in this category participants who were reported to abuse their own children directly, who were present while another person abused them, or who allowed others to abuse them out of their presence. Severe physical beating, and punishment or neglect which resulted in injury to the child through burns, falls, and the like, were counted as abuse.

If we adjust for overlap amongst the first three categories, we find, in sum, that two-thirds or 66 percent (31/47) of the women classified as high risk for disorders of mothering had experienced some form of abuse while growing up. Not surprisingly, this early abuse correlated significantly with abuse in adult life, supporting the contention that being abused as a child leads to abuse as an adult. The correlation between a woman having been physically abused as a child and becoming abusive toward her own children was $r = .31$ ($p = .017$), accounting for 10 percent of the variance between abusing and nonabusing mothers. The correlation between witnessing abuse and being abusive was even stronger, $r = .44$, $p = .001$. Together, 20 percent of the variance is accounted for. Further, a significant relationship was found between being abused as a child and being abused as an adult, $r = .33$, $p. = .012$. This correlation is even higher when we include those participants who witnessed abuse, $r = .48$, $p = .001$, accounting for almost 25 percent of the variance between abusing and nonabusing mothers. The high incidence of abuse also led us to examine this variable in relation to race and income, but here no significant relationships were found. The only correlation which approached significance was between the participant's physical abuse/neglect of her own children and her income level. Women in the lower income category were somewhat more likely to be abusive ($r = .20$, $p. = .09$). This, however, is not a very substantial relationship.

Disruption of Significant Relationship Prior to Age 12

On the assumption that object losses during childhood would contribute to the high-risk status of our mothers, we examined the disruption of significant relationships prior to adolescence. We found, in fact, that 69 percent (31/47) experienced such disruptions before the age of 12. Disruption was defined as the occurrence of an unexpected and relatively enduring separation from a nuclear family member or surrogate parent, although not necessarily through death. For example, if parents divorced and one moved out of state and did not maintain contact with the participant, we counted these events as a significant disruption. If, on the other hand, parents divorced but the participant was able to maintain contact with both parents, we did not list a disruption. It should be kept in mind that this item is only concerned with the disruption of a relationship and does not speak at all to the quality of that relationship. Grandparents were also excluded so as not to inflate our figures with losses that, while perhaps meaningful, would be common to a wide variety of children and not simply characteristic of this high-risk group.

In 78 percent of the cases where disruption did occur, it came about through death, abandonment, or placement in a home other than that of the participant's parents. In only 22 percent of the cases where there was disruption did it occur

TABLE 8-4
Patterns of Abuse

Abuse of or by Mother	
Exposed to Abuse below Age 18	66.0% (31/47)
Physical Abuse or Severe Neglect	44.7% (21/47)
Sexual Abuse	32.0% (15/47)
Witnessed Abuse of Other Family	38.0% (18/47)
Above Age 18	
Abused by Partners or Other Family	53.2% (25/47)
Abuses or Severely Neglects Children	45.0% (21/47)

through the divorce of the parents. Fifteen and a half percent (7/45) of our participants had been placed in foster settings at least once before age 12.

Psychosocial Functioning

In keeping with our interest in the antecedent variables contributing to the high-risk status of our mothers, we examined their adjustment during childhood and adolescence. Our findings are based on the clinicians' process notes and debriefing interviews during several years of work with participants.

PSYCHOSOCIAL FUNCTIONING BEFORE AGE 18

We evaluated three areas of psychosocial functioning before and after the age of 18: within the family, within the peer group, and at school or work. Seventy-nine percent (34/43) of our women were judged to have been impaired in at least one of these areas before age 18. Seventy-six percent (32/42) were judged to be impaired in one or more of these areas after the age of 18. Of the 32 participants who were rated as impaired in adulthood, 94 percent (30/32), were also rated as having been impaired in childhood. For this group of women, at least, time did not heal all wounds.

FAMILY FUNCTIONING BEFORE AGE 18

Seventy-three percent of the women (32/44) were deemed impaired in this category, defined as the presence of one of the following repeated episodes (three or more) of running away from home, violent outbursts in the home, chronic argumentativeness in the home, chronic rule breaking as the predominant ongoing daily characteristic of home life, or being the object of physical/sexual abuse.

FUNCTIONING IN PEER GROUP BEFORE 18

Half of the women (20/40) were rated as impaired in this category, which included difficulties in making and/or keeping friends, being scapegoated by peers, "purchasing" of friendship through inappropriate means, or having been labeled a bully by the peer group.

FUNCTIONING IN SCHOOL

Almost half (49 percent, 21/43) of the women experienced significant difficulties in school. This high proportion appeared to exceed what would be expected on the basis of estimated cognitive capacity. The criteria for impaired school functioning were: repetition of at least two grades, failure to perform to level of estimated IQ, and a history of chronic school phobia and/or truancy.

A significant relationship was found between psychiatric hospitalization as an adult and impaired psychosocial functioning before age 18. As many as 93 percent of those participants who were hospitalized as adults were rated as having been impaired in childhood (14/15, $\chi^2 = 3.85$, p = .05). Only nine women were judged to be without significant impairment in family, peer, and school functioning before age 18 (21 percent, 9/43). It remains to be seen whether the psychological profiles of these women and their course and outcome in the CIDP is markedly different from those deemed impaired in childhood.

FAMILY FUNCTIONING AFTER AGE 18

Seventy-eight percent of our mothers were rated as being significantly impaired in their functioning within their own families after age 18 (35/44). A finding of impaired functioning was based upon the presence of one or more of the following: the participant's inability, at times, to provide food or clothing for her children; involvement in serious and chronic arguments with other family members; physical or sexual abuse of her children; or periodic withdrawal, with children left unattended. Because these criteria are fairly coarse, not all of the participants were rated as being impaired in family functioning, even though close clinical assessment of maternal functioning had judged *all* the participants to be impaired enough to warrant inclusion in the high-risk group.

PEER GROUP FUNCTIONING AFTER AGE 18

Forty-nine percent (20/41) of the women were impaired in their functioning within their peer group at the time they entered the program. Impaired functioning was based on the inability to establish meaningful relationships outside of the family or on relationships with peers which involved being scapegoated or otherwise taken advantage of. Once again, the criteria were gross and probably underestimated the true incidence of disordered functioning in the peer group.

WORK FUNCTIONING

Forty percent (17/42) were judged to be impaired in their ability to work. This was evidenced by frequent job changes, chronic argumentativeness at their place of employment, holding a job significantly below what one would expect on the basis of education, or on history of work outside the home even though the participant was not occupied as a primary homemaker.

ANTISOCIAL BEHAVIOR

While a number of our mothers had difficulties with impulse control and regulation, only a relatively small proportion of women were deemed to be chronically antisocial, 17.5 percent, 7/40. We used the criteria for antisocial character disorder specified in the *Diagnostical Statistical Manual* (DSM-III), including a history of continuous and chronic antisocial behaviors in which the rights of others are violated. Apart from the question of true psychopathy, 23 percent (8/35) of our participants had been expelled from school and 32.5 percent were judged to have been chronic rule violators at home and/or at school prior to age 15.

Twenty-four percent (10/42) of our mothers were rated as unimpaired in psychosocial functioning as adults according to the above criteria even though we considered them to be high risk. As indicated above, we believe this was due to the gross criteria used, and it remains to be seen whether the clinical course and outcome of this group of participants is significantly different from those judged to be impaired.

TABLE 8-5

Psychosocial Functioning

All Areas		
Below 18	79%	(34/43)
Above 18	76%	(32/42)
Both above and below	94%	(30/32)
Family		
Below 18	73%	(32/44)
Above 18	78%	(35/44)
Peer Group		
Below 18	50%	(20/40)
Above 18	49%	(20/41)
School or Work		
Below 18	49%	(21/43)
Above 18	40%	(17/42)

THE INDEX OF MISFORTUNE

The incidence of traumatic events in the lives of the women we found to be high risk is remarkable. Clearly, as a group they represent the "multirisk" individuals referred to and often stereotyped in professional literature.

In order to capture, if only in a limited fashion, the degree to which multiple risk or antecedent variables come together for each individual participant, we constructed an index of occurrence of such events in the lives of these women prior to their entry into the program. The index is simply a frequency count of the occurrence of 18 misfortunes represented by the antecedent variables divided by 18 to derive a percentage. Thus, an index of 0 would indicate that none of these particular misfortunes had occurred in the life of the individual while an index of 1 would indicate that all of the events had occurred. The antecedents are listed in Table 8-6.

TABLE 8-6
Antecedent Variables Utilized in the Index of Misfortune

1. History of psychiatric illness in participant's family of origin
2. Psychiatric hospitalization
3. Physical abuse/neglect of participant before age 18
4. Physical abuse of participant before age 18
5. Sexual abuse of participant before age 18
6. Witness of the abuse of others before age 18
7. Physically abused by mate
8. Participant physically abuses/neglects her own children
9. Disruption of significant relationship before age 12
10. Impaired functioning in family before age 18
11. Impaired functioning in peer group before age 18
12. Impaired functioning in school before age 18
13. Impaired functioning in family after age 18
14. Impaired functioning in peer group after age 18
15. Impaired functioning in work after age 18
16. Chronic antisocial behavior
17. Expelled from school
18. Chronic rule violator at home/at school before age 15

An examination of the index of misfortune (Table 8-7) provides convincing evidence that our participants do indeed belong to the category of multirisk, multiply traumatized individuals. Rather than a negative exponential distribution as might be expected in the case of events of relative rarity, the index is distributed almost normally. The median value of the index is .49 (mean = 47). What this means is that 50 percent of these women experienced nine or more of these misfortunes before they entered the program. In contrast, the median value for the index of misfortune for the low-risk group is .09 (Group A). That is, the women in the low-risk group generally

TABLE 8-7
Index of Misfortune

PCT	N	LOW BND
2.1	1	.0000
6.4	3	.0497
2.1	1	.0994
.0	0	.1491
4.3	2	.1988
4.3	2	.2485
4.3	2	.2982
10.6	5	.3480
12.8	6	.3977
4.3	2	.4474
14.9	7	.4971
8.5	4	.5468
10.6	5	.5965
4.3	2	.6462
2.1	1	.6959
2.1	1	.7459
2.1	1	.7953
.0	0	.8450
4.3	2	.8947

Total N = 47   Valid N = 47

had none of these events occur in their lives. In fact the maximum value for the index of misfortune in the low-risk group is .21, 3.7 occurrences. In contrast, 15 percent of the high-risk women had an index of .65 or more; that is, experiencing almost 12 of the 18 events prior to joining the program.

The index of misfortune is intended to serve as an efficient means of describing our participants in terms of an array of life events which may be related to psychiatric disorder. In addition, however, we would expect that this index will serve as a predictor of certain outcomes in mother and child. Thus, we anticipate a linear relationship between maternal index of misfortune and the index child's development. We intend to explore the relationship between this maternal index on a variety of maternal and child outcomes in a future paper. We should note at this time that there was a moderate relationship between the index of misfortune and the rating of maternal functioning ($r = -.34$, $p = .01$) and also between the index and the participant's capacity to engage in a therapeutic relationship ($r = -.34$, $p = .01$). The fact that our index correlates, though moderately, with these two independent measures of psychiatric status at entry leads us to believe that it may have some predictive utility.

Psychiatric Status at Entry: Clinical Ratings

The initial clinical evaluation of each mother was conducted during the first four to six contacts with her. As was indicated above, these evaluations were not conducted in the traditional format of psychiatric interviews in an office setting but in the process of engaging and forming relationships with the mothers while responding with help they wanted. During meetings in their homes or while taking participants to health or social service agencies our clinicians could ask questions and make observations of their general and maternal functioning. This would lead to more formal opportunities for interviews, testing, and observations in our office. Each contact was reported in narrative process form. Although the course each evaluation took varied somewhat from mother to mother, the information gathered, when summarized, resulted in a complete psychiatric evaluation and a team consensus on the risk status, group assignment, and diagnosis of the mother. All clinical evaluations, with one exception, were completed during the last trimester of the participants' pregnancies.

Because we could not use the form of the clinical evaluations for quantitative purposes, we devised an independent and objective evaluation by a team of clinicians who had no previous contact with the mothers in order to validate our clinical assignment and to quantify various psychiatric dimensions for statistical purposes.

We developed 20 rating scales (see Table 8-8) which represented the psychological and functional issues we considered most pertinent to understanding the maternal functioning and experiences of our high-risk women and were derived from our theories of development and intervention. The 20 ratings pertained to four major dimensions: (1) overall devel-

TABLE 8-8
Clinical Rating Scales

I. Overall Developmental Level
   1. Regulation and control of drive, affect, and impulse
   2. Defensive functioning
   3. Overall developmental level
II. Maternal Identification and Capacities
   1. Capacity for nurturance
   2. Capacity for symbolic and representational thinking
   3. Capacity for reading complex affective signals
   4. Differentiation of maternal schema
   5. Integration of maternal schema into other parts of personality
   6. Self/object differentiation
   7. Valence of maternal schema
   8. Locus of control for maternal behavior
   9. Attitude toward pregnancy
III. Ability to Engage in Therapeutic Relationships
   1. Therapeutic relationship: process
   2. Therapeutic relationship: regularity and stability
   3. Therapeutic relationship: attachment
IV. Overall Risk and Future Prediction
   1. Global risk
   2. Maternal functioning
   3. Prediction to therapeutic process
   4. Prediction to attachment
   5. Prediction to regularity and stability

opmental level†; (2) maternal identification and capacities; (3) the ability to engage in therapeutic relationships; and (4) the overall risk status of the mother in terms of predicting her future on the basis of the three other dimensions. We realized there would be some overlap within the dimensions but felt they contributed independently to the mother's functioning. (See Appendix 2 for specific ratings.)

The ratings were constructed as visual analogue scales (Folstein and Luria, 1973).*

Procedure for the Ratings

Our team of raters consisted of four experienced doctoral level clinicians (three psychologists and a psychiatrist) all of whom were blind to outcome and did not know any of the participants personally. Three of the raters were brought in as consultants from outside the program; the fourth rater, though working in the program, was carefully screened from any contact with the participants and from attendance at any clinical conferences.

The material rated consisted of the first six process narratives dictated by the primary clinician from the time the participant entered the program to a point shortly before the birth of the index child. These narratives were generally lengthy and quite rich in detail. In the narratives the clinicians described what was known of the mother's life history, her current mode of behavior and affective life, her family situation, and the responses to the clinician and to the program in general. Because these reports were intended as clinical

†That is, a line 100 millimeters long was placed in the center of a piece of paper. On either side of the unbroken line was an anchor point with the extreme definitions written out. The raters' task was to make a mark on that point of the line which they felt corresponded to the degree to which a participant possessed the attribute which was being rated. A mark on the line was then assigned its equivalent in millimeters from the end of the line and this number was treated as a score. The range of possible scores was 99; that is from 1 to 100.

*The three scales of overall developmental level were patterned after scales developed by L. Bellak et al., 1973.

records, the sorts of events and the type of information given varies from record to record and from clinician to clinician. We felt, however, that the information available was sufficient to allow skilled clinicians to make judgments about psychiatric status. Both high- and low-risk mothers who had clinical evaluations were rated.

Seven cases were picked at random as training cases. During the initial training the raters met and rated cases together, attempting to achieve a group consensus and understanding of the meaning of the ratings and the use of the visual analogue scale as a rating instrument. After this task was accomplished the second step was the initial reliability check, during which raters rated 20 cases independently on all the ratings. Our initial reliabilities were satisfactory. In order to minimize halo effects we then utilized a randomized rating procedure on the remaining cases. The procedure involved: (1) splitting the cases in half randomly; (2) randomly assigning the four raters to two rating teams; and (3) assigning, on a random basis, two ratings to be rated; one by each team on half the cases. When each team had rated its half of the cases on one of the ratings they would then rate the other half on the second rating. After two ratings had been accomplished in this manner there was a complete rerandomization of teams and cases and two more of the remaining ratings were selected at random and the entire procedure repeated until all cases had been rated on all ratings. We used pairs of raters so that we could have a continuous assessment of drift at our weekly meetings. In the end, we achieved adequate reliability on all 20 scales (see Table 8-9).

Assignment of Risk Level Using the Entry Ratings: Two Independent Tests

As indicated above, the initial evaluation of the risk status of the mother and her assignment to the low-risk group (A) or one of the two risk groups (B, C) was accomplished through a standard clinical assessment. This assessment employed the

TABLE 8-9
Reliabilities for Ratings of Psychiatric Status at Entry
(Intraclass Correlations, N = 30)

	Alpha
1. Regulation and Control of Drive, Affect, and Impulse	.84
2. Defensive Functioning	.79
3. Overall Developmental Level	.89
4. Differentiation of Maternal Schema	.88
5. Self/Object Differentiation	.90
6. Integration of Maternal Schema	.88
7. Valence of Maternal Schema	.81
8. Locus of Maternal Schema	.90
9. Capacity for Nurturance	.90
10. Capacity for Reading Complex Affective Signals	.86
11. Capacity for Symbolic and Representational Thinking	.90
12. Attitude toward Pregnancy	.80
13. Maternal Functioning	.94
14. Therapeutic Relationships: Regularity and Stability	.80
15. Therapeutic Relationships: Attachment	.80
16. Therapeutic Relationships: Process Level	.84
17. Global Risk	.85
18. Prediction to Therapeutic Regularity and Stability	.84
19. Prediction to Therapeutic Attachment	.64
20. Prediction to Therapeutic Process	.79

clinical consensus of senior clinicians and supervisors working with the participant and with her children. At the time of the evaluation no attempt was made to quantify the judgment or determine the reliability of the judgment among the various clinicians. In order to cross-check our original group assignments we did two independent tests using only the entry ratings.

In the first analysis we employed a stepwise discriminant function procedure. The problem was to classify the cases on the basis of their entry ratings into high risk or low risk. The procedure was a stepwise analysis where the computer follows an iterative procedure in which the first variable put into the equation is that which provides the greatest degree of group discrimination when taken by itself. The next variable entered into the program is that which is the next best discriminator and so forth. It keeps adding variables until no further increment in discrimination between the groups is accomplished. In this analysis the criteria for discrimination was that set of variables which most minimizes Wilk's λ, a measure of the discriminating power contained in the variables. The *lower* the Wilk's λ, the higher the information content in the set of variables, that is, the greater their discriminating power. In this analysis, the program stopped entering variables when there was no significant reduction in Lambda upon the inclusion of new variables.

The stepwise discriminant analysis wound up using six of the 20 variables for the discriminant function. The standardized discriminant function is given below:

Regulation and control of drive, impulse, and affect	.689
Differentiation of self and object	− .624
Locus of control of maternal behavior	− .681
Global risk	− .357
Capacity for nurturance	1.068
Capacity for reading complex affective signals	.632

The canonical discriminant functions at the group means was: low risk, 2.43; high risk, − .70.

The canonical correlation for the discriminant function is .798. The square of this correlation indicates that approximately 64 percent of the variance in the discriminant function can be accounted for by group membership. This rather adequate discrimination is mirrored in the Wilk's λ of .36 for the variables ion the equation.

The essential fact in all of this is that the assignment to the high- and low-risk groups based on the entry ratings was nearly identical to the assignment made at the time of the participants' entry into the program. The discriminant function based upon the six entry ratings classified 95 percent of the cases with the same risk assignment that was made at time of entry into the program. Only one individual from the original high-risk group was reclassified as low risk on the basis of the ratings (that is, 2.2 percent) whereas two individuals who were initially low risk were classified as high risk on this basis (15.4 percent). This replication of group assignment using different raters and a different means of classification thus validates the original process of risk evaluation (see Table 8-10).

Although the discriminant function analysis of risk level using the entry ratings had provided support for the original assignment of participants into high and low risk, it was able to do so employing only six of the 20 ratings. The question remained as to whether the entire set of 20 ratings could discriminate between the high- and low-risk groups or whether any of the ratings would not discriminate between the high and low risk women. In order to answer these questions, we performed a Multivariate Analysis of Variance (Manova). The results, as expected, did not differ from those obtained in the discriminant analysis. The overall multivariate

TABLE 8-10
Classification of Mothers into Low- and High-Risk Groups Based on Clinical Ratings

| | | Predicted Group Membership | |
Actual Group	No. of Cases	Low Risk	High Risk
Low Risk	13	11 (84.6%)	2 (15.4%)
High Risk	45	1 (2.2%)	44 (97.8%)

Percent of cases correctly classified: 94.83%

test of significance gave results quite close to that of the discriminant analysis: Wilk's λ = .326; df = 20,37; F = 3.826; significance = .000. Over and above the multivariate result, the univariate tests of significance on each of the 20 ratings were all significant beyond .000. This means that each of the ratings had a significantly different mean score for the high- and the low-risk group.

Conclusion

We recruited our participants on the basis of demonstrated difficulty in providing adequate mothering rather than on the basis of identifiable psychiatric or psychosocial disability. Nevertheless, as this chapter makes clear, disorders in mothering in our sample more often than not occurred jointly with rather serious psychiatric and psychosocial morbidity. Over 75 percent of the women in our sample had psychosocial difficulties at the time they presented as well as historically. The adverse experiences we called the "index of misfortune" occurred exceedingly often to our women: 64 percent of our participants were born into families where identifiable and severe psychiatric dysfunction was present; there was a disruption in a significant relationship in 69 percent of our participants' lives before the age of 12 years; 66 percent of our participants were exposed, in some fashion, to physical and/or sexual abuse as children.

We do not propose that all women who have difficulty in providing adequate mothering come from the population which we have described. Our impression, however, of the developmental trends indicates that multirisk factor families are rarely able to negotiate an infant's development into the second year of life without difficulties which require specific treatment services.

While we do not suggest that every child who is experiencing developmental difficulties comes from a background similar to that of our mothers, we do suggest that our sample may represent an important segment of the population.

9

A Model for Comprehensive Preventive Intervention Services for Infants, Young Children, and Their Families

Stanley I. Greenspan, M.D.

The Clinical Infant Development Program's (CIDP) study of infants in multirisk families offered comprehensive service approaches to severely disturbed families in an effort to reverse maladaptive patterns which in some cases had persisted for generations. Because these families had not found it possible to use the traditional, sometimes fragmented, array of services in the community, our comprehensive effort combined either directly or through collaborating elements seldom found in a single agency. These included:

- services responding to concrete survival needs such as food, housing, and basic medical care;
- a planned effort to meet the need of the family and the child for an ongoing, trusting human relationship;
- specific clinical techniques and services that focused on the many lines of a child's development and that were tailored to the child's tasks at each developmental subphase; and
- a special support structure to provide, at one site, partial or full therapeutic day care for the child, innovative outreach

to the family, and ongoing training and supervision of program staff.

As we increased our understanding of the developmental challenges facing a young child and his family, we also acquired a basis for conceptualizing therapeutic intervention at both the service system and clinical levels.

Compelling empirical evidence does not yet exist as to whether what will be described below as a comprehensive preventive intervention model is indeed more effective than more traditional unidimensional programs. Unfortunately, comprehensive programs have been implemented so infrequently that research comparing them with other programs is nonexistent. However, there are strong theoretical reasons and much clinical experience to suggest that such programs have the best chance for success; particularly in multirisk families where both child and parent(s) are suffering from or at risk for physical, emotional, and/or cognitive impairment.

Rationale for a Comprehensive Intervention Model

The rationale supporting the need for comprehensive intervention program models is based on two primary assumptions, the first of which is that human development follows multiple patterns including, for example, physical and neurological growth, cognitive or intellectual development, the development of human relationships, and the capacity to organize and differentiate experience (coping and adaptive capacities). An intervention which accounts for the existence of multiple lines of development will approach a presenting problem in ways that will facilitate development in all areas of the infant's life. For example, a baby born with an auditory and/or tactile hypersensitivity will tend to withdraw when held or talked to. A comprehensive approach would combine gentle exposure to the potentially noxious stimuli in low doses with soothing experiences, such as rocking, and soothing sounds. Simultaneously, recognizing the youngster's tendency to withdraw, patterns of care would be taught to the parents to help them "woo" the baby into greater emotional relatedness. In contrast, an approach which focused only on "cognitive stimulation" might attempt to enliven a withdrawn, seemingly "slow" baby through sensorimotor stimulation. Yet if the infant actually suffers from sensory hypersensitivity, he or she could become even more irritable and less available for human relationships as a consequence of this type of intervention.

Furthermore, failure to account for multiple lines of development in infancy may lead to impairment at a later age even though problems are not pronounced during infancy. For example, a youngster who responds to human stimulation with irritability, rigidity, and gaze aversion may very well be alert and show interest in the inanimate world. From the point of view of physical and neurological development, such a youngster might develop adequate cognition during the first 12 to 18 months. However, the later development of human relationships and capacity to organize and differentiate animate experience (coping and adapting skills) might be severely impaired. Unfortunately, such impairments might not become clearly noticeable until the latter part of the second or early in the third year when unsocialized behavior or patterns of withdrawal (refusal to play with others) become evident.

A second assumption which forms the basis for a comprehensive intervention approach views the infant in a context that includes not only his or her own multiple lines of development, but also mother, father, other family members, and relevant social structures. This might be termed an interactional (as opposed to an isolated) approach. An interactional intervention incorporates the parents' predominant attitudes and feelings, family relationships, and other crucial contextual factors, such as the system of health and mental health services and relevant community structures. More "isolated" intervention strategies, while working, for example, to stimulate an infant's cognitive capacities, may limit intervention with parents to help only with issues such as food and housing.

Based on the foregoing two assumptions, a comprehensive intervention approach would include a regular pattern of services and the following: (1) organizing existing service systems (e.g., food, housing, and medical care) on behalf of the family's survival needs; (2) providing a constant emotional relationship with the family; and (3) most importantly, at pivotal junctures when the infant's development may be in jeopardy, providing highly technical patterns of care to deal with the infant's and family's individual vulnerabilities and strengths along multiple dimensions. As a part of this service pattern it is often useful to provide partial or full therapeutic day care for the child, innovative outreach to the family, and ongoing training and supervision of the program staff. We found it useful to visualize preventive service approaches as a pyramid (see Figure 9-1) which includes concrete survival services, an

FIGURE 9-1. The Service Pyramid

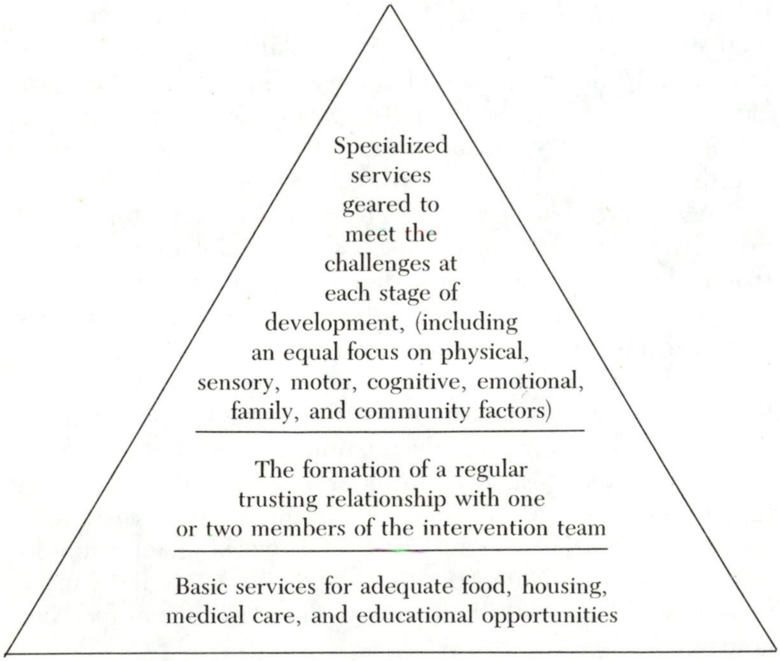

Specialized
services
geared to
meet the
challenges at
each stage of
development, (including
an equal focus on physical,
sensory, motor, cognitive, emotional,
family, and community factors)

The formation of a regular
trusting relationship with one
or two members of the intervention team

Basic services for adequate food, housing,
medical care, and educational opportunities

ongoing relationship and technical approaches). It is useful to think of service requirements in terms of the stages of a child's development (see Table 9-1). The tasks at each stage of development imply that certain components of the service system must be available to assure appropriate support for the function of that stage.

Homeostasis

At the base of the pyramid are certain essential services that involve the major elements of the services system. These must work cooperatively to facilitate an integrated approach to infants and their families. Thus, the tasks of homeostasis (i.e., a baby achieving regulation and interest in the world) imply providing adequate nutritional, medical, and overall physical care to the infant; providing a protective environment; and at the same time, providing an environment which permits the infant to engage the world in a comforting and self-regulating manner. These tasks imply certain essential support services, including optimal pediatric care, "good enough" housing, and, when necessary, legal protection on behalf of the infant: in sum, all the services that enhance human development. If infants' basic needs are to be met, service system planning at this level must be based, not on the easiest, but on the *most difficult* case; that is, the multiproblem, hard-to-reach family which does not make itself available to the traditional service system. Often only when a new infant comes to our attention through a protective service intervention with an older child, or through the public health nurses' involvement with neglected children does the service system become alert to the multiple service needs of such a family. The challenge here is to have each of the components of the service system working together synergistically.

In addition to all the social services (including protective

TABLE 9-1

Schematic Illustration of Levels of Development and Corresponding Service System Requirements and Expected Shifts in the Therapeutic Relationship

Time	Interagency Collaboration	Basic Requirements	Therapeutic Relationship
		Representation, Differentiation, and Consolidation	
24–40 months	Services to permit, as appropriate, more independent functioning and new relationships (e.g. nursery schools).	Facilitation of representational capacity and reality orientation.	Work on capacity to shift between fantasy and reality and integrate wide range of affective and thematic issues.
		Representational Capacity	
17–30 months	Services to permit direct psychotherapeutic work with toddler on as intensive basis as necessary.	Engagement of evolving representational (symbolic) capacities across a wide thematic and affective range.	Work on capacity to use and elaborate fantasy.
		Behavioral Organization, Initiative, and Internalization	
9–18 months	New services to permit direct exploratory work with the toddler now useful. Remedial educational approach should also be available.	Secure availability while admiring and supporting greater behavioral organization initiative and originality.	Further work on self-observing capacity permits integration of affective polarities around dependency and aggression and passivity and assertiveness.
		Somatopsychological Differentiation	
8–10 months	Services incl. educative and psychotherapeutic, and as necessary, auxiliary caretaker to facilitate reading of infant's communications.	Reads and responds contingently to range of affective and behavioral cues.	Includes work on capacity for self observation to facilitate empathetic reading of the "other."
		Attachment	
2–8 months	Special services to support consistent affective caretaker–infant relationship.	Rich investment in human world; woos and is wooed.	Evolves an attachment that survives negative feelings.
		Homeostasis	
0–2 months	Health, Mental Health, Social Service, Educational, Legal.	Protection, care, engagement in world.	Has a pattern that is predictable, regular, comforting.

service, the legal system, the education systems, and the health and mental health systems) working in an integrated manner, two more pivotal components are needed to offer the appropriate service in support of homeostatic capacities. The first involves active and skillful outreach programs with personnel who can make home visits on a daily basis, if necessary. The second, which we have found to be crucial to our work, is a project headquarters, such as an Infant Center, to which the most vulnerable multirisk families, often with severe psychopathology in the caretakers, can come every day. Here structure can be provided for parents and support offered for the vital needs of their infant. Here the infant can be worked with in the context of a supportive environment, and other adults are available to support the infant's need for physical care and protection and his capacity for regulation and engagement. This kind of care can often help the family avoid the cycle of foster care, which is not proving to be a viable alternative at this time in our country. Such integrated, extensive service patterns often make it possible for the family to attain the strength to stay together and to avoid the later patterns that can lead to severe debilitating psychological, social, and intellectual difficulties and even institutional care.

Attachment

The next level in the pyramid conceptualizes the services necessary to support the family's capacity to provide a satisfying, loving attachment for the growing infant. All the aforementioned services are needed, as well as specific services which may involve skilled psychotherapeutic support for the parents, and again, additional complimentary adult care for the infant. Systematic availability in the relationships with the parents should be established along with offers of help with practical issues such as housing, etc., in order to minimize acute stresses and resolve crises. When these stresses are eased, parents can become more available for involvement in a relationship with their new infant.

Somatopsychological Differentiation

At the third level in the pyramid, that of somatopsychological differentiation (i.e., helping the infant establish purposeful or "cause and effect" type communication patterns), in addition to the concrete services and the supportive intimate relationship which facilitates an attachment, specific clinical approaches must be made available in order to help a family read their infant's signals and respond emotionally and empathetically in a reciprocal manner. This is especially true for the most impaired families if they are to learn to observe both cognitive and emotional communications in their infant. In order to be able to observe these capacities in their infants, they must often be able to observe them first in themselves. Thus, the opportunity to establish a human relationship with a skilled clinician, where *the observing function and the capacity to observe their own feelings become possible, is essential*. As we have described earlier, this capacity is predicated on the parent(s) first having established a *warm and trusting enough* relationship with the clinician so that they can meet on a regular basis.

This relationship must be able to tolerate negative feelings such as disappointment and anger, without interrupting its regularity and certainty. It is the task of the service system to provide the sophistication necessary to enable a clinician to work with parents toward this self-observing function (which is not always possible for them to achieve at the emotional level). Sometimes, simple support in combination with educative approaches teaches parents at least to read the infant's signals at the cognitive level. However, the optimal goal for the self-observing function should continue to be cognitive *and* effective "observing" as this capacity is necessary to support all further stages of development. Infant specialists, nurses, and if necessary specially trained homemakers can facilitate the development of this capacity.

Behavioral Organization, Initiative, and Internalization

The next level of the pyramid, the fourth, is the stage of behavioral organization, initiative, and internalization. During this stage, the family is called upon not only to be able to read the baby's relatively "simple" emotional and cognitive signals, but now to understand complex emotional and social overtures and to interact in an organized reciprocal manner. They must now not only support the toddler's new behavior and emotional organization and emerging ability for greater autonomy (i.e., read the baby's emotional and cognitive signals), but also support the toddler's continuing dependency by being available for continuing nurturance. Here the capacity for reading more complex emotional signals is of prime importance. Parents must now be able to maintain the self-observing function over a wide range of affective experience and complicated behavioral patterns. In working with a woman with an underlying thought disorder, for example, we observed that she was capable of maintaining a self-observing function and reality orientation with simple communication. But once emotions became complicated (e.g., a mixture of love and aggression), she became overwhelmed, and her self-observing function and ability to read signals deteriorated. In such a case the individual must be engaged beyond the level of the basic attachment which permits and tolerates negative feelings and beyond the level of some limited capacity for self-observation. Individuals must be helped to strengthen their capacity for self-observation of their own emotional signals and to tolerate highly complex emotions (including ambivalence).

Unfortunately, many therapeutic programs often attempt this task only at the educative level, by teaching parents to read the more cognitively oriented communications of the toddler. It might be more useful to recognize that even "impersonal" communications take place in an emotional context and can therefore lead to confusion. The difficult goal of emotional understanding cannot be ignored, and should be striven for, even if the results are not perfect. In this instance, as with the earlier goals, the service system must now make available a new level on the pyramid—a specialized clinical team which operates at the educative as well as dynamic-emotional level and can help parents deal with and learn to observe and understand their own and their infant's and toddler's feelings and communications.

It is often not necessary for parents to resolve fully all their own difficulties (including conflicts, characterologic limitations, tendencies toward fragmentation, etc.) in order for them to maintain their observing function and be able to read correctly those aspects of their own emotional lives that infringe on their infant's or toddler's emotional life. If they can understand those areas of feelings that relate specifically to their relationships to their infants and toddlers and parallel aspects of their relationship to the therapist, other nonrelated areas can be dealt with later. Often this island of experience (e.g., therapist–parent–child) can be separated to some degree from the parent's other difficulties, particularly with the continuing support of the therapist, and the relationship with the infant–toddler can become facilitating and growth-producing for the toddler even when other relationships in the parents lives remain worrisome. In some sense, the therapist facilitates the relationship with the infant and toddler as a first step so that it may become relatively free from the more conflicted aspects of the caretaker's personality. Often direct work with a toddler in a toddler's group or on an individual basis (by a trained clinician-educator) can be helpful here. A free-play setting offers the opportunity to help the toddler deal with complex emotions and social interactions. Remedial occupational therapy or special education is indicated for sensory, motor, or language lags.

Representational Capacity

At the next level of the pyramid, the fifth, we observe the emergence of the young child's representational capacity (i.e., the ability to use ideas to label feelings and guide behavior) which becomes elaborated and then differentiated. Here, as we go another step higher in the pyramid, the service system must be able to support the parents' growing capacity for symbolic elaboration. Often we note that if we can help the parents represent their own experiences in *words, fantasies, and rich mental imagery*, they can then interact and engage their growing child in this mode. Where this is not possible, parents often maintain a concrete way of relating which undermines the natural development of the symbolic capacities in their toddlers and young children. At this level, the clinical service approach permits a therapeutic relationship to go on with the parents for a period of time sufficiently long to help them develop the capacity for mental imagery, if they never had that capacity in the first place, or when the parent's capacity for mental imagery is restricted by characterological limitations or conflict, to "liberate" this ability, at least in regard to the relationship with the toddler. This effort requires sophisticated therapeutic work, in which the parent's own fantasies are permitted to emerge. The parents are encouraged in their relationship with their therapist to observe their own way of handling fantasy and mental imagery, and, also, to become aware of this emerging capacity in their children. The important parallel is that if the parents can observe the function of fantasy and imagery in their relationship to the therapist, they can then understand how it may also relate to their child. Here, if necessary, direct work with the toddler in a free-play setting can offer an invaluable experience for the child to use his symbolic capacity in different emotional contexts (e.g., the hungry or mad or happy doll or bear).

Reality Orientation

The capacity for reality orientation and differentiation of representational capacities takes us to the sixth step in the pyramid. Here the task is not simply to help parents develop and elaborate mental imagery, but also to be able to differentiate that imagery which pertains to the outside world and that which pertains to their own inner life. With this differentiation they can begin to understand how to facilitate a similar reality orientation in their youngsters. It permits them to make pivotal judgments about when limit-setting is important, and when pointing out the reality of the situation is important, and when supporting the internal "make-believe" play of toddlers and children may be most useful. Although these subtle distinctions are not easy to make, healthy, competent parents make them intuitively.

When parents have characterologic constrictions, severe conflicts, or tendencies toward fragmentation, intensive therapeutic work may be required. The establishment or strengthening of these capacities in the caretakers may then serve as a foundation for the establishment in the child of such basic ego functions as reality testing, impulse regulation, mood stabilization, and a capacity for focused concentration and attention. Both preschool programs and individual therapy can provide opportunities for children to practice these new capacities.

We have outlined here six steps of a developmental pyramid. At the base of the pyramid is an integrated service system that can provide the services necessary to support the integrity of the family, including supplying missing pieces when necessary, in order to assure basic homeostatic capacities and early capacities for attachment. We have also noted that each step up the pyramid demands very specialized services to help facilitate the special developmental needs of the growing infant, toddler, and young child at that stage. It must be emphasized, for example, that for the 8-month-old child, simply helping the family with concrete supports, assuring adequate housing and nutrition, and helping to alleviate crises is often not sufficient to maintain development. The youngster now often needs more differentiated experience. In some families, where financial or other crises are interfering with an otherwise natural capacity to provide the "higher level" experiences, more concrete services may be all that are needed. In most cases we have observed, however, this is not so. Where individuals and/or families are chronically fragmented, disorganized, and in repetitive crises, a combination of the concrete services at the base of the pyramid to stabilize the family is only the first step. Then a successive number of specialized services are necessary to support the types of experiences needed to facilitate the child's growth at each stage of his or her development (e.g., reading of communications, representational elaboration and differentiation).

Most often, in our experience, we have found that the various levels of experience that need to be supported in the family can be made possible through a program that integrates the existing network of community support services. Such a clinical infant development program serves as a focal point for other community services. While providing, at each level of the pyramid, the specific kinds of technical expertise that will further the youngster's development, the program also provides an integrating focus for the total service system. As suggested, both a center and outreach capacities are necessary to augment more traditional program approaches, because the hardest to reach, most challenging families often require intensive daily care, and, depending on their level in the pyramid, highly specific clinical approaches.

It is well worth emphasizing that strengthening a family sometimes involves working directly with the youngster. This work, too, undergoes a number of successive stages, helping the youngster, when the parents cannot, to learn to engage the world and regulate; to become involved with people rather than just things; to read human communications; to take pleasure and pride in a growing behavioral organization and initiative; to use an emerging symbolic capacity, and to differentiate this capacity along adaptive lines. These are all tasks that can be enhanced through direct work with the infant and the young child, although it is more advantageous to the child to have the parents in the therapeutic program as well, and have them supporting their child's development. If the parents are not available during the important stages of the child's early development because of their own psychopathology or other circumstances, direct work with the youngster can help strengthen his adaptive capacities, enabling him often to be a "stronger team member" in the family unit. The child can then help the parents help him. For example, the youngster who sends his signals in a weak fashion, or who has a parent who does not read his signals at 8 months, may, through work with an infant specialist, be taught to strengthen his signals. He can then relate more readily to his depressed mother. As she gets more feedback from her child, she can be drawn out of her depression somewhat, and in turn relate to her infant more. Another example of such direct work involves the youngster at 22 months who has already had a history of difficulties and has a tendency toward negativistic avoidance and fragmented aggressive behavior. Using the existing symbolic modes he may have available, he can explore through play and other symbolic communications the repetitive or maladaptive patterns he may have learned as a way of dealing with stress. Even at a nonverbal level these patterns can be played out symbolically and alternatives presented: in the course of treatment working with a toddler who made her doll "run away" all the time, the therapist took the doll and showed it moving in a more assertive direction toward the parent—reaching out to rather than avoiding the family.

10
Dimensions and Levels of the Therapeutic Process

Stanley I. Greenspan, M.D.
Serena Wieder, Ph.D.

Although a primary treatment modality used in the Clinical Infant Development Program (CIDP) involved individual psychotherapy for the mothers on a once or twice weekly basis, we used a range of treatment programs, which were individually tailored to each family. We offered not only individual psychotherapy but also group therapy for mothers, marital and family therapy, mother–infant treatment, individual treatment of the infant, day treatment and day care, and educational programs for the mothers and children.

Our years of work with these high-risk, hard-to-reach women helped us to recognize and delineate what we believe to be the most basic elements of the therapeutic process. We conceptualized three parallel dimensions of the therapeutic relationship and work, each of which can be evaluated independently at any point in time. These dimensions include (1) regularity and stability; (2) attachment; and (3) process. Each dimension includes a number of progressive steps or stages. By considering each dimension separately, one can focus on the very earliest stages of intervention: engaging and facilitating a patient's interest, establishing a regular pattern of meeting, evolving an affective relationship, promoting purposeful communication, and helping the patient tolerate discomfort without the usual avoidance. These steps may be generic to any therapeutic relationship, applicable to work in complex parent–infant situations as well as to more usual problems with work and relationships which come to the attention of mental health professionals.

The framework for specifying steps generic to the psychotherapeutic process emerges from our studies of adaptive and maladaptive human development. As outlined in this chapter, the developmental structuralist approach describes how development proceeds from the earliest stages of infancy into adulthood in terms of the way the human organism organizes experiences at successively higher levels of integration. The proposed model, as will be seen, suggests that the development of specific human relationships follows a sequence not dissimilar to the development of human relationships in general. The therapeutic relationship, it will be suggested, begins at the most fundamental levels with the patient's interest in the therapeutic program, emotional investment in both the person of the therapist and the program of therapy; engagement in an exchange of signals that are purposeful and organized (as a minimum basis for embarking on the techniques specific to the particular therapy), and learning to tolerate whatever discomfort may be specific to the particular treatment (e.g., uncomfortable feelings, facing phobic fantasies or situations, etc.). At higher levels, the therapeutic relationship provides a context in which the patient can observe various behavioral and emotional patterns, relinquish maladaptive patterns, and embrace newer ways of functioning. It is at these higher levels that therapeutic techniques, such as psychoanalytic treatments or behavioral reality-oriented approaches, begin to vary, each having its own steps to altering old patterns.

The First Dimension of the Therapeutic Relationship: Regularity and Stability

Regularity and stability, the first dimension of the therapeutic relationship, are often assumed in models of treatment where patients voluntarily present themselves with a problem to work on and agree to meet with the therapist on a regular basis. But even in these instances, the regularity of meeting is occasionally disrupted during the course of treatment. In the beginning, this may be due to ambivalence regarding treatment; later, discomfort within the treatment process may result in cancellations, "no shows," and disruptions. In any case, it is possible to evaluate the regularity and stability of treatment sessions. At first a patient's interest in the therapeutic process or the person representing it is demonstrated by coming to sessions, or, if home visiting is involved, being available for appointments and opening the door. At this elementary level, for example, one would expect a mother to be able to engage in a simple conversation about occurrences of daily living or an infant's feeding patterns. Even at this beginning level, one can distinguish the person who will only occasionally attend a session or only occasionally let the home visitor in the door from one who will be regularly available. Clearly, there is also a difference between a person who appears alert, interested, and engaged with the therapist and one who falls asleep repeatedly or withdraws into a state of self-absorption, withholding even minimal interest in the therapist or the program he or she offers.

The specific steps involved for a patient in establishing regularity and stability are listed below, followed by clinical examples:

I Expressing willingness to meet with an intervenor or therapist to hear about services or to convey concrete concerns, (no commitment to future contacts).

II Expressing willingness to schedule future meetings.

III Meeting according to some predictable pattern, even

though an agreed upon schedule is not maintained; for example, missing every other scheduled session.

IV   Meeting on a regularly scheduled basis with occasional disruptions; for example, cancellations when fears of getting "too close" arise or the content of sessions is too disturbing.

V   Meeting regularly with no disruptions.

Clinical Illustrations

1. Madeline, a depressed young mother of four children (see Chapter 6 for full case study), initially told the CIDP clinician to visit her because she liked "a little company sometimes," but rarely could she be found (Step I). For months Madeline moved from place to place with her children, desperately seeking refuge but antagonizing those who took her in. The clinician and infant specialist pursued her with food, diapers, and offers of transportation. Madeline was rarely surprised when the clinician arrived at one of her temporary headquarters, as if the clinician should be expected to know where she was and respond to her need. Although she never called or informed the therapists of her next move, she would be angry if they did not come to see her. There was no regularity in her life, nor could there be any in the therapeutic process at this stage. Only after eight months of persistent pursuit did some pattern of regularity begin to form, as Madeline became less frightened and grew able to tolerate some predictable contacts with the clinician. The contacts were for the most part concrete, focusing on day-to-day survival and acquiring some life skills to enhance Madeline's poor self-esteem. Although Madeline never acknowledged that she needed therapy or other help and was unable to talk about her life, she was willing to be with the therapist to be nurtured (Step III). As regularity of contact stabilized (Step IV) and her attachment grew, however, she began to reveal some of her history and reported events in her life which up to that point the clinician had to witness to be aware of them at all.

2. Suzanne was married at 17 and proceeded to have one child after another. She stayed within the confines of a small apartment while her husband negotiated the outside world. She did not shop, handle any accounts, or leave the apartment except for occasional trips to church or to the clinic. Suzanne was referred to us following a severe marital crisis, which involved a brief stay in a women's shelter before reconciliation with her husband took place. The CIDP therapist offered concrete help to Suzanne, as well as the opportunity to discuss her concerns. Suzanne never said no and never expressed any suspiciousness, allowing the clinician to schedule meeting after meeting (Step II). On the day of each visit, however, Suzanne would take 20 or 30 minutes to answer the door. If the clinician called before leaving the office or telephoned from a booth when there was no answer at the door, the phone would ring 20 to 30 times before Suzanne answered. Once the clinician was admitted to the apartment, Suzanne would graciously invite her to sit down, but then would excuse herself and disappear to a back room for half an hour or more while the clinician sat waiting. When she finally returned, Suzanne, an articulate and bright woman, would ask the clinician questions about her children's problems and the influence of her own past but refuse to discuss these issues. Even the mildest comment by the clinician regarding Suzanne's behavior or feelings was met with denial and even longer waits at the door or on the phone.

The clinician persisted, however, responding sensitively on Suzanne's terms. Soon Suzanne began to call for rides and accepted our referrals for her children. She started to answer the door within 10 or 15 minutes and took less time to adapt to the clinician's presence in her home, joining her somewhat more quickly. Many cancellations and interruptions still took place, and for every two or three contacts one was missed (Step III). And if Suzanne saw the infant specialist that week she would not meet with the clinician in the same week. Eventually, the contacts stabilized and Suzanne could meet regularly on a twice weekly basis (Step IV). By this time she had formed a strong attachment to the team, whose members she now trusted. She also began to tolerate the fears and other feelings aroused by her own questions and protected her time to explore these further, even though she continued to be secretive and to insist on control of the process.

3. In contrast to the two cases above, months of persistence and pursual did not lead to regularity or attachment with Anita, another young mother. She was the victim of abuse and had lived in numerous foster homes by the time she reached adolescence and began to have children. When we met her, she was again pregnant, living in her boyfriend's truck, and had two daughters in foster care. Anita was also under the scrutiny of both protective services and her boyfriend's family, who, in her view, hated her and turned her children against her. At first, Anita seemed to accept our help and met with us sporadically before her baby was born and during the first months postnatally (Step I). Our services were concrete, as we tried to stabilize her living situation and coordinate efforts with other agencies. Anita, however, remained distant and unrevealing. Once her son was born, she could not contain streams of projections regarding his "badness, orneriness," and all "the evil" he was doing her. When the baby turned away, she shook and jostled him in frustration. Despite our many efforts to maintain contact and offer help, Anita fled from address to address, and unlike Madeline, left no trail to pursue.

Almost two years after her son's birth, Anita walked into our center and asked us to assess her child. She would not reveal why or tell us about her whereabouts. After the assessment we shared some concerns regarding the severe developmental delays he evidenced and urged her to return so that we could do a more complete evaluation and be of help to her and her child. She did not return. We got in touch with everyone who had been involved but could not find her again.

As these vignettes illustrate, maintaining even a minimal

degree of regularity and interest in a therapeutic relationship is an achievement for many patients which should not be underestimated. Given the nature of their early experiences, fears, and psychological disturbances, many people in need of help are not capable of making even this level of commitment.

Programs of therapy which assume that all patients can and should be responsible for coming regularly for treatment and label those who do not do so as "unmotivated" or "unworkable," are therefore likely to fail many patients. Similarly, therapeutic programs which ignore the first steps in establishing a relationship and attempt to engage the patient at higher levels of process, such as the discussion of complex feelings, before regularity and stability are achieved, may be building a house on a very shaky foundation.

It is important to note that once regularity is established, its stability is still vulnerable to disruption. Initially, regularity may simply be some predictable pattern of contact rather than a weekly meeting. In the example above, Suzanne's initial pattern was to permit contact, subject to her various delays and manipulations. Later she could tolerate beginning each contact more promptly but would cancel every third session or would refuse to meet with both the clinician and infant specialist during the same week. As her treatment progressed and the sessions were stabilized, the process was disrupted by intermittent cancellations due to anxiety and anger related to the clinician and the content of her sessions. These occasional cancellations continued during the entire course of treatment until termination approached and she no longer wanted or needed to miss any more contacts. While the significance of the missed sessions could be addressed and interpreted in these later stages of treatment, in the beginning Suzanne, like many other women in the program, would have experienced any comment as an attack or criticism to be responded to with further avoidance.

Karen, another mother who reached the highest steps of

regularity, recalled that during her second year of treatment she disrupted the pattern of her sessions (Step IV). She said:

> I must have gotten to the point where I really couldn't deal with what we were talking about because I would find that every time it seemed like we got on a sticky subject, I would not come back the following week for one reason or another. And, it just got to the point where I didn't come back for weeks. And then during one of the periods I was away she (clinician) went on vacation. And then I started feeling like I desperately needed some help again and I came back for assessments but I wouldn't come back for the therapy.

Karen later resumed therapy with another clinician and examined this pattern closely. She no longer missed sessions and committed herself to the regularity (Step V), including:

> I just couldn't stay at home (after an upsetting point) where either I'm going to get better or I'm going to get worse. And I definitely don't want to be a crazy old lady.

When an independent interviewer asked CIDP participants at the conclusion of the program what aspects had been most important to them, one mother's comment was typical: "You came back again and again, even when I told you to go away." Our pursuit and reaching out represented the most crucial tool for establishing the first dimension of regularity, eventually enabling many high-risk women to meet regularly and participate in psychotherapy.

The Second Dimension of the Therapeutic Relationship: Attachment and the Emerging Affective Relationship

The second dimension of the therapeutic relationship involves the affective relationship that develops between the patient and the clinician. This process may include several steps.

I. *In the first step, the patient may be interested only in what the clinician or program can provide in very concrete terms, in "What can you do for me?"* (Forms of this question include: Can you help me get my welfare check, cure my physical illness, make my husband stop picking on me, make my children better, help with food, housing, or other survival issues, buy me presents?) At this step it may not matter which therapist offers the services and there is little evidence of specific interest in or acknowledgement of the therapist. (This stance is not uncommon among clients who continually have to meet with numerous and unpredictable staff to get social services.) When the therapist remains stable, however, some emotional expectations appear to develop. These expectations may be positive, as the patient asks for and begins to depend on the therapist for help, or negative when the patient is angry and attacks the therapist for failing to do enough even though there has not been the opportunity to do more. What is important to note is the evidence of emotional involvement entering the relationship, and the nature of the involvement will suggest what prior experiences the patient has had.

For example, Barbara, the primary caregiver of a severely handicapped 5-year-old son and an active 2-year-old toddler, and pregnant again, rarely answered a question in more than mumbled monosyllables. Nor did she look at or even sit directly across from the clinician. At times she appeared so withdrawn and depressed that it was not clear whether she heard the clinician's questions. Barbara initially asked for help for her oldest child but claimed not to need anything else. She did not have a phone and would not let the clinician in although she could be seen peeking through the venetian blinds as the clinician knocked repeatedly at her door. Barbara would accept help when *she* wanted it: She often called the CIDP a half-hour before an appointment, expecting to be driven there. Furthermore, the clinician soon realized Barbara was angry if the clinician did not guess what she needed, even though she had said nothing. For many months the

clinician absorbed Barbara's glares and other signs of rejection. These behaviors appeared to shift, however, and Barbara
began to dress up when she visited the Infant Center. She
also appeared disappointed if her clinician was not waiting for
her (although she continued to deny it mattered) and she
refused offers of help from other staff members. It was evident
that the person of the clinician had taken on a specific meaning
and an attachment was definitely forming.

Barbara's expectations about therapeutic engagement
hardly included the traditional processes of "mutual collaboration" and "self-exploration." But there is no question that
many people like Barbara are quite capable of benefiting from
a therapeutic process if given the opportunity to develop attachment.

II. *The second step of the therapeutic relationship involves an affective quality beyond the concrete level of wishes
for food, housing, and transportation.* By covert or overt
indications, the patient communicates that he is emotionally
interested in the therapist. A positive feeling tone may be
indicated by a joyful look on the patient's face when she comes
in for a session, by a statement about a newly forming friendship outside the therapeutic situation accompanied by a glance
at the therapist indicating that perhaps the patient has similar
feelings about the therapist, or by general references to
warmth and closeness. At this step the patient may perceive
the therapist as someone she feels good with, like a sister or
friend. Emotional relatedness may also be indicated by highly
personalized statements (e.g., "You hurt my feelings") of distrust, annoyance, and irritability (e.g., a sense of closeness is
developing even though it is initially with negative feelings).

III. *The third step involves a human affective tie with
purposeful communication.* Here the patient uses the therapeutic relationship to communicate in a logical and purposeful
manner, in at least an elementary fashion. A patient at this
stage may share factual information about paying a bill; discuss
concrete matters such as how to buy food in a store, get a

welfare check, diaper one's baby, or arrange transportation to get to the session; or ask for advice. Both patient and therapist, at least for some of the session, engage in logical communication, either at a verbal or nonverbal level, demonstrating they are operating in a purposeful, logical manner. However, the person who sits quietly and passively and does not say a word for three-quarters of the session but at the end looks up at the therapist and talks about the time of the next session, has also made a logical and purposeful communication. This step should be distinguished from higher levels of the therapeutic relationship where complex feeling states such as love, empathy, jealousy, and rivalry are discussed.

IV. *The fourth step involves forming a therapeutic relationship which tolerates discomfort and/or "scary" emotions.* This step characterizes a relationship which is sufficiently stable to allow the patient to tolerate uncomfortable feelings of anger, frustration, and remorse, or aspects of pleasure and joy which may be frightening, such as precocious sexual longings, without a major disruption in the relationship. While minor perturbations, disruptions, or upsets, including missed sessions, may occur, the overall relationship and the affective investment survive. Typical of this stage is the patient who misses a session or two after a separation from the therapist (but does not stop treatment for 6 months) and is able to talk about the experience directly (e.g., "I need to 'be in control' of myself and others"). It should be noted that although negative affects, such as anger, remorse, and suspiciousness, and feelings of being exploited are the most potentially disruptive to a therapeutic relationship, for many patients feelings of intimacy, warmth, or sexual longing are most frightening, and patterns of avoidance, including disruption of treatment, occur when such feelings emerge. It is in such situations that the dimension of attachment and affective contact, even though such contact may take on an angry, suspicious, or passive dependent form, suggests this fourth level of attachment has been reached.

V. *The fifth step involves a state in which the patient feels secure in being "known" by the therapist in both positive and negative aspects.* This highest level of therapeutic attachment supports continued exploration and tolerance of uncomfortable affect states. The relationship with the therapist thus involves many different current emotions which permit the patient to compare them with others and work through maladaptive patterns. At the highest step one observes satisfaction and often affection in the therapeutic relationship along with a sense of accomplishment of a task jointly well done.

At these highest steps the therapeutic attachment may overlap the higher level process steps described below, but the focus in this dimension is on the depth of feeling and degree of differentiation in the attachment. The patient acknowledges the depth and meaning of the attachment, which has been reparative and healing, often the very first relationship to be trusted and sustained by the patient.

Looking at our records of CIDP mothers for examples of levels of therapeutic attachment beyond the first step, we find Marian, who responded to a question about what her infant specialist meant to her by saying:

> My sister told her [clinician] about me and the next thing I know she was coming to my house, talking to me and everything and I was going through a rough time. She just kept coming and I got to know her. I don't know. It's nice. . . . Sometimes I feel like I owe my whole life to her. If it wasn't for her, I don't know where I'd be at or end up at. (Marian later adds) I just like seeing her. It feels good to have her around.

Another mother, Janette, described the evolving process of the relationship with her clinician as follows:

> She made me feel like [she was] an older sister, I

kind of had that feeling about her, yeah, an older sister type. I saw what she was trying to do [help me] and it made me really feel good, you know, when I saw she was trying to show me, so she was glad and I was glad (Step II).

While these "sisterly feelings" supported the therapeutic efforts and helped stabilize regular contacts, Janette continued to be guarded in her attachment. She articulates her reasons:

Well, I've come to learn that's just something [the attachment], you should really allow, because if you don't it takes away a whole lot, it really does. It takes away the chance of having shared part of your life with that person, and part of your time with that person and of that person having shared part of their time with you.

Janette also expresses her ambivalence:

So a lot of times I really feel kind of left out, I just felt kind of uncomfortable she [clinician] had to end the conversation and had to go in with somebody else, like you go a psychiatrist and your time is up. You have this feeling that you don't really want to get too close because when you do they are not there anymore. . . . She [the clinician] showed me that, because it was really difficult for me to really open up with her, I guess because I really felt, I wasn't really aware that I had gotten so close to her. . . . So you say, wow, how did that happen, how did I get attached to this person? She's not part of my family, she's just a professional person . . . how did that happen? How did you cross that barrier? That's not supposed to happen because she's a professional and I'm just a mere layman, you know. It happened, it happened, and I've worked with a lot of [other] professional people and I would get to the point where I just wouldn't, you know, go so far.

The importance of the attachment in helping another mother work through her difficulties was conveyed in the following way:

> You know, I mean there are some people who do a job because it is a job and they get paid for it. But you [clinician] really care. And that is a good feeling because I have always grown up feeling that people didn't really give a damn. And nobody, people do certain things for you out of a certain, because they have to, but nobody really cared you know. Now I don't feel that way.

Therapeutic Process Level

The third dimension of the therapeutic relationship focuses on the "process" and level of communication and includes traditional aspects of the therapeutic process such as self-observation and connecting past to present, elaborated here systematically in operational terms. It also encompasses aspects of regularity and affective investment, dimensions described earlier.

I. *Preliminary communication at the first step simply involves any general communication or initial sharing of information.* While outreach and concrete services are often involved, communication at this level moves toward verbal support and information gathering. The therapist observes and comments on the patient's functioning, struggles, and availability. As some trust develops, patients begin to talk, however selectively, about what has happened in their lives.

Louise, the CIDP mother described in Chapter 3, for example, turned down offers of concrete help with housing or health care even after she was evicted, but let the clinician find her after she had moved on her own and seemed to make use of some of the concrete information she had been given, although she never acknowledged this directly. The clinician went to Louise's weekly, bringing cigarettes; the two women would smoke and drink coffee, saying very little beyond chatting about the weather or a TV soap opera. After several months, Louise seemed more willing to share information and gave some details regarding her boyfriend, daughter, and some of the work she was doing, but she stayed away from talking about her past. It took several more months for Louise to reveal that she had been abandoned as an infant and had attempted suicide after learning of her original family, who resided only blocks away from where she was raised. The clinician had to temper her responses and empathy carefully, guided by Louise's defense patterns. Although an emotional tie slowly formed, based on the sensitive acceptance of Louise's painful and guarded experiences of the human world, and regular contacts were established, the process level remained at the earliest stages. As further details emerged, the critical experience of Louise's abandonment and its consequences to her as a woman and mother were to be reworked at every subsequent process level.

II. *The second step involves the patient's ability to observe and report single behaviors or action patterns.* This early level of self-observation does not necessarily involve observing complex feelings such as love, hate, and anger, or the mixtures of love and hate involved in ambivalent feelings. Rather, this level involves a far simpler type of communication: the patient's report of behavioral patterns. For example, a patient may report "I wanted my wife to take care of the baby and she didn't. I then went out and got drunk and came home and beat her up." This report of a pattern shows that the patient is able to observe a complex series of behaviors and report them, aware at some level that the recognition of this behavior pattern and the reporting of it will somehow be useful to the therapeutic work. This type of report is, clearly, much different from a more advanced form of self-observation, such as that offered by the patient who says, "I wanted my wife to take care of the baby and I got angry: I then *felt scared* and ran out and got drunk and came back and beat her up."

In this latter example, the patient is able to recognize an internal feeling state, while in the former example the patient simply reports a behavioral pattern and, at most, implies some cause and effect between one piece of behavior and another.

The initial self-observing function is evident when the patient, in collaboration with the therapist, goes beyond simply saying "I want you to take care of me" or "I want you to help me with my welfare check," to describing his own or others' behavioral patterns. This ability of the patient enables the therapist to recognize some of his other adaptive and maladaptive behaviors and their accompanying affects (although the accompanying affects may not be explicit). For example, during one session a mother, Barbara, comments:

> Everybody tells me I'm so quiet. People just come around, they try to take advantage of me, you know, I'll just sit back and look at them. (Clinician asks: What happens if somebody makes you mad?) They can look at me and tell that I'm mad. I just give them this nasty look you know. (And then?) Well, I just get over it.

Barbara cannot directly express her feelings but is able to describe her behavior. This is important information for the therapist, who can relate it to the frequent silent glares he has absorbed for many months with no clue as to their meaning. At a subsequent session the therapist continues to explore Barbara's expectation that she will be taken advantage of and asks, "What do you do when you want to say *no* to people?" Now Barbara is at a higher level of self-observation and is able to recognize some internal states and relate them to her behavior. She reports:

> See, I feel bad if I say no, but then again I do want to say it, and then again I feel bad about doing it. If somebody wants to borrow some money or this or that, I'll tell them I don't have it, you know. Then I feel badly

because I don't have it to give to them, you know. Then I'll call back and still want to give it to them because I feel bad because I couldn't, you know. Because if I got anything I'm not actually mean, I like to give it up, you know.

Barbara cannot yet recognize the many conflicts which underlie her report or how they relate to her current life situation, which includes staying with an abusive boyfriend and rejecting her healthy children while she meets the physical needs of her handicapped children. Nevertheless, the report indicates that she had taken a significant step in the therapeutic process from the days of her silent glares, and can now both observe her behavior and indicate how she feels.

III. *The third step involves focusing on the relationships involved in the descriptions of behavior patterns given earlier.* At this level, the patient uses his emerging capacity for self-observation to describe his behavior in terms of the key people in his life and the relationship of these people to the treatment objectives. If, for example, improving a mother's relationship with the infant is a treatment objective, it is particularly notable when the patient is able to begin describing behavioral patterns that involve her infant, as opposed to simply talking about how she behaves at work, with her boyfriend or husband, or her reaction to her favorite soap opera. The ability in a session to shift back and forth—even at a behavioral level—and to report, "I hit my infant, then I hit my boyfriend, then I ran out and got high"—shows that the patient is beginning to link the various sectors of her life and most importantly, is attending to the troubled relationship which presumably caused her to come into treatment.

The kind of communication characteristic of this step is demonstrated by Melissa, the mother of two sons and a daughter under the age of 4, who was extremely upset by her boyfriend's behavior because he was failing to meet the needs of the family and preferred one of his children to the others. She describes his behavior and her ensuing rage, which led her to walk out and leave the children with him.

> He was drinking again. We had $5.00 for the weekend, till Monday when he got paid. . . . We needed diapers, we needed food, I needed cigarettes, the kids needed stuff and we had $5.00 and he came home with a 6-pack of beer, and I really got hot. I mean you take this money and spend it on yourself and what about us? You know and I got really mad and I stayed on him for 8 hours and he told me, I mean I wasn't that mad but I mean I just wanted him to know how much I hated when he did this, and I had him, I had him to the point where he was going to leave but then he decided he wasn't going to leave, he was going to make it miserable for me and he was going to do what he wanted to do whenever he wanted to do it. . . . He wouldn't even let me take my medicine, he wouldn't go to the doctors, he wouldn't do *nothing* for me and the kids, and I just told him that I'm leaving. I said I want to get out, I want to get away from you, I want to get away from the kids, I'm going, I don't know where I'm going, but I'm going. I said I can't put up with this —— anymore. I can't take it, I'm sick and tired of you doing this. I said if you think you're a better parent, then fine, here are the kids, keep them, I'm going. I didn't even know where I was going.

Melissa left but soon returned to retrieve two of her children while her boyfriend held onto his favorite. As her tirade indicates, she could observe the destructive patterns in her relationship with her boyfriend and the use of the children as pawns in their battles. Yet while she could describe what happened, Melissa's ability to link the various sectors of her life, understand what had led to her current situation, and see how she contributed to it currently was, at best, at its earliest stages of development.

The Range of Thematic Affective Expressions

Two additional aspects need to be considered at subsequent steps of the therapeutic process: first, the range of relationships examined in the context of observing and reporting behavioral events, and second, whether the report is polarized or representative of a balanced range of different themes. (For example, the person who enters therapy to improve his relationship with his spouse may begin to describe his relationship with his spouse and then describe a similar action pattern at work.)

The range of relationships in the patient's life to be identified include (1) the infant; (2) other children; (3) spouse; (4) other important relationships; (5) nuclear family members; (6) work relationships; (7) the therapist; and (8) others. To determine whether behavioral patterns at this step, or feelings at later steps, are polarized, consider whether patients talk about only one dimension of their lives, such as anger or suspiciousness. One patient may produce many vignettes about how he hit someone or someone hit him or he yelled at someone or someone yelled at him or how somebody picked on him unfairly or he picked on someone unfairly. At the other extreme, a patient might focus only on dependency: he needs this person and this person needs him, or he is holding onto this or that person or this or that relationship. If the person is polarized, seldom in the single 15–20 minute sequence would one hear descriptions of different dimensions of human functioning such as anger, assertiveness, dependency, love, and pleasure. In other words, even at the behavioral level of communication one can distinguish a person who reports behaviors that are characteristic of one dimension of life from a person who reports a range of behaviors characteristic of a number of dimensions of life.

IV. *The fourth step in the therapeutic process involves the capacity for self-observation in relationship to feelings.* This step is reached when the person goes beyond the level of behavioral description and talks about feeling states. The patient is able to say, "I was angry at him after he didn't show up for our date," or "I got angry with my baby when he wouldn't eat," or "I felt very disappointed when my boss criticized me for my work." Here, there is a clear statement of feelings rather than a description of behavioral patterns alone. The person has moved beyond seeing the world as a series of behaviors ("I messed up the work and my boss yelled at me,") and can include feelings in his world view ("I was upset and couldn't work well and therefore my boss got angry and I felt disappointed").

One mother, Vera, describes how she cannot wait to get to work in the mornings after getting her children off to school because her husband lashes out at her, expecting her to meet his every need and is critical of whatever she does. She reports:

> But he's always saying little silly things that sort of start my day or upset it and the only way it doesn't is if we have no communication. I just jump up, get dressed, get the kids out and disappear and then he will be all to himself. Some days I am not able to do that because I don't work every day. It's too much pressure between the kids and him and I don't think I can handle being home every day.

At a later point in the treatment Vera recognizes the mood swings which accompany the feelings of pressure but when asked if she gets angry, she says:

> Probably I suppress it [anger] a lot and then when I suppress it it reaches a point where I get very depressed, and then that's not good for me, cause I get—it's very, a very painful feeling.

All that is needed to reach this fourth level is the reporting of simple feelings. More complex feelings (such as subtle gradations between levels of anger), mixed feelings, and empathy need not be evident at this step. Nor do explorations of interaction between feeling states within oneself and between the self and others need to occur to reach this step. The shift from communications at the behavioral level to the use of feeling states in description is key. As indicated earlier, it is useful under this category as well to note how significant others are brought into the therapeutic discussion and to evaluate the degree of polarization versus integration.

V. *The fifth step of the therapeutic process pertains to the use of self-observation in relationship to complex and interactive feeling stages.* This level is reached when a person is able to talk about complicated feelings and interactions among feelings. The person goes beyond saying simply, "I was mad," and is able to explore the fact that "I may have gotten a little bit mad and therefore withdrew from my boyfriend. I can therefore see where he felt saddened and perhaps got discouraged. That's why he told me he didn't love me anymore." This highly complex statement of interactions among feelings is characteristic of this next level. While it may not be easy to judge the difference between levels IV and V, the more advanced state in the therapeutic process is characterized by the ability to see how the world works in terms of interactions among feelings. In addition, this level is characterized by the patient's ability to make subtle judgments about gradations of feelings. For example, the patient may say, "I felt only slightly annoyed the first time he was late, but by the fifth time he missed his appointment with me I was furious," or "I like Tom but love Bill because of how well we understand each other."

Natalie reported early in her therapy that she had been sexually abused by her uncle between the ages of 13 and 16. She could not discuss the details or the impact it had for several years except to note that she had had stomach problems ever since. After several years of treatment in the CIDP, Natalie recognized the complex feelings which were involved.

I didn't handle it. . . . Because I had mixed feelings
of guilt because I felt it was my fault. There was nobody
I could talk to and say, "Hey, you know—." At that time
I wanted my father's love, my mother's love, but my
mother was so busy doing everything else she just didn't
have time for me, and my father, being an artist, didn't
really have much time for me, so when this guy came
along it was mixed feelings, it was between wanting to
be loved but yet knowing that it was wrong and this kind
of guilt.

Although Natalie believed her mother was aware of what
was going on she never expressed any anger at her mother.
"Oh, I'd keep it inside or go in my room and then get at
myself for not letting it out."

VI. *The sixth step in the therapeutic process involves
using self-observation for thematic and affective elaboration.*
Here we look for the person's ability to use the observing
functions not only to report complex feelings in interpersonal
situations but to elaborate these themes in a deep and rich
manner. This calls for complicated judgment. The ability to
talk about a theme in relation to multiple people in the patient's life, as well as in historical context, is the key indicator
of this level. A person may use the historical context to deepen
the understanding of particular emotions and themes and or
discuss a number of relationships which deal with the same
theme. A person may talk about a theme in a relationship to
friends, family (including her own baby), and individuals from
the past. The person who talks about anger, intimacy, or love
in relationship to his spouse, baby, boss, and/or any historical
figures in his life has reached this step. Of course, a reference
to the person of the therapist may also indicate the range and
depth of thematic elaboration.

After several years in therapy and many, many attempts
to reconcile a sadomasochistic relationship with her husband
of 14 years, Rita finally reaches the rage which she has turned
inward all her life. She tells her clinician:

And it's just, it's just at the point now I don't care. I don't you know, I don't care. I'm 36 and I don't have to live like that. Now, he's going away again and, you know, he knows I'm going to be waiting for him this time. I'm just not, you know. I want to be happy too. I mean, my kids are not everything that makes me happy, and I want something out of life. I'm just not going to stay still and be the humble little wife, like . . . Lord, like my mother. I'm not like my mother in ways of when my father used to fight her and she never fought back. Well, when he used to cuss or beat her, she never cussed him back. I'm not like that.

Taking this therapeutic step was a turning point for Rita, who went on to work through her long-standing depression and "martyr" behavior. As she differentiated herself from various relationships in her life, she could use her talents and capacity for hard work to establish her independence and a new home for her family.

VII. *The seventh step pertains to the capacity for using observation to make connections between the key relationships in one's life, including the therapeutic relationships.*

We look at this state for the ability to begin making connections among emotions and themes elaborated at the sixth step. Characteristic of this level is the ability to make connections among the therapeutic context (the person of the therapist), the historical context (past relationships with parents, friends, and relatives), and current interpersonal situations (including key people in the present, with special reference to the key problem areas). For example, if a person is coming for treatment because of developmental problems with her baby or young child, the capacity to deal with feelings toward her child in the relative context of historical relationships, the therapeutic relationship, and other current relationships would indicate achievement of this level. If the primary problem area is a person's relationship to his spouse,

then one would look for the ability to begin making connections among his problems with his spouse, historical relationships, the therapeutic relationship, and relevant others in his
life to see if this level has been reached.

Dolores, a CIDP participant, did not reveal an incestuous
relationship with a family member for several years of treatment. She feared to reveal what was happening until a
younger sister was also raped and her anxiety was triggered
by her young children, who were beginning to ask questions
about their bodies and sex differences. While exploring why
she did not "scream out," Dolores said tearfully:

> I was afraid of getting in trouble—you [even] got
> spanked for something you know you didn't do wrong.
> You don't trust anybody to talk to them about it. I didn't
> know and I was afraid of getting into trouble, it was like,
> you know, so I didn't know what to do, so of course I
> didn't say anything. But that's the reason why I say, you
> know, I talk to the kids about it [i.e., not letting anyone
> touch their bodies]. I feel like I tread a very thin line
> now. Tell them enough but don't scare them to the point
> where they are afraid to go out.

In addition to being able to deal with her past in relation
to her wish to protect her children, Dolores also makes the
connection to her current sexual relationship with her husband:

> I'm kind of like hot water. Off and on, it's like some
> days I am very sexually attracted to my husband, I'm
> very responsive and then I get to the point where I just
> can't do it. I just cannot feel close. I feel close enough
> to touch him and that, but not close enough to make
> love, to be sexually responsive. It bothers me, confuses
> me, and even in some of the things you [the clinician]
> say, it's like—there is something there because you are

young, you are healthy, you have no business not feeling like it or whatever. It concerns me. I'm not really angry but I'm not sexually motivated either.

Dolores proceeded to work on these feelings in couples therapy as well as individually.

It should be noted that the way in which a person makes connections may vary considerably from one person to another and even for the same person from time to time. Sometimes connections may be straightforward—"Aha, I feel jealous toward my baby the same way I feel jealous toward you (my therapist), the same way I feel toward my husband/boyfriend, and the way I felt jealous toward my siblings and my parents." On the other hand, connections may be indirect. A patient may talk for the first 10 minutes of a session about how she is angry at her baby and how she loves the therapist and her parents, how happy she is that she has people she can love, although her baby and boyfriend are frustrating to her, and so forth. The therapist may then comment that there are those who frustrate her and make her angry and those who support her, like the therapist and her parents, and make her feel good. Subsequently, what emerges is a spontaneous connection between relationships that are all loving and all frustrating. While separating her feelings keeps her world simple and concrete, the patient discovers that in fact she feels both ways toward her infant (loving and angry), both ways toward her therapist, and both ways toward her parents, but has been hiding this from herself by overpolarizing in order to protect the more vulnerable relationships.

VIII. *The eighth step involves the capacity to use the identification of patterns in their current therapeutic and historical relationships to work through problems and difficulties and facilitate new growth and development.* This level is achieved when the patient is able to use the therapeutic relationship to explore current, ongoing patterns and their historical antecedents, and repetitively examine these pat-

terns in multiple contexts. A person at this level, in essence,
can spontaneously report, "here it happened again" and immediately can see the transference and historical basis for
behaviors and feelings and how "it happened again" with his
girl friend, baby, best friend, or colleagues at work.

The repetitive exploration of patterns at this level leads
to the tendency to begin relinquishing old patterns of maladaptive functioning, including patterns which were used to
attain compromise gratifications, and to work through the fears
of achieving new satisfactions, associated with more mature
functioning.

One mother who entered the program because of fears
of her own potential for child abuse described the process of
repeatedly exploring patterns in her life in group and individual therapy in the following way:

> I felt like a ragbag, that everybody had pulled all
> these rags out and that at the end of the hour I was left
> to pick up all the rags and stuff them into the bag and
> make it through the rest of the week. . . . It was getting
> that deep and that emotional and I didn't know whether
> I could handle it and I seriously considered not coming
> and I thought, "Oh God, that's a cop-out, I can't do
> that." . . . It was very hard and I realized that I felt like
> a ragbag, all the little pieces all over the place, spread
> out everywhere. Not only were they spread out, every-
> body could see them. . . . I could no longer bury them,
> it was really hard! That is when I didn't know myself
> anymore. I knew I wasn't this bad mother anymore. I
> guess I could have said I was a good mother, or pretty
> good mother anyway.

She continued:

> After we messed through my ragbag for a few weeks, I
> started to, like, I left a few rags behind. I didn't need

them anymore. And some of the other things that were in there I didn't know about. I took them back. I'm still not sure what they are, I just know, well this looks like a good rag, I'll keep it. This one is not a good rag, I don't need it anymore. So I know some new parts of me. I know that I love my kids. I know that I'm not supermom. I'd like to be a better mom than I am, most people go through life wishing to be a little bit better at something than they are. But I'm not a bad mom. I'm not a bad wife. I'm not a bad person.

This question illustrates the shift to new ways of relating and experimenting with new, developmentally higher level patterns of satisfaction. At this level for example, the person who is locked into sadomasochistic styles of relating to the therapist, his spouse, and his own child sees the pattern common to all relationships and begins to relinquish it, taking a chance on more frightening, albeit higher level satisfactions (e.g., greater intimacy and collaboration in his relationships). *New* feelings, thoughts, and associative trends representative of more advanced developmental levels are evidenced in the sessions and behavioral patterns outside the session reflect a greater, more age-appropriate range of affect, thought, and relationships.

At this level, one expects to see comfort with dependency and intimacy; a capacity for pleasure; and freedom to explore, to be assertive and curious, and to mobilize and regulate anger in a variety of age-appropriate interpersonal contexts.

IX. *The ninth step of the therapeutic process is the consolidation of new patterns and levels of satisfaction and the preparation for separating from the therapeutic relationship.* This level is reached when the participant is consolidating new adaptive patterns of relating, feeling, and behaving in all sectors of his life and feels that he or she can continue without the therapeutic relationship. Arrival at this state is signaled by recurrent reports of the consolidation of gains, a sense of satisfaction in these gains, and a sense of security that these gains can be maintained. At this level, as on all earlier levels, fears and anxieties in anticipation of the loss of the therapeutic relationship appear. There may be short-term regressions to earlier stages in the therapeutic process or to earlier styles of functioning. However, one sees a capacity to recover once the regressive experience and its purpose (often to prevent the sense of loss associated with anticipated separation and with unresolved fears of functioning at a higher level of development) are identified.

Anticipating the termination of therapy, Dorothy had a crisis when her clinician was away briefly. The clinician confronted Dorothy with this old pattern as they continued to work on the themes and fears of separation. During the clinician's vacation Dorothy reflected:

> This time not only have we not had any problems but things have gone along rather well. I think it's like I've been preparing myself that someday she [the clinician] is not going to be here and it's not going to be that long away and so I'm going to have to do it on my own and think I can. We've been through a lot together. There was one time I called in and said I wasn't coming in, I didn't have anything to wear, which was true, I didn't, but I didn't want to come in and [clinician] called and said, "wear your black and white sundress." I said, "I don't even know where it is." She said, "You're coming in if I have to come and get you." So I found the dress. Later I told her, I'm going to take this dress home and burn it! I hated her then but she really stuck by me. She knows everything about me, more than I know myself sometimes, and she's changed my life. I'm not afraid of getting down close to them [children] and if you come into a confrontation, relax. I feel I can handle it. We worked hard and I'll never forget her.

Another mother struggles with her fears of separation and termination:

I think at the beginning I had a very deep problem about separation like my daughter shared when she was younger about separation from me. I had a terrible separation problem, not just from my husband but from people in general that I felt close with. It would take me a long time to get over it and even with her [clinician] I had a hard time accepting there were times we wouldn't see each other and there were times I was really angry about it. There were times that maybe subconsciously I deliberately didn't make arrangements to see her either. I said, okay, this is not going to last so why should I make an effort to really get dependent on something that is not going to be there. I got to be strong. I got to be able to cope after this is over and I have to start weaning myself away from her . . . [starts to cry] I don't know where I would be right now if I hadn't worked with her . . . it was not that I wished I never got involved, I appreciate and really enjoyed the time that we had and though I guess I really don't want it to end I can cope with it and I will.

These women are able to experience and describe love, dependency, warmth, and intimacy as well as curiosity and assertiveness and can clearly integrate the two. Their statements connecting both sets of feelings as they terminate from the program reflect this capacity.

X. *The highest step in the therapeutic process is the capacity for full consolidation of gains in the context of separating from the therapeutic relationship and experiencing a full sense of loss and mourning.* This state of the therapeutic relationship is characterized by further consolidation of gains and the full emergence of issues of loss and separation from the therapeutic relationship. There is usually an enhanced capacity for mature mourning, as well as confidence in the ability to maintain the therapeutic momentum already achieved. While regressions may also occur, the patient demonstrates a ready capacity to reorganize and understand quickly the various maladaptive maneuvers he may tend to employ. Feelings of affection and a sense of accomplishment in a task jointly well done may be expressed in the therapeutic relationship.

Quantifying the Dimensions for Research: Three Scales

The major significance of the therapeutic relationship dimensions is that they define where therapy begins, what the subsequent therapeutic tasks must be, and when the patient arrives at the end of treatment, as well as the levels which a patient has attained at any given point during the course of therapy. In contrast to the assessment of other psychological variables, such as ego strength, or of aspects of psychopathology such as paranoia, all of which, of course, may have bearing on the course of treatment, the therapeutic dimensions directly define the work that needs to be done. Further, the profile suggests which treatment approaches, such as outreach, home-based treatment, milieu supports, or range of individual and group treatment modalities, may be most effective for the patient at a particular step. The dimensions address generic steps in the therapeutic process which form the basis for any kind of therapeutic work. Because use of the dimensions allows one to recognize the steps most basic to a therapeutic relationship and to appreciate even small improvements, mental health professionals may become more sanguine about the abilities and "motivation" of many people needing help. Also, predictions of outcome can be evaluated by using the specific steps to measure patients' progress along the dimensions.

The reports of the women in the CIDP which we have quoted above convey a sense of the variety of their experiences of the therapeutic relationship. Some needed extensive outreach in order to be engaged with some regularity and, despite our efforts, continued to be guarded and to show little awareness of their difficulties or how their past experiences related to their present lives. Others leaped at the opportunity to be helped, feeling relieved that someone would try to understand their pain, and immediately expressed fears that they could not be different from their mothers.

When she entered the program and began the treatment process, every CIDP participant presented a unique profile with regard to the three dimensions of the therapeutic relationship. Our task became to quantify the dimensions for research purposes. This effort required developing reliable measures, or scales, of the three dimensions. The objectives of these measures were to rate the women on their ability to engage in the therapeutic relationship during the first four to six weeks of contact, to predict the progress they would make if they could be engaged in treatment and to assess independently their outcome at the conclusion of the program. A line 100 millimeters long was placed at the center of a piece of paper and on either side of the line an extreme definition was written out to serve as an anchor point. The rater's task was to mark the point on the line which corresponded to the degree to which the participant possessed the dimension being rated. The mark on the line was then measured in millimeters and this number was treated as a score. The range of scores was 1 to 100. The therapeutic relationship scales were developed as part of the group of 20 clinical ratings described below of various psychiatric, maternal, and developmental measures made of the participants in the program at entry and at outcome.

The Therapeutic Relationship Scales

These scales represent each of the three dimensions (Regularity and Stability, Attachment, and Process Level) described earlier. See Table 10-1 for an overview of these dimensions and the steps in each one. They were used to rate the intervention efforts described during the entry phase of the CIDP. Although the entry data are concerned with the initial evaluation of participants joining the CIDP, the efforts reported to engage and evaluate each participant give us in-

TABLE 10-1

Dimensions of the Therapeutic Relationship: Steps in the Therapeutic Process

Regularity and Stability	Attachment	Process
I. Willingness to meet with an interviewer or therapist to convey concrete concerns or hear about services.	I. Interest in having concrete needs met and can be provided by anyone (e.g., food, transportation, etc.).	I. Preliminary communication, including verbal support and information gathering.
II. Willingness to schedule meetings again.	II. Emotional interest in the person of the therapist (e.g., conveys pleasure or anger when they meet).	II. Ability to observe and report single behaviors or action patterns.
III. Meeting according to some predictable pattern.	III. Communicates purposefully in attempts to deal with problems.	III. Focuses on relationships involved in the behavior–action pattern.
IV. Meeting regularly with occasional disruptions.	IV. Tolerates discomfort or scary emotions.	IV. Self-observing function in relationship to feeling.

V. Meeting regularly with no disruptions.

V. Feels "known" or accepted in positive and negative aspects.

V. Self-observing function in relationship to complex and interactive feeling states.

VI. Self-observing function for thematic and affective elaboration.

VII. Makes connections between the key relationships in life including the therapeutic relationship.

VIII. Identification of patterns in current, therapeutic, and historical relationships to work through problems and facilitate new growth.

IX. Consolidation of new patterns and levels of satisfaction and preparing to separate from the therapeutic relationship.

X. Full consolidation of gains in the context of separating and experiencing a full sense of loss and mourning.

formation about the way participants were engaged in the program and the level at which they presented themselves, their histories, and their thoughts and feelings about themselves and others. The ratings of these scales should not be limited to the traditional parameters of therapeutic process; that is, verbal office sessions. Instead, all the clinical material presented during the first four to six contacts should be rated along the following three dimensions.

1. THERAPEUTIC RELATIONSHIP—REGULARITY AND STABILITY

Rate the degree to which the participant has established some regularity and stability in her contacts during the entry phase. At the low end of this scale participants may permit contacts at times, following outreach, but whether they are in the program is questionable. Their interest or ambivalence remains unclear but they do not lock the clinician out or reject the program entirely. Follow-up contacts that do occur may feel as if nothing has taken place. As you move up the scale you will be rating whether the participant permits contacts and demonstrates some interest in the program, however disguised. Assess whether there is regularity or some pattern of contacts (which may be intermittent, such as just seeing the clinician every other week or for every other appointment) is evidenced. Regularity at this point may take the form of a regular pattern but has some predictability or relationship to outreach, concrete services, etc.

At later points along this dimension will be participants who begin to commit themselves to regular appointments and are able to account for their availability or cancellations. If there are disruptions at this point the participant and clinician are able to acknowledge these as part of the process going on between them. At the high end of this scale the participant and clinician are working in a stable and intensive fashion, whatever the frequency may be. The therapeutic work is stable and the patient can tolerate whatever is going on with infrequent or no unplanned disruptions.

Rater ID _____ Subject ID _____

Therapeutic Relationship—Regularity and Stability
___ *Prediction*

No predictable therapeutic contact. Subject may permit contacts at times but it is questionable whether they are or are not in the program (even if they have signed a consent form). Their interest in the program remains unclear but they do fall just short of locking out the clinician or rejecting the program entirely. Contacts that do occur may feel like first-time events as if earlier meetings had never taken place.

Contacts are regular and stable with sessions occurring as scheduled with no unplanned interruptions. The stability reflects the tolerance of the participant to deal with unpleasurable affects during the continual reexamination of patterns in the therapeutic relationship and with others. Short-term regressions in response to terminations are identified and can be worked through.

2. THERAPEUTIC RELATIONSHIP—ATTACHMENT

This dimension is concerned with the affective bond which develops between the participant and the therapist. In its earliest stages this may take the form of some interest in the *program* without any specific interest in the therapist; it would appear as if any clinician could be coming to see that participant. As this interest develops it moves from the impersonal to a more differentiated affect quality specific to the therapist; the participant is relating in a more personal way, recognizing the therapist as someone with specific meaning to her. The relationship between the participant and therapist continues to progress from specific attachment to recognition of signals and feelings between them. At this point, the participant might feel that the therapist "knows" her because the therapist can anticipate her behavior or feelings. Early signs of trust are taking the place of earlier ambivalence and fear of letting the therapist get too close. As this relationship develops the participant is able to tolerate uncomfortable feelings or frightening affects without major disruption or flight from treatment. Because her attachment and relationship feel more secure, the participant can tolerate feeling "known" and accepted by the therapist even though she is experiencing uncomfortable affect states. Reserve the upper end of this scale for those participants who can make connections between the therapeutic relationship and other key relationships following examination of what is going on between them and the therapist. At this stage the participant can compare and differentiate patterns in her other relationships from those in the therapeutic relationship and sees how these patterns guide her behavior. At the highest end of the scale, one would observe satisfaction and often affection in the therapeutic relationship with a sense of accomplishment of a task jointly well done.

3. THERAPEUTIC RELATIONSHIP—PROCESS LEVEL

This scale is concerned with the process observed in the content of the meetings between the participant and the ther-

Rater ID _____ Subject ID _____

Therapeutic Relationship—Attachment
_____ *Prediction*

Participant views the therapist in an impersonal manner with little evidence of an affective or specific relationship between them. Continuous outreach is needed to maintain contacts and interest in the therapist is impersonal or ambivalent at best.

Relationship between therapist and mother is secure and tolerates continuous examination and exploration of pleasant and unpleasant affects. Often there is a great deal of affection and a sense of accomplishment of task jointly well done.

Rater ID ———   Subject ID ———

Therapeutic Relationship—Process Level
Prediction

———

Interventions are centered around outreach, concrete services, and information gathering. Therapists must initiate and structure most of the contact or are drawn into crisis-type interventions. Work is supportive but participant's capacity to reflect or observe feelings remains very limited.

Therapeutic process is focused on self-observing feelings, behaviors, and the therapeutic relationship, recovering and reconstructing early historical experiences, repetitive exploration and reworking old patterns related to maladaptive and compromised functioning moving toward higher level patterns of satisfaction.

apist. At its earliest stages it may take the form of concrete services and outreach, moving toward supportive and information gathering phases. These are generally initiated and moved along by the therapist's interest and concrete emotional support. Next the participant increases her ability to report interactions and behaviors with others on her own and permits feelings to be recognized and named by the therapist. This may develop into more self-observing reports to the therapists and would be followed by the participant's capacity to report not only what happened to her but how she felt about it. This may pertain to events within as well as outside the therapeutic process; the participant may talk about how she felt about a prior session or this session. The observing function develops and is used to understand the mother–infant relationship in a more selective and organized manner; the mother can now observe and record her feelings in relation to her infant as well as to other people in her life. More complex feelings enter the therapeutic process here, such as loss, jealousy, and competition. The observing function appears more stable and the participant begins to recognize complex and ambivalent feeling stages in her various relationships. As the participant moves up on this scale you would expect to see connections made between the therapeutic relationship and other key relationships through the use of transference. The participant is now using the therapeutic relationship as a vehicle for learning and understanding more about her emotions and interactions. She can continually reexamine patterns in this relationship and relate these to patterns with others as well as to patterns reflected in her history. It is at this point that the therapeutic process moves to remembering, recovering, or reconstructing early experiences, which help her see the historical continuity involved in these patterns. This historical perspective offers depth and further understanding to emotional experiences involving the participant and the therapist, their babies, and others. The highest level of this process is illustrated by the participant's capacity to use the identification of patterns in her current life, reorganize historical antecedents, and repeatedly explore these patterns in multiple settings as she works through her difficulties. The participant recognizes "here it happened again" and sees the historical base as well as the current ramifications of behavior and feelings. Repetitive exploration leads to the participant beginning to relinquish old maladaptive and compromised patterns of functioning in favor of new ways of relating and experimenting with higher level patterns of satisfaction. The final point of this scale would reflect the consolidation of new patterns and the participant's feeling secure that the gains she has made can be maintained and have become adaptive in all parts of her life. This would be followed by dealing with separation and termination of therapy, demonstrating the capacity to work through the sense of loss and mourning and move forward.

11

A Developmental Diagnostic Approach for Infants, Young Children, and Their Families

Stanley I. Greenspan, M.D.
Robert A. Nover, M.D.
Alfred Q. Scheuer, M.D.

One of the goals of the Clinical Infant Development Program's (CIDP) study of normal and disturbed developmental patterns in infancy was the development of a more comprehensive classification of adaptive and maladaptive infant and family patterns than had previously existed. Over the years, we devised a multiaxial approach to diagnosis for infants, young children, and their families, based on a developmental structuralist conceptual framework. Our hope is that such an approach to diagnosis may facilitate communication among the clinicians from many disciplines who work with this population. This chapter includes a review of the historical and theoretical foundations of a clinical developmental approach, an overview of the developmental structuralist framework, outlines of infant and caregiver characteristics at various stages of development which provide an opportunity to make a developmentally based diagnosis of disturbed functioning, and case vignettes which illustrate the application of this diagnostic approach.

Work with the multirisk families and their infants and other risk groups (i.e., low birthweight babies), as well as competent infants and families, provided us with a range of experiences that led to a conceptual framework to categorize adaptive and maladaptive infant and family patterns.

Ideally, a diagnostic framework would encompass all of the clinically relevant lines of human development. These include physical, neurologic, and cognitive lines, human relationships, and capacities for organizing and differentiating experience (adaptive and coping strategies). This framework would lend itself to an understanding of the range and variation in human functioning from the normal to the pathologic.

Several existing developmental frameworks have provided enormous understanding of individual lines of development in infancy and early childhood; for example, Sigmund Freud (1905), Erikson (1959), Piaget (1962), Sander (1962), Anna Freud (1965), Kohut (1971), Mahler, Pine, and Bergman (1975), and Kernberg (1975); in addition, there has been empirical research. These foundations, together with the rapidly growing body of clinical experience with infants and their families, provide direction for a much-needed integrated approach encompassing the multiple lines of development in the context of adaptive and disordered functioning.

These contributions have led to an integrated clinical approach based on a developmental structuralist framework (Greenspan, 1979, 1981; Greenspan and Greenspan, 1985) and to the classification of adaptive and pathologic personality organizations and behaviors in infancy and early childhood. This in turn provides a basis for understanding adaptive and maladaptive environments and principles of preventive and therapeutic intervention.

Traditional approaches to the classification of adaptive functioning, disordered functioning, and intervention are based on the clustering of certain symptoms and/or on an understanding of the etiologic basis of the disorder. However, while necessary, the etiologic and symptom-complex approaches to classification and diagnosis are in themselves insufficient. For example, the same etiologic factor can result in different behavioral outcomes or symptoms: As an illustration, a reaction to a given allergen or stress may differ depending on individual differences in response proclivity. Conversely, several different etiologic agents may result in the same symptoms: for example, an allergen, an infectious agent, or a series of external events can all produce a similar gastrointestinal disturbance.

In considering adaptive and maladaptive personality development, we do not yet have a complete framework for delineating the pathogenic and adaptive processes. There is, therefore, a need for another classification which would focus on the organism's individual way of processing, organizing, integrating, and differentiating experience, that is, the pathways that lead to certain behavioral outcomes. This "final common pathway" connects the influence of multiple etiologic factors with varying outcomes and suggests something fundamental about the individual organism's manner of organizing its experience of its world, internal and external, animate and inanimate.

Thus the study of psychopathology in infancy is a new area, even though the historical foundation for identifying disturbances in the early years of life is very impressive. Constitutional and maturational patterns which influenced the formation of early relationship patterns were already being noted in the early 1900s, with descriptions of "babies of nervous inheritance" who exhaust their mothers (Cameron, 1919) and infants with "excessive nerve activity and a functionally immature" nervous system.

Winnicott, who as a pediatrician in the 1930s began describing the environment's role in early relationship problems (1931), was followed in the 1940s by well-known studies describing the severe developmental disturbances of infants brought up in institutions or in other situations of emotional deprivation (Lowrey, 1940; Hunt, 1941; Backwin, 1942; Spitz,

1945; Bowlby, 1952). Spitz's films resulted in laws in the United States prohibiting care of infants in institutions.

The role of individual differences in the infant based on constitutional maturational and early interactional patterns (i.e., "nervous" infants described by Cameron [1919] and Rachford [1905]) again became a focus of inquiry, as evidenced by the observations of Burlingham and A. Freud (1942); Bergman and Escalona's descriptions of infants with "unusual sensitivities" (1949); Escalona and Heider (1959); Cravioto and DeLicardie's descriptions of the role of infant individual differences in malnutrition (1973); Murphy's vulnerability index (Murphy and Moriarity 1976); Thomas and Chess's temperament studies (1978). There is the impressive emerging empirical literature on infants (Gewirtz, 1961; Rheingold, 1961, 1966, 1969; Sander, 1962; Lipsitt, 1966; Brazelton, Koslowski, and Main, 1974; Stern, 1974a, 1974b; Emde, et al., 1976). More integrated approaches to understanding disturbances in infancy have been emphasized in descriptions of selected disorders and very insightful clinical case studies (e.g., Fraiberg, 1980; Provence, 1983; Provence and Naylor, 1983).

A Developmental Basis for Psychopathology and Adaptation in Infancy and Early Childhood

The adaptive and maladaptive infant and family patterns which we observed in the Clinical Infant Development Program (CIDP) beginning in 1975 are summarized in the following chart. The narrative description of these patterns which follows is presented in more detail in the first volume of Clinical Infant Reports, as well as in other writings by Greenspan, Lourie, and Nover (1979), Greenspan (1979), Greenspan and Lourie (1981), and Greenspan and Porges (1984).

The capacities described by the stages on the chart are all present in some rudimentary form in very early infancy. The sequence presented suggests not when these capacities begin, but when they become relatively prominent in organizing behavior and furthering development. In this classifi-

TABLE 11-1a
Developmental Basis for Psychopathology and Adaptation

Stage-Specific Tasks and Capacities	Capacities		Environment (Caregiver)	
	Adaptive	Maladaptive (Pathologic)	Adaptive	Maladaptive
Homeostasis (0–3 mo) (Self regulation and interest in the world)	Internal regulation (harmony) and balanced interest in world	Unregulated (e.g. hyperexcitable), withdrawn (apathetic)	Invested, dedicated, protective, comforting, predictable, engaging and interesting	Unavailable, chaotic, dangerous, abusive: hypostimulating or hyperstimulating: dull
Attachment (2–7 mo)	Rich, deep, multisensory emotional investment in animate world (especially with primary caregivers)	Total lack of, or nonaffective, shallow, impersonal, involvement (e.g. autistic patterns) in animate world	In love and woos infant to "fall in love": affective multimodality pleasurable involvement	Emotionally distant, aloof, and/or impersonal (highly ambivalent)
Somatopsychologic differentiation (3–10 mo) (Purposeful, cause & effect" signaling for communication)	Flexible, wide-ranging affective multisystem contingent (reciprocal) interactions (especially with primary caregivers)	Behavior and affects random and or chaotic, or narrow, rigid, and stereotyped	Reads and responds contingently to infant's communications across multiple-sensory and affective systems	Ignores infant's communications (e.g. overly intrusive, preoccupied, or depressed) or misreads infant's communication (e.g. projection)

TABLE 11-1a (continued)

Developmental Basis for Psychopathology and Adaptation

Behavioral organization, initiative, and internalization (9–24 mo)	Complex, organized, assertive, innovative, integrated behavioral and emotional patterns	Fragmented, stereotyped, and polarized behavior and emotions (e.g. withdrawn, compliant, hyperaggressive, or disorganized toddler)	Admiring of toddler's initiative and autonomy, yet available, tolerant, and firm: follows toddler's lead and helps him organize diverse behavioral and affective elements	Overly intrusive, controlling: fragmented, fearful (especially of toddler's autonomy): abruptly and prematurely "separates"
Representational capacity, differentiation, and consolidation (1½–4 yr) (The use of ideas to guide language, pretend play, and behavior and eventually thinking and planning)	Formation and elaboration of internal representations (imagery) Organization and differentiation of imagery pertaining to self and nonself; emergence of cognitive insight Stabilization of mood and gradual emergence of basic personality functions	No representational (symbolic) elaboration; behavior and affect concrete, shallow, and polarized; sense of self and other fragmented and undifferentiated or narrow and rigid; reality testing, impulse regulation, mood stabilization compromised or vulnerable (e.g. borderline psychotic and severe character problems)	Emotionally available to phase-appropriate regressions and dependency needs: reads, responds to, and encourages symbolic elaboration across emotional behavioral domains (e.g. love, pleasure, assertion) while fostering gradual reality orientation and internalization of limits	Fearful of or denies phase-appropriate needs; engages child only in concrete (nonsymbolic) modes generally or in certain realms (e.g. around pleasure) and/or misreads or responds noncontingently or nonrealistically to emerging communications (i.e. undermines reality orientation); overly permissive or punitive

TABLE 11-1a (continued)
Developmental Basis for Psychopathology and Adaptation

Capacity for limited extended representational systems and multiple extended representational systems (middle childhood through adolescence)	Enhanced and eventually optimal flexibility to conserve and transform complex and organized representations of experience in the context of expanded relationship patterns and phase-expected developmental tasks	Derivative representational capacities limited or defective, as are latency and adolescent relationships and coping capacities	Supports complex, phase- and age-appropriate experiential and interpersonal development (i.e. into triangular and posttriangular patterns)	Conflicted over child's age-appropriate propensities (e.g. competitiveness, pleasure orientation, growing competence, assertiveness, and self-sufficiency): becomes aloof or maintains symbiotic tie: withdraws from or overengages in competitive or pleasurable strivings

Source: Stanley I. Greenspan, *Psychopathology and Adaptation in Infancy and Early Childhood; Principles of Clinical Diagnosis and Preventive Intervention, Clinical Infant Reports*: No. 1. New York: International Universities Press, 1981.

S. I. Greenspan and N. T. Greenspan, *First Feelings; Milestones in the Emotional Development of Your Infant and Child from Birth to Age 4*. New York: Viking Press, 1985.

cation the first stage is the *achievement of homeostasis*, that is, self-regulation and emerging interest in the sights, sounds, smells, tastes, and textures of the world through the senses. Once the infant has achieved some capacity for regulation in the context of engaging the world, and central nervous system (CNS) maturation is increasing (between 2 and 4 months of age), he becomes more attuned to social and interpersonal interaction. He is more able to respond to the external environment and to form a special relationship with the significant primary caregivers. Thus a second, closely related stage is that of *forming a human attachment*. If an affective and relatively pleasurable attachment (an investment in the human, animate world) is formed, then, with growing maturational abilities, the infant develops complex patterns of communication in the context of this primary human relationship.

As he develops his relationship to the inanimate world and begins to understand basic schemes of causality (means/ends relationships) (Piaget, 1962), the infant at the same time becomes capable of complicated human communications (Charlesworth, 1969; Tennes, Emde, Kisley, and Metcalf, 1972; Brazelton et al., 1974; Stern, 1974a).

When there have been distortions in the attachment process (e.g., if a mother responds in a mechanical, remote manner and/or projects some of her own dependent feelings onto her infant), the infant may not learn to appreciate causal relationships between people at the level of compassionate and intimate feelings. This can occur even though causality seems to be developing in terms of the inanimate world and the impersonal human world. We have observed infants who are differentiated in the assertive, impersonal domain of human relationships but who are relatively undifferentiated in the intimate, pleasurable domain.

That causal relationships have been established between the infant and the primary caregiver can be seen in the infant's growing ability to discriminate significant primary caregivers from others. He also becomes able to differentiate his own actions from their consequences, affectively, somatically, behaviorally, and interpersonally. Usually by 8 months of age or earlier, the process of differentiation begins along a number of developmental lines (e.g., with sensorimotor integration, affects, relationship). A third state therefore may be formally termed *somatopsychologic differentiation* to indicate processes occurring at the somatic (e.g., sensorimotor) and emerging psychological levels. (In this context, psychologic refers to higher level mental processes characterized by the capacity to form internal representations or symbols as a way to organize experience.) While schemes of causality are being established in the infant's relationship to the interpersonal world, it is not at all clear whether these schemes exist at an organized representational or symbolic level. Rather, they appear to exist mainly at a somatic level (Greenspan, 1979), even though we do observe the precursors of representational capacities. Some are perhaps even prenatally determined (Lourie, 1971).

With appropriate reading of cues and systematic differential responses, the infant's or toddler's behavioral repertoire becomes complicated and communications take on more organized, meaningful configurations. By 12 months of age, the infant is connecting behavioral units into larger organizations as he exhibits complex emotional responses such as affiliation, wariness, and fear (Bowlby, 1969; Ainsworth, Bell, and Stayton, 1974; Sroufe and Waters, 1977). As the toddler moves farther into the second year of life, in the context of the practicing subphase of the development of individuation (Mahler et al., 1975), there is an increased capacity for forming original behavioral schemes (Piaget, 1962) and imitative activity and intentionality.

A type of learning through imitation evidenced in earlier development now seems to assume a more dominant role. As imitations take on a more integrated personal form, it appears the toddler is adopting or internalizing attributes of his caregivers. To describe these new capacities it is useful to consider a fourth stage, that of *behavioral organization, initiative, and internalization*.

As the toddler moves into the end of the second year, with further central nervous system maturation, we notice an increased capacity to form and organize mental representations (i.e., ideas). Internal sensations and unstable images become organized in a mental representational form which can be evoked and is somewhat stable (Gouin-Décarie, 1965; Bell, 1970; Piaget, 1962). While this capacity is initially fragile (i.e., between 16 and 24 months), it soon appears to become a dominant mode in organizing the child's behavior, and a fifth stage can be documented, that of *forming mental representations or ideas*. As a clarification of related concepts, it should be pointed out that the capacity for "object permanence," referring to the toddler's ability to search for hidden inanimate objects, is relative and goes through a series of stages (Gouin-Décarie, 1965). Representational capacity refers to the ability to organize and evoke internal, organized, multisensory experiences of the animate object. The capacities to represent animate and inanimate experiences are related and depend both on CNS myelination and appropriate experiences. The process of "internalization" may be thought of as an intermediary process. Internalized experiences eventually become sufficiently organized to be considered representations.

At a representational level the child again develops his capacities for elaboration, integration, and differentiation. Just as causal schemes previously were developed at a somatic and behavioral level, now they are developed at a representational level. The child begins to elaborate and eventually differentiate those feelings, thoughts, and events that emanate from himself and those that emanate from others. He begins to differentiate what he experiences and does from the impact of his actions on the world. This gradually forms the basis for the differentiation of "self" representations from those which embody the external world, animate and inanimate, and also provides the basis for such crucial personality functions as distinguishing what is real from unreal, impulse and mood regulation, and the capacity to focus attention and concentrate in order to learn and interact.

The capacity for differentiating internal representations becomes consolidated as object constancy is established (Mahler et al., 1975). In middle childhood, representational capacity becomes reinforced, with the child's ability to develop derivative representational systems tied to the original representation and transform them in accord with adaptive and defensive goals. This permits greater flexibility in dealing with perceptions, feelings, thoughts, and emerging ideals. Substages for these capacities include representational differentiation, the consolidation of representational capacity, and the capacity for forming limited derivative representational systems and multiple derivative representational systems (structural learning [Greenspan, 1979]).

At each of these stages, in varying degrees, pathologic as well as adaptive formations are possible. These may be considered as relative compromises in the range, depth, stability, and/or personal uniqueness of the experiential organization consolidated at each stage. The infant can form adaptive patterns of regulation in the earliest stages of development. His internal states are harmoniously regulated and he is free to invest himself in the animate and inanimate world, thereby setting the basis for rich emotional attachments to his primary caregivers. On the other hand, if his regulatory processes are not functioning properly and he cannot maintain internal harmony in the context of being available to the world, the infant may withdraw. From relatively minor compromises such as a tendency to withdraw and/or be hyperexcitable under stress, to a major deviation such as an overwhelming avoidance of the animate world, we can observe the degrees to which the infant, even in the first months of life, achieves a less than optimal adaptive structural organization.

Thus, the early attachments can be warm and engaging, or shallow, insecure, and limited in their affective tone. In the early reciprocal relationships, we can observe differences between an infant who reads the signals of the caregivers and responds in a rich, meaningful way to multiple aspects of the communications (with multiple affects and behavioral communications), and one who can respond only within a narrow range of affect (e.g., protest) or who cannot respond at all in a contingent or reciprocal manner (e.g., the seemingly apathetic, withdrawn, and depressed child who responds only to his own internal cues). As the toddler, optimally, becomes behaviorally more organized and complex patterns appear which reflect originality and initiative in the context of the separation and individuation subphase of development, we can observe toddlers who manifest this full adaptive capacity. They may be compared with others who are stereotyped in their behavioral patterns (reflect no originality or intentionality), who remain fragmented (never connect pieces of behavior into more complicated patterns), or who evidence polarities of affect, showing no capacity to integrate emotions (e.g., the chronic negativistic, aggressive toddler who cannot show interest, curiosity, or love).

As a capacity for representational organization is reached, we can distinguish the child who can organize, integrate, and differentiate a rich range of affective and ideational life from one who remains either without representational capacity or undifferentiated (i.e., deficits with reality testing, impulse control, focused concentration, or who may form and differentiate self and object representations only at the expense of extreme compromises in the range of tolerated experience (e.g., the schizoid child who withdraws from relationships). Similar adaptive or maladaptive structural organizations can be observed in later childhood (the triangular phase), latency, and adolescence.

Developmental Morbidity in Children in Multirisk Families

Infants and young children in multirisk families, we discovered, show significantly less than optimal development in the first years of life. Expanding on the public health concept of infant morbidity, we called this pattern "developmental morbidity." While, in general, babies in the CIDP had been at risk prenatally, at the time of their mothers' enrollment prenatal intervention had assured adequate nutrition and other supports, including appropriate medical care. Patterns of perinatal development were normal. However, as early as the first few days of life, babies whose weight, size, and overall physical health were satisfactory had difficulty in regulating social responsiveness, establishing habituating patterns, and organizing their motor response.

Pediatric, neurological, and Brazelton neonatal examinations at 1 month of age showed developmental progression but not the increased capacity for orientation characteristic of a normative population. By 3 months of age, instead of a capacity for self-regulation, organization, and an interest in the world, a number of babies in multi-risk families showed increased tendencies toward lability, muscle rigidity, gaze aversion, and an absence of organized sleep–wake, alert, and feeding patterns. Their caregivers, instead of having an overall capacity of offering the babies comfort, protection, and an interest in the world, tended either to withdraw from them and avoid them or to overstimulate them in a chaotic fashion.

Between 3 and 9 months of age, in the multiproblem families, children's behavior and affects remained under the control of internal states in random and chaotic or narrow, rigid, and stereotyped patterns of interaction. The child's environment, instead of offering the expected optimal contingent responsiveness to the child's varied signals, tended to ignore or misread them. The child's caregivers were overly preoccupied, depressed or chaotic.

Toward the end of the first year of life and the beginning of the second, a child in a multirisk family, instead of showing an increase in organized, complex, assertive, and innovative emotional and behavioral patterns, tended to exhibit fragmented, stereotyped, and polarized patterns. These toddlers were observed to be withdrawn and compliant or highly aggressive, impulsive, and disorganized. Their human environment tended to be intrusive, controlling, and fragmented. These toddlers may have been prematurely separated from their caregivers or the caregivers may have exhibited patterns of withdrawal instead of admiringly supporting the toddler's initiative and autonomy and helping the organization of what would become more complex capacities for communicating, interacting, and behaving.

As the toddler's potential capacities continued to develop in the latter half of the second year and in the third (18–36 months), profound deficits could be more clearly observed. The child did not develop capacities for internal representations (imagery) to organize behavior or feelings, differentiating ideas and feelings and thoughts pertaining to the self and the nonself. These children either developed no representational or symbolic capacity or, if the capacity did develop, it was not elaborated beyond the most elementary descriptive form so that the child's behavior remained shallow and polarized. The sense of the emerging self, as distinguished from the sense of other people, remained fragmented and undifferentiated. The child's potentially emerging capacities for reality testing, impulse regulation, and mood stabilization seemed either to be compromised or to become extremely vulnerable to regression. In other words, patterns either consistent with later borderline and psychotic personality organization or severe asocial or antisocial impulse-ridden character disorders were observed.

At this stage, the underlying impairment manifested itself in the child's inability to use a representational or symbolic mode to organize his behavior. In essence, the distinctly human capacity of operating beyond the survival level, of using internal imagery to elaborate and organize complex feelings and wishes and to construct trial actions in the emotional sphere, and of anticipating and planning ahead, were compromised. In many of the research families, the parents simply did not have these capacities themselves. Even when they were not under emotional distress or in states of crisis or panic, they did not demonstrate a symbolic mode, as evidenced in the lack of verbal communication (only one aspect of symbolic communication) and in the lack of symbolic play. Such families tended to be fearful and to deny and fail to meet their children's needs. They engaged the child only in non-symbolic modes of communication, such as holding, feeding, and administering physical punishment, and at times they misread or responded unrealistically to the child's emerging communication, thus undermining the development in the child of a sense of self and a flexible orientation to reality.

Needless to say, the mastery by the children in these families of higher level developmental tasks would become even more difficult. At each new level of development, the infants and toddlers who, for a variety of reasons, had survived earlier developmental phases intact invariably would challenge the multirisk environment with their new capacities, such as their capacity for symbolic communication. The healthier the toddler, the more challenging and overwhelming the child was likely to be. In a pattern frequently observed, the child would move ahead of the parent (engaging, for example, in symbolic play around themes of dependency or sexuality), and the parent would become confused and either withdraw from, or behave intrusively toward the child. Soon, unless other more skillful caregivers became available, the child would begin to regress to presymbolic modes of behaving.

The children may be able to consolidate higher level capacities when they begin to receive support from other systems, such as the school, and when they become capable of understanding parental limitations. These capacities, however, can only develop when the child is a little older. The youngster who experiences developmental failures, including the failure to develop a fully representational or symbolic capacity (the basis for formal school experience later on) will unquestionably be handicapped in all subsequent opportunities for learning.

An Outline of the Diagnostic Categories

The overview of the developmental basis for psychopathology and adaptation in infancy and early childhood and the discussion of developmental morbidity presented previously provide the necessary background for the description of a diagnostic classification system for disturbances in infancy and early childhood (see Tables 11-1b—11-15). As with all systems of classification, the approach presented should be viewed as a set of hypotheses derived from clinical observations and abstractions of what appeared to be the most relevant patterns. These descriptions are open to further revisions and need to be tried out in larger population studies.

While the focus of this approach to classification is the developmental diagnosis and the explicit criteria for each developmental category, the approach described is also a multipronged one, based on the assumption that a complete approach to diagnosis must involve describing the patient's symptoms in the context of the patient's overall developmental level. The patient's symptoms and developmental level in turn must be seen in the context of caregiver and familial functioning as well as the child's physical, neurological, and psychosocial patterns of adaptation. To this end, information is collected regarding symptoms, developmental diagnosis, physical and neurological systems, and the extenuating or contributing factors, including a diagnosis of caregiver and familial patterns. The caregiver patterns include both a developmental statement (the degree to which the caregivers facilitate or undermine phase specific functioning), and a formal (i.e., *Diagnostic and Statistical Manual* [DSM-III] or *International Classification of Diseases* [ICD-9] type) diagnostic judgment for individual adult or child family members.

In using this approach it will also be evident that the developmentally oriented diagnostic impression of the caregiver's abilities parallels the developmental needs of the infant and young child at each stage of development. There is a parallel between the youngster's phase specific tasks and the caregiving environment's hypothesized supportive attributes. The developmental diagnosis, with degree of disorder or deficit, ascertained for the caretaker should be made at the same level of functioning as exists for the child. For example, if the child's disorder is at the level of somatopsychological differentiation, a diagnosis for the caretaker should be made at that same level as well as at earlier levels of development if warranted. In making a diagnosis for the caregiving environment, it may prove practical to put this outline side by side with the outline of the child's functioning at each age and describe both simultaneously.

The reader's attention should also be drawn to the categories describing acute, subacute, and chronic as an additional level of description of the nature of the disorder. It may not always be possible to make this differentiation but where possible, it may help to clarify the type of disorder present.

The outlines also provide an opportunity for indicating a "subtype" of the disorder. This may prove useful where a limitation in a particular sensory mode or affect system is present.

In using the following outline, please note that there is an overview outline for both the infant's functioning and the caregiver's functioning. This overview outline is followed by detailed descriptions of the developmentally based diagnostic categories (see Tables 11-1b and 11-9).

The framework is aimed at providing a systematic frame of reference for describing a child's functioning relative to his competencies and his vulnerabilities. Its goal is to make it possible to diagnosis difficulties in infants and young children in a detailed manner, to provide both a series of diagnostic statements and a set of "codes" for a system of medical records with sufficient information (inherent in the various diagnostic judgments) to allow one to recreate, for example, from a com-

APPROACH TO DIAGNOSIS WITH INFANTS AND THEIR CAREGIVERS

TABLE 11-1b

Overview Chart—Infant Functioning

Symptomatic (Presenting symptoms)	(Methods of organizing and differentiating experience)	Review of Systems (Additional medical, or developmental diagnosis or findings based on history and examination should be listed here; e.g., congenital defects, middle ear infection, maturational motor lag, neurological asymmetry.)	Modulating Factors (Etiological, precipitating, exacerbating, or attenuating factors) More than one group of modulating factors may be listed as primary or secondary to indicate degree of contribution.
Sleep	A defect is present if both direct observation and history confirm the patterns or if three successive observations at different times confirm this pattern. (An observation is a 10–15 minute free interaction sequence between caregiver and infant.)	a. There are no additional diagnoses	a. Constitutional or maturational (list here biological vulnerabilities not already listed such as hyperlability, sensory hypersensitivities, hypoarousal, motor delays, etc.)
Eating		b. There are additional diagnoses but they have no known bearing on main disorder (list diagnosis)	1. Biological vulnerabilities
Change in Weight (Gain or Loss)		c. There are additional diagnoses and they contribute to main disorder (list diagnosis)	2. No biological vulnerabilities
Bowel or Bladder			b. Caregiver, family support system vulnerabilities
State Regulation			1. Competent caregiver family and support
Motor			
Sensory Processing			
Sensory Motor	A. General (See Tables 11-2–11-8 for Guidelines)		
Cognitive	1. Severe		
Speech	a.		
Social	b.		
Affective	c.		
Delayed Physiologic Functioning	2. Moderate		
Organ Dysfunction (without Tissue Damage: Psychogenic)	a.		
	b.		
	c.		
	3. Mild		
	a.		

TABLE 11-1b (continued)
Overview Chart

b.

c.

B. Subtype (use this rating only when a
subtype is clearly evident)
(See Table 10-8 for Guidelines)
Sensory
Motor
Affective Range
Affective Stability
Affective Space and Time

C. Duration

1. Acute (pattern only within last
month)

2. Subacute (pattern exists for more
than one month but there is
history of better functioning)

3. Chronic (pattern is present either
since birth or for as long as history
is obtainable)

individual differences

2. Caregiver, family or
support system is
compromised in
facilitating phase specific
developmental
challenges. If 2b is
present, fill out caregiver,
family support system
diagnosis (See Table 10-
16 and Tables 10-8–10-13)

TABLE 11-2

Developmental Diagnosis—Homeostasis (0–3 months)

Competent functioning is based on the following observations or historical information about the infant.

Relaxed and sleeps at regular times; recovers from crying with comforting. Is able to be very alert; looks at one when talked to; brightens up progressively more when provided with appropriate visual, auditory, and/or tactile stimulation as he goes from 0–3 months.

Disordered functioning is based on the following observations and historical information.

1. Severe Disorders	2. Moderate Disorders	3. Mild Disorders: Functioning between competent and moderate
Type A—Sleeps almost all the time. Shows no interest in anyone; does not respond to interesting stimuli; e.g., lights, colors, sounds, touch or movements.	Type A—Seems apathetic or sad, uninterested in anything. Responds a little to touch or movement, but not very interested in seeing or hearing objects nearby.	Type A—Use descriptions from Moderate Disorders and Competent Functioning.
Type B—Always upset or crying; stiff and rigid. Becomes completely distracted by any sights, noises, touch, movement; gets too excited and cries.	Type B—Upset and crying most of the time. Is too alert; looks at too many things; gets somewhat distracted by things he can see, hear, or feel.	Type B—Use descriptions from Moderate Disorders and Competent Functioning.
Type C—Mixed type. Shows a mixture of above with neither predominating.	Type C—Mixed type. Shows a mixture of above with neither predominating.	Type C—Mixed type. Use descriptions from Moderate Disorders and Competent Functioning.

Severe   Mild

Type _____

Indicate with a line where on the continuum the disorder lies and list type (e.g., A, B, C).

TABLE 11-3
Developmental Diagnosis—Attachment (2–4 months)

Competent functioning is based on the following observations or historical information about the infant.

Very interested in people, especially mother or father, and other key caregivers; looks, smiles, responds to their voices, their touch with signs of pleasure and interest such as smiling, relaxing, "cooing" or other vocalizations indicating pleasure. Seems to respond with deep feeling and with multiple sensory modalities (e.g., with vision, audition, tactile senses, movement, olfactory senses, etc.).

Disordered functioning is based on the following observations and historical information.

1. Severe Disorders	2. Moderate Disorders	3. Mild Disorders: Functioning between the Competent and Moderate Range.
Type A—Disinterested in people, especially mother, father, and/or other primary caregivers (e.g., always looks away rather than at people); looks withdrawn (as though eyes are turned inward); human approaches (i.e., holding) lead to rigidity and turning away or further withdrawal. Chronic flat affect.	Type A—Only occasionally looks at people or responds to their voices with show of interest, either a smile or putting hand out or kicking. After, however, shows no special interest in human world. No comfort in being held. Flat affect a good deal of the time.	Type A—Use descriptions from Moderate Disorders and Competent Functioning. Type B—Use descriptions from Moderate Disorders and Competent Functioning. Type C—Mixed type. Use descriptions from Moderate Disorders and Competent Functioning.
Type B—Insists on being held all the time; will not sleep without being held.	Type B—Seems almost too interested in people; clinging to mother, father or other primary caregiver; cries easily if not held; goes to strangers and holds on as if they were parents. Not very interested in playing alone (e.g., exploring new toy).	
Type C—Mixed type. Shows a mixture of above with neither predominating.	Type C—Mixed type. Shows a mixture of above with neither predominating.	

Severe _____ Mild

Type _____

Indicate with a line where on the continuum the disorder lies and list type (e.g., A, B, C).

TABLE 11-4

Developmental Diagnosis—Somatopsychological Differentiation (3–10 months)

Competent functioning is based on the following observations or historical information about the infant.

Able to interact in a purposeful (i.e., intentional, reciprocal, cause and effect type) manner; smiles in response to a voice; able to initiate signals and respond purposefully using multiple sensory modalities, the motor system. Purposefully employs a range of emotions (e.g., pleasure or protest, assertion, etc.); at the same time able to get involved with toys and other inanimate objects.

Disordered functioning is based on the following observations and historical information.

1. Severe Disorders	2. Moderate Disorders	3. Mild Disorders: Functioning between the Competent and Moderate range.
Type A—May interact but not purposefully. Seems oblivious to caregivers' signals; does not respond to their smile, voice, reaching out; "Marches to the beat of a different drummer."	Type A—Responds occasionally to caregivers' signals, such as smiles or sounds, but hard to predict when; very intermittent, often random rather than purposeful social responses, or limited only to one type of signal, such as caregiver's voice, but not smile.	Type A—Use descriptions from Moderate Disorders and Competent Functioning.
		Type B—Use descriptions from Moderate Disorders and Competent Functioning.
Type B—Demands constant interaction, cannot tolerate being alone at all; has temper tantrums or withdraws if caregiver does not respond to his signals or initiate interactive signals all the time.	Type B—Able to interact, but seems overly sensitive to any emotional communication of caregiver; looks sad and forlorn at slightest sign that caregiver is preoccupied; gets very easily frustrated if signal (e.g., smile and hand reaching out) is not responded to. Disorganized.	Type C—Mixed Type. Use descriptions from Moderate Disorders and Competent Functioning.
Type C—Mixed type. Shows a mixture of above with neither predominating.	Type C—Mixed type. Shows a mixture of above with neither predominating.	

Severe   ┼————————————————————————————————————┼   Mild

Type ————

Indicate with a line where on the continuum the disorder lies and list type (e.g., A, B, C).

Developmental Diagnosis—Behavioral Organization, Initiative, and Originality (10-17 months): Behavioral Organization

Competent functioning is based on the following observations or historical information about the infant.

Manifests a wide range of socially meaningful behaviors and feelings including warmth, pleasure, assertion, exploration, protest, anger, etc., in an organized manner. For example, can play or interact with parents stringing together a number of reciprocal interactions into a complex social interchange such as a game where parents and child take turns chasing each other around the house, or where looking at pictures together contains interest and curiosity in the context of a warm interchange with parents and child taking turns viewing, pointing or vocalizing. Able to go from interacting to separation and reunion with organized affects including pleasure, apprehension and protest.

Disordered functioning is based on the following observations and historical information.

1. Severe Disorders

Type A—Rarely initiates behaviors and/or emotions; mostly passive and withdrawn or seemingly uninvolved or excessively negativistic. Flat affect may predominate.

Type B—Behavior and affect completely random, chaotic. Toddler almost always appears "out of control" with aggressive affects predominating in context of highly disorganized behaviors. No sense of purpose.

Type C—Mixed type. Shows a mixture of above with neither predominating.

2. Moderate Disorders

Type A—Can manifest a few socially meaningful behaviors in narrow range (e.g., can only protest, or only compliantly "go along"); involved only with social interaction around inanimate world (exploring a new object); no capacity for integrating pleasure, warmth, assertiveness and anger in social context.

Type B—Lots of behaviors and feelings manifested but in poorly organized unmodulated manner; shifts behaviors and moods rapidly; only occasionally involved in socially meaningful interactions. No focused curiosity.

Type C—Mixed type. Shows a mixture of above with neither predominating.

3. Mild Disorders: Functioning between competent and moderate range.

Type A—Use descriptions from Moderate Disorders and Competent Functioning.

Type B—Use descriptions from Moderate Disorders and Competent Functioning.

Type C—Mixed type. Use descriptions from Moderate Disorders and Competent Functioning.

Severe _____|_____ Mild

Type _____   Indicate with a line where on the continuum the disorder lies and list type (e.g., A, B, C).

TABLE 11-5b

Developmental Diagnosis—Behavioral, Organization, Initiative, and Originality (10–17 months): Behavioral Initiative and Originality

Competent functioning is based on the following observations or historical information about the infant.

Initiates complex, organized, emotionally and socially relevant interactions, yet also accepts limits. Continually surprises parents in a "delightful way" with new behaviors, capacities, social skills, complex emotions (e.g., can initiate cuddling with parents; can bring favorite game or puzzle and convey desire to play). Can explore new objects, and after a "warmup," new people, especially when parents are available.

Disordered functioning is based on the following observations and historical information.

1. Severe Disorders
Type A—Passive; compliant; withdrawn
Type B—Usually out of control, with aggressive behavior, disregarding limits and others' feelings.
Type C—Mixed type. Shows a mixture of above with neither predominating.

2. Moderate Disorders
Type A—Occasionally takes initiative, but usually only responds to others' initiative and may also be negativistic; little or no originality (i.e., no surprises or new emotions or behaviors); instead tends to be repetitive. No focused curiosity.
Type B—Takes initiative but is demanding and stubborn; tends to repeat rather than develop new behaviors or interactions.
Type C—Mixed type. Shows a mixture of above with neither predominating.

3. Mild Disorders: Functioning between competent and moderate range.
Type A—Use descriptions from Moderate Disorders and Competent Functioning.
Type B—Use descriptions from Moderate Disorders and Competent Functioning.
Type C—Mixed type. Use descriptions from Moderate Disorders and Competent Functioning.

Severe |——————————————|—— Mild

Type ———————

Indicate with a line where on the continuum the disorder lies and list type (e.g., A, B, C).

TABLE 11-6
Developmental Diagnosis—Use of Thoughts and Ideas: Representational Elaboration—Symbolic Capacities (17–30 months)

Competent functioning is based on the following observations or historical information about the infant.

Representational elaboration in descriptive and social-emotional interactive contexts. For example, either uses words or wordlike sounds to indicate wishes and intentions; can use dolls or other objects to play out a drama (e.g., feeding scene or shooting scene, etc.). Symbolic elaboration appears to cover a range of emotions including love, closeness, dependency, assertion, curiosity, anger, and protest.

Disordered functioning is based on the following observations and historical information.

1. Severe Disorders

Type A—No symbolic behavior such as words, symbolic play (e.g., one doll feeding another), complex actions implying planning and anticipation, etc. Behavior fragmented or stereotyped.

Type B—Symbolic activity, but totally disorganized and fragmented, totally used in the service of discharge type hyperactivity; words or play activities *never* develop into an organized drama.

Type C—Mixed type. Shows a mixture of above with neither predominating.

2. Moderate Disorders

Type A—Some symbolic behavior such as a few words or doll play. This capacity mostly limited to descriptive use of symbolic mode (e.g., naming objects or pictures); little or no capacity for social, emotional, interactive use of thoughts and ideas (the child can name objects or even describe cars crashing but is unable to use ideas in an emotional sense. He is unable to say "no, I like this or want this").

Type B—Symbols used (e.g., words or play) but often in chaotic, disorganized fashion; dramas have only fragments of discernible meaning.

Type C—Mixed type. Shows a mixture of above with neither predominating.

3. Mild Disorders: Functioning between competent and moderate range.

Type A—Use descriptions from Moderate Disorders and Competent Functioning

Type B—Use descriptions from Moderate Disorders and Competent Functioning

Type C—Mixed type. Use descriptions from Moderate Disorders and Competent Functioning

Severe ——————————— Mild

Type ——————

Indicate with a line where on the continuum the disorder lies and list type (e.g., A, B, C).

TABLE 11-7
Developmental Diagnosis— Purposeful, Realistic Use of Thoughts and Ideas: Representational Differentiation and Consolidation (26–36 months)

Competent functioning is based on the following observations or historical information about the infant.

Relates in balanced manner using the representational mode to people and things across a range of emotions (e.g., warmth, assertiveness). Is able to be purposeful, know what is real from unreal; accepts limits; can be self-limiting and also feel good about self; switches from fantasy to reality with little difficulty.

Disordered functioning is based on the following observations and historical information.

1. Severe Disorders

Type A—Withdrawn; unrelated to people; uses words or symbolic play only with "things." If words or symbolic play with people are used, then real from unreal is unclear. No sense of purpose or intention in social use of symbolic mode.

Type B—Relates to people and things symbolically in totally chaotic, unrealistic manner; no reality testing or impulse control. Self-esteem and mood is labile.

Type C—Mixed type. Shows a mixture of above with neither predominating.

2. Moderate Disorders

Type A—Relates slightly to people with words, play, or other symbols, but in narrow range of emotions. Some purposefulness and reality orientation is present but toddler is vulnerable to the slightest stress.

Type B—Relates to people and things using words or play across a range of emotions and themes, but in a chaotic, unreality oriented manner; can only relate to reality orientation with structure (e.g., needs lots of limits and repeated help with what is pretend and what is real).

Type C—Mixed type. Shows a mixture of above with neither predominating.

3. Mild Disorders: Functioning between competent and moderate range.

Type A—Use descriptions from Moderate Disorders and Competent Functioning.

Type B—Use descriptions from Moderate Disorders and Competent Functioning.

Type C—Mixed type. Use descriptions from Moderate Disorders and Competent Functioning.

Severe ├─────────────────────────┤ Mild

Type _____

Indicate with a line where on the continuum the disorder lies and list type (e.g., A, B, C).

TABLE 11-8

Amplification of Subtypes for the Developmental Diagnosis (As Listed under "B" in Col. 2, in Table 11-1b)

Subtypes—a subtype is present when a phase specific difficulty is either caused, intensified, or most evidenced by one or more *focal* difficulties in the use of the various senses, sensory motor capacities, or an affective potential in relationship to the normative tasks of that developmental phase.

a. Sensory System:
1. Visual
2. Auditory
3. Tactile
4. Olfactory
5. Proprioceptive
6. Motion

b. Motor (Sensory Motor)
1. Localized (e.g., arms or legs or trunk, etc.) (specify)
2. Global—full body response (e.g., inability to mold)
3. Integrate age expected capacities (e.g., crawling) into phase specific task

c. Affective Range (This Identifies Missing Components from the Age-Expected Affective Range)
1. No interest in inanimate world (e.g., no brightening up or alerting to appropriate stimuli—flat affect)
2. No interest in human world (e.g., no brightening up or alerting—even without smile or inspection—to the human world: flat affect)
3. No pleasure or satisfaction—after 2 months no real smile or show of joy. Neutral to sad looking
4. Clearly sad looking
5. No satisfying dependency (i.e., no comfort from being held, or touched, or talked to, or played with), neutral to sad looking
6. No focused explorative curiosity (assertiveness) (e.g., passive, laid back infant who never seeks or examines objects)
7. No protest or anger, even in mild forms (e.g., pulling or pushing objects of discomfort or yelling angrily or crying angrily or biting, pinching, hitting, etc.)

TABLE 11-8 (continued)

Amplification of Subtypes for the Developmental Diagnosis (As Listed under "B" in Col. 2, in Table 11-1b)

d. Affective Stability (Phase Appropriate Stability of Affect System)
  1. Markedly unstable shifting affect states (e.g., joy to protest to disinterest)
  2. Intermittently unstable and shifting affect states, below age expectations or inconsistent with situational context

e. Affective Space and Time (Use of Affects to Communicate Across Space and Time)
  1. No use or limited use of proximal modes—holding, touching, etc.
  2. No use or limited use of distal modes (eye signaling, facial and motor gesturing, affective gesturing, vocalizations and language)
  3. No use or limited use of imitation
  4. After 15 months no use of delayed imitation
  5. After 17 months no capacity to abstract functions of objects (e.g., spontaneous use of telephone, toothbrush, or comb realistically as part of play) or no indication of a prevailing attitude toward caregiver suggesting awareness of the person's "functions"
  6. After 22 months no evidence of "representational mode" as illustrated through "pretend play" (e.g., doll is mother or child pretends to be parent or TV character, etc.) or language

Overview Chart—Caregiver Functioning

Functional Approach to Caregivers	Developmental Level of Primary Caregiver	Formal Diagnosis*
Record this for each primary caregiver. Indicate approximate percentage of time spent with child.	For each primary caregiver indicate	For Caregivers (Where Appropriate As Found in DSM-III or ICD-9 and other nuclear family members, if appropriate
A. Primary caregiver (See Charts X–XV for guidelines)	a. Overall developmental level Rating . . . (See Apprendix 2 for Outline)	a. Primary caregivers (List the different caregivers, i.e., mother, father, sister, aunt, and if appropriate, their diagnoses) 1. 2. 3. etc.
a. Severe b. Moderate c. Mild a. a. a. b. b. b. c. c. c.	b. Developmental level of maternal schema Rating . . . (See Appendix 2 for Outline)	b. List other family members and if appropriate, their diagnoses. 1. 2. 3. etc.
Note [Only list the criteria on top for caregiver]		
B. Using above approach, record diagnosis for entire family as a unit in terms of their Functional Ability (i.e., include siblings, etc.). If it is no different from individual caregiver, indicate "same."		
C. Record functional diagnosis for family plus currently available support system using above approach. If it is the same as the family, indicate "same."		

*Formal diagnosis may prove useful for record keeping, research, and reimbursement for services.

TABLE 11-10

Functional Approach to Caregivers—Homeostasis (0–3 months)

Competent Caregiver

Excellent at helping infant to become fully regulated and comforted; can use multiple sensory and motor modes, voice, vision, movement (rocking), as well as a variety of affect states and empathetic skills in ways that tune into the individual differences of infant in a regulating manner. Interests infant in a variety of animate and inanimate stimuli. Gains infant's attention in a relaxed, focused manner and helps infant use multiple sensory and motor modalities, such as vision, sound, touch, movement, as a way to explore the human and inanimate world. Caregiver stress generally does not interfere, except temporarily, with this capacity.

Disordered functioning is based on the following observations and historical information.

1. Severe Disorders	2. Moderate Disorders	3. Mild Disorders: Functioning between competent and moderate range.
Type A—Completely unavailable to comfort infant (e.g., aloof, self-absorbed, very depressed, etc.). Caregiver presents no interesting stimuli, animate or inanimate.	Type A—Intermittently available (e.g., can comfort for brief periods or when infant is not too upset). Other times is withdrawn, aloof, or otherwise unavailable. Intermittently interesting to infant; gains his attention on occasion.	Type A—Use descriptions from Moderate Disorders and Competent functioning.
Type B—Grossly hyperstimulating and chaotic; undermines infant's own regulatory capacity.	Type B—Tries to comfort, but out of synchrony with infant or with lack of mutuality; overly intrusive, occasionally hyperstimulating. Gains infant's interest, but intermittently chaotic and distracting (e.g., too many stimuli or too intense).	Type B—Use descriptions from Moderate Disorders and Competent functioning.
Type C—Mixed type. Shows a mixture of above with neither predominating.	Type C—Mixed type. Shows a mixture of above with neither predominating.	Type C—Mixed type. Use descriptions from Moderate Disorders and Competent functioning.

Severe ___|___ Mild

Type ___

Indicate with a line where on the continuum the disorder lies and list type (e.g., A B C)

TABLE 11-11

Functional Approach to Caregivers—Attachment (2–4 months)

Competent caregiver

Optimal attachment with deep rich emotional investment expressed through smiles, looks, touch, talk, etc. Loving interest can accommodate occasional anger and disappointment, and survive caregiver stress (e.g., illness, tiredness, etc.)

Disordered functioning is based on the following observations and historical information.

1. Severe Disorders

Type A—Totally unavailable; lacks emotional warmth (e.g., mechanical or disinterested; does not look at, smile, talk to, or touch infant).

Type B—Slightly chaotic emotional investment; overwhelming, intrusive, hypomanic quality; seems impervious to infant's moods or states.

Type C—Mixed type. Shows a mixture of above with neither predominating.

2. Moderate Disorders

Type A—Intermittent emotional interest as reflected in some looking, cuddling, talking to, and/or stroking; may be limited to one modality (e.g., looking only, or holding and touching only). Whatever emotional contact that does exist is very vulnerable to caregiver stress.

Type B—Appears very interested in infant, but seems overly anxious and overprotective (e.g., always smiling, stroking) and worried that infant be "happy."

Type C—Mixed type. Shows a mixture of above with neither predominating.

3. Mild Disorders: Functioning between competent and moderate range.

Type A—Use descriptions from Moderate Disorders and Competent functioning.

Type B—Use descriptions from Moderate Disorders and Competent functioning.

Type C—Mixed type. Use descriptions from Moderate Disorders and Competent functioning.

Severe   ┼──────────┼ Mild

Type ─────

Indicate with a line where on the continuum the disorder lies and list the type (e.g., A, B, C).

TABLE 11-12

Functional Approach to Caregivers—Purposeful Communication (Somatopsychological Differentiation) (3–10 months)

Competent caregiver

Reads and responds causally and with empathy to entire range of infant's communications across all sensorimotor modalities and affect states. For example, reads and responds causally or reciprocally to smiles, vocalizations, glances, facial expressions, motoric behaviors in context of pleasurable dependency, as well as to protest and assertiveness. This capacity is resilient to stress.

Disordered functioning is based on the following observations and historical information.

1. Severe Disorders

Type A—Impervious to infant's communications. Fails totally to recognize or respond purposefully (causally) to infant's signals in any modality (e.g., no responsive smile; no responsive looks; no responsive vocalizations; no appropriate reaching out in response to infant's inviting gesture).

Type B—Misreads and overresponds to all signals. There is a chaotic intrusive quality.

Type C—Mixed type. Shows a mixture of above with neither predominating.

2. Moderate Disorders

Type A—Responds causally and purposefully only intermittently or in one modality but not another (e.g., only sometimes responds to smile; may totally misread or misinterpret [i.e., not respond to] entire areas of affect such as assertiveness or tenderness, etc.).

Type B—Overresponds and/or misreads some signals. When anxious, tends to confuse own feelings with infant's feelings. This is either limited to certain affects or sensorimotor modalities or states of stress. For example, responds contingently to smiles but overresponds to infant's protests by overfeeding child (i.e., sees protest as hunger).

Type C—Mixed type. Shows a mixture of above with neither predominating.

3. Mild Disorders: Functioning between competent and moderate range.

Type A—Use descriptions from Moderate Disorders and Competent functioning.

Type B—Use descriptions from Moderate Disorders and Competent functioning.

Type C—Mixed type. Use descriptions from Moderate Disorder and Competent functioning.

Severe ─────┼─────────────────────┼───── Mild

Type ─────── Indicate with a line where on the continuum the disorder lies and list type (e.g., A, A, B, C).

Functional Approach to Caregivers—Behavioral Organization and Initiative (10–17 months): Behavioral Organization

Competent caregiver

Can interact in complex organized manner and help child organize one step further. Able to do this across a wide range of themes (e.g., love, dependency, separation, anger, etc.). Can incorporate many themes into one interaction sequence, including polarities of love/hate and passivity/activity. Recovers well from stress, tolerates frustration and child's negativism and is able to pursue and be available without being overly controlling.

Disordered functioning is based on the following observations and historical information.

1. Severe Disorders

Type A—Unavailable to child as child is organizing complex behavior (e.g., withdraws, feels "the child doesn't need me anymore").

Type B—Always becomes intrusively confused and mildly disorganized when child's behavior or affect becomes complex, such as the child introducing a number of themes or signals. For example, cannot switch with child from one game to another or tends to switch and introduce new ideas too quickly, confusing and disorganizing the child. Cannot tolerate toddler's intensity of feeling or becomes too easily ashamed of themes such as sex or aggression and becomes intrusive or disorganized.

Type C—Mixed type. Shows a mixture of the above with neither predominating.

2. Moderate Disorders

Type A—Can interact in organized manner around a few limited themes or when not under any stress. For example, will play organized, interactive games around love, but withdraws as soon as aggression or assertion comes to center stage.

Type B—Intermittently tends to become intrusively confused and mildly disorganized when child's behavior becomes complex or introduces a theme—aggression—that caregiver finds frightening. Intermittently, cannot switch with child from one game to another or tends to switch and introduce new ideas too quickly, confusing and disorganizing the child.

Type C—Mixed type. Shows a mixture of the above with neither predominating.

3. Mild Disorders: Functioning between competent and moderate range.

Type A—Use descriptions from Moderate Disorders and Competent functioning.

Type B—Use descriptions from Moderate Disorders and Competent functioning.

Type C—Mixed type. Use descriptions from Moderate Disorders and Competent Functioning.

Severe ┤————————————————————————————————————┤ Mild

Type _____ Indicate with a line where on the continuum the disorder lies and list type (e.g., A, B, C).

TABLE 11-13b

Functional Approach to Caregivers—Behavioral organization: Initiative (10–17 months)

Competent caregiver

Admires (with gleam in eye) child's initiative; can follow child's lead; encourages child to go one step further (e.g., a great noncontrolling coach), and can do this across thematic areas, which include dependency, assertion, curiosity, aggression, pleasure, etc.; at the same time can set limits effectively to help child take initiative in self control. Permits separation; remains available and knows when to pursue child lovingly.

Disordered functioning is based on the following observations and historical information.

1. Severe Disorders

Type A—Withdrawn and unavailable to any initiative by child, however appropriate.

Type B—Totally overwhelms child. Provides no opportunity for child's initiative. Becomes chaotic and physical. Undermines and over-controls. Does the initiating in all areas.

Type C—Mixed type. Shows a mixture of the above with neither predominating.

2. Moderate Disorders

Type A—Intermittently unavailable to child's initiative, depending on thematic area (e.g., will encourage initiative around play with puzzles). May "pull away from" child's initiative around pleasure, including interest in the human body, sexual parts, sucking, etc. Easily disorganized by stress.

Type B—Intermittently tends to overcontrol and undermine initiative. Tends to be anxious and intrusive.

Type C—Mixed type. Shows a mixture of the above with neither predominating.

3. Mild Disorders: Functioning between competent and moderate range.

Type A—Use descriptions from Moderate Disorders and Competent functioning.

Type B—Use descriptions from Moderate Disorders and Competent functioning.

Type C—Mixed type. Use descriptions from Moderate Disorders and Competent functioning.

Severe ————————————————— Mild

Type ——————

Indicate with a line where on the continuum the disorder lies and list the type (e.g., A., B, C).

Functional Approach to Caregivers—Representational Capacity and Elaboration (17–30 months)

Competent caregiver

Interacts in representational (symbolic) mode across a variety of age-appropriate themes using multiple sensorimotor capacities (e.g., can interact using language and/or symbolic play in all thematic areas such as love, pleasure, dependency, aggression, competition, envy, hate, curiosity, etc. Can supportively pursue thematic areas which may be mildly frightening to a child. Can gradually develop richer and deeper symbolic communication (e.g., caregiver can further child's play sequence without assuming the initiative). Caregiver can maintain representational (symbolic) mode in face of stress.

Disordered functioning is based on the following observations and historical information.

1. Severe Disorders

Type A—Lacks all capacity to engage child symbolically; engages child in concrete fashion only (e.g., can deal with feeding and cleanliness), but cannot interact imaginatively, as with words, to describe feelings, or through play with dolls to represent people, or activities.

Type B—Symbolic capacity supported in chaotic, fleeting, hypomanic manner (e.g., mother keeps switching topics, etc.). Often totally misreads child's communication.

Type C—Mixed type. Shows a mixture of the above with neither predominating.

2. Moderate Disorders

Type A—Some symbolic interactive capacity but limited only to some themes, dependency but *not* curiosity or assertiveness and/or to one or two sensorimotor modalities (e.g., can play symbolically, whereas language use is concrete only). Withdraws if child tries to engage in "avoided area."

Type B—Interacts symbolically but only along own agenda, thereby undermining the child's capacity for elaboration; may do this in only some thematic areas (e.g., when child develops play where two dolls feed each other, caregiver becomes anxious and switches to a shooting game). Easily undermined by stress. Controls by activity and intrusiveness.

Type C—Mixed type. Shows a mixture of the above with neither predominating.

3. Mild Disorders: Functioning between competent and moderate range.

Type A—Use descriptions from Moderate Disorders and Competent functioning.

Type B—Use descriptions from Moderate Disorders and Competent functioning.

Type C—Mixed type. Use descriptions from Moderate Disorders and Competent functioning.

Severe _____|_____ Mild

Type _____   Indicate with a line where on the continuum the disorder lies and list the type (e.g., A, B, C).

TABLE 11-15

Functional Approach to Caregivers—Representational Differentiation and Consolidation (26–36 months)

Competent caregiver

Able to interact symbolically in a purposeful (causal, reciprocal) manner to wide range of themes, including love, dependency, pleasure, assertion, aggression, impulsivity, curiosity, etc. Can respond in flexible manner, including support, encouragement, empathy and firm limit-setting. Stress does not interfere except briefly.

Disordered functioning is based on the following observations and historical information.

1. Severe Disorders

Type A—Unable to use symbolic mode in logical or causal manner (e.g., depressed mother only interacts occasionally and never completes interaction in a logical sequence). For example, when child shows doll being "naughty," mother cannot finish sequence, even with child's encouragement, to show how child is either punished or learns a lesson, etc. Mother cannot use language to set limits and thereby help child see consequences of actions; similarly, unable to convey through language a sense of pleasure or pride in child's accomplishments.

Type B—Totally disorganized symbolic interactions (e.g., mother with severe thought disorder or very manic).

Type C—Mixed type. Shows a mixture of the above with neither predominating.

2. Moderate Disorders

Type A—Intermittently compromises in purposeful symbolic communications due either to stress, inability to deal with certain thematic areas or for other reasons (e.g., no limit-setting in response to anger or explosiveness; but able occasionally to interact meaningfully to child's symbolic expressions of dependency).

Type B—Interacts symbolically, but frequently not purposefully or causally (caregiver "marches to the beat of his own drummer"). Intermittently tends to be disorganized in communication patterns.

Type C—Mixed type. Shows a mixture of the above with neither predominating.

3. Mild Disorders: Functioning between competent and moderate range.

Type A—Use descriptions from Moderate Disorders and Competent functioning.

Type B—Use descriptions from Moderate Disorders and Competent functioning.

Type C—Mixed type. Use descriptions from Moderate Disorders and Competent functioning.

Severe _____ |_____|_____ Mild

Type _____   Indicate with a line where on the continuum the disorder lies and list the type (e.g., A, B, C).

puterized medical record system, the likely clinical description of a youngster's pattern of functioning.

Using a Developmental Diagnostic Approach: Case Illustrations

The case vignettes which follow illustrate the application of a developmental diagnostic approach to infants and their caregivers. Descriptions of presenting problems, assessment approaches, and interventions are followed by diagnostic impressions and developmental diagnosis. The first four examples are summaries of the cases presented in Chapters 3–6 of this volume, including the developmental diagnostic approach to their problems. The next five cases were selected from outpatient child psychiatry and pediatric practices. All represent challenges to the attainment of homeostasis, attachment, somatopsychological differentiation and/or representational differentiation. The approach to elucidating the contributory factors is applicable to many different problems of development. In each instance, intervention emanated from a defined process of assessment and diagnosis. Treatment recommendations to alter the pathologic state must always, it should be noted, be subject to constant revision in the light of the child's ongoing maturation and the caregivers' changing emotional capacities and relationships.

CASE #1

Louise and Robbie were a mother–infant dyad in which each partner's vulnerability affected the other. Louise's life, as documented in Chapter 3, was marked by abandonment, physical abuse, and psychological rejection, all themes repeated in the relationship with the clinician during the prenatal period, when intervention efforts were directed toward the establishment of a therapeutic relationship.

Louise herself was born out of wedlock and raised by neighbors who lived nearby. She was beaten by her "mother,"

who died of cancer when Louise was eight. Little is known
of her later childhood and adolescence except that as a teenager she felt isolated, unwanted, and became increasingly
suspicious of people's motives and overtures. She began outpatient psychiatric treatment at 20 and received several antipsychotic medications. At 23 she was hospitalized briefly for
depression.

Louise was 25 when she gave birth to Robbie, her second
child. Delivery was uncomplicated; a local anesthesia was administered, Robbie was of average weight, his Apgar 8/9. The
Brazelton at 3 days revealed an infant who had difficulty orienting, was not readily consoled, and showed tremors and
startles. The Brazelton at 30 days showed further difficulty in
orientation; there was gaze aversion, muscle tension, and less
cuddliness than on the initial assessment.

At this time Louise was depressed and angry, particularly
at her boyfriend, Robbie's father, and these feelings affected
her attitude toward her son. She did not look at Robbie, was
stiff and wooden when holding him, and shared little pleasure
in his overtures. Louise was fearful of rejection by her baby
and frightened by her own dependency needs. By 4 months
Robbie showed pronounced gaze aversion, was fretful, had
few vocalizations, and held himself in a stiff and rigid position
much of the time. Intervention efforts (as illustrated in the
case) were tried to "win him back to the human world" and
help him relax his own body. A formal developmental assessment (Bayley) at 4 months showed that his tactile exploration was entirely limited to mouthing. Motor movement was
disorganized and there were few vocalizations. The MDI was
in the low average range.

Robbie had frequent changes of caretakers while Louise
worked. At 5 months, he entered the therapeutic Infant Center where intervention efforts were directed at helping him
to relax his muscles, integrate cross-sensory and sensory-motor experience, and to learn to find satisfying human relationships. In contrast to his experience at home with his

mother, at the Center he found an environment that learned to read his changing affective signals and provide purposeful feedback. His mother continued in psychotherapy with the team social worker, holding down two jobs and participating with Robbie in the Center after work. Disruptions occurred from time to time as a result of upheavals in Louise's personal life when she would keep him home or change baby-sitters.

By 8 months Louise's behavior toward Robbie was variable. When preoccupied or angry at her boyfriend or the clinician she would reject her son's overtures for physical closeness; at other times, when not depressed, she would be warm and intimate with him. In Robbie there emerged intense interest in the human world, an increase in his self-regulation, selective affective interest in his mother, and contingent reciprocal interaction. Robbie's cognitive and sensorimotor functioning showed adequate development. Vocalizations, however, were below age level and he showed a perseverative banging of objects that interfered with manipulation and visual exploration.

As Louise explored painful issues in her therapy, particularly around themes of separation and loss, she became more available to Robbie. The therapeutic intervention by the Center staff to whom Robbie was attached and his mother's increasing affective availability were reflected in the 12-month developmental assessment. Interactive play between mother and child showed the beginnings of an organized pattern of reciprocal behavior as well as the emergence of initiative and originality. On the Bayley he was at age level for performance.

During the next six months Louise gradually came to appreciate the causal relationship between her own feelings and behavior and Robbie's development. For his part Robbie continued to respond to the stability and consistency of the therapeutic center, although his behavior from day to day fluctuated with the episodic upheavals in his mother's life.

The 18-month evaluation reflected Robbie's steady improvement. While he had a tendency (thought to be a reflection of a constitutional vulnerability) to become easily overstimulated and easily distractable, he was now warm and engaging, had a capacity to play out themes in complex interactive games, and exhibited age-appropriate fine motor skills and developing language ability. Mother for her part was now able to recover from personal rejections and reach out to Robbie physically and emotionally instead of withdrawing or becoming disorganized.

Diagnostic Impressions

The diagnostic impressions in the first months of life for Robbie were presenting symptoms of difficulty in orientation, gaze aversion, lack of molding and muscle tension, a developmental diagnosis of a severe disorder of homeostasis (Type C, chronic) and attachment (Type A, chronic, Table 11-2) with a subtype diagnosis of b2 (Table 11-8). The primary caretaker, the mother, had a severe caretaker disorder of homeostasis and attachment (Type C, chronic, Tables 11-10 and 11-11) with unipolar depression. Especially noxious to Robbie was his mother's own early object loss and need for her own nurturing, her episodic affective availability, and tendency to feel rejected with subsequent withdrawal from human relationship, including that with Robbie.

By 18 months Robbie had reached the age-appropriate level of behavioral organization initiative and originality with only mild evidence of a disorder at that developmental level (Type C, Table 11-5b). His constitutionally based tendency to become distracted and overstimulated remained but was markedly diminished. His mother had also progressed developmentally. She was able to integrate affect polarities and maintain a long-term relationship with another person, the clinician, in which she was able to explore and work through her own emotional conflicts. Louise at this time had a moderate caretaker disorder of representational capacity and elaboration (Type C, chronic, Table 11-14).

CASE #2

Betty was a vulnerable infant with a family history of severe mental disorder (mother, father, maternal grandfather, and uncle were schizophrenic) who was born into a disturbed, chaotic household that was ill-equipped and unprepared to provide her with the essential physical and emotional nutriments. She was less than a week old when she was first introduced to her mother's primary clinician. Her parents, Mr. and Mrs. Lake, had joined the CIDP at the time Mrs. Lake was five months pregnant and hospitalized with a diagnosis of paranoid schizophrenia. Mrs. Lake, 34, had had psychiatric symptoms since she first began hearing voices as an 18-year-old. Since that time she had developed an organized delusional symptom that centered around a particular voice which, she felt, controlled her thoughts and actions. Her husband, 40 years old and deaf since 15 as a result of streptomycin therapy, was chronically unemployed, in conflict with his three adolescent children, schizoid in his social adjustment, and determined to attribute all of the family's multiple problems to his wife's "craziness." The Lake family was not organized to provide adequate practical support in time for Betty's arrival. As a result the CIDP treatment efforts were directed toward facilitating interagency collaboration and anticipatory guidance, especially with Mrs. Lake, in anticipation of the baby's arrival.

Betty was small for gestational age (37 weeks), 6 pounds, 3¼ ounces, Apgar 9/9. The Brazelton exam at 7 days revealed a sallow, scrawny baby, irritable when disturbed from sleep, with brief alert states requiring a great deal of stimulation, and a limited capacity to interact, with only momentary brightening to animate and inanimate auditory stimuli. She molded well, had self-consoling capacity, and tolerated mild stress. The second Brazelton at 13 days showed only minimal improvement.

Mrs. Lake gradually decompensated following the birth of her daughter. Betty deteriorated physically and emotion-

ally. Frequent visits to the home by the public health nurse
and CIDP staff were not sufficient to reverse the downward
cycle, and Betty was hospitalized for a week at 6 weeks of age.
At that time she had gained only 13 ounces, was difficult to
console, and showed little interest in the animate and inanimate world.

An extensive interagency network was initiated by the
CIDP. Nonetheless Betty was finally removed from her parents' home a short time later and spent the next several
months in two foster care homes, returning to her parents
when she was 6 months of age. In the meantime a reentry
plan was forged by the CIDP between the parents and the
local health and mental health agencies involved with the
Lakes. Mrs. Lake began taking antipsychotic medication,
Mellaril; visits to the Infant Center began; the parents and
Betty were encouraged to interact, exercises and social games
between mother and baby were initiated, and couple and
family sessions were begun.

Betty responded dramatically to the foster care and the
CIDP intensive intervention. At the 4-month Bayley assessment Betty was noted to have gaze aversion, was lethargic,
and had muted, sullen affect. With much effort she was responsive to the examiner's overtures. Upon her return home
from foster care at 6 months, Betty showed an increasing
capacity to respond with pleasure to social interaction. Mrs.
Lake also began to evidence pleasure in the capacity of her
daughter for increasingly complex social interactions. The infant specialist on the CIDP team, through direct interaction
with Betty, acted as a role model, and Mrs. Lake gradually
began to imitate her style and pattern of interaction with
Betty.

The parents continued to attend therapy sessions with
the primary clinician and a psychiatric social worker trained
to communicate with deaf individuals. When Betty was 7
months old, Mrs. Lake announced a new pregnancy, trigger-
ing staff concern for her capacity to care for two infants, a

toddler, and three adolescents. Since the primary clinician also became pregnant at this time, the responsibility for the case, including working with the parents, shifted to the infant specialist team member. Mrs. Lake discontinued the Mellaril, fearing the adverse effects on her unborn child; almost immediately she suffered a severe psychotic regression with frequent breaks from reality.

Betty's developmental assessment at 8 months (Bayley) showed marked improvements in sociability, affective range, and cognitive performance. Mrs. Lake was preoccupied and was not able to respond to her daughter's efforts at eye contact. Intervention efforts were continued to help Mr. and Mrs. Lake engage their daughter. When she was 11 months old her brother Phil was born. He weighed 6 pounds 14 ounces, Apgar 7/9 and was 37 weeks gestational age. At the time of the Brazelton (3 days), he was felt to be a responsive, alert, social infant, capable of self-consoling and organized responses to stimulation. Concern for the Lake family's ability to care for the next infant was so high, however, that the newborn was placed in the protective custody of Mrs. Lake's sister. Betty and the parents resumed their infant room visits four mornings a week. Although initially reluctant, Mrs. Lake gradually became involved with Phil in a normal, socially appropriate manner. Antipsychotic IM medication (Prolixin) was begun. She developed Parkinsonlike side effects which triggered a temporary setback in her emotional involvement with her children.

When Betty was 12 months old, developmental assessments were conducted (Bayley and Uzgiris Hunt) which showed her as a cognitively and socially competent toddler. Of concern was her expressive language, which was 5 months below age level. While Mrs. Lake showed interest in her daughter's assessment performance, her spontaneous interactions were stereotypic and repetitive. She seemed to find it easier to enjoy her daughter through the distance of observation rather than through direct interaction.

When Betty was 14 months old, Phil, now 10 weeks, returned home. The work of the CIDP team continued with the Lakes and their two small children.

Diagnostic Impressions

The diagnostic impression (use Tables 11-1b—11-15 as shown for Case 1, p. 470) of Betty in the first months of life were presenting symptoms of irritability, low energy, minimal spontaneous response to animate and inanimate stimuli, failure of adequate weight gain, and a persistent gaze aversion with a muted sullen affect. The developmental diagnosis was a severe disorder of attachment (Type A, chronic) with a subtype diagnosis of a2 and c3–4 (Table 11-8). The primary caretaker, Mrs. Lake, was a chronic paranoid schizophrenic. Her disordered caretaker functioning was in homeostasis and attachment (Type C, severe). Mr. Lake was a deaf, borderline psychotic individual with a disordered caretaker functioning in behavioral organization and initiative (Type A, moderate).

Betty only approached minimal developmental adequacy in her second six months of life. By a year of age she was considered to have a moderate disorder of somatopsychological differentiation (Type C, chronic) with an expressive language delay of five months. Her mother, while still psychotic and given to idiosyncratic interpretations of her daughter's overtures and behaviors, was able to show some pleasure and interest in her play. Mother continued to have a moderate to severe disorder in homeostasis, attachment and somatopsychologic differentiation (Type A, chronic).

CASE #3

The case of Amy and her mother, Christine M., particularly the direct intervention with the child, has been reported in detail in an earlier volume (Sally Provence, ed., *Clinical Infant Reports: Report No. 2, Infants and Parents: Clinical Case Reports*). The chapter in this volume, in contrast, focuses more specifically on the psychotherapy with the mother, particularly her personality functioning and the evaluation of the treatment process. The following is a summary of Amy's development, together with the salient features of her mother's caretaking patterns, and intervention efforts by the primary clinician.

Amy was the second child of a moderately intelligent, single, 25-year-old woman. Mrs. M. joined the infant program during her twenty-first week of pregnancy. She was depressed, self-absorbed to such a degree that aspects of reality testing were impaired, and had a long history of marijuana use and a socially chaotic life-style. Mrs. M. had marked ambivalence about her pregnancy. She feared having a daughter, feeling that she might be as "overprotective" of her baby as her own mother was of her.

In fact Mrs. M.'s mother had been abandoning and neglectful of her during much of her childhood. Mrs. M.'s early life history, her chaotic relationship with important figures in her current life, and the vicissitudes of her therapeutic relationship with the primary clinician are well documented in the current case report. Gradually, over the course of treatment, she developed a capacity for self-observation and an appreciation of the effect of her personality and behavior on Amy's development. While she remained vulnerable to regression in the face of external and internal stress, there were major shifts in personality organization, particularly a capacity for object constancy as reflected in the therapeutic relationship, a diminished view of the world as divided into good and bad, as well as pride, admiration, and empathy for her daughter.

Amy, for her part, was a psychologically vulnerable infant. Although she was constitutionally sound during the first month of life, experiential factors, particularly poor physical and emotional nurturing, severely compromised her chances for reasonable developmental progress.

Amy was full term, and labor and delivery were uneventful. She weighed 6 pounds, 14 ounces at birth with Apgar scores of 8/9. The Brazelton Neonatal Behavior Assessment Scale at 3 days revealed a constitutionally sound infant; however, Amy suffered in a number of ways, leading to deterioration in her physical and emotional development. By 1 month mother distanced herself from Amy, returning in marijuana smoking and moderate alcohol consumption. Her pattern of breast-feeding was erratic and consistent with a steady deterioration in her physical caretaking. Her emotional involvement with her daughter became more and more ineffective as she did not look at, talk to, stroke, or in other ways engage Amy. Amy began to appear lethargic and apathetic with a weak suck, ineffectual coping behaviors, and symptoms associated with the onset of "failure to thrive." At 3 months, weekly visits by the infant nurse specialist were initiated with concrete caretaking advice to Mrs. M., and auditory and visual stimulation with Amy.

By 4 months Amy revealed increasing signs of neglectful caretaking by her mother including cradle cap and frequent diaper rashes. She was somber and quiet; her mouth and eyes were her main perceptual organs. After an abrupt move out of the area when Amy was 6 months old, Mrs. M. returned 2 months later, more responsive to the team interventions. Amy had gained only 8 pounds from her original birth weight. She appeared fragile, listless, and apathetic. She did, however, have a long attention span, demonstrating resilience in her persistence at certain tasks on the Bayley. Intervention efforts with Mrs. M. continued with simultaneous daily attention to Amy by a visiting homemaker from the program. The focus was on sensory, motor, and cognitive exercises and interactive games with Amy which had as their goal emotional interchange and nutritional planning with mother.

By 1 year Amy had improved in motor control and overall cognition and was vocalizing. However, she remained easily upset, was still sober and withdrawn, and overreacted to the disappearance of objects. At 17 months Amy began attending the therapeutic Infant Center as mother was now able to make a more regular commitment. At that time Amy could not discriminate human objects, was aimless, and her affects were undifferentiated. She was the victim of others' aggression, as well as defenseless against her own angry feelings. Christine's care, as documented in the present case report, was intermittently overstimulating and withdrawn. Although Mrs. M. was primarily concerned with meeting her own needs, she appeared more willing to involve herself in the activities of the Infant Center.

In the following year and a half Amy made significant gains as for the first time she began relating to others with trust and even joy. She was helped in this process by twice weekly therapeutic play sessions. By 3½ she manifested a facility with pretend play and language and used these capacities to explore feelings. She was more comfortable with her aggression, and developing capacities for assertiveness, empathy, and sharing.

Throughout the course of her own therapy Mrs. M. slowly developed a beginning capacity for self-observation and observation of her children's needs, along with control of her own urges to overcontrol them. Her care of other children in a new job in a day care setting, realistic planning for her new son, and delight in his responsiveness to her in the first months of life were signs of further potential emotional growth for Mrs. M.

Diagnostic Impressions

The diagnostic impression (use Tables 11-1b—11-15 as shown for Case 1, p. 470) of Amy in her first months of life were presenting symptoms of weak suck, difficulty in self-consoling, apathy, withdrawal, and poor vocalization, with a developmental diagnosis of moderate disorder of homeostasis (Type C, subacute) and severe disorder of attachment (Type A, chronic), with a subtype diagnosis of limitation of affective range, c3 (Table 11-8). The primary caretaker, her mother, had a borderline character disorder with narcissistic features.

Her patterns of care in the early months of life induced the symptoms in Amy associated with a "failure to thrive" syndrome. Her disordered caretaking functioning was in attachment (Type C, severe). As described in the text, Amy was a low-energy but competent baby whose developmental deterioration in the first four months of life was directly attributed to her mother's caretaking patterns and lack of emotional involvement.

At 18 months Amy had a developmental diagnosis of a moderate disorder of both somatopsychological differentiation and behavior and organization (Type B, chronic). Mrs. M.'s disordered caretaking functioning was still in attachment (Type C, severe); however, she showed a willingness to have others (the CIDP staff) interact with her daughter. By age 3½ Amy had made much progress and now only evidenced some characteristic constrictions and therefore had resolved early difficulties and had a developmental diagnosis of mild disorder of representational differentiation and consolidation (Type C, chronic). Mrs. M. was now more responsive to her daughter's cues and signals and showed a capacity for self-observation of her own emotional patterns and their effects on her children. Therefore she was greatly improved and had only mild compromises in representational differentiation (Type C, mild).

CASE #4

Anita was a full-term healthy infant, weighing 7 pounds, 9 ounces at birth; delivery was uncomplicated, Apgar 9/10. The 3-day Brazelton assessment revealed a sturdy, alert infant, extremely responsive to animate and inanimate stimuli. Motor maturity and good muscle tone were evident. Anita exhibited good state control and was able to self-console with minimal effort. The intervention in the first weeks (as described in the case report) consisted of providing her mother Madeline, whose four other children were in foster care, with basic caretaking skills while freeing her emotionally to take pleasure and invest in her competent infant.

At 1 month, Anita was progressing quite well. She could now use animate visual stimuli to console herself and could also draw adults into her world. Her mother, on the other hand, was stiff and wooden in the expression of her feelings and appeared unable to attend to her daughter's signals or maintain eye contact with her. She was chronically depressed and generally uncommunicative with the staff and her baby. Her own anger and feelings of deprivation prevented her from offering Anita emotional nourishment.

Anita at 4 months was brought daily to the therapeutic Infant Center, whose staff provided support to the mother while offering Anita an adequate caretaking environment. Major treatment efforts were modeling caretaking patterns and helping Madeline to read her baby's signals. Although Madeline participated actively, she neither recognized nor acknowledged the emerging reciprocal attachment that was forming with her daughter or the impact of her personality on Anita's emotional development. The 4-month Bayley showed Anita to be in the average range of cognitive and motor performance. Although Anita persisted in trying to "woo" her mother in the free-play interaction, Madeline was not able to respond to Anita's overtures.

Intervention efforts for the next several months were aimed at trying to widen Madeline's responses to Anita and to teach Madeline basic physical and emotional caretaking patterns with an infant. By 8 months, Anita was in the superior range for mental and motor functioning, and mother and infant had developed a capacity for relating warmly to each other. The baby demonstrated emotional resilience and persistence, and had a "take charge" quality. By a year the emotional relationship between Madeline and Anita was firmly established. Madeline was interactive, rather than withdrawn and distant in her responses; mother and daughter took pleasure in each other.

During the second year of life the treatment challenge was to facilitate in Anita what was lacking in her mother, the use of organized emotional patterns and the beginning of play and language to communicate wish and feeling. At the same time the treatment was sensitive to preserving the attachment between the two: we did not wish Anita's progress to threaten the mother's sense of control. As Anita showed progress Madeline began to use her own words to set limits and did not, as she had with her other children, retaliate when Anita directly expressed anger. At the 18-month assessment Anita was engaging, assertive, and organized. Her negativism was also prominent but did not interfere with her cognitive performance. However, she did poorly in expressive language. Madeline was preoccupied at this time and was unable to enhance her daughter's performance. For the next six months intervention efforts were concentrated on encouraging Anita in pretend games across a range of emotions and in her expressive language and imagination. Parallel efforts were made with Madeline, who used facial gestures rather than words as a preferred mode of communication.

By 24 months Anita was a warm, exuberant toddler with good capacity for assertiveness as well as self-control. She was in the average range cognitively, with good persistence. Madeline was able, by this time, to be an active participant in a rich array of play experiences. Anita's language, however, was still delayed (four months). At 30 months she was vivacious, assertive, and playful with a range of fears, pleasures, and impulses appropriate to her age. She functioned in the average range cognitively on all areas of the McCarthy. Most impressive was her motoric competence and ability to imitate words and gestures. In addition language delay was no longer in evidence.

Diagnostic Impressions

The diagnostic impression for Anita at 4 months was of a sound, physically healthy infant who had a developmental diagnosis of competent functioning at the level of homeostasis and early attachment. Her mother Madeline was a chronically depressed young mother with a developmental diagnosis of severe caretaker disorder of homeostasis and attachment (Type A, chronic, use Tables 11-1b—11-15 as shown for Case 1, p. 470). By 1 year of age Anita had a developmental diagnosis of competent functioning at the level of somato-psychological differentiation while Madeline, through her progress in therapy and participation at the Infant Center, showed a moderately disordered caretaker functioning at the attachment level (Type A).

When Anita was 30 months she showed a developmental diagnosis of competent functioning at the level of representational use of thoughts and ideas. Her mother, responding to the continued therapeutic intervention, was capable of interactive play with her daughter but still lacked the capacity for a full range of emotional expressiveness and had a developmental diagnosis of moderately disordered caretaker functioning at the level of behavioral organization and initiative (Type A) and a moderate to severe disorder in representation capacity and elaboration (Type A).

CASE #5

Mrs. K. was an obese, quite depressed, borderline woman who gave birth to a healthy, competent infant. Although somewhat on the sluggish and passive side, Jill was an adorable little girl, smiling, alert, and easily soothed. Initially, Mrs. K. sought to care for Jill by anticipating her every need, interpreting her every cry as a signal of hunger, and occasionally overfeeding her to the point of regurgitation. A rich attachment developed, observable in selective synchronous smiles and mutual longing looks. Overall physical care seemed to be adequate.

By 6 months, however, Jill began to lag developmentally. Expected capacities for crawling, vocalizing, and for initiating reciprocal affective interchanges (by smiling reciprocally and so on) had not appeared. While Mrs. K. seemed quite capable of rhythmically rocking her infant and looking at her with a broad smile, we noticed that every time Jill pushed herself away so as to get a better view of her mother, perhaps to begin a pattern of reciprocal communication, Mrs. K. forcefully brought Jill back to her shoulder saying, "She needs to be comforted." This pattern was observed on three subsequent visits one week apart and was consistent with reports from home. Despite occasional, mutually synchronous smiles during the observation session, Jill seemed to ignore her mother, moving her arms, trying to crawl, glancing at mother but with affective expressions that were independent of mother's expressions.

Discussion with Mrs. K. often revealed a need to "fill her baby up." References to eating and feeding dominated her view of how she must care for her infant. Attempts to point out to her that Jill was trying to communicate with her through smiles, glances, and sounds, and that it was important for Jill to begin developing her motor capacities, met with general agreement but were always qualified by Mrs. K.'s assertion that Jill was a "little bit slow" and needed "more taking care of." While Mrs. K. had formed a solid relationship with her clinician, she could take little distance from her own picture of her infant and her own feelings toward the world.

There were no findings on physical or neurologic exams suggestive of an organically based difficulty (e.g., no asymmetries) and the Bayley mental items were handled in an age appropriate manner.

Mrs. K. had experienced a number of separations early in life, but, at least on an intermittent basis, seems to have been satisfied—"filled up" as she once again put it. She was married to an alcoholic, a man whom now she felt she took care of.

As she became more involved with her therapist, she attempted to dominate the sessions and would frequently interrupt him. When he pointed out the parallel between her interference with his own attempts at communication and her interference with her baby's attempts, she was at first quite annoyed and then said that the therapist only wanted to talk in order to hurt her. The idea that people might hurt her if they were permitted to communicate on their own, if they were not controlled by her, then became the focus of the treatment. As she became able to confront this fear and to see that overfeeding Jill was an attempt on her part to ward off her own anticipation of being hurt, she began to be able to permit her daughter to initiate communications, to which she responded contingently. By 12 months of age Jill was functioning phase-appropriately in the cognitive as well as affective spheres.

This case illustrates the relationship between therapeutic work with the mother and her ability to deal with a new stage of development in her infant. While Mrs. K. was quite capable of establishing an early nurturing relationship with Jill characterized by adequate homeostatic patterns and adequate attachment, her own conflicts made it hard for her to facilitate her daughter's differentiation. The development of an observing ego permitted the caregiver to perceive and respond to her infant's needs in an appropriate way.

Diagnostic Impression

The diagnostic impression for the infant was a presenting symptom of a major lag, a developmental diagnosis of a moderate disorder of somatopsychological differentiation (Type A), chronic type (use Tables 11-1b—11-15 as shown for Case 1, p. 470), with a subtype diagnosis of limitation of use of affective space (i.e., lack of distal modes) (Table 11-8 e2). A moderate caregiver disorder of somatopsychological differentiation, Type B, was a modulating factor.

CASE #6

Tom's pediatrician referred him to the child psychiatrist after several attempts to reassure an anxious but capable mother and father as to the reasons their infant seemingly would not express a social smile. Both parents and pediatrician had tried without success to elicit a smile or other evidence of an ongoing affective exchange between infant and adult; whenever an adult cooed or spoke cheerfully to him, Tom continued to look dour. Several well-baby physical examinations convinced the pediatrician of the basic biological integrity of the baby. He was also aware of the parents' capacity to provide emotional as well as physical nurturing, reflected in the competence of their two older sons. They were more than "good enough parents." In this case the child psychiatrist, as a subspecialty consultant, functioned much as the pediatrician would have, to elicit, through current and past history, as well as observation of the infant and parents, the nature of the child's disorder.

The pregnancy and delivery had proceeded uneventfully. There was a mild ABO incompatibility noted at birth. Tom spent 8 days in the intensive care nursery, including 4 days with phototherapy. The indirect bilirubin reached 17.3 early in the course of hospitalization. The mother pumped breast milk, the parents visited the infant in the intensive care unit, and handled the baby in the isolette. Tom was discharged on his ninth day of life. By 8 weeks the mother noted that Tom was more difficult to engage than her other two sons, now ages 2 and 4½. For example, Tom would imitate her spontaneous facial movements only occasionally, in contrast with her experience with her other babies. Although interested in his toys and other objects and the world around him, he showed little animation when his brothers would play with him in his crib. The mother was convinced that there was something "wrong" with the baby, although the pediatrician, in his office visits, had not been able to observe anything of particular note. The baby appeared interested in the world around him and maintained good eye contact (also noted by the pediatrician). He seemed more interested in inanimate than animate objects, more involved with the rattle and other toys than with the parents' facial expressions. A pediatric neurological exam done at 8 weeks was felt to be within normal limits, and there were no stigmata noted of mental retardation or genetic abnormalities. By 8 weeks Tom's mother had also noted the beginning of a small, flat, red growth on the baby's forehead which was diagnosed by a dermatologist as a benign lesion. Although surgery was not immediately advised lest it be traumatic for the infant, it was suggested that the lesion should be removed between ages 4 and 5 to prevent "pre-cancerous" changes. By 5 months, despite their efforts, the parents reported that they could only occasionally elicit any smiling or spontaneous reciprocal babbling and voiced their concerns during a well-baby visit with the pediatrician. At their urging, the pediatrician decided to refer the case for consultation.

Tom was an attractive, alert youngster when seen in the office. He was particularly active in the visual perceptive mode, spending most of his time looking around, craning his neck, and interested in what was going on in his surrounds. Mother seemed mildly depressed, as evidenced by her slow speech, furrowed brow, and dampened enthusiasm for her son. Father was an engaging, gregarious individual. Tom played quietly with plastic and cuddly toys that the parents had brought with them. He showed appropriate sensory, gross- and fine-motor development, but did not seem more interested in inanimate toys than in the parents or the examiner. He was easily comforted and became more active when held by the examiner in the upright position.

Physical contact with the infant was undertaken at this point, both to develop a hands-on picture of the infant's muscle tone, molding, etc., and also to demonstrate any elicited responses by the examiner to the parents. This produced no brightening of affect: Tom appeared flat and sober. Twenty minutes of effort failed to produce smiling or cooing, although there was no gaze aversion noted. Tom explored the examiner's face in an impersonal fashion. He alerted to the voice and rattle, and there did not appear to be any hearing deficit.

(The pediatrician had already done more extensive hearing tests before the infant was referred and had felt Tom's hearing was within the normal range.) During the session Tom became hungry and the parents, upon request, took turns feeding him (he was being breast-fed but a bottle was brought for the visit). He molded, enjoyed the interaction, and fed vigorously. When placed supine on the floor, Tom looked actively around. A diaper was placed over his face and produced appropriate defensive maneuvers, but it proved too heavy for Tom to remove himself. At this point, 45 minutes into the session, a piece of tissue was substituted for the diaper over Tom's face. It brought dramatic results. The baby pulled the tissue off his face, looked up in a surprised manner at the examiner, laughed (the child psychiatrist laughed also), and offered the first audible sounds of the session. Repeated tries, turning this maneuver into a game, elicited a range of babbling sounds, spontaneous cooing, and, ultimately, synchronized movements of his arms and legs to the examiner's voice. The parents were surprised and pleased to see this degree of spontaneous reciprocal play and sound production, which they had been unable to elicit before.

The psychiatrist saw Tom as a child who was not taking obvious pleasure in animate interaction and who was making minimal spontaneous efforts on his own to engage the animate world. He did not send intense signals to his parents to engage or capture their attention. The parents were encouraged to join the child psychiatrist on the floor, to repeat the "tissue game" and to look for other patterns incorporating the element of *surprise* and *novelty* to engage their son. Peekaboo, for example, and the use of a facelike mask were suggested to the mother, with the mother then substituting her own face for the mask.

Further discussions revealed that mother had been preoccupied with the suggestion of Tom's possibly precancerous lesion. On further inquiry, the history revealed that a cousin, after whom Tom was to have been named, had died of cancer at age 22, 6 months prior to Tom's birth. This death had been prominent in the mother's mind when she was told about Tom's spot, although she hadn't revealed this to the pediatrician. The lights in the newborn nursery and the elevated bilirubin level had also made the parents fearful. When asked, "Did anyone tell you why they did that procedure or what the dangers were?" they responded, "No." Mother revealed, however, that she had herself worried that Tom was mentally retarded, and this concern was inhibiting her from more active engagement with her son.

Mother's unexpressed concerns and fantasies had led to a general dampening of her emotional interaction with Tom. As she attempted to engage him, his own lack of receptivity and low sending power further confirmed the mother's worry that there was "something wrong."

The parents were instructed to continue to play a series of affective interactive games with Tom, particularly to employ the element of visual surprise paired with affective auditory and kinesthetic experiences. The infant's initial responses to the examiner, together with the parents' successful efforts to elicit responses, were heartening and supported their efforts.

A follow-up visit a month later revealed dramatic changes. Tom now cooed and babbled spontaneously, was smiling and alert, and was interested equally in the animate and inanimate world. Mother was more rewarded by his responses and greatly relieved in the transient nature and reversibility of Tom's presenting symptoms. The child was referred back to the primary care pediatrician for further follow-up, with the advice of periodic observation of interaction of mother, father, and child in his waiting room and office in order to assess Tom's further developmental progress.

A final note regarding this case is in order. The importance, in this instance, of careful history taking and studied observation of the infant in relation to the examiner, as well as to his parents, provided the opportunity for this infant to reveal the mode(s) of intervention which were ultimately successful. The child psychiatrist's observation of the infant's pleasure and surprise in removing the tissue was capitalized upon and turned into an active mode of intervention. In this case it was important that he used an active, hands-on approach with the infant, seeking to read his signals and elicit those responses which would activate Tom's interest in the animate world. Having done so, he also needed to demonstrate the infant's capacity to the parents, to invite them to repeat the experience themselves in his presence, and to deal with the related history and feelings.

Diagnostic Impression

The diagnostic impression for the infant was a presenting symptom of the absence of a social smile, a developmental diagnosis of a mild disorder of both attachment and somato-psychological differentiation Type A, chronic type (use Tables 11-1b—11-15 as shown for Case 1, p. 470), with a subtype diagnosis of limitation of affective range (i.e., no show of pleasure or satisfaction) (Table 11-8, c3). The primary caretaker, the mother, was felt to have a depressive character disorder.

CASE #7

Andrew was a 9-week-old infant brought to the pediatrician for evaluation with the chief complaint of "colic."

The child had been delivered without complications at term after an uneventful pregnancy. Birth weight had been 7½ pounds and Apgar scores 8/9. Andrew's mother had noted concerns about her son almost immediately on his coming home: fussiness, crying spells, erratic feeding and sleep habits, and much gastrointestinal discomfort with loose stools and gas. Multiple changes of formula, including hypoallergenic brands, and the intermittent use of antispasmodics and phenobarbital prescribed by his previous pediatrician had provided only slight relief and led to the conclusion that there was no obvious milk allergy. By excluding these other possibilities, including those of genetic origin, the pediatrician concluded that Andrew had a functional gastrointestinal immaturity. Parental concerns mounted as forceful regurgitation supervened, and the baby appeared to be losing weight.

His mother presented as an anxious woman of 19 years whose recollections of the pregnancy and perinatal period were sketchy but significant. She complained bitterly that Andrew had kicked vigorously and incessantly during the latter half of gestation. Her most vivid memory of the hospitalization was the nurse's announcement that Andrew was a "screamer." She volunteered that this description fitted Andrew perfectly. The mother was tired, frustrated, unhappy, and afraid that she was raising "a monster."

Questioning revealed complicated family patterns. Andrew's parents had married four months prior to delivery at the insistence of both their families. Andrew's father was a salesman whose work required him to be away for extended periods. Indeed, he had been unavailable to accompany his wife to the consultation because of business commitments. The couple had few close friends in the area, and the mother felt she had no one with whom to share the burdens of caring for her demanding child. Although both sets of grandparents lived reasonably close, visits from them were awkward. Specifically, Andrew's mother felt unable to elicit from her mother any helpful information to aid in coping with the problems her son presented.

Observation of mother and child demonstrated intense mutual anxiety. Interaction consisted of mother's attempts to shift Andrew from one uncomfortable position to another either on her lap or shoulder while the infant wriggled incessantly, arching himself away from her, and passing large volumes of gas. Mother's awkwardness was accentuated by her repeated attempts at rhythmic rocking while she was seated in a straight-back chair. An attempt at feeding was punctuated by repeated regurgitations. Her pats on the baby's back, initially gentle, became more aggressive and punishing as the mother became more frustrated by her inability to comfort the screaming child.

Examination of the child revealed a healthy, alert, and vigorous 2-month-old. Despite parental concerns, weight and length increments were adequate. The neurological exam was normal except for the obvious fussiness, slightly increased tone, occasionally violent startles, and recurrent tremors of the chin with handling. No attempts at self-comforting either through sucking on his hands or focusing on the pediatrician were noted.

In this case, attainment of homeostasis was frustrated by a combination of factors inherent in the child as well as in the parental environment. The infant's constitutional inability to modify or defend against noxious stimuli was exacerbated by the inexperience, intense anxiety, and style of handling of his primary caregiver, his mother. Discussions with Andrew's mother after the examination focused on her worries about herself as a conscientious caregiver and how her worries led her to feel tense and "out of control" and therefore impatient with her infant. Intervention included practical suggestions for engaging someone to give mother periods of rest; including father in the baby's care when he was at home; establishing short frequent feedings in a quiet, semidarkened environment; providing consistent rhythmic experiences, rather than abrupt changes in position; and directing Andrew's mother to a discussion group with other young mothers where she could compare notes, share her worries, and learn techniques of comforting, such as slow and steady rocking with her infant in a horizontal position, gentle and consistent pressure on his larger muscles, and soft rhythmic vocalizations. These interventions were based in part on the conclusion that Andrew's irritability and eating disorders were not primarily the result of organic factors and that emotional issues were primarily contributing to his disorder. With this therapeutic program, a sense of comfort between mother and child increased, and Andrew's symptoms abated.

Ongoing contact with this mother eventually led to her sharing the fantasy that Andrew's early difficulties represented retribution for her premarital indiscretions. It was felt that immediate referral to a psychiatrist was not warranted, although it was obvious that the mother's vulnerability to recurrent guilt could affect her chances for emotional intimacy with her baby.

It is important to note an assessment of this baby's tendency toward hyperreactivity earlier on may have alerted medical personnel to the potential for interactional difficulties. An examination of those newborns who demonstrate traits such as excessive screaming, gastrointestinal distress, or poor alerting responses could sensitize professionals to the need to give extra guidance to the mother–infant dyad.

The pediatrician's contribution to the resolution of this situation was twofold. First, he sided with that part of the mother's ego which wanted to be a source of nurturance for the child. By concentrating initially on practical aids, he supported her without ignoring the problems inherent in her inexperience and ambivalence. In addition, the ongoing, nonthreatening contact allowed her to feel comfortable enough to discuss previously unspoken anxieties.

Diagnostic Impression

The diagnostic impression for the infant was one of gastrointestinal irritability, a sleep disturbance, and difficulty in state regulation, a developmental diagnosis of severe disorder of homeostasis, Type B, chronic type (use Tables 11-1b—11-15 as shown for Case 1, p. 470). A moderate caregiver disorder of homeostasis, Type B was a contributing factor.

CASE #8

Six-month-old Gregory was referred to both a pediatrician and child psychiatrist because of lack of interpersonal responsiveness as evidenced by chronic gaze aversion. The referring family practitioner was frustrated by his inability to answer the family's anxious questions concerning Gregory's poor weight gain and apparent unwillingness to engage socially. The child's medical and social histories were quite complicated, and while both consultants reviewed the data in depth individually it was decided early on to divide the consultant responsibilities. Thus, pediatric input was directed to establishing a relationship with the child and providing practical help in child-rearing techniques, while psychiatric intervention was aimed at supportive therapy for the parents during the acute crisis and more in-depth treatment later on.

Gregory was the product of an unplanned twin gestation. His parents were both professionals in their later twenties who worked for a large corporation. Married 2 years, struggling to keep up with mortgage and car payments, they had contemplated having only one child 5 years hence. The pregnancy, however, had been without complication until, as the mother put it, her obstetrician "dropped the bomb." The parents had felt they could manage one child, but twins seemed to present insurmountable problems. Gregory was the junior of the pair, weighing 4 pounds, 10 ounces at birth; Apgar scores were 4/7. Medical problems became apparent almost immediately. Several cardiac abnormalities were discovered and prompted swift transfer from a community hospital to a tertiary care center. His mother saw him only briefly in the delivery room; postpartum complications as well as the demands of the other healthy twin precluded her visiting Gregory for 2 weeks. Although father made heroic attempts to promote an emotional relationship between Gregory and his mother, by bringing her photographs and frequent reports on his condition, mother described the neonatal period as devoid of any sense in her mind that she was the parent of more than one child.

During his first 5 months, recurrent hospital admissions necessitated by surgery and treatment of various complications had prevented Gregory from spending more than about 3 weeks at home. A review of nurses' notes from several of these inpatient intervals showed a consistent characterization of him as sleepy, quiet, and hypotonic except when various procedures were being performed; at these times he was said to exhibit a piercing cry and to require inordinate amounts of physical comforting. He rejected a pacifier, did not mold when being held, and seemed apathetic. Twice during the first month of life, Brazelton behavioral assessments were performed which confirmed the child's poor visual and auditory responsiveness as well as an inability to maintain an alert state. His mother's visits to the hospital were unrewarding for her. Moreover, her attempts to engage him were inhibited by her lack of assurance that he would survive early infancy. After a while she came to feel that Gregory viewed her as just another person who would inflict physical pain.

Upon the child's arrival home at 2 months, his mother noted that he paid little attention to her, often averting his gaze when she approached. Despite her initial efforts to follow the advice of hospital personnel about engaging her son, Gregory's mother began to feel that he was actively rejecting her. Daytime routine was chaotic, and mother felt she could not cope with both a well child and another whose medical status demanded much from her but who gave little in return. She said she had essentially decided to provide custodial care for Gregory but otherwise leave him to entertain himself. She saw as her primary responsibility the child whose chances for survival were, in her mind, appreciably greater.

Examination of Gregory at 6 months showed a frail infant held on his mother's lap but well away from her trunk and facing the examiner. His face was expressionless and his gaze alternated between the floor and the wall over the examiner's shoulder. His hands were held limp at his sides. Initial attempts to engage him visually met with definite gaze avoidance. When cuddled, Gregory felt floppy and made no attempt to prolong physical contact. Forty minutes of quiet talking while holding Gregory physically close produced an occasional sidelong glance at the examiner. Use was then made of a brightly colored furry stuffed animal to attract Gregory's attention, at which point the examiner moved his face in line with the child's gaze. Initially able to tolerate only the briefest of such visual contact, Gregory began to relax, and after three daily sessions of such games could sustain *en face* contact for up to several minutes.

Intervention strategies grew from the demonstrated success during the evaluation. Gregory's parents were taught techniques of capturing his attention as well as methods of promoting mutually pleasurable bodily contact. For example, they were encouraged to place a stuffed animal in front of his face and when it attracted his interest, to drop the toy in favor of their own faces. It was suggested to mother that when Gregory squirmed on her lap she allow him to find a position of comfort rather than force him into the crook of her arm. Consistent nursing care allowed Gregory to work on engaging with one particular adult for extended periods each day. Plans for a daily interaction between infant and parents at home included techniques to encourage more active use of musculature to allow him to become more aware of his body. For example, the parents were told to try rolling Gregory over from stomach to back repeatedly until he learned to roll for himself, to pull him from lying to sitting, and to play with him in this new position, to play games of bounce on their knee, and to try to encourage him to bounce and move about in pleasurable ways. Helping him to relearn the efficacy of hand to mouth stimulation as a tool for self-comfort proved quite rewarding.

Psychotherapy for the parents to deal with their disappointment, rage, and guilt at having produced a damaged child was also begun after Gregory's discharge. Frequent discussions among the pediatrician, parents, and homemaker allowed shifts in intervention strategies as the child progressed. Steady improvement in relatedness, pleasure in exploration and play, and sustained weight gain resulted despite temporary setbacks during periodic hospitalizations.

Diagnostic Impression

The diagnostic impression at 5 months for the infant were the presenting symptoms of inadequate weight gain, gaze aversion, and poor state regulation, a developmental diagnosis of a severe disorder of homeostasis and attachment, Type A chronic type (use Tables 11-1b—11-15 as shown for Case 1, p. 470) with a subtype diagnosis of diminished sensory system responsiveness (Table 11-8, 1a, 2a, visual and auditory and diminished motor response, 2b). In addition, congenital heart defects were present from birth. A severe caregiver disorder of attachment, Type A (see Table 11-11) was a contributing factor.

CASE #9

Laura was 17 weeks old when brought for evaluation of a sleep disorder. Both parents accompanied the child, and interaction between them and Laura seemed spontaneous and reciprocal as evidenced by their gentle handling and her willingness to go readily from one to the other. Her mother, although quite voluble, appeared sad. Without prompting she stated that Laura had been conceived primarily because of her husband's wish to have children. The couple had been married for 7 years; Laura's mother was a successful attorney who had given little thought to starting a family. She described the pregnancy as uneventful, labor and delivery as devoid of problems, and the first week at home as blissful. Birth weight was 7 pounds, with Apgars of 9/9. The infant had nursed eagerly and had begun to sleep for three to four hours at a time at night. During Laura's third week, the couple noted less, rather than more, regularity in her pattern of sleep. Her three daytime naps decreased from 3 hours in duration to 30 minutes each. Falling asleep at night progressed from a spontaneous occurrence following the last feeding to a prolonged routine in which Laura had to be rocked, jiggled, and patted for up to an hour. Her mother volunteered that the child's changing sleep habits had aroused in her a feeling that Laura might be becoming ill and suddenly stop breathing. When awake, Laura was described as being comfortable, cuddly, and sociable; a few smiles had been noted at 5 weeks of age and the baby had begun to coo by 7 weeks. Review of subsequent developmental history showed the child to be progressing normally although her parents agreed that she seemed more vocal with her father when he played with her in the evenings than with the mother.

Since Laura's birth her mother had been on leave from her law firm and had not yet made a definite decision regarding the date of her return. She described her daily activities as centering around household chores and nursing Laura. Nursing, in fact, seemed to consume endless hours during which mother and child would lie together in bed. The parents had not socialized during these 4 months and mother's time out of the house had been limited to once-a-week shopping trips.

Examination of the child showed her to be thriving and neurologically intact. After a moderately prolonged warm-up period, she engaged the examiner in reciprocal cooing and demonstrated occasional chuckles and screeches. Sensory-motor functioning was adequate, and Laura demonstrated appropriate interest in rattles and teething rings. After 30 minutes of interaction she seemed to tire and began to comfort herself by sucking her fingers. On return to her mother she became fussy; her mother's attempts to quiet her with a few brief pats on the back were done without pleasure or enthusiasm. When her father finally intervened, he comforted her easily and effectively.

In a session with Laura's mother alone, reevaluation of this history gave a different picture from the one previously obtained. Mother now spoke bitterly of her rejected attempts to end the pregnancy: without success she had appealed to her husband for an abortion; her obstetrician had also been unwilling to discuss in much depth the possibility of abortion. On reviewing the pregnancy again, she admitted that while uncomplicated by physical problems, it had been a time of deep personal sorrow. She had learned during the sixth month of pregnancy of the terminal illness of a maternal aunt whom she described as her psychological mother. The aunt had succumbed to metastatic cancer within five weeks of the diagnosis. Laura had been named after this relative at the mother's insistence and over her husband's objections. The immediate postpartum period had, in fact, not been blissful. Laura's mother had been tired, tearful, and anxious. Both her physician and the pediatrician had reassured her that "the blues" were common and would be overcome. In fact, she could acknowledge that her sadness had not lifted. Household chores had become burdensome, and she had left more and more responsibilities to her husband.

Her concerns about Laura's well-being during the night had progressed rapidly from listening to the child's breathing outside the nursery door to actually going to the side of the crib. Often Laura would awaken, and mother would then spend up to an hour getting her back to sleep. Although vague in her story, she eventually revealed that she would continue to hold and rock Laura even after the child had settled down. She had recently read several articles on sudden infant death syndrome and had contemplated installing an intercom system to monitor her daughter's sleeping more efficiently.

Laura had progressed through the stage of homeostasis but with a disruption of her pattern of sleep as a result of ongoing maternal depression and worry. In contrast to the previous cases, Laura's problems in homeostasis appeared functional in nature.

It seemed appropriate to suggest psychiatric intervention for both mother and child because of evidence that Laura's mother would resist referral for herself alone. Although angry at the child she had not wanted, mother was willing to accept therapy to promote her daughter's emotional growth. A referral was made to a child psychiatrist for joint twice-weekly parent–infant psychotherapy. Laura's sleep problem rapidly diminished as her mother quickly focused the discussions on her own anxieties, including the crisis for her of being both a professional and a first-time parent. Mother became less worried about Laura's well-being while asleep and less intrusive; she continued in psychotherapy for another year after she stopped bringing her daughter. In this case direct work with Laura was not necessary, although the therapist would highlight how mother's tension was communicated to her daughter.

Diagnostic Impression

The diagnostic impression for the infant was a presenting symptom of an irregular sleep pattern, a developmental diagnosis of a moderate disorder of homeostasis, mixed Type C, subacute (use Tables 11-1b—11-15 as shown for Case 1, p. 470). No subtype was noted because Laura was felt to be constitutionally sound, and her disorder was felt to be based on maternal dysfunction. A moderate caregiver disorder of attachment, Type C, mixed with reactive depression was a contributing factor. Especially noxious to Laura was mother's intermittent reinvolvement and subsequent withdrawal.

Conclusion

We have presented an approach to diagnosis for infants, young children, and their families which attempts to understand the infants' presenting symptoms, antecedents, and family and environmental patterns in the context of his or her developmental progression. The infant's developmental progression can be seen as a sequence of organizational levels; for each of these levels we have attempted to describe the adaptive and maladaptive features. Based on a developmental structuralist framework, this multiaxial approach to diagnosis should be viewed as a preliminary attempt to facilitate communication among clinicians interested in characterizing early adaptive and maladaptive infant and family patterns.

12

Conclusions: Theoretical Perspectives on Research Regarding Psychopathology and Preventive Intervention in Infancy

Stanley I. Greenspan, M.D.

The complexity of the infant is perhaps matched only by the challenge of conducting research on infants and their families in complex, naturalistic, and clinical settings. Yet, accepting the difficulties and embracing the complexity of such a research subject, as we attempted to do in the Clinical Infant Development Program (CIDP), can yield gratifying results.

After providing a theoretical perspective on mental health research in general, this chapter will propose an agenda for clinically relevant research concerning infancy and place the work of the CIDP in this context. We will then show how some of the patterns, classification systems, and concepts which emerged from our clinical research are proving useful in interpreting previously collected data sets and in evaluating a whole body of early intervention research.

Theoretical Perspectives

Mental health research is, in part, struggling with an appropriate scientific identity. One behavioral science tradition has focused on studying functional relationships between predefined groups of measurable variables. The value of this approach is that one knows in advance one will clearly get a result: the functional relationship will or will not be demonstrated. As is well known, however, what is measurable may not always be meaningful, and what is meaningful may not always be measurable. This approach runs the risk of either avoiding areas of relevance to clinical practice or of studying some problems in an oversimplified or even misleading manner.

The clinical, descriptive, and psychodynamic tradition, in contrast, does not begin with preconceived notions of relevant or measurable variables but seeks to describe complex, naturally occurring phenomena. Then, through a series of gradual approximations, it attempts to abstract meaningful patterns and to classify these patterns, describing their vicissitudes under natural and other (e.g., intervention) conditions. While a special asset of this approach is the opportunity it affords to discover phenomena relevant to challenging clinical problems (.e.g., discovering and classifying new syndromes), it also has an important limitation; namely, that one is betting on the ingenuity of the investigator to describe the phenomena and recognize the patterns. There is no guarantee that useful descriptions, abstractions, patterns, and subsequent classifications will occur.

Both approaches are obviously necessary to study complex mental health problems. These approaches may be integrated through the following sequence:

1. Describe the complex natural, clinically relevant phenomena.
2. Abstract relevant patterns (e.g., identify the relevant variables).
3. Develop useful classification systems (e.g., further codification, definition and grouping of the relevant variables).
4. Develop instruments and protocols to recognize, measure, or quantify the *relevant* variables and dynamics referred

to above. (Note: One should not avoid the challenge by developing instruments to measure factors less significant and relevant because they are "easier" to develop and validate.)

5. Describe variations in these classified patterns under natural and special (e.g., intervention) conditions.
6. Develop new "special conditions" (e.g., intervention) at a descriptive level that, on a case-by-case basis, appears to shift patterns toward more optimal configurations.
7. Study the functional relationships between these new *clinically relevant*, predefined, measurable variables. (For example, studies would include such functional relationships as those between etiological variables and syndromes, treatment approaches and outcomes, and interrelationships among pathologic and adaptive patterns at biological, behavioral, experiential, and environmental levels, etc.)

The exploration of these functional relationships divides into two components:

a. *Basic Research* which looks at relationships among
    i. Etiological variables and syndromes;
    ii. Antecedent developmental patterns and disordered functioning;
    iii. Mechanisms responsible for disordered functioning at biological, behavioral, and experiential levels;
    iv. Mechanisms responsible for adaptive functioning at biological, behavioral, and experiential levels; and
    v. Mechanisms of action of various therapeutic agents and approaches to their use in improving adaptive functioning and reversing pathologic trends.
b. *Applied Treatment and/or Preventive Intervention Research* (e.g., clinical trials; Greenspan and Sharfstein, 1981, for further discussion) which looks at relationships among
    i. Defined interventions and clinically valid outcomes;

ii. No intervention or hypothesized "less optimal" intervention and outcomes;

iii. Intervention "process" steps and outcomes; and

iv. Developmental level of patient's personality, diagnosis
and outcomes.

An Agenda for Research

The assumptions which distinguish clinical from other
approaches also suggest certain research strategies which,
emerging from the context of clinical work, are likely to be
clinically useful (i.e., for interventive planning); discrimina-
tive of subtle differences in the range of functioning observed
(particularly in the high-risk multiproblem population); and
sensitive to social and cultural differences.

Ideally, clinically relevant research concerning infancy
should strike a balance between the comparatively easier-to-
study problems that involve single (or even multiple), but
readily identifiable, risk factors and related conditions, and
the more complicated situations that involve multiple-risk factors in the context of complex developmental and social problems. For example, developing a research strategy to study
the developmental patterns associated with prematurity, low
birth weight, or early chronic medical illness, while challenging, may be relatively easy in comparison to developing
research strategies for understanding developmental variations, clinical and service requirements, and the relative efficacy of preventive intervention strategies for the most high-
risk groups of multirisk, multiproblem infants and their families.

An approach to studying these more complex questions
involves a number of steps designed to tease out the relevant
groups of variables and their potential relationships. Rather
than attempting to acquire instant understanding of functional
relationships between groups of variables (e.g., etiological
variables and disordered functioning, or treatment variables
and outcome), such an approach would try to obtain a greater

understanding of (1) the nature of the disorders and their course during development; (2) the preventive and treatment strategies required; and (3) the ones most likely to be successful. More classical preventive studies would constitute a fourth stage of research.

Therefore, step A (corresponding to stages 1–4 of the sequence outlined above) would require investigators to understand the range in variation of adaptive and disordered functioning in infants, toddlers, young children, and their families along multiple developmental lines.

It is especially important to obtain an understanding of the range and variation of these patterns in the most high-risk populations, including groups whose members traditionally do not come for services in routine settings and usually do not participate in research studies. Often it is only possible to reach them by offering innovative services which will enlist their cooperation, and by providing a setting that will allow one to observe how development unfolds in an interactive service context. Even then the challenge is great. Without understanding the ranges and variations in developmental patterns in these infants, toddlers, and their families, one has no way of knowing the "natural history" (in a relative sense) of an important host of disorders.

Step B (corresponding to stages 5 and 6) would entail gaining an understanding of both the clinical techniques and service system strategies required in relationship to the above developmental patterns and interactions. For example, what clinical strategies are required for the hyperactive or labile infant who has difficulty in focusing concentration; or the infant who tends toward withdrawal and apathy and has difficulty alerting to routine auditory and visual stimuli; or the infant with special tactile, auditory, or visual sensitivities; or the infant who at 3 or 4 months is evidencing muscle rigidity and severe gaze aversion in relation to the human world? To complicate matters further, what clinical strategy is required to work with the above-mentioned withdrawn infant with a similarly withdrawn and depressed mother, who feels helpless and inadequate, who interprets her baby's behavior as further evidence that she is "worthless," and who therefore becomes immobilized and unable to try to find a way to reach out and interest her infant in her world? What clinical strategy is suggested for the hyperactive, unfocused infant whose father has paranoid ideation, views his baby's lability as an "aggressive attack," and perceives anyone who is interested in his baby, such as a pediatrician or a clinical program for infants and their families, as an enemy?

At the service system level, what type of interagency collaboration and pattern of care is most useful for the recently discharged chronic schizophrenic mother who intermittently loses the capacity for reality testing and may not always be able to attend to the most basic needs of her infant for physical care and protection? How does one involve the protective service, social service, and/or foster care system in the context of a service system approach that is in the best interest of the infant? What type of service system approach is necessary for the youngster with early nonspecific lags in sensorimotor development, or for the neglectful and intermittently abusing family that has given up some children to foster care and is intermittently using the foster care system for their newest infant? Multiproblem families with infants of worrisome constitutional and early developmental patterns may involve a dozen or more agencies in ways sufficiently fragmented to parallel the fragmentation that already exists in the family.

Step C in research (also stage 6), once the developmental variations and the range of clinical and service requirements are identified, is the in-depth study on a case-by-case basis of optimal clinical and service system strategies and their relative efficacy. Case studies may often be thought to yield data of low reliability and generalizability. Yet where the state of knowledge is such that the natural history of disordered functioning is not yet known and only a handful of detailed, indepth clinical studies exists in the literature, the case study becomes a crucial first step toward gaining an in-depth understanding of the nature of maladaptive and adaptive functioning in various multirisk families and toward developing reasonable hypotheses regarding the types of clinical and service system experience required and likely to work. Optimally, general principles would be abstracted from such in-depth studies to form the basis of a new clinical science of preventive intervention.

Those who argue that the state of knowledge has passed the case study method have the obligation to provide a body of clinical literature that delineates in depth, and from physical, cognitive, and social–emotional perspectives, the variations in developmental patterns in multiproblem, multirisk factor families and the clinical and service system strategies found to be most successful. What, for example, is the course of development in the labile, distractible infant with an auditory hypersensitivity and a paranoid father? What types of clinical strategies have been found most successful? In how many cases? Such a collection of reported clinical experiences is not available. While there have been some studies of this population, by and large they have not included an in-depth understanding of the developmental patterns of infants along multiple lines. There is a great deal of fragmented clinical information (e.g., on the family but not on the infant's development; or on one aspect of infant development, but not another). While hypotheses abound, the most relevant types of hypotheses and first-order constructs are still being formulated.

After the three areas outlined above are most fully explored, it will become possible to conduct classical prospective studies which look for functional relationships between treatment, etiological, and developmental factors and outcomes at various stages of development (stage 7 in the sequence). These types of studies, it must be emphasized, are only possible when a field has reached the point where there are useful functional categories. For example, categories of risk factors must be understood in the context of the range and variations of adaptive and disordered development. A typology of disordered functioning along multiple developmental lines must be used, such as the developmental structuralist model described in Chapter 11. Using existing classification schemes where such schemes are not applicable may only confuse rather than clarify functional relationships. Similarly, to conduct treatment assessment research, the most likely efficacious clinical and service strategies must first be clearly documented.

Level D of the study involves the more classically designed longitudinal studies of the efficacy of treatment and the relationship between the various etiological and developmental factors and outcome. But if such D level studies are to address the compelling, complex problems of human beings' capacities to organize and differentiate experience and to develop relationships, as these capacities appear in naturalistic settings, they must be based on a solid foundation of exploratory research which has delineated patterns, classification systems, and instruments to assess the relevant variables in the field. It is a serious error to apply research designs which assume an understanding of relevant groups of variables, until one is reasonably certain that the most relevant variables, from the perspectives of etiology, developmental patterns, and prevention and treatment approaches, have in fact been identified.

The CIDP's Research Approach

As we approached the area of mental health problems in infancy and early childhood in the late 1970s, we were influenced by this framework and agenda. Where within these steps were we in our knowledge of clinical approaches to diagnosis, prevention, and treatment? Did we have sufficient knowledge of the way in which patterns were organized, and therefore could be classified and measured, in order to study functional relationships, or did we need to start at a descriptive level, and immerse ourselves in complex clinical phenomena and bet that the clinical researcher's educated guesses would lead to the extraction of meaningful patterns and techniques and the development of new methods? We were influenced by what we felt had been premature attempts at narrowing the field of observation in work with infants and their families. There were programs, for example, that intervened or that measured outcomes but looked at only one dimension of development. Often sensorimotor or cognitive development, or aspects of social adaptation were the focus and investigators ignored in-depth emotional and psychological features of child development, not to mention family functioning. We reasoned that if the areas of development most sensitive to preventive intervention concerned the formation of human relationships and the development of effective coping strategies, then assessments which looked only at cognition or at limited aspects of social adaptation might be like the efforts of the proverbial drunk who looks under the street light, where he can see, for the wallet that he dropped further down the block, where it is dark.

We were also struck by the fact that many programs seemed to be grouping participants, both infants and families, into pseudohomogeneous groups based on somewhat undifferentiated criteria. Parents and children might be grouped according to educational and economic status or other demographic variables with little attention given to their clinical condition (i.e., the presence or absence of psychopathology) even though clinical status often accounts for much of the variance in most areas of functioning.

Front-line workers in day care and educational programs often told us of a subgroup that they "couldn't get to," who were "unmotivated," or "the mother seemed strange and would never come in and cooperate." This seemingly high, high-risk group within the general-risk population would tend to pull down the group's scores on outcome evaluations, giving the appearance that a particular intervention had been ineffective. Not having used clinical dimensions to categorize the participants, researchers could not easily, after the fact, divide the group of program participants and include these high, high-risk individuals in a separate group. In fact, many programs had no systematic ratings, even of the "difficult behavior they presented" (Greenspan and White, in press).

Using the definitions, assumptions, and research agenda outlined above, we placed ourselves at the beginning of the research sequence. We therefore developed our study to describe the characteristics and classify the patterns of a range of infants and their families; to examine on a case-by-case basis their service needs and the clinical techniques likely to be helpful; to observe on a case-by-case basis which clinical techniques and service approaches worked best; and to develop a data base which would also lend itself to looking at functional relationships between treatment techniques, process, outcome, etiological factors, and antecedent developmental patterns and subsequent adaptive and maladaptive functioning.

We did, fortunately, have some concepts to guide our observations. These included increasingly sophisticated concepts of infant development and the concept of "developmental morbidity," discussed in Chapter 11, and the notion of the multiproblem or multirisk family developed by previous researchers.

Characteristics of the Multirisk Family

While we wanted to focus on a wide range of infants and families, we were especially interested in including the multirisk and multiproblem families because of the major public health challenge they present. Our clinical impression was that families at the high-risk end of the spectrum in respect to any single-risk factor, such as substance abuse or poor nutrition, often evidence multirisk factors. Such families have also been described as "multiproblem," "hard to reach," "crisis-oriented," and so forth (Buell, 1952; Curtis, Simon, Boykin, and Noe, 1964; Geismar and LaSorte, 1964; Riessman,

Cohen, and Pearl, 1964; Minuchin and Montalvo, 1967; Minuchin et al., 1967; Pavenstedt, 1967; Zilbach, 1971). In addition, they have been classified by the way they use the service system and according to the kinds and number of problems they have. Results of the latter approach suggest that poverty or welfare status is not the only identifying characteristic, since families across the socioeconomic strata evidence the same multiproblem characteristics (Mazer, 1972).

In spite of definitional differences, there has been general consensus on the clinical characteristics of these families. They tend, for example, to think only in concrete terms, to be need oriented, and to have difficulty in anticipating the future and conceptualizing the consequences of their actions. The parents operate on a survival basis, often competing with their children for concrete, as well as psychological and social, supports (Levine, 1964; McMahon, 1964; Pavenstedt, 1967; Minuchin and Montalvo, 1967; Geismar, 1968; Zilbach, 1971; La Vietes, 1974). Although most of the families share these characteristics, an individual family may differ in some respects. Some of the families evidence clearly diagnosable mental illness and some, a predominance of severe antisocial and asocial personality patterns. Others are characterized by passivity and inadequacy in coping with life's daily challenges. Individual clusters of symptomatic behaviors also characterize the families—psychotic symptoms, child abuse, spouse abuse, marital difficulties, crime, delinquency, alcoholism, physical illness, and suicide (Buell, 1952; Geismar and LaSorte, 1964; Pavenstedt, 1967; Minuchin et al., 1967; Mazer, 1972).

Before 1975 few in-depth studies had been conducted of the development of the children in multirisk families. In Pavenstedt's (1967) classic descriptive study, only 13 of such families (which had 40 to 50 children between the ages of 2½ and 6 years) were studied. Nevertheless, the clinical impressions from the study were striking. Almost all the children showed social and psychological characteristics more consistent with 1½ to 2 year olds in their egocentricity and need orientation.

Their ability to use a symbolic (or representational) mode to plan for their own needs and to consider the needs and actions of others was limited, and they had variable self-esteem. They tended to think in fragmented, isolated units, rather than in cohesive patterns. They were not capable of goal-directed organized action and were limited in their ability to socialize and interact appropriately for their age. The children already had an ingrained defeatist attitude and the core of either asocial or antisocial personality structure.

Recognizing Relevant Variables

The importance of (and the uncertainties involved in) identifying, examining, and struggling to measure the *relevant* factors affecting infant development have been mentioned earlier. Our conviction in the CIDP was that a comprehensive clinical approach must begin with an assessment consisting of a number of conceptually consistent categories that take into account multiple lines of development in a longitudinal manner. This approach attempts to deal with the full complexity of clinical phenomena and therefore has methodological limitations when it comes to research. For example, the ideal assessment protocol would define a limited number of key outcome criteria and specify reliable and valid instruments to assess them. The variables (e.g., mother–infant interaction) assessed to plan interventions would differ from variables employed to assess outcome in order to avoid the possibility of "teaching to the test." However, a clinical orientation demands a detailed study of a minimum number of key clusters of personality variables for both clinical planning and assessment. Therefore, rather than prior selection of a few variables, the following six core areas of assessment must in one way or another be described.

PRENATAL AND PERINATAL VARIABLES

These variables all have some relative impact on the infant's constitutional status and developmental tendencies, although the extent of the impact is unknown. The prenatal variables include familial genetic patterns; mother's status during pregnancy, including nutrition, physical health and illness, personality functioning, mental health, and degree of stress; characteristics of familial and social support systems available; characteristics of the pregnancy; and the delivery process including complications, time in various stages, and the infant's status after birth. The perinatal variables include maternal perceptions of her infant, maternal reports of the emerging daily routine, and observations of the infant and maternal–infant interaction.

PARENT, FAMILY, AND ENVIRONMENTAL VARIABLES

These variables include evaluations of parents, other family members and individuals who relate closely to the family along a number of dimensions. These assessments include each member's personality organization and developmental needs, child-rearing capacity, and family interaction patterns. Evaluation of the support system (e.g., extended family, friends, and community agencies) used or available to the family and of the total home environment (both animate and inanimate components) are also included.

PRIMARY CAREGIVER AND CAREGIVER-INFANT/CHILD RELATIONSHIP VARIABLES

Evaluations in this area focus on the interaction between the infant and his or her important nurturing figure(s). Included are the quality of mutual rhythm, feedback, and capacity for joint pleasure, as well as their flexibility in tolerating tension and being able to return to a state of intimacy. Later in development, capacities to experience differentiation, form complex emotional and behavioral patterns, and construct representations are important.

INFANT VARIABLES—PHYSICAL, NEUROLOGICAL, PHYSIOLOGICAL

These variables include the infant's genetic background and status immediately after birth, including the infant's gen-

eral physical integrity (size, weight, general health), neurological integrity, physiological tendencies, rhythmic patterns,
and levels of alertness and activity. Special attention should
be paid to the infant's physical integrity and how this factor
could foster or hinder the child's capacities to experience internal and external stimulation; regulate internal and external
experience and reach a state of homeostasis; develop human
relationships; interact in cause and effect reciprocal patterns;
form complex behavioral and emotional patterns; and construct representations to guide behavior and feelings.

INFANT VARIABLES—SENSORY, MOTOR AND COGNITIVE

The variables in this category include the development,
differentiation, and integration of the infant's motor and sensory systems, and the relationship of the infant's sensorimotor
development to the infant's cognitive development.

INFANT VARIABLES—FORMATION AND INTERNALIZATION OF HUMAN RELATIONSHIPS

The following variables involve the interrelationships and
capacities for relationships among the infant, parents, and
other family members. These early relationships help the infant develop the capacity for a range of emotions (dependency
to assertiveness) in the context of a sequence of organizational
stages. These stages include the capacity for purposeful interactions, complex, organized social and emotional patterns,
constructing representations, and differentiating internal representations along self versus nonself, time and space dimensions.

There also are variables which focus on the mother and
involve the mother's capacity to reach out and foster attachment to provide physical comfort and care; to perceive basic
states of pleasure and discomfort in her infant; to respond
with balanced empathy, that is, without either overidentification or isolation of feeling; and to perceive and respond
flexibly and differently to the infant's cues, foster organized

complex interactions, and support representational elaboration and differentiation.

Developing Concepts

As we worked intensively on a case-by-case basis with our families and looked, just as intensively, at this range of variables, we eventually developed a number of concepts which we hoped would be powerful enough to have both explanatory and predictive value. These included the model for comprehensive services (described in Chapter 9); the dimensions and levels of the therapeutic process (Chapter 10); the developmental structuralist approach to diagnosis (Chapter 11); and the "index of misfortune" (described in Chapter 8). These concepts enlarged the original notions which had helped inform our thinking as the CIDP began. The developmental structuralist approach provided a framework which could take complexity into account yet still provide a succinct system of classification. The scales for rating dimensions and levels of the therapeutic process and the "index of misfortune" not only provided powerful insights into the psychological, family, and interactional patterns which characterize multirisk families but also suggested ways to approach and measure the effectiveness, however gradual, of psychological intervention with these families. They enabled us to say more about multirisk families than that they were "hard to reach." The model for comprehensive services helped us to order the variety of treatment modalities we mixed, matched, and invented during the program and to understand how approaches which had been effective had addressed the specific needs of infants and their families at particular stages in their lives. The model then provided a basis against which to measure other kinds of preventive interventions.

In addition to helping CIDP staff clarify their thinking and improve clinical practice over time, the concepts developed in the program enabled us to collaborate with other researchers in looking at previously collected data from a new

perspective and in evaluating a large body of work on outcomes of early interventions in the light of our understanding
of multirisk families and of the essential elements of comprehensive intervention approaches.

Application of Multirisk Clinical Criteria to a Nonintervention High-Risk Population

The CIDP's findings about the multiple misfortunes experienced by many of our high-risk mothers before they became parents and our observations of developmental failure
or morbidity in their offspring beginning as early as the first
days of life stimulated interest in a collaborative effort. This
collaborative effort with Sameroff and colleagues involved
again looking at data from a nonintervention population of 215
multirisk families who had been followed since pregnancy.
The study demonstrated that, controlling for socioeconomic
states (SES), family, psychological, and infant interactional
patterns correlated with poor outcomes at age 4. It further
showed that cumulative risk patterns during infancy can be
used to predict an as many as 25-fold increase in the probability of poor outcomes at age 4 (Sameroff, Seifer, Barocas,
and Greenspan, mimeographed manuscript available) and
that, indeed, it is cumulative risk factors that place infants
and families at greatest risk.

The findings of the Sameroff study are paraphrased in
some detail because of the important implications they have
for predicting poor outcomes in high-risk populations. The
population for this study, although recruited with the original
aim of looking at the effects of different types of parental
emotional disturbance on development in the offspring, was
consistent with the patterns found in multiproblem or multirisk families described above. Of 215 families followed since
pregnancy, all of Hollingshead's SES groupings were represented, some with greater portions in groups 3, 4, and 5. They
were divided between white (131), black (79), and Puerto
Rican (5), with family sizes ranging from 1 to 10 children.

Approximately 54 of the women were either single, separated, or divorced. Their education ranged from advanced college degrees to completion of only the third grade. The children were well distributed between boys and girls with slightly more boys.

Ten variables that appeared to be clinically relevant from prior studies and that were measured in this study were selected to categorize the families into high- and low-risk families.

Multirisk status was defined operationally in this study by the number of high-risk variables in any one family (0–8). A relationship was found between the degree of risk defined by number of risk factors and verbal IQ at age 4. The linear trend analysis was significant ($F = 100.24$; $df = 1$; $p =$

TABLE 12-1

Variables Used for Calculating Cumulative Risk Scores for Families of 4-Year-Old Children

Risk Variable	Low Risk	High Risk
Chronicity of Illness	0–1 Contact	1 or More Contacts
Anxiety	75% Fewest	25% Most
Parental Perspectives	75% Highest	25% Lowest
Interaction	75% Most	25% Least
Education	High School	No High School
Occupation	Skilled	Semiskilled
Racial Status	White	Nonwhite
Family Support	Father Present	Father Absent
Life Events	75% Fewest	25% Most
Family Size	1–3 Children	4 or More Children

<.01). The deviation from linear trend was nonsignificant (F = <1).

It is interesting to note that multirisk patterns had far greater impact than any one risk factor alone. For verbal IQ outcomes at age 4, there were two standard deviation differences between the lowest- and highest-risk groups.

Perhaps the most important finding of this study, however, is the fact that interactive, familial, and psychological variables, as measured by multiple-risk criteria, impact on later developmental outcomes even within SES groups. Confirming the clinical impressions and risk factor analyses of the CIDP, this study demonstrates that, contrary to earlier belief in SES as the major predictor of developmental outcomes, interactive psychological and family patterns account for poor

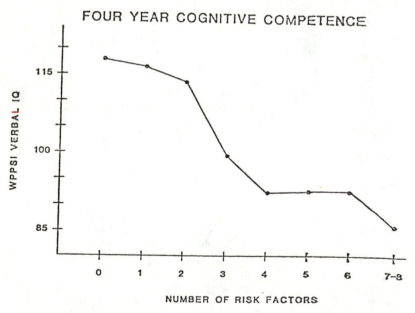

FIGURE 12-1: Means of 4-year-old children's verbal IQ scores for each cumulative risk score. Cumulative risk scores are total of high-risk factors present in each child's family.

developmental outcomes even when socioeconomic status is
held constant.

Trend analysis was significant for high (F = 7.65; p
<.01) and low (F = 24.88; p < .01) SES groups.

In another analysis, to highlight these findings, families
were divided into low risk, moderate risk, and high risk depending on the number of risk factors that characterize the
family. A most striking finding is that if a family is in the high-
risk group, characterized by four or more risk factors, they
have a 25 times greater probability of falling into the low IQ
category.

It should also be pointed out that the same trends described here for intellectual performance were also found for
aspects of emotional and social functioning at age 4 (Sameroff
and Seifer, 1983). The linear relationships, while significant,

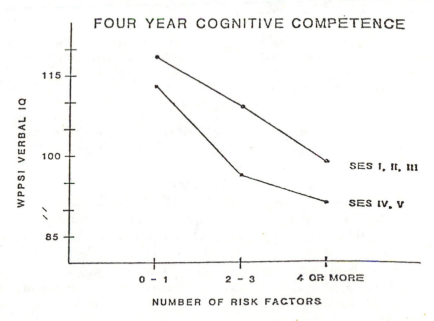

FIGURE 12-2: Means of 4-year-old children's verbal IQ scores within high
SES (I, II, III) and low SES (IV, V) groups in three cumulative risk categories:
low (0–1 risk factors), medium (2–3 risk factors), and high (4 or more risk factors).

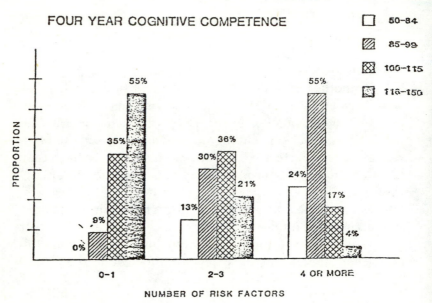

FIGURE 12-3: Percentages of 4-year-old children whose verbal IQ scores were low (50–84), low average (85–99), high average (100–115), and high (116–150) in three cumulative risk categories: low (0–1 risk factors), medium (2–3 risk factors), and high (4 or more risk factors).

were not as dramatic, however. This is most likely due to the types of measures used rather than a lesser degree of impairment in emotional functioning.

In summary, when multirisk criteria derived from in-depth clinical studies of individual infants and families were applied to a nonintervention sample of multirisk families, we found that familial, psychological, and interactive variables early in the first year of life predict aspects of intellectual and social performance four years later. Furthermore, familial, psychological, and interactive variables operate independent of socioeconomic class. When taken together, familial, psychological, and interactive variables and social class variables can predict a 25-fold increase in the probability of having a poor developmental outcome at age 4. It should be noted that tapping this predictive power was only possible after in-depth clinical research had uncovered the prevalence of familial, psychological, and interactive problems in multirisk families and suggested the significance of the impact of cumulative risk factors on development. Further research establishing probabilities of poor developmental outcomes associated with specific familial, interactive, and constitutional patterns in infancy has the promise of bringing to developmental diagnosis and preventive intervention a degree of specificity which has only been possible for a limited number of disorders in general medicine.

Reviewing Preventive Intervention Efficacy Studies from a Comprehensive Services Perspective

Our experience in using a comprehensive preventive intervention approach with the families of the CIDP also offered us a perspective from which to interpret the findings of a major review of prevention intervention studies with children from birth to age 3.

A collaboration (White and Greenspan, in press; Greenspan and White, in press) which reviewed the results of a meta-analysis of all preventive intervention studies with 0- to 3-year-olds found in the literature revealed that early interventions have been shown to be working at the time the intervention stops. Yet the lack of comprehensive approaches to both intervention and evaluation in most studies limited the conclusions one could make about the duration of effect and about which types of programs do best for which types of infants and families.

White and Casto analyzed data on 162 early intervention studies, including studies in which interventions were compared to no interventions and in which one intervention was compared with another. These studies also included different types of problems and populations ranging from high-risk populations (socially, emotionally, and/or economically disadvantaged) to infants and children with developmental delays and handicaps.

The overall results were quite interesting (a mean = .44,

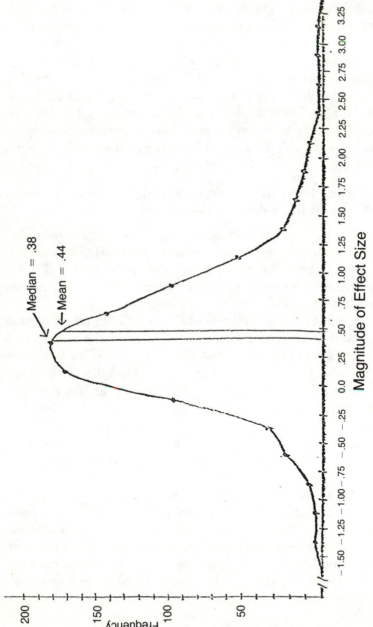

FIGURE 12-4: Frequency distribution of effect sizes from intervention versus control early intervention efficacy studies.

a median = .38, standard deviation − .68). From Figures 12-
1 & 2 it can be seen that the average impact of early intervention is quite impressive. It suggests that at the time they
are completed, most interventions have impact. The average
impact is approximately half of a standard deviation. When
the interventions for developmentally delayed and handicapped and disadvantaged or otherwise stressed children are
looked at separately, it can be observed that the amount of
effect is higher for the handicapped than for the disadvantaged. However, if only "good quality" studies are included,
the average effect size is no different for both disadvantaged
(or "stressed") families and handicapped infants and young
children.

But how enduring are the effects of preventively oriented
interventions? Unfortunately the data is insufficient to draw
conclusions about duration of effect and will need to be addressed in further research. Not only the limited number of
studies with follow-ups, but also the lack of clinically valid
follow-up measures to study the diversity of long-term effects
presents a problem in looking at duration of intervention effect. While studies of disadvantaged children seem to show
declining effects of intervention, it is important to note that
these variables, such as overall social adaptation which do
"hold up" long term, were usually not measured.

Limitations in Preventive Intervention Efficacy Research

One of the major limitations in preventive intervention
efficacy research is a lack of comprehensiveness in both the
intervention and the outcome variables. Many programs for
disadvantaged families, for example, often work only with the
infant, not with the family, or work only on an educational
curriculum with the family and not with day-to-day social and
psychological stresses.

In an attempt to document this impression about preventive intervention research, the existing studies were reviewed from the perspectives of types of measures used,

TABLE 12-2
Average Effect Size for Intervention versus Control Early
Intervention Efficacy Studies for Subgroups of Data

	Handicapped*			Disadvantaged		
	ES	Ses	Nes	ES	Ses	Nes
All studies	.56	.06	143	.42	.02	751
Only good quality studies	.39	.13	23	.41	.03	188
Only good quality studies with immediate posttest	.43	.15	20	.51	.04	121

ES = mean effect size; Ses = standard error of the mean for ES; Nes = number of ES's on which a calculation is based.

duration of intervention, and target of intervention. Additionally the review looked at the number of studies which attempted to work with multiple domains of functioning.

Tables 12-3 and 12-4 show the number and percentage of effect sizes in relationship to the type of measures used, the duration of the intervention, and the time interval lapsing after the intervention when outcome was assessed. One might have thought that studies of shorter duration would focus more on cognitive variables and those of longer duration on psychosocial and familial variables. One may have also thought that longer-term follow-ups would focus more on non-IQ measures. As can be seen from Tables 12-3 and 12-4, this is not the case. There is a predominant focus on limited outcome measures regardless of the duration of the intervention or the time of follow-up.

The different types of intervention and the targets of the intervention are also of interest. By types of intervention it is meant whether the focus is on motor, language, social development, combinations of these, focused physical or occu-

TABLE 12-3

Number and Percentage of ES's Categorized by "Type of Measure" and "Duration of Intervention"

Duration of Intervention in Weeks	Type of Measure										
	IQ	Motor	Language	Soc./Emo.	ITPA	Academic	Attitude	Parent-Skill	Health	School Progress	
1–24	106/ 6.5%	42/ 2.6%	36/ 2.2%	44/ 2.7%	7/ 0.4%	3/ 0.2%	5/ 0.3%	9/ 0.6%	8/ 0.5%	2/ 0.1%	290/ 17.9%
24–52	281/ 17.3%	43/ 2.6%	118/ 7.3%	37/ 2.3%	44/ 2.7%	122/ 7.5%	10/ 0.6%	7/ 0.4%	6/ 0.4%	5/ 0.3%	720/ 44.3%
52–104	175/ 10.8%	28/ 1.7%	28/ 1.7%	27/ 1.7%	29/ 1.8%	71/ 4.4%	0/ 0.0%	6/ 0.4%	1/ 0.1%	10/ 0.6%	379/ 23.3%
104+	92/ 5.7%	10/ 0.6%	41/ 2.5%	19/ 1.2%	3/ 0.2%	35/ 2.2%	2/ 0.1%	4/ 0.2%	6/ 0.4%	19/ 1.2%	235/ 14.5%
Total	654/ 40.3%	123/ 7.6%	223/ 13.7%	127/ 7.8%	83/ 5.1%	231/ 14.2%	17/ 1.0%	26/ 1.6%	21/ 1.3%	36/ 2.2%	1624/ 100.0%

TABLE 12-4

Number and Percentage of ES's Categorized by "Type of Measure" and "Time of Measure"

Months After Intervention Completed, Outcome Was Measured	Type of Measure										
	IQ	Motor	Language	Soc./Emo.	ITPA	Academic	Parent-Skill	Health	School Progress		Total
Immediate	339/ 21.1%	103/ 6.4%	159/ 9.9%	90/ 5.6%	70/ 4.4%	46/ 2.9%	12/ 0.7%	23/ 1.4%	19/ 1.2%	10/ 0.6%	929/ 58.0%
1–12	101/ 6.3%	16/ 1.0%	18/ 1.1%	14/ 0.9%	9/ 0.6%	31/ 1.9%	5/ 0.3%	2/ 0.1%	1/ 0.1%	4/ 0.2%	201/ 12.5%
12–24	77/ 4.8%	0/ 0.0%	17/ 1.1%	2/ 0.1%	2/ 0.1%	40/ 2.5%	0/ 0.0%	1/ 0.1%	1/ 0.1%	4/ 0.2%	144/ 9.0%
24–36	42/ 2.6%	1/ 0.1%	9/ 0.6%	0/ 0.0%	0/ 0.0%	33/ 2.1%	0/ 0.0%	0/ 0.0%	0/ 0.0%	2/ 0.1%	87/ 5.4%
36–60	42/ 2.6%	0/ 0.0%	9/ 0.6%	4/ 0.2%	2/ 0.1%	31/ 1.9%	0/ 0.0%	0/ 0.0%	0/ 0.0%	8/ 0.5%	97/ 6.1%
60 +	44/ 2.7%	0/ 0.0%	10/ 0.6%	14/ 0.9%	0/ 0.0%	50/ 3.1%	0/ 0.0%	0/ 0.0%	0/ 0.0%	6/ 0.4%	145/ 9.0%
Total	645/ 40.2%	120/ 7.5%	222/ 13.8%	124/ 7.7%	83/ 5.2%	231/ 14.4%	17/ 1.1%	26/ 1.6%	21/ 1.3%	34/ 2.1%	1603/ 100.0%

pational therapy, diet counseling, etc. Because of the limited number of studies in some areas, studies of medical, social skills, physical and occupational therapy, and diet counseling categories were all put into "another" category.

The majority of the studies focused on the child and preschool skills. Where the parent is a major intervenor, this involved very little parent training or parent treatment. There is relatively little focus on having the parents become better "copers" in terms of overall family adjustment or to develop their own coping skills to facilitate the development of their children. Parents tended to focus on carrying out particular curricula where the parent is the intervenor or where the child is the direct recipient of the curriculum.

As another way of looking at the degree to which comprehensive approaches were included in the studies to date, the review looked at the studies which had outcomes in four or more domains. Of the 14 out of 162 studies including outcomes in four or more domains, 12 included outcomes in five domains, six included outcomes in six domains, and one study included outcomes in seven domains. Even with multiple outcome studies (which only constitute a very small percentage of the total studies conducted), the comprehensiveness of intervention approach was quite limited. Not surprisingly, because of the narrow intervention focus, the effect sizes for programs with multiple outcome measures was consistent with the effect sizes for the overall group of studies.

From the White and Casto (1985) analysis it seems clear, therefore, that preventive interventions have a positive effect when compared to comparison groups receiving other interventions or control groups. What is not clear, however, is the duration of this effect and the potentially enhanced value of having individually tailored comprehensive approaches to both intervention and outcome evaluation. It is disturbing that so few "comprehensive" programs, which simultaneously address physical, cognitive, emotional, and family functioning, have even been attempted, making it difficult to draw conclusions about longer-term effectiveness or ingredients which favor one type of intervention over another. For example, the "staying power" of the intervention cannot be readily assessed because the way in which an intervention manifests itself would be in the overall functioning of a child, not necessarily in the child's motor or intellectual functioning alone. Similarly, the effect of family involvement cannot be ascertained unless one knows more about the quantity and quality of the family involvement. Family approaches which pay attention to the emotional factors of the family, as well as engaging the family in the instructional curriculum, have not been adequately studied. These are remaining challenges for future studies.

Directions for Further Research

The CIDP attempted to describe the complex lives of infants and parents in multirisk families, to abstract meaningful patterns for study, and to suggest directions for future research. We found that an in-depth case by case approach not only helped us to identify the range in variation of adaptive and disordered functioning in the families we saw and to devise appropriate clinical and service system strategies, but also yielded basic demographic data which would be likely to elude more traditional research designs if used with multirisk families. Building on this foundation, we were able to develop concepts which have proved useful tools for collaboration with other researchers.

We believe we have made some progress along the research sequence described at the beginning of this chapter. There are also enormous challenges that lie ahead. It has been demonstrated that preventive interventions are generally efficacious in spite of the narrow focus of most programs. Yet little is known about the degree to which preventive interventions hold up over time and the efficacy of specific types of interventions for specific types of problems. Furthermore, models which demonstrate how to work with multiple aspects of development—that is, physical, cognitive, emotional and social and familial—are few and far between. The application of such models to a range of common challenges in primary care settings for infants, children, and their families including motor and language delays, high-risk parenting situations, and emotional–social disorders have not been implemented and evaluated with sufficient rigor.

In addition, while the normative developmental landmarks have been well delineated, studies documenting disturbed patterns in development have been relatively scarce. Such basic questions as the relative contributions of fine and gross motor delays to emotional problems or the contributions of difficulties in sensory processing to emotional, social, and intellectual difficulties have not been well studied. The demarcation of a developmental timetable involving cognitive, emotional, and social functioning now permits the study in greater detail of the factors that determine poor versus optimal developmental outcomes in both short- and long-term studies. In addition, the ability to follow development from each phase to the next will permit short-term studies to have more meaning for longer-term ones.

It is time to undertake new integrated programs of research which could simultaneously look at the efficacy of comprehensive approaches to preventive intervention and offer the prospect of integrated approaches to understanding the pathogenesis of psychomotor, cognitive, and emotional difficulties.

An Example of a Specific Developmental Hypothesis Regarding Disorders of Thought and Affect

An integrated developmental approach has led us to specific hypotheses about disorders of thought and affect. Consider a child who has a problem at the early homeostatic-regulatory level and again at the ideational interpretative level. Imagine that the child cannot abstract or sequence (i.e., decode) auditory signals (an infantile version of a learning

disability). He has a very specific, selective disturbance; he
cannot make sense of his auditory world. In addition he has
a well-intentioned but anxious and intrusive parent, who is
inflexible and talks more and more (rather than using visual
cues) and faster and faster to "get a reaction." Confused and
overwhelmed, the infant turns away, and forms a weak and
shallow attachment. He then has failures at the 8-month cause-
and-effect stage because he is not invested in the human world
and has no basis for "decoding" interactive vocal signals. As
he grows older, the family is so anxious that they *distort*
meanings for the youngster. In addition, because he also has
auditory sequencing problems, even if they label feelings correctly, he may experience their reactions as confusing. His
representational system is therefore not elaborating or differentiating. He therefore has problems on at least two levels—his
signals (sound coming in, getting processed, and sent up for
interpretation)—are *confused* signals because he is not discriminating well at the periphery. Auditory "affect" signals
perhaps are especially confusing (more than nonaffect signals).
His interpretive system (his representational system), which
labels sensations is also not well developed because he is living
in a world of confused meanings (i.e., chaotic, poorly differentiated family patterns). He therefore has problems at both
the early somatic level and the later representational–interpretive level. It is not surprising, depending on the degree
of the processing and interpretive limitations, that one may
see varying degrees of disturbances in thinking and behavior.

Disturbances of affect regulation (e.g., manic depressive
illness, "acting out" behavior disorders), may emerge from a
different constitutional maturational pattern and set of early
experiences. Affect regulatory disturbances, it may be hypothesized, are related to early motor regulatory and
visual–spatial sequencing or processing difficulties. Such babies have difficulty regulating *intensity* of experience. They
may be excellent in auditory processing, but have difficulty
in visual–spatial processing. Decoding the meaning of affect

may be more of an auditory pathway challenge, whereas decoding intensity may be more of a visual–spatial pathway task (Caron and Caron, 1982). A visual–spatial processing lag and poor state of affect intensity modulation, however, may be compensated for with an unusually empathetic caregiver who balances empathy with limit setting. A failure of empathy and limit setting, however, together with a visual–spatial processing limitation, it may be hypothesized, will lead to an affective regulation disorder. Thought disorders emerge from auditory–verbal processing difficulties coupled with caregivers providing confused meanings. Affective regulation disorders emerge from visual–spatial processing difficulties coupled with a lack of empathy and limit setting. These illustrative developmental hypotheses are further discussed elsewhere (Greenspan, 1985) and are mentioned briefly here to show how integrated approaches may lead to less polarized (all biology versus all experience) and more clinically relevant hypotheses and research strategies.

Summary and Conclusions

Developmental disturbances during infancy and childhood are invariably a product of multiple factors, including biological, developmental, familial, and social–cultural.

There are converging findings from both human and animal studies that the vast majority of developmental problems in infancy are influenced by both biological and experiential environmental factors and that the optimal time for prevention and treatment is early in the course of the disorder. Yet there is still a large gap in the development of clinical techniques and tools to assess, diagnose, and intervene in a comprehensive manner. At the level of practice, for example, sensory or motor irregularities are still viewed as a static form of brain damage in isolation from experiential, that is, familial factors. Interventions often begin much later than they should, except for the most extreme cases, and rarely include the full range of appropriate modalities. Similarly, family and interactional problems likely to undermine development are rarely considered in relationship to the individual differences in the infant's and young child's constitutional and maturational patterns. Counseling for a family with an infant diagnosed as "failure to thrive" or as having an attachment disorder, will, for example, usually not recognize, or will fail to integrate into the treatment plan observations of sensory or motor differences in the infant as well as possible emotional sequelae to the primary disorder.

Another major challenge concerns the service delivery system. At present, while there is growing recognition among service providers of the importance of health, mental health, and educational components in a comprehensive approach to developmental problems, models to integrate these components around the care for specific infants, children, and families have not been sufficiently developed and demonstrated. Furthermore, an even larger gap exists in getting much needed services to those at most risk. Families who are the most at risk for developmental problems are often those who are limited in their ability to make use of available services. Innovative outreach programs, coordination of service agencies, and consultation efforts are essential.

There is therefore a need to integrate in clinical research and service system approaches the health and mental health factors vital to understanding the etiology, course, prevention, and treatment of a variety of health and mental health problems first evident during early childhood.

An important series of challenges lies in studying how the various factors (from the infant's constitutional status to the structure of the family and community) work together to promote healthy adaptation or disordered functioning.

How the various aspects of early functioning influence one another is not always self-evident. For example, as indicated in the case studies, infants, early in their development, evidence different characteristics in their sensory, motor, and affective patterns. Some infants are hypersensitive and others hyposensitive to tactile or auditory experiences. In addition, clinically, we have observed some infants who appear to have difficulty decoding auditory experiences, but abstract visual patterns well, while other infants are just the opposite. Parent–infant interaction patterns may reflect sensitivity to an infant's individual differences and developmental, phase-specific requirements, or a misreading of cues and needs (as exemplified by the distractible infant who is engaged in a hyperstimulating interaction pattern only at the tactile and motoric level with no opportunities for organizing vocal and affective interchanges).

Some parents are very patient and will "woo" or pursue even a "slow-to-warm-up" infant, while other parents feel easily "rejected" and withdraw. Other caregivers see their infants as aggressive and exploitative and, therefore, are intrusive and overcontrolling. In some families, there is an adaptive support network where the whole is greater than the sum of the parts. There is, for example, empathy and support for a depressed parent and another adult to help out and offer age-needed experiences to facilitate the child's development. In other families, there is either no support or patterns of conflict and chaos which undermine the availability of phase-appropriate experiences for a child. The structure of the neighborhood, community, and service system is also highly variable and, in some instances, may support development, while in others it may contribute to compromises. Schematically, one may observe the factors which influence development (see Figure 12-5).

It is obviously difficult for diagnostic and preventive intervention approaches to deal with the full complexity of factors outlined above. In isolating manageable groups of variables, approaches often tend to be too narrow and as these cases illustrate research and demonstrations that are intended to have clinical relevance may especially need to consider the interactions among a number of relevant factors. With these considerations in mind, a number of important questions may

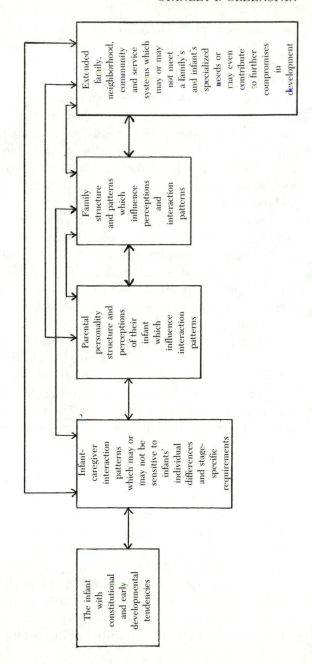

FIGURE 12-5
Factors influencing development

be usefully addressed. They may be conceptualized into four broad areas of challenge: (1) the capacity to screen for developmental and emotional difficulties in primary care settings; (2) greater understanding of the relative contributions of infant, interactive, parent, family, and community variables in disordered functioning; (3) improved models of comprehensive approaches to diagnosis and preventive intervention; and (4) approaches to training and technical assistance.

Specifically, some of the following objectives may be considered:

I. Screening for emotional and developmental difficulties in primary health care settings.
    A. Brief screening and observational guidelines for primary care professionals.
    B. Guidelines for parents.
    C. Validation of brief screening criteria.
    D. Data on the incidence and prevalence of selected developmental and emotional difficulties in primary health care settings.
    E. Data on current approaches to preventive services.
II. Comprehensive approaches to the diagnosis and identification of etiological and contributing factors for developmental and emotional difficulties in various groups of infants and their families.
    A. Groups may include:
        1. Those at special risk, such as:
            a. low birth weight (including SGA infants);
            b. perinatal complications;
            c. being an offspring of a parent with a severe emotional disorder, such as manic depressive and/or schizophrenic illness.
        2. Those with disordered functioning, such as:
            a. regulatory difficulties;
            b. attachment problems;
            c. motor delays.

B. Goals may include:
   1. Developing and applying new approaches to assessing sensory and affective processing in infants.
   2. Refining and applying infant–caregiver interaction observational approaches.
   3. Studying family and extended family patterns.
   4. Studying relationships between numbers 1 and 3 above.
III. Models of comprehensive approaches to preventive intervention.
   A. Demonstrating how a model program works, in terms of types of infants and families seen, patterns of service offered, liaison with existing health, educational, and mental health programs, and patterns of service support from private and public sources.
   B. Studies of the efficacy of comprehensive preventive interventions for selected developmental and emotional problems, in comparison to less comprehensive approaches. Comprehensive preventive interventions may include:
      1. Providing specialized experiences that help an infant master and, where appropriate, use specific vulnerabilities to progress toward age- and stage-expected adaptive capacities.
      2. Encouraging infant–caregiver interactions that are sensitive to individual differences and developmental stage-specific challenges.
      3. Facilitating accurate caregiver perceptions and overall personality growth.
      4. Improving availability and utilization of the service system, and facilitating adaptive extended-family and community relationships.
IV. Training and technical assistance on comprehensive approaches to infants and young children.
   A. Working with states and communities toward integrating health, mental health, and educational ap-

proaches, in terms of structure, organization, and planning of services.

B. Training and incentive building for the variety of professionals and paraprofessionals responsible for the care of infants, young children, and their families.

C. Educational approaches for parents and other caregivers.

Clinical case studies always bring home the reality of the complexity of human functioning. This brief overview of some challenges that may be of current importance in improving preventive approaches for infants, young children, and their families reflects the enormous effort needed. But it also reflects identifiable and achievable goals.

Appendix 1
A Model for Cost-Effectiveness Analysis of Services for High-Risk Families and Infants

Nancy Thorndike Greenspan, M.A.*

Introduction

How the value of a health services program is judged depends upon one's perception. The clinician considers the improved functioning of all the patients involved; an individual patient and his family looks at his own degree of improvement; the policymaker weighs the costs of running the program against the benefits which accrue. Oftentimes, a determination made by any one of these parties is nondefinitive because of the complexities of the problem and the lack of complete information. Although, over time, the value of the program may become clearer, in the short run decisions about what course of action to follow for a particular case, a particular group of cases, or the entire program is often ambiguous.

Other chapters in this volume have given information useful to health care providers in determining the value of the services provided. However, especially in the present political

*The statements and data contained in this paper are solely those of the author and do not express any official opinion of or endorsement by the Health Care Financing Administration nor by the U.S. Department of Health and Human Services.

and financial environment, policymakers at the local, state, or federal level may still be skeptical of the value of intervention programs vis-à-vis other funding choices.

One method helpful to these policymakers in making decisions and determining trade-offs is cost-effective (or cost-benefit) analysis. Unfortunately, in the area of programs for high-risk parenting, only rarely have such analyses been undertaken, leaving a void in a particularly important decision area. As an initial step toward facilitating more of this kind of analysis, this paper will present a model for cost-benefit analyses for the Clinical Infant Development Program (CIDP).

The model is based on broad assumptions regarding the social benefits derived from the program and modifications of the standard cost-effective approaches. It is intended to be an illustration of an approach, *not* a definitive measure of outcome for the CIDP. The assumptions and modifications, necessitated by the lack of longitudinal data, are clearly enumerated in this chapter so as to allow an interested person who disagrees with the assumptions, the option to vary them and develop his own expected net benefits. Given that most intervention programs in the area of high-risk parenting are fairly recent and have not had time to gather longitudinal data, those interested in performing other cost-effectiveness or cost-benefit analyses may wish to consider an approach similar to that outlined in this paper.

Is it worthwhile to spend federal and state funds in funding services needed by high or multirisk families and their infants? A cost benefit analysis of CIDP at-risk families and infants in Prince Georges County, MD will, it is hoped, shed some light on this question.

The Primary Concerns

The primary concerns of the CIDP's intervention efforts were the physical and mental health and development of the infant and the functioning of the parents and family. Staff personnel at the Center included social workers, psychologists, infant specialists,[1] therapeutic day care workers, and on a part-time basis, a pediatrician and a psychiatrist. The facilities are comprised of therapy or testing rooms (some of which are specially equipped for videotaping) and an all- or part-day treatment room. A number of the families brought their newborn infant to the Center twice a week for 3 to 4 hours each time, during which period the mother and/or father was seen by the social worker and infant specialist for an hour each and spent the remaining time in the day treatment room parenting the infant under the guidance of the specially trained personnel.

A cost-benefit analysis of this type of program is particularly difficult because there are many unknowns. For example, because of the relative newness of this type of program, no longitudinal data on outcomes (extended into adulthood) are available; also, because of ethical and medical constraints on having prospective control groups, it is not possible to know what the person's ability to function would be if the intervention had not occurred. In order to perform the analysis, a range of assumptions will be made about these and other variables.

Another problem is that each case differs and, consequently, costs are not similar for each. As part of a preliminary approach to these challenges, an analysis will be done on two cases, one considered a difficult case requiring very intensive intervention (the Lakes) and a moderate one requiring an "average" amount of intervention (the Smithsons). For each of these cases, expected benefits and cost-benefit ratios will be calculated.

Costs of the Program

THE LAKES

Mrs. Lake came to the attention of the Center while she was in a state psychiatric hospital where she had been com-

---

[1]The infant specialist was usually a nurse or a special education teacher specially trained by the Center to help the mothers care for their babies and, at times, provide care themselves directly to the babies.

mitted by her family. She was 4 months pregnant at the time of commitment and had four other children (three teenagers and one toddler). Her husband was deaf and the family lived on his Social Security disability income; he also did repair work in exchange for food. He was diagnosed as a borderline psychotic personality disorder with strong passive aggressive traits.

When she was 6 months pregnant, Mrs. Lake was released from the hospital and entered the program. For the 3 months prior to birth, she was seen by a social worker either at the Center or at home. During these sessions, she told of auditory hallucinations and also indicated no interest in the arrival of the baby. Mr. Lake only sometimes participated in the home sessions. Because of his deafness, his involvement necessitated writing out questions.

A healthy baby girl named Betty was born; however, Mrs. Lake failed to notify the Center staff of the birth. Not until a clinician visited her, after the clinician's vacation, did they find out. At that point, Mrs. Lake was back home from the hospital with Betty.

Sessions for the parents and infant started at the Center soon after birth. Mrs. Lake was delusional and her delusions extended onto the infant. For instance, Mrs. Lake thought "the bugs" she saw would crawl on the baby. After a few weeks, it was also recognized by Center personnel that the infant was undernourished and dehydrated and, therefore, at 6 weeks, the baby was hospitalized. Soon after returning home from the hospital, she was placed in a temporary foster home by the county welfare agency. Throughout the four months in foster care, the parents came to the Center daily to see the baby (who was brought from the foster home by Center personnel) and to learn parenting skills. When the baby finally went home, the baby and parents started to come to the Center three mornings a week.

In addition to the therapy time, the Center staff was involved in extensive coordination efforts with local public agencies. Weekly meetings were held with the public agencies involved in the case and the core team from the Center (social worker, infant specialist, psychologist, psychiatrist, and pediatrician). Because the local agencies were also providing services (e.g., protective services because of the foster care, and homemaker services), it was extremely important for all those involved to coordinate and integrate their efforts. At one time, there were 16 different public agencies consulting and/or working on the case.

The therapy sessions continued at the intensive rate of three mornings per week in order to keep the family stabilized. This level was necessary because in addition to caring for little Betty, Mrs. Lake found herself pregnant again and was also coping with her three older children who were in trouble with the law and were periodically suspended from school. (One daughter was sent to a Job Corp Camp, from which she ran away and then became pregnant.)

When the next baby, Phil, arrived, Mr. and Mrs. Lake were incapable of caring for him; and, for similar reasons as Betty, Phil also went to a foster care home but for a shorter duration than Betty. Coordination efforts again started with local agencies and similar daily sessions at the Center occurred until the baby returned home.

The Lakes continued in the Center program for another year but on a more sporadic basis. The last developmental assessment showed Betty to be at age appropriate levels physically, cognitively, and affectively.

In addition to the therapy sessions for the parents (both individual and couples), the Center provided a specialized treatment program to help the parents; individualized patterns of care for Betty who, by 4 months of age, tended to withdraw, have gaze aversion, and evidenced poor muscle tone and flat affect; a therapeutic day program for their 3-year-old boy while they were at the Center; periodic developmental assessments of the baby; elaborate coordination of all local welfare agency involvement such as the public health nurse and protective services agency; transportation for the family to come to the Center; a social worker for the father who knew sign language for the deaf; and staff to attend the court hearings concerning foster care.

Table A-1 shows a detailed breakdown of hours spent by various types of personnel at the Center for the three years of treatment for the Lake family. Costs are calculated using an hourly rate derived from average yearly salaries.[2] Total direct labor costs are $22,226. Overhead[3] is then added to this amount making the total costs for the three years $32,228.

This total cost may seem high; however, it must be remembered that this case was very difficult to treat and unusual in the complexity of the problems presented. The next case is more typical of the degree of intervention required for a high-risk family.

The Smithson Case

Mrs. Smithson entered the program when she was 4 months pregnant. At that time, she had a 1½-year-old son and a "psychotic" husband (diagnosed during a brief hospitalization) who was in prison for arson (for trying to burn down his own house). He had also physically abused the child and the child was being monitored by the county's protective service agency. Mrs. Smithson was seen frequently prenatally and was also brought to the prison to meet with her husband a few times (she did not have her own transportation).

A boy, Michael, was born, who was physically and neurologically competent at birth. However, shortly after bring-

[2]Yearly salaries are: social worker, $22,000; infant specialist, $20,000; psychologist, $24,000; psychiatrist and pediatrician, both $50,000 each; therapeutic day care personnel at $3 per hour for each child. These salaries are representative of those in the different specialties. In some cases, the actual salaries at the Center were less because time was volunteered. These volunteered hours, however, were costed out at the opportunity cost (i.e., cost of opportunities foregone because of involvement in this activity).

[3]The overhead rate is 45 percent which includes rent, utilities, videotape personnel and equipment, transportation, secretarial support, and fringe benefits.

TABLE A-1
Cost of Three Years of Intervention for the Lakes (in Hours)

	Social Worker	Infant Specialist	Psychiatrist	Psychologist	Pediatrician	Therapeutic Day Care Personnel
Therapy* Sessions	506	359	34	5	3	942
Supervision	32	5	37	0	0	0
Record Keeping & Telephoning	200	145	5	5	1	0
Meetings†	77	75	63	15	30	0
Total Hours	815	581	139	25	34	942
Hourly Rate	$11	$10	$25	$12	$25	$3
Costs	8,965	5,810	3,475	300	850	2,826

Total Costs: $22,226 × 1.45 = $32,228

*Includes travel time if therapist is driving to family's home or taking patient some place.
†Includes collaborative agency meetings, case conferences and team meetings.

ing the baby home, the mother complained that Michael was spitting up. The Center staff determined that Mrs. Smithson was overfeeding Michael and the infant specialist counseled her about feeding patterns.

Three weeks after the birth, Mr. Smithson returned from prison. A staff social worker started couple's therapy with them, in addition to individual sessions with the mother and baby. However, the father had serious emotional problems and, during his first six months after returning from prison, he was hospitalized in the state psychiatric hospital three times. Many of the problems resulted from his violent outbursts when he would threaten to kill people. The instability of these few months was compounded by Mr. Smithson's penchant for changing residences for himself and his family. At four months, Michael's developmental assessment showed signs of problems regulating, difficulty being calmed, and lack of ability to focus, a deterioration from earlier test results.

As much as possible throughout this time period, the social worker and infant specialist continued to see Mrs. Smithson and Michael twice a week at the Center where the older son received therapeutic day treatment. The therapists also responded to the various crises by providing additional therapy, coordinating the efforts of the county welfare and health agencies, ensuring that Mr. Smithson was taken to the hospital, and providing transportation for his wife to visit him. Finally, Mrs. Smithson separated from her husband and eventually found a boyfriend who was more stable than her husband. Therapy continued more intermittently. When Michael was last tested at the age of 2½ he was physically, cognitively, and emotionally quite competent. At the boyfriend's insistence, therapy stopped shortly after this assessment.

The 3 years of labor costs for this case are shown in Table A-2. The total labor costs are $12,416. With overhead added on, the total direct and indirect costs are $18,003 for the 3 years.

TABLE A-2
Cost of Three Years of Intervention for the Smithsons (in Hours)

	Social Worker	Infant Specialist	Psychiatrist	Psychologist	Pediatrician	Therapeutic Day Care Personnel
Therapy* Sessions	272	164	7	12	1	402
Supervision	40	5	45	0	0	0
Record Keeping & Telephoning	104	56	2	8	.5	0
Mothers Group	0	0	3	3	0	0
Meetings†	44	48	48	12	13.5	0
Total Hours	460	273	105	35	15	402
Hourly Rate	$11	$10	$25	$12	$25	$3
Costs	5060	2730	2625	420	375	1206

Total Costs: $12,416 × 1.45 = $18,003

*Includes travel time if therapist is driving to family's home or taking patient some place.
†Includes collaborative agency meetings, case conferences and team meetings.

Benefits

Because of the excellent records kept by the Center, the costs of the intervention program were relatively easy to derive. As noted earlier, the difficult aspect is deriving the benefits. Determining the benefits is done by comparing the cost of services required both in the presence and the absence of intervention; that is, by subtracting the cost of services needed after the intervention from the cost of services required had there been no early intervention. (Losses to society due to crimes such as robbery or murder are not included because of the already complex method of determining the benefits. However, they are a legitimate social cost and should be included.) Both sets of costs could include lost worker productivity and other social costs, such as those of the correctional system. If Betty and Michael require fewer services than they would have with no intervention, the difference between the costs of the two outcome paths will give the benefit of the intervention program to society.

As noted earlier, the problem in determining the benefits is the lack of longitudinal information on the functioning of the principal patient in adulthood given the intervention and their functioning if there had been no intervention. In order to circumvent this problem, five different plausible scenarios of possible outcomes, ranging from the worst to the best, will be hypothesized for adulthood. Also, for each scenario will be given the probability of its occurrence in the presence of intervention and in the absence of intervention. For instance, for the most severe outcome—chronic psychoses requiring fairly frequent hospitalization—the probability for that outcome may be 10 percent for Betty with intervention and 35 percent without it. The costs associated with this outcome would be weighted by the different probabilities.

In a more typical cost-effectiveness analysis of medical treatments, there is usually a clearer delineation of success or failure resulting from a particular intervention. However, with psychiatric treatment, results are more relative. The probabilities attached to the outcomes mean that, in 100 cases, 10 percent would be described by Outcome 1 (the worst), for example. Therefore, by multiplying the cost of each outcome by the probability of its occurrence and by adding the resulting five amounts, one determines the average benefit if data were obtained from 100 cases. The benefits of any one particular case could be better or worse than this average, depending on which outcome the person actually matches.

The methodology for determining the costs in childhood and adolescence will be slightly different from that used for adulthood. One scenario will be given for the outcome associated with intervention and a different scenario for the outcome associated with no intervention. Ranges are *not* being given because there is better ability to predict the earlier outcomes based on the known family dynamics. For instance, it is almost a certainty that with no intervention of the Center or the local agencies, Betty would have died. Although the intervention of the health department alone may have altered this outcome, it is highly unlikely that Betty would have been cared for by Mrs. Lake, given her delusional state pre- and postnatally and her previous record of not taking her medication. Therefore, the childhood outcome in the absence of intervention appears almost a certainty—foster care. It is unnecessary to iterate other outcomes for her.

The remainder of this section will first describe Betty Lake's case, giving the two childhood and adolescent scenarios, and then the range of five scenarios for adulthood in order to determine the benefits. The benefit analysis for Michael Smithson will follow and will be described in the same sequence of stages.

The Lakes

DESCRIPTION OF CHILDHOOD AND ADOLESCENCE WITH NO INTERVENTION

Betty spent much of her childhood in and out of foster homes because Mr. and Mrs. Lake were not stable enough to provide sufficient care. (Mrs. Lake was frequently hospitalized.) The frequent separations and turmoil caused learning problems and acting out behavior in elementary school. With adolescence, there was a problem of truancy along with signs of disturbed behavior that resulted in arrest for aggravated assault at age 16. She was put on probation for one year. She was admitted to a state psychiatric hospital at age 18.

Present Value Cost: $155,093 (see Table A-3).

DESCRIPTION OF CHILDHOOD AND ADOLESCENCE WITH
INTERVENTION

At the age of 2½ years, little Betty was exhibiting age appropriate behavior and developmental functioning. Although the parents still had serious psychiatric problems, the mother was, for the first time, taking her medication on a regular basis and was able to care for the family. It is probable that the mother would require hospitalization some time in the future and that during these episodes a homemaker would be needed to help care for the children; however, with this service, it is probable that Betty and her younger brother would have remained out of foster care.

In adolescence, there were some problems with truancy and signs of emotional problems. Betty received regular outpatient therapy for two years at a childhood mental health clinic. At age 18, she graduated from high school.

Present Value Cost: $50,340

FIVE ADULTHOOD SCENARIOS USED FOR OUTCOMES WITH AND
WITHOUT INTERVENTION

Outcome 1.

Betty had severe chronic mental disorders similar to her mother's, which resulted in frequent periods of hospitalization. She married but her husband, who was unskilled and an alcoholic, was unable to keep a job. Most of the time, the family was on Medicaid or unable to pay for medical treatment. They relied on public support. Betty and her husband

TABLE A-3
Costs and Present Values for Outcomes for Betty Lake

Childhood and Adolescence (ages 0–18)	Unit Cost (1981)	Total Cost (1981)	Present Value of Total Costs*
Without Intervention			
a. Foster care for Betty and younger brother, 6 years	$3,011/yr	$36,132	$27,622
b. Betty's mother's psychiatric hospitalization for 6 mo each at Betty's ages of 2–5, 7, 8, 10, 12, 13, 16	17,654/6 mo	176,540	114,385
c. Court costs and probation for 1 yr for Betty at age 16	1,733/yr	1,733	682
d. Betty's psychiatric hospitalization for 1 yr at age 18	35,405/yr	35,405	12,404
Total Present Value			155,093
With Intervention			
a. Foster care for Betty for 2 mo and for younger brother when Betty was 1 yr	$495/2 mo	$990	$962
b. Betty's mother's psychiatric hospitalization for 4 mo each at Betty's ages of 4, 7, 10, 11, 13, 15	11,640/4 mo	69,840	39,907
c. Homemaker services while mother in hospital, at Betty's ages 4, 7, 10, 11	3,360/4 mo	13,440	8,241
d. Outpatient psych. therapy for Betty for 3 yr from ages 15 to 17—once a week	1,040/yr	3,120	1,230
Total Present Value			50,340

TABLE A-3
Costs and Present Values for Outcomes for Betty Lake

Adulthood (ages 17–70)	Unit Cost	Total Cost	Present Value
Outcome 1			
a. Medicaid—routine health needs at Betty's ages 19–70	$1,121/yr	$58,292	$6,229
b. Betty's psychiatric hospitalization for 3 mo each at Betty's ages 20, 22, 26, 31, 33, 35, 38, 40, 45, 52, 60	8,730/3 mo	96,030	14,033
c. Food stamps for Betty and family at ages 19–70	1,068/yr	55,536	5,935
d. General assistance for Betty and family at ages 19–70	2,224/yr	115,648	12,359
e. Foster care for Betty's children for 1 yr each at same periods as her hospitalizations up through age 35	3,011/yr	54,198	11,836
f. St. juvenile institution for 8 and 7 mo in aftercare for Betty's child at Betty's ages of 35 and 36	21,535/8 mo 4,800/7 mo	26,335	3,391
g. Court hearing and 6 mo probation for another child at Betty's age of 38	1,239/6 mo	1,239	135
h. Residential treatment for 1 yr for one of Betty's children at Betty's age of 36	67,890/yr	67,890	8,333
i. No productive employment for Betty from ages 19–60, measured at median income	13,165/yr	552,930	131,179
Total Present Value			193,430

TABLE A-3

Costs and Present Values for Outcomes for Betty Lake

	Unit Cost	Total Cost	Present Value
Outcome 2			
a. Medicaid—routine health needs at Betty's ages 19–70	$1,121/yr	$58,292	$6,229
b. Food stamps for Betty and family at ages 19–70	1,068/yr	55,536	5,935
c. AFDC for Betty and family at ages 19–42	3,887/yr	93,288	17,091
d. General assistance for Betty at Betty's ages 43–70	2,223/yr	62,244	2,578
e. Betty's outpatient psych. therapy at ages 27, 29, 30, 32, 33, 35, 37, for once a week	1,040/yr	7,282	1,158
f. Correctional day care for child for 4 mo at Betty's age of 34	4,015/4 mo	4,015	554
g. AFDC for daughter at Betty's ages of 39–41	3,887/yr	11,661	1,136
h. No productive employment for Betty from ages 19–60, measured at median income	13,165/yr	552,930	131,179
Total Present Value			165,860

TABLE A-3
Costs and Present Values for Outcomes for Betty Lake

	Unit Cost	Total Cost	Present Value
Outcome 3			
a. Unemployment comp. for Betty for 3 mo each at ages 20, 23, 30	$1,368/3 mo	$4,104	$1,023
b. Betty's outpatient psych. therapy at ages 24 and 25	1,040/yr	2,080	499
c. Public health use for Betty and family at Betty's ages of 19–70	1,121/yr (for 19–40) 300/yr (for 41–70)	33,662	5,131
d. Outpatient psych. therapy for Betty's child for 2 yrs at Betty's ages of 36 and 37	1,040/yr	2,080	248
e. Truancy and school problems for Betty's child for 3 yrs	NA†	NA†	NA†
f. Betty's lost marginal productivity for ages 19–60, measured at median income minus poverty level income	4,454/yr	187,068	44,381
Total Present Value			51,282
Outcome 4			
a. Betty's lost marginal productivity at ages 19–21 and 27–60, measured at 15% above poverty level subtracted from median income	$3,147/yr	$116,439	$25,209
b. Truancy and school problems for Betty's child	NA†	NA†	NA†
Total Present Value			25,209

†No data available for these costs.

SOURCES OF COSTS AND NOTES FOR TABLES A-3 AND A-5

SOURCES

1. Psychiatric hospitalization and residential treatment—Maryland State Hospital at Spring Grove (1981 data)
2. Foster Care—Montgomery County, MD (1981 data)
3. Correctional—*Reports of the National Juvenile Justice Assessment Centers* (1977 data)
4. Medicaid—Medicaid Program Statistics (1979 data)
5. AFDC and General Assistance—*1980 Statistical Abstract*, p. 354, No. 570 (1979 data)
6. Outpatient psychiatric—MD Medicaid reimbursement (1981 data)
7. Unemployment Compensation—*1980 Statistical Abstract*, p. 350, No. 566 (1979 data)
8. Productivity—*1980 Statistical Abstract*, p. 462, 463, No. 767 (1979 data)
9. Homemaker Service—Montgomery County, MD (1981 data)
10. Food Stamps—Montgomery County, MD (1981 data)
11. Public Health Facilities—same as Medicaid

NOTES

1. All figures inflated to June 1981 levels, using all goods and services component of the Consumer Price Index.
2. Years are measured from age of principal patient.
3. Costs of childhood and adolescence include only those that differ between the intervention and nonintervention scenarios.
4. Adulthood costs of principal patient include costs of their children up through age 18.
5. Productivity levels (measured by income) are not adjusted for different earnings levels in different phases of life.

had three children very close together, the first when Betty was 20. Betty, who had only occasionally received effective parenting from a foster parent, had very few mothering skills. The younger children went to foster homes while Betty was hospitalized and they all had problems with delinquency as teenagers. One spent eight months in a state juvenile institution for a second offense; one was arrested and placed on probation for six months, and another spent a year in a residential psychiatric treatment facility. (This most severe outcome is closely patterned after the behavior of Betty's parents and her older siblings; the latter had school and delinquency problems.)

Present Value Cost: $193,430

Outcome 2.

Betty became an unmarried mother at age 19. (This outcome is loosely taken from Betty's older sister's history.) She qualified for Aid to Families with Dependent Children (AFDC) and remained on welfare. During her twenties, she had various boyfriends, some of whom she lived with. A second child resulted from one of these relationships. By her late twenties she was receiving outpatient psychiatric care, which continued on and off for the next 10 years. Her children remained with her throughout this time but showed signs of learning disorders and troublesome school behavior. One child had trouble with the law as a teenager and spent four months in a correctional day care program. One daughter ran away, became pregnant, and returned home with her newborn baby.

Present Value Cost: $165,860

Outcome 3.

Betty married immediately after high school and found a low-paying job doing domestic work. Her husband worked as a janitor. Shortly, she became pregnant. After taking off from work for a few months, she returned to her job and brought her baby with her. Both she and her husband were sometimes on unemployment and had no health insurance. They relied on public facilities for health care. After the birth of her second child, Betty had a serious depression and required outpatient psychiatric help for two years. Although minor bouts of depression had troubled her during her adulthood, she had not sought treatment until this point. Betty was an adequate mother to her two children most of the time (that is, she was able to care for their physical well-being but was unable to provide much warmth and emotional nourishment). Her husband also helped care for them. One of the children required psychiatric help for two years in high school and the other caused problems in school and was truant.

Present Value Cost: $51,282

Outcome 4.

Betty had learned secretarial skills in high school and upon graduation found a job as a typist. However, she was only marginally adept at the job because of learning problems, which had bothered her throughout her school years. She changed jobs frequently. She was never able to advance very far in her profession but she was able to find work most of the time. In her early twenties, she married and had three children very quickly. She stopped working for five years and then returned to her former occupation. She never needed psychiatric help and she and her husband were always able to support the family on an income just slightly above the poverty line. Her children had some learning problems but were well behaved. One daughter had behavior problems in high school and was an occasional truancy problem.

Present Value Cost: $25,209

Outcome 5.

After finishing high school, Betty took a secretarial job, which she performed competently, and enrolled in a night course at a community college. Here she took courses in business accounting. After three years she graduated and found a job in a firm doing accounting work. She worked hard and was given promotions. She married, had three children, and did not require any psychiatric help or public assistance, nor did the rest of her family.

Present Value Cost: None

The costing out of the above outcomes appears in Table A-3. The probabilities associated with each outcome by presence or absence of intervention are shown in Table A-4. Be-

TABLE A-4

Two Sets of Probabilities for Mary Fawley's Adulthood Scenarios

Outcome	Present Value	Probabilities With Intervention	Col. 1 × Col. 2	Probabilities Without Intervention	Col. 1 × Col. 4
1	$193,430	.10	$19,343	.35	$67,701
2	165,860	.15	24,879	.35	58,051
3	51,282	.25	12,821	.20	10,256
4	25,209	.35	8,823	.08	2,017
5	0	.15	0	.02	0
Weighted average			$65,866		$138,025

Adulthood and Childhood/Adolescence Benefits from Intervention ($176,912)—Cost of Intervention ($32,228) = Average Expected Net Benefit ($144,684)

Outcome	Present Value	Probabilities With Intervention	Col. 1 × Col. 2	Probabilities Without Intervention	Col. 1 × Col. 4
1	$193,430	.10	$19,343	.30	$58,029
2	165,860	.20	33,172	.35	58,051
3	51,282	.35	17,949	.20	10,256
4	25,209	.25	6,302	.10	2,521
5	0	.10	0	.05	0
Weighted average			$76,766		$128,857

Adulthood and Childhood/Adolescence Benefits from Intervention ($156,844)—Cost of Intervention ($32,228) = Average Expected Net Benefit ($124,616)

cause the assignment of the probabilities are subjective, Table A-4 contains two possible sets of probabilities in order to provide a range of net benefits. In both sets of probabilities, it is assumed that there is a lasting impact from the intervention. Although making this assumption can be questioned, it is based on early developmental assessments done on Betty. As noted earlier, at 4 months of age, she had deteriorated in functioning, showing systems of gaze aversion, withdrawal, and flat affect. These trends are rarely reversed without intensive therapy with the parents and the infant, and if left untreated, result in serious psychological adjustment problems. Given that the testing done on Betty at age 2½, after intensive intervention, showed normal, age-appropriate functioning, it can be presumed that Betty had a better chance of a psychologically stable existence than would have occurred with no intervention. Therefore, the purpose of this cost-benefit analysis is not to determine if the intervention program had a positive effect (that is presumed), but rather to determine if the resources spent on the program are outweighed by the benefits received. As can be seen from Table A-4, the expected net benefit for this case ranges from $124,616 to $144,684, depending on the probabilities. (The respective cost benefit ratios are 1:4.9 and 1:55.) The small variation (16 percent) in the sets of net benefits mainly stems from the high costs of foster care and Betty's mother's hospitalization during Betty's childhood and adolescence. Since these costs are not weighted as the adulthood ones are, they neutralize the impact of varying the probabilities.

The Smithsons

DESCRIPTION OF CHILDHOOD AND ADOLESCENCE WITH NO INTERVENTION

Michael's childhood consisted of a series of moves (often staying in one place for no more than a few weeks), periodic absences of his father who was either in jail or a state psychiatric hospital, the witnessing of his father's violent outbursts, and subjection to occasional physical abuse. At one point, the protective services agency placed Michael and his brother in a foster home for six months while his father received outpatient psychiatric help. Mrs. Smithson finally left her husband when Michael was 6. (Although Mrs. Smithson actually left her husband when Michael was about 2 years old, it is highly unlikely that she would have done so at this point without the support and therapy from the intervention program.) This step made a large improvement in the environment but Michael had already developed some emotional problems. School officials had difficulty controlling Michael and, at age 13, he was placed in a residential treatment center for two years. When he was discharged at age 15, he continued to receive outpatient psychiatric care for another year.

Present Value Cost: $64,474 (For the costs of the different outcomes, see Table A-5.)

DESCRIPTION OF CHILDHOOD AND ADOLESCENCE WITH
INTERVENTION

Michael continued to do well after his mother left his father and moved in with her new boyfriend. Although the boyfriend had some character pathologies, he was far more stable than Mr. Smithson. Even though therapy stopped, Mrs. Smithson had learned to be a competent mother during the 2½ years and Michael received adequate parenting. During grade school, he was an average student; during high school, he had some problems with aggressive behavior and received outpatient therapy for a year.

Present Value Cost: $434

FIVE ADULTHOOD SCENARIOS USED FOR OUTCOMES WITH AND
WITHOUT INTERVENTION

Outcome 1.

In his late teens, Michael began showing signs of a temperament similar to that of his father. He found an unskilled job after graduating from high school, but lost it after a few

TABLE A-5

Costs and Present Values for Outcomes for Michael Smithson

Childhood and Adolescence (ages 0–18)	Unit Cost	Total Cost	Present Value
Without Intervention			
a. Foster care for Michael and older brother for 6 mo at Michael's age of 5	$1,501/6 mo	$3,002	$2,244
b. 2 yrs of psychiatric residential treatment for Michael at ages 13 and 14	67,850/yr	135,700	61,821
c. 1 yr of outpatient psych. therapy for Michael at age 16	1,040/yr	1,040	409
Total Present Value			$64,474
With Intervention			
a. 1 yr of outpatient psych. therapy for Michael at age 15	1,040/yr	1,040	434
Total Present Value			$434
Adulthood (ages 19–70)			
Outcome 1			
a. Medicaid—routine health needs at Michael's ages 21–70	$1,121/yr	$56,050	$5,508
b. Unemployment comp. for Michael for 2 mo each at ages 20, 21, 23	912/2 mo	2,736	791
c. General assistance for Michael at ages 21–25 and 43–70	2,224/yr	73,392	5,501

TABLE A-5
Costs and Present Values for Outcomes for Michael Smithson

Childhood and Adolescence (ages 0–18)	Unit Cost	Total Cost	Present Value
d. AFDC for Michael's wife at Michael's ages of 26–42	$3,887/yr	$66,079	$9,489
e. Food stamps for Michael's wife at Michael's ages of 26–42	1,068/yr	18,156	2,607
f. Michael's court hearing and 1 yr probation at age 20	1,734/yr	1,734	541
g. Michael's jail sentence of 6 mo at age 21	13,650/6 mo	13,650	4,015
h. Michael's jail sentence of 18 mo at age 23	27,300/yr	40,950	10,518
i. Michael's psych. hospitalizations for 3 mo each at ages 24, 28, 30, 33, 35, 38, 40, 45, 51, 57	8,690/3 mo	86,900	11,601
j. St. juvenile institution for 8 mo and aftercare for Michael's son for 7 mo at Michael's age of 38	21,535/8 mo 4,800/7 mo	26,335	2,847
k. Psych. residential treatment for Michael's daughter for 6 mo at Michael's age of 41	33,925/6 mo	33,925	3,298
l. 1 yr of outpatient psych. therapy for Michael's daughter at Michael's age 41	1,040/yr	1,040	95
m No productive employment for Michael at ages 21–60, measured at median income; lost marginal productivity at ages 19 and 20	11,000/yr & 19,857/yr	816,280	185,066
Total Present Value			$241,877

TABLE A-5

Costs and Present Values for Outcomes for Michael Smithson

Childhood and Adolescence (ages 0–18)	Unit Cost	Total Cost	Present Value
Outcome 2			
a. Medicaid—routine health needs at Michael's ages 22–70	$1,121/yr	$54,929	$5,178
b. General assistance for Michael ages 22–70	2,224/yr	108,976	10,277
c. Food stamps for Michael's ages 22–70	1,068/yr	52,332	4,935
d. Michael's psych. hospitalizations for 2 mo each at ages 19, 20, 21	5,793/2 mo	17,379	5,425
e. Michael's outpatient therapy for 4 mo for every age from 22–70	340/4 mo	16,660	1,571
f. Lost marginal productivity for ages 19–21; no productive employment for ages 22–60	11,000/yr & 19,857/yr	807,423	181,179
Total Present Value			$208,565
Outcome 3			
a. Unemployment comp. for Michael for 2 mo each at ages 20, 22, 25, 28, 30, 34, 38, 45, 50, 60	$912/2 mo	$9,120	$1,456
b. Public health agencies for Michael and family at ages 19–70	1,121/yr (19–40) 300/yr (41–70)	33,662	5,131
c. Food stamps for Michael and family at same ages as (a)	178/2 mo	1,780	286
d. Michael's outpatient therapy for 6 mo each at ages 19, 23, 25, 26, 28, 31, 32, 36, 40, 42, 43, 50, 58, 65	520/2 mo	7,280	964

TABLE A-5
Costs and Present Values for Outcomes for Michael Smithson

Childhood and Adolescence (ages 0–18)	Unit Cost	Total Cost	Present Value
e. Correctional day care for Michael's child for 5 mo at Michael's age of 39	$5,018/5 mo	$5,018	$517
f. Michael's lost marginal productivity at ages 19–60, measured median income minus poverty level income	11,000/yr	462,000	109,606
Total Present Value			$117,960
Outcome 4			
a. Lost marginal productivity for ages 19–60, measured at 15% above poverty level minus median income	$9,791/yr	$411,222	$97,559
b. School problems for Michael's child	NA*	NA*	NA*
Total Present Value			$97,559

*No data available for these costs.

months because of his aggressive and hostile behavior. A pattern of unemployment and aggressive behavior followed, resulting in frequent arrests for assault. For the first offense he was put on probation for a year, the second time he was jailed for 6 months, and the third time he was jailed for 18 months. In between jail sentences, he managed to get married (at age 21). After returning home from his final jail sentence, he was hospitalized frequently. During the times Michael was in jail, the family relied on welfare and Medicaid. Eventually his wife and children left him. At this point, Michael would alternately disappear and then spend time in psychiatric hospitals. He did not contribute to the support of the family. Michael's wife received AFDC. (This most severe outcome is patterned after Michael's father's life.) Both of the children had severe adjustment problems. The son was arrested at the age of 15 for robbery and after his second offense, he was placed in a state juvenile institution for 8 months. When released, he received aftercare for seven months. The daughter spent 6 months in a psychiatric residential treatment center and received outpatient therapy for one year following discharge.

Present Value Cost: $241,877

Outcome 2.

Michael tried to work after he graduated from high school but severe psychological problems kept him from holding a job for more than a few months. Finally, after being hospitalized four times for about two months each, he went on general assistance payments. He did not marry, but continued to live on welfare using outpatient psychiatric therapy in times of emotional crises.

Present Value Cost: $208,565

Outcome 3.

Michael found a job as dishwasher and busboy after high school but was frequently unemployed, both because of his constant tardiness and absenteeism and his troublesome personality. In between times, he received unemployment compensation. Occasionally, he would become very depressed and would seek outpatient psychiatric care. He married and had three children. Much of the time the family used public health agencies, food stamps, etc. One of the older children was delinquent and spent five months in a correctional day care program.

Present Value Cost: $117,960

Outcome 4.

Michael became a construction worker after high school but changed jobs often, mostly because the mediocre quality of his work did not allow the advancement which he was looking for. He married and had two children. His wife worked part-time. Between the two of them, they were able to support the family on an income slightly above the poverty level. Michael never sought psychiatric help, but occasionally subjected the family to violent emotional outbursts. The oldest daughter had behavior problems throughout her school years and spent many sessions with the school counselor.

Present Value Cost: $97,559

Outcome 5.

Michael apprenticed as an electrician after graduating from high school. He performed his job well and became a licensed electrician working for a large company. In his spare time, he moonlighted, doing electrical repairs for friends. He married at the age 23 and had three children. He was able to support them and provide a secure and stable environment. The children did not have any adjustment problems and successfully completed high school.

Present Value Cost: None

Table A-5 shows the costing out of the above scenarios for Michael Smithson. The two sets of probabilities associated with the outcomes are given in Table A-6. The expected net benefits given in Table A-6 range from $93,369 to $133,983.

TABLE A-6

Two Sets of Probabilities for Michael Smithson's Adulthood Scenarios

A*

Outcome	Present Value	Probabilities with Intervention	Col. 1 × Col. 2	Probabilities without Intervention	Col. 1 × Col. 4
1	$241,877	.10	$24,188	.35	$84,657
2	208,565	.15	31,285	.35	72,998
3	117,960	.25	29,490	.20	23,592
4	97,559	.35	34,146	.08	7,805
5	0	.15	0	.02	0
Weighted average			$119,109		$189,052

*Adulthood and Childhood/Adolescence Benefits from Intervention ($133,983)—Cost of Intervention ($18,003) = Average Expected Net Benefits ($115,980)

B*

Outcome	Present Value	Probabilities with Intervention	Col. 1 × Col. 2	Probabilities without Intervention	Col. 1 × Col. 4
1	$241,877	.10	$24,188	.30	$72,563
2	208,565	.20	41,713	.35	72,998
3	117,960	.35	41,286	.20	23,592
4	97,559	.25	24,390	.10	9,756
5	0	.10	0	.05	0
Weighted Average			131,577		178,909

*Adulthood and Childhood/Adolescence Benefits from Intervention ($111,372)—Cost of Intervention ($18,003) = Average Expected Net Benefit ($93,369)

(The respective cost-benefit ratios are 1:6.7 and 1:7.4.) Here, unlike with Betty, changing the probabilities on the adulthood outcomes does affect the net benefits. The variation of 44% is mainly due to two factors: a smaller cost differential between the childhood/adolescence scenarios and higher costs for the adulthood outcomes, due primarily to the cost of not being a productive member of the labor force. Although Betty's scenarios also included costs of lost worker productivity, the median income for a woman, which was used to measure her productivity, is considerably lower than that of a man.

Conclusion

The expected net benefit and cost-benefit ratio findings from these two cases strongly suggest that early intervention for high-risk infants is very cost-effective. Depending on the case, the results show a savings to society of between $93,000 and $145,000 *in present value terms*, which means that the actual dollar amounts saved in the future are considerably higher but because money in the future is valued less than in the present, it is necessary to deduct part of the future savings. It is as though someone offered you $250,000 in 18 years or the present-day equivalent of $150,000 (the approximate values for total cost and present values for Betty in childhood without intervention, Table A-3).

In addition, it should be noted that it is quite possible to have much higher social costs than those enumerated in the five scenarios. Should any scenario contain serious social problems such as robbery, homicide, or drug abuse, costs escalate quickly. For instance, it has been estimated that by curing a heroin addict, the *present value* of the benefit to society of the foregone theft due to heroin addiction is $332,000. When added to the $56,000 benefit to society from future earnings, the total benefit is $388,000. Therefore, if Michael Smithson were a rehabilitated heroin addict in Outcome 1, the present value for that scenario would be $629,877 and would cause the average expected net benefit (using the first set of probabilities in Table A-6) to be $230,983. Just including heroin addiction in one scenario increases the *average* expected net benefit by 72 percent, showing how conservative the above estimates are. Court and correctional facility costs for serious crimes are even greater, especially when considering the harm to the victim. In 1981, the construction costs alone of a maximum security cell in a federal prison were estimated at $75,000.

Although the above approach needs to be replicated for additional cases in the CIDP in order to determine if they are representative of the program as a whole, the findings for the two cases are consistent and suggest a positive social value. In conclusion it should be emphasized that this chapter presents a new model and illustrates the application of this model to two cases. It is not intended to draw conclusions about the outcomes of the CIDP, but rather to show how a model can be created to deal with *assumptions* and that within the model these assumptions can be shifted and relationships examined.

Acknowledgments

I would like to thank Delise Williams, Robert Nover, and Stanley Greenspan for their effort in relaying information about the Clinical Infant Development Program and the two cases. I would also like to thank Laurie Feinberg of the Health Corp. Financing Administration, and Thomas Hodgson of the National Center for Health Statistics for their review of the paper.

Appendix 2
Clinical Infant Development Program Clinical Entry Ratings

Serena Wieder, Ph.D.
Stanley I. Greenspan, M.D.

Developmental Level

TIME PARAMETERS FOR CLINICAL RATING:

These attempt to measure the relatively enduring aspects of personality. Therefore, when rating the participants on the various subscales below, the rater should consider the participant's entire developmental history as well as current functioning. The rater should consider information about the participant's childhood, adolescence, and early adult years, as well as her current history around the time of the entry into the project and the current pregnancy. For example, if a participant had a history of impulsive acting out throughout adolescence, this should be factored into her rating of the regulation of drive impulses and behavior. This should be the case even if the participant had no such episodes for several years and seems currently to be functioning more adequately. The point is that the rater should attempt to derive an overall Gestalt based on the total life history of the participant and not only consider current life situation.

The first rating is concerned with the regulation and control of drives, affects, and impulsive behavior. The rating should reflect how adequately the participant is able to regulate and control their behavior, affects, drives, and impulses going from low to high. The second rating is concerned with the overall developmental level or diagnosis of the participant. This rating should be based on the evaluation of psychosexual and drive development as well as structural organization. Thus the scale would move from pregenital to genital levels and from no capacity for ideas and imagery with primitive and concrete structure to symbolic and representational levels in the postoedipal phases. In other words, your rating here should reflect a developmental diagnosis of the participant.

1. REGULATION AND CONTROL OF DRIVES, AFFECTS, IMPULSES, AND BEHAVIOR

This function refers to the extent to which delaying and controlling mechanisms allow drive derivatives to be expressed in a modulated and adaptive way, characterized, optimally, by neither under- nor overcontrol.

Evidence here is from overt behavior, associated or indirect behavioral manifestations, fantasies and other ideation, dreams, and inferences made from symptoms, defenses, and controls.

Regulation and control might very well be regarded as one aspect of defensive functioning, but since our concerns here are limited to behavioral and ideational indices of impulse expression and since drives and impulses may be controlled and channeled by ego structures other than defenses, regulation and control would appear to merit a scale of its own. Defensive functioning also relates in its own way to dealing with anxiety and intrapsychic conflict, thus differing from regulation and control.

Among the drives under consideration are the libidinal and aggressive, in both their developmentally earlier and more advanced forms. Included also are impulse expressions deriving from superego pressures such as guilt and self-destructive urges, ranging from suicidal tendencies to less extreme manifestations of depression, then moral and instinctual masochism. (Developmental Scales excerpted, with modification, from Bellak et al., 1973, p. 446.)

Rater ID _____ Subject ID _____

Regulation and Control of Drives, Affects, Impulses, and Behavior

Strong urges are usually acted upon. Sometimes, although present, they are not experienced at all, and knowledge of them can only be deduced from behavior. There may be sporadic rages, tantrums, or binges, as with alcohol, food, or sex. Affects and moods may be very labile, crying one moment laughing the next. May be psychopathic personality. May be hyperkinetic, or need to be physically on the go all the time.

When general behavior and interests are aggressively and sexually oriented, it is with effective sublimation and neutralization (e.g., physical assaultiveness occurs only in the interest of survival of self and others when there is no other alternative). Intercourse is the preferred outlet for sexual urges. Unusual or aggressive behavior is seen only under extreme provocation or prolonged stress.

---

2. OVERALL DEVELOPMENTAL LEVEL

This rating should reflect your developmental diagnosis based on your overall impressions of the developmental status of the participant. Two major features should be considered here. The first pertains to the structural organization of the personality. Consider the participant's capacities for ideas and imagery. If the participant is very concrete or limited to somatic expressions then her structure is at the most primitive level and would be rated at the lowest point. If the participant reflects symbolic and representational capacities which they utilize in the complex and multiple aspects of their functioning, then they have reached the higher developmental levels. The second feature to consider pertains to the psychosexual level of the participant, ranging from the pregenital early arrests or fixations at the oral, anal, and phallic stages to the more oedipal triangular and posttriangular phases at the higher levels.

Rater ID————————————Subject ID————————————

Overall Developmental Level

Structural level is primitive, exhibited by concrete and somatic expression with no capacity for ideas and imagery. Overall developmental level is pregenital. There are major arrests and/or fixations at oral, anal, and phallic stages. Basic issues of aggression, sexuality, self-esteem, etc., are unresolved and permeate personality functioning. Pathology is manifested in the psychoses and the severe character disorders.

Structural level is symbolic and representational. Overall development is at the genital level. While there may exist focused conflicts around oedipal, sexual, aggressive issues, basic aspects of sexuality, aggression, self-esteem, etc., have been resolved. While there may exist areas where functioning is impaired, the basic capacity to love and to work is intact. Relationships are reflected by triangular and posttriangular patterns. Pathology is manifested in the neuroses and the mild character disorders.

Functional Approach to Caregivers—Developmental Level for Caregiving Orientation

The following two scales* attempt to go beyond the caregiver's overall level of ego development and focus on the maternal or caregiving orientation in terms of: (1) presence and differentiation of maternal attributes and (2) valence (i.e., positive or negative). These scales are aimed to help understand the differences in caregiving ability between individuals with equally primitive character structures or equally mature character structures.

*These two scales were developed by Serena Wieder, Ph.D., and Stanley Greenspan, M.D.

3. PRESENCE AND DEGREE OF DIFFERENTIATION OF MATERNAL ORIENTATION

This subscale simply attempts to rate the degree to which there exists a well differentiated, vivid maternal orientation. How well supplied with affects, thoughts, wishes, etc., is the orientation? How stable is the orientation? Is there a sense that the orientation is fairly energized and alive for the subject or does the subject appear not to attend much to thoughts, feelings, etc., about herself as a mother. Two extreme examples might be the woman who is often thinking about her children, who, when she is pregnant, thinks about what the child will be like, who thinks about what her own experiences with her mother were like, etc. Contrast this with the pregnant woman who expresses no special feelings or thoughts about being pregnant, "It's just a baby," and who makes no special preparation for the birth of the child, etc.

Rater ID_____ Subject ID_____

Degree of Differentiation of Maternal Orientation

Maternal schema is poorly differentiated; lacks vividness and is relatively unstable. The subject's maternal schema is not well supplied with feelings, thoughts, memories, wishes, impulses, etc.	Maternal schema is well differentiated; is vivid and relatively stable. The schema is well supplied with feelings, thoughts, memories, wishes, impulses, etc.

---

4. VALENCE (POSITIVE OR NEGATIVE) OF MATERNAL ORIENTATION

When rating the degree of differentiation of maternal schema, do not be pulled by the positive or negative aspects of these schemata, but stay focused on the degree of differentiation. For example, if a mother presents very intense and angry feelings about her own mother's rejection and abandonment of her, and this predominates—the presentation of issues which may pertain to maternal identification—do not rate her necessarily at the lower end of this scale unless there is a great paucity of other feelings, thoughts, wishes or images pertaining to this experience. Again, the purpose of this rating is to note how complex and rich and differentiated maternal schema are. Consider the range of maternal schema as well as the depth and how well supplied it is with maternal feelings, thoughts, memories, etc.

Rater ID_____ Subject ID _____

Valence of Maternal Orientation

Essentially negative: maternal schema is bound up with unpleasurable feelings and thoughts. Subject might, for instance, experience mothering as assaultive, humiliating or depriving.

Essentially positive: while there is an openness to negative feelings and thoughts, the mother can deal with this ambivalence and the predominant experience associated with the maternal self is positive.

Maternal Identification

5. CAPACITY FOR NURTURANCE

To what extent has the subject worked through issues around nurturance so that she can attend to the needs of her children in a relatively undistorted and empathic manner? Here again, we are focusing on the internalized thoughts, feelings, anxieties, wishes, and so on which are connected with the subject's experiences of nurturance. What is being rated here then is not strictly the behavioral capacity of the mother to provide for the child's needs. For instance, it may be the case that someone feels terribly needy and related to her child principally as a vehicle for reparation of her own neediness. While such a person may be driven to provide for what she perceives to be the needs of her child, such a person would be scored on the more pathological end of this scale because the nurturance she gives is primarily rooted in her internal pressures which lead her to care for her infant when she needs to rather than responding to the needs and signals of her infant.

Rater ID_____ Subject ID_____

Capacity for Nurturance

Because of her own difficulties with nurturance/dependence mother is unable to tolerate nurturant aspects of mothering without a great deal of distortion: she may experience child as competitor for supplies, she may need to view herself in an over-idealized fashion as a "good mother" who meets every need of the child in a magical fashion.

Mother has worked through issues around nurturance and dependence in a phase-appropriate fashion. Nurturant aspects of mothering are experienced in a positive fashion. Mother herself feels enriched and grateful by the act of nurturing her child.

---

6. CAPACITY FOR READING COMPLEX AFFECTIVE AND BEHAVIORAL SIGNALS

This rating is concerned with the mother's capacity to read and respond contingently to her infant's communications and behavior during the emerging stages related to separation, autonomy, and assertiveness. During this stage the infant or toddler's repertoire of behavior becomes more complex and communications take on more organized and meaningful form. There is increased imitative activity and intentionality as well as more assertive and autonomous behavior. The infant or toddler will no longer just cry as a way of communicating but will make his needs known in more complex behaviors. It is crucial for the mother to be able to respond to these behaviors in order to promote cause and effect experiences and greater organization and initiative. When the mother ignores or withdraws from these new behaviors, or she misreads her infant's communications because of her own projections and becomes overly intrusive, preoccupied, or too depressed to respond, she would be rated at the low end of the scale. In contrast the mother who is admiring of her infant or toddler's initiative and autonomy, but is yet available and tolerant and firm in setting limits to protect him, is at the other end of this scale and reflects the capacities to support autonomy and assertiveness as well as to organize diverse behavioral and affective elements.

Rater ID_____ Subject ID _____

Capacity for Reading Complex Affective and Behavioral Signals

Mother's capacity to read her baby's communications is impaired because of projection and overly intrusive and controlling tendencies. She may be fearful of her baby's autonomy and/or abruptly and prematurely "separate" when she senses the baby's strivings for autonomy and assertiveness.

Mother has capacity to admire her baby's initiative and autonomy yet is available, tolerant, and firm. She follows her baby's lead and helps organize diverse behavioral and affective elements, supporting his strivings for autonomy and assertiveness.

---

7. CAPACITY FOR SYMBOLIC AND REPRESENTATIONAL THINKING

This scale is concerned with the mother's capacity to utilize symbolic and representational forms in her interaction with her child. The mother who is fearful of or denies phase appropriate needs and impulses, particularly in relation to emerging sexual and aggressive impulses, may only be able to engage her child in concrete and nonsymbolic modes. Or she may misread or misunderstand these impulses and behaviors, responding noncontingently or nonrealistically to her child's communications with the result that she is overly permissive or punitive. In contrast, the mother who has greater capacities in this area is more likely to be emotionally available to her child's emerging capacities in the formation and elaboration of internal representations or imagery as well as in dealing with sexual and aggressive themes. She will be able to read and respond to these issues encouraging symbolic elaboration and across emotional and behavioral domains such as love, pleasure, and assertion. By pretending and imitating she fosters her child's representational capacities as well as a gradual reality orientation and internalization of limits through representational modes.

Rater ID_____   Subject ID_____

Capacity for Symbolic and Representational Thinking

Mother has capacity to engage child only in concrete (nonsymbolic) modes resulting in shallow and polarized affects and behavior. Mother is fearful of, denies, or misreads phase-appropriate needs related to sexuality and aggression, undermining the development of reality orientation and responding by being punitive and/or overly permissive.	Mother has capacity to read, respond to, and encourage symbolic elaboration across emotional and behavioral domains. Responds appropriately to phase-related impulses such as sexuality and aggression as well as regression and dependency; fosters reality orientation and internalization of limits.

---

8. LOCUS OF REINFORCEMENT FOR MATERNAL SCHEMA

This is perhaps the most behaviorally based on the subscales. The question here is what experiences seem to most enhance the subject's sense of herself as a mother. Do these experiences occur mostly within the context of the developing mother–child relationship or do they mostly occur outside of this relationship? It may be that for some subjects the act of mothering itself has little bearing on their feelings about themselves as mothers and is reinforced and sustained by the expectations and demands of others to be "mothers." In contrast to this external locus is the mother who reinforces herself because of the internal gratification she derives from being a mother and her relationship with her child.

Rater ID _____   Subject ID _____

Locus of Reinforcement for Maternal Schema

Predominantly extrinsic: Those experiences which most enhance the subject's sense of herself as a mother occur outside of the dyadic mother–child relationship. For example, the times when she most feels like a mother are when other people ask her about her children or when she watches other people interact with her children, or when she must "be" a mother because of the expectations of others; e.g., the grandmother, nurse, teacher, etc.

Predominantly intrinsic: Those experiences which most enhance the subject's sense of herself as a mother occur in the context of the developing mother–child relationship. For example, subject most feels like a mother when helping child with a task or when providing for the child's needs.

---

9. GLOBAL RISK FOR MOTHER–INFANT OUTCOME

On this scale the rater is to make a judgment of the global risk status of the mother and infant's future outcome. This pertains to the maternal capacities to support the infant's development and the consequences of her capacities if they are less than optimal. In other words, how high is the risk for this mother and infant dyad with respect to deficits in primary maternal functions such as providing basic protection, physical protection, and care to the infant as well as to the maternal capacities to meet her infant's emerging developmental needs in a balanced, empathic manner. The highest risk would include the former, mainly those mothers who are impaired in meeting the basic needs of their infants, while the lowest risk would be for those mothers who are functioning optimally and can respond and promote the development of their infants empathically and appropriately. To make your evaluation of this risk status include the following list of possible sources:

1. Psychiatric disturbance or psychological resources
2. Environmental supports or stresses
3. Adequacy of prenatal care and nutrition
4. High-risk pregnancy including substance abuse by the mother
5. Family stresses
6. Educational level
7. Current maternal functioning with existing children
8. Historical antecedents

The above list includes various sources which contribute to your assessment of risk and are not presented in a hierarchical order. Following your rating of the global risk, please list the three main sources of risk which led to your ratings. Be sure you do your global estimate before noting these sources.

Rater ID_____   Subject ID_____

Global Risk for Mother-Infant Outcome

High risk mother seems almost certain to experience great difficulties in maintaining even a minimally acceptable level of functioning and will have severe difficulties in dealing with her infant's basic care or reading signals of pain and attachment.

Low-risk mother presents little risk with respect to her capacities to nurture and promote the development of her infant empathically and sensitively. She is also likely to be resilient.

Level of Caregiver Adaptive and Maladaptive Functioning

Most maladaptive
10   **Ego Defects**
         Basic physical organic integrity of mental apparatus (perception,
integration, motor, memory regulation, judgment, etc.) ·

         Structural psychological defects and defects in ego functions
         Reality testing and organization of perception and thought
         Perception and regulation of affect
         Integration of affect and thought

**7.5 Defect in Integration and Organization and/or Differentiation of
         Self and Object Representations**

6.5   **Major Constrictions and Alterations in Ego Structure**
              Limitation of experience of feelings and/or thoughts in major life
areas (love, work, play).
              Alterations and limitations in pleasure orientation
              Major externalizations of internal events; e.g., conflicts, feelings,
thoughts
              Limitations in internalizations necessary for regulation of im-
pulses, affect (mood) and thought
              Impairments in self-esteem regulation
              Limited tendencies toward fragmentation of self-object differ-
entiation

5   **Moderate Constrictions and Alterations in Ego Structure**
              Moderate versions of major constrictions listed above
3   **Encapsulated Disorders**
         Neurotic symptom formations
              Limitations and alterations in experience of areas of thought
                (hysterical repression, phobic displacements, etc.)
              Limitations and alterations in experience of affects and feelings
                (e.g., obsessional isolation, depressive turning of feelings
                against the self, etc.)
         Neurotic encapsulated character formations
              Encapsulated limitation of experience of feelings, thoughts, in
                major life areas (love, work, play)
              Encapsulated alterations and limitations in pleasure orientation
              Encapsulated major externalization of internal events (e.g., con-
                flicts, feelings, thoughts)
              Encapsulated limitations in internalizations necessary for regulation

of impulses, affect (mood), and thought
Encapsulated impairments in self-esteem regulation

2   **Age and Phase Appropriate Adaptive Capacities with Phase
Specific Conflicts**

1   **Age and Phase Appropriate Adaptive Capacities with Optimal
Phase Expected Personality Functioning**

Most Adaptive

This framework can also be used quantitatively on a scale from 1 to 10 to reach an approximation of degree of impairment. See column at left (scale), where 10 indicates the most severe psychopathology.

Source: S. I. Greenspan and W. J. Polk (1981), A developmental approach to the assessment of adult personality functioning and psychopathology. In: *The Course of Life: Psychoanalytic Contributions Toward Understanding Personality Develop-ment*, Vol. III. Washington, DC: Government Printing Office.

---

*See Table 11-9, Overview Chart of Caregiver Functioning, middle column.

Therapeutic Relationship Rating

The therapeutic relationship scales are concerned with three aspects of the intervention efforts:

10. REGULARITY AND STABILITY

Rate the degree to which the participant has established some regularity and stability in contacts during the entry phase. At the low end of this scale the participant may permit contacts at times following outreach but not really be part of the program. The interest or ambivalence remains unclear but the clinician is not locked out or the program rejected entirely. Contacts that do occur may feel like first time events as if earlier meetings did not take place. As you move up the scale you will be rating whether the participant permits contacts and demonstrates some interest in the program however disguised. Assess whether the regularity or some pattern of contacts which may be intermittent such as just seeing the clinician every other week or every other appointment, is evidenced. The regularity at this point may take the form of an irregular pattern, but has some predictability or relationship to outreach, concrete services, etc. At later points along this dimension will be the participants who begin to make a commitment to regular appointments and is able to account for availability or cancellations. If there are disruptions at this point the participant and clinician are able to acknowledge these as part of the process going on between them and the participant is moving in the direction of tolerating regular and stable contacts without having to disrupt the process as frequently. At the high end of this scale the participant and clinician are working in a stable and intensive fashion, whatever the frequency may be. The therapeutic work is stable and can tolerate whatever is going on with infrequent or no unplanned disruptions.

Rater ID_____ Subject ID _____

Therapeutic Relationship Scale: Regularity-Stability

_____Prediction

No predictable therapeutic contact—subject may permit contacts at times but it is questionable whether they are or are not in the program (even if they have signed a consent form). Their interest in the program remains unclear but they do fall just short of locking out the clinician or rejecting the program entirely. Contacts that do occur may feel like first-time events as if earlier meetings had never taken place.

Contacts are regular and stable with sessions occurring as scheduled with no unplanned interruptions. The stability reflects the tolerance of the participant to deal with unpleasurable affects during the continual reexamination of patterns in the therapeutic relationship and with others. Short-term regressions in response to terminations are identified and can be worked through.

11. ATTACHMENT—RELATIONSHIP

This dimension is concerned with the affective bond which develops between the participant and the therapist. In its earliest forms this may take the form of some interest in the program but without any specific interest in the therapist and it would appear as if any clinician could be coming to see that participant. As this interest develops it moves from the impersonal to a more differentiated affect quality specific to the therapist and the participant is relating in a more personal way recognizing the therapist as someone specific to them. The relationship between the participant and therapist continues to grow through the specific attachment just noted to recognizing signals and feelings between them. At this point the participant might feel that the therapist "knows" them because the therapist can anticipate their behavior or feelings and early signs of trust are emerging whereas until now there was greater ambivalence and fear of letting the therapist get too close. As this relationship develops the participant is able to tolerate uncomfortable feelings or scary affects without major disruption or flight. The participant tolerates feeling "known" and accepted by the therapist even though they are experiencing uncomfortable affect states because their attachment and relationship feels more secure. Reserve the upper end of this scale for those participants who can make connections between the therapeutic relationship and other key relationships following examination of what is going on between them and the therapist. At this stage the participant can compare and differentiate other patterns in their relationships with that of the one with the therapist which also has the force of current emotions as with others and sees how these patterns guide their behavior. At the highest end one would observe satisfaction and often affection in the therapeutic relationship with a sense of accomplishment of a task jointly well done.

Rater ID_____   Subject ID_____

Therapeutic-Relationship Scale: Attachment-Relationship

Participant views the therapist in an impersonal manner with little evidence of an affective or specific relationship between them. Continuous outreach is needed to maintain contacts and interest in the therapist is impersonal or ambivalent at best.	Relationship between Participant and therapist is secure and tolerates continuous examination and exploration of pleasant and unpleasant affects. Often there is a great deal of affection and a sense of accomplishment of a task jointly well done.

---

12. THERAPEUTIC PROCESS

This scale is concerned with the process as observed in the content of the meetings between the participant and the therapist. At its earliest stages it may take the form of concrete services and outreach, then moving toward supportive and information gathering phases. These are generally initiated and moved along by the therapist's interests and concrete and emotional support. Next the participant increases her ability to report interactions and behaviors with others on their own and permits feelings to be recognized and named by the therapist. This may develop into more self-observing reports to the therapist and would be followed by the participant's capacity to report not only what happened to her but how she felt about it. This may pertain to events outside of the therapeutic process as well as within the therapeutic process such as talking about how she felt about a prior session or this session. The observing function develops and is now utilized to better understand the mother–infant relationship in a more selective and organized manner so that the mother can now also observe and record her feelings in relation to her infant. More complex feelings enter the therapeutic process here such as loss, jealousy, competition, etc. The observing function appears more stable and the participant begins to recognize complex and ambivalent feeling states in their various relationships. As the participant moves up on this scale you would expect to see connections being made between the therapeutic relationship and other key relationships through the use of the transference. The participant is now using this relationship as a vehicle for learning and understanding more about her emotions and interactions and can continually reexamine the patterns in their relationship and relate these to patterns with others as well as patterns reflected in their history. It is at this point that the therapeutic process moves to remembering, recovering, or reconstructing early experiences which help them see the historical continuity involved in these patterns. This historical perspective offers depth and further understanding to emotional experiences between the participant and the therapist, their babies, and others. At the highest level of this process is the participant's capacity to use the identification of patterns in her current life, reorganize historical antecedents, and repeatedly explore these patterns in multiple settings as she works through her difficulties. The participant recognizes "here it happened again" and sees the historical base as well as the current ramifications. The repetitive exploration leads to her beginning to relinquish old maladaptive and compromised patterns of functioning to new ways of relating and experimenting with higher level patterns of satisfaction. The final point of this scale would reflect the consolidation of new patterns and the participant's feeling of security that the gains she has made can be maintained and have become adaptive in all parts of her life. This would be followed by dealing with the separation and termination with the capacity to work through the sense of loss and mourning and move forward.

Rater ID _____ Subject ID_____

Therapeutic-Relationship Scale: Therapeutic Process

Interventions are centered around outreach, concrete services, and information gathering. Therapist must initiate and structure most of the contact or is drawn into crisis-type interventions. Work is supportive but participant's capacity to reflect or observe feelings remains very limited.

Therapeutic process is focused on self-observing feelings, behaviors, and the therapeutic relationship, recovering and reconstructing early historical experiences, repetitive exploration, and reworking old patterns related to maladaptive and compromised functioning moving toward higher level patterns of satisfaction.

References

Ainsworth, M., Bell, S., & Stayton, D. (1974), Infant–mother attachment and social development: Socialization as a product of reciprocal responsiveness to signals. In: *The Integration of the Child Into a Social World*, ed. M. Richards. Cambridge, England: Cambridge University Press, pp. 99–135.

American Psychiatric Association (1980), *Diagnostic and Statistical Manual* (DMS-III). Washington, DC: American Psychiatric Association.

Argles, P., & Mackenzie, M. (1970), Crisis intervention with a multi-problem family: A case study. *J. Child Psychol. Psychiat.*, 11:137–195.

Backwin, H. (1942), Loneliness in infants. *Amer. J. Dis. Child*, 63:30–42.

Bayley, N., (1969), Manual for the Bayley Scales of Infant Development. New York: Psychological Corporation.

Bell, S. (1970), The development of the concept of object as related to infant–mother attachment. *Child Develop.*, 41:219–310.

Bellak, L., Hurvich, M., & Gidiron, H. (1973), *Ego Functions in Schizophrenics, Neurotics, and Normals: A Systematic Study of Conceptual, Diagnosis and Therapeutic Aspects.* New York: Wiley.

Bergman, P., & Escalona, S. (1949), Unusual sensitivities in very young children. *The Psychoanalytic Study of the Child*, 3/4:333–352. New York: International Universities Press.

Berstein, B. (1964), Social class, speech systems, and psychotherapy. *Brit. J. Sociol.*, 15:54–64.

Bowlby, J. (1952), *Maternal Care and Mental Health*, WHO Monograph No. 2. Geneva: World Health Organization.

——— (1969), *Attachment and Loss.* New York: Basic Books.

Brazelton, T., Koslowski, B., & Main, M. (1974), The origins of reciprocity: The early mother–infant interaction. In: *The Effect of the Infant on Its Care Giver*, ed. M. Lewis & L. Rosenblum. New York: Wiley, pp. 49–76.

Buell, B. (1952), *Community Planning for Human Services.* New York: Columbia University Press.

Burlingham, D., & Freud, A. (1942), *Young Children in Wartime.* London: Allen & Unwin.

587

Cameron, H. (1919), *The Nervous Child*. London: Oxford Medical Publications.

Caron, A.J. & Caron, R.F., (1982), Cognitive development in early infancy. In: *Review of Human Development*, ed. T. Fields, A. Huston, H. Quay, L. Troll, & G. Finley. New York: Wiley, pp. 107–147.

Charlesworth, W. (1969), The role of surprise in cognitive development. In: *Studies in Cognitive Development: Essays in Honor of Jean Piaget*, ed. D. Elkind & J. Flavell. London: Oxford University Press, pp. 257–314.

Cravioto, J. (1980), Malnutrition in infants: A developmental perspective. Paper presented at the scientific meeting of the Mental Health Study Center of the National Institute of Mental Health, Adelphi, MD.

——— DeLicardie, E. (1973), Environmental correlates of severe clinical malnutrition and language development in survivors from kwashiorkor or marasmus. In: *Nutrition, the Nervous System and Behavior*, PAHO Scientific Publication No. 251. Washington, DC: Pan American Health Organization.

Curtis, J., Simon, M., Boykin, F., & Noe, E. (1964), Observations on 29 multiproblem families. *Amer. J. Orthopsychiat.*, 34:510–516.

Edelstein, R. (1972), Early intervention in the poverty cycle. *Soc. Casework*, 53:418–424.

Ekman, P. (1972), Universals and cultural differences in facial expressions of emotion. *Nebraska Symposium on Motivation*. Lincoln: University of Nebraska Press.

Emde, R., Gaensbauer, T., & Harmon, R. (1976), Emotional expressions of infancy: A biobehavioral study. *Psychological Issues*, Monograph No. 37. New York: International Universities Press.

Erikson, E. (1959), Identity and the Life Cycle. *Psychological Issues*, Monogr. 1. New York: International Universities Press.

Escalona, S. (1968), *The Roots of Individuality*. Chicago: Aldine.

——— Heider, G., (1959), *Prediction and Outcome: A Study in Child Development*. New York: Basic Books.

Fantl, B. (1958), Integrating psychological, social, and cultural factors in assertive casework. *Social Work*, 3:30–37.

Folstein, M., & Luria, R. (1973), Reliability, validity and clinical application of the visual analogue mood scale. *Psycholog. Med.*, 3:476–486.

Fraiberg, S. (1965), *The Magic Years: Understanding and Handling the Problem of Early Childhood*. New York: Scribner.

——— (1980), *Clinical Studies in Infant Mental Health: The First Year of Life*. New York: Basic Books.

Freud, A. (1965), Normality and Pathology in Childhood. *The Writings of Anna Freud*, Vol. 6. New York: International Universities Press.

Freud, S. (1905), Three essays on the theory of sexuality. *Standard Edition*, 7:135–242. London: Hogarth Press, 1953.

——— (1911), Formulation on the two principles of mental functioning. *Standard Edition*, 12:218–226. London: Hogarth Press, 1958.

Geismar, L. (1968), The results of social work intervention: A positive case. *Amer. J. Orthopsychiat.*, 38:444–456.

——— LaSorte, M. (1964), *Understanding the multiproblem family: A conceptual analysis and exploration in early identification*. New York: Association Press.

Gewirtz, J. (1961), A learning analysis of the effects of normal stimulation, privation and deprivation on the acquisition of social motivation and attachment. In: *Determinants of Infant Behavior*, Vol. 1, ed. B. Foss. London: Methuen, pp. 213–299.

——— (1965), The course of infant smiling in four child-rearing environments in Israel. In: *Determinants of Infant Behavior*, Vol. 3, ed. B. Foss. London: Methuen, pp. 205–260.

——— (1969), Levels of conceptual analysis in environment-infant interaction research. *Merrill-Palmer Quart.*, 15:9–47.

Gouin-Décarie, T. (1965), *Intelligence and Affectivity in Early Childhood: An Experimental Study of Jean Piaget's Object Concept and Object Relations*. New York: International Universities Press.

Greenspan, N. (1981), Funding and cost-benefit analysis for a preventive intervention program. Paper presented at Pediatric Round Table on "High-Risk Parenting," sponsored by Johnson & Johnson Baby Products Co., Key Biscayne, FL.

Greenspan, S. (1979), Intelligence and Adaptation: An Integration of Psychoanalytic and Piagetian Developmental Psychology. *Psychological Issues*, Monogr. 47/48. New York: International Universities Press.

——— (1981), *Psychopathology and Adaptation in Infancy and Early Childhood: Principles of Clinical Diagnosis and Preventive Intervention. Clinical Infant Reports: Report 1*. New York: International Universities Press.

——— (1985), The development of psychopathology: Perspectives from clinical work with infants, young children and their families. In: *Toward a Comprehensive Model for Schizophrenic Disorders*, ed. D. Finesilver. Hillsdale, NJ: Analytic Press.

——— Greenspan, N. (1985), *First Feelings: Milestones in the Emotional Development of Your Infant and Child from Birth to Age 4*. New York: Viking Press.

——— Lieberman, A. (1980), Infants, mothers and their interactions: A quantitative clinical approach to developmental assessment. In: *The Course of Life: Psychoanalytic Contributions Toward Understanding Personality Development*, Vol. I—*Infancy and Early Childhood*, DHHS Publication No. [ADM] 80-786. Washington, DC: Government Printing Office, pp. 271–312.

——— ——— Poisson, S. (1983), Greenspan–Lieberman Observation System for Assessment of Caregiver–Infant Interaction During Semi-structured Play (GLOS). Division of Maternal and Child Health, HRSA, DHHS, Rockville, MD.

——— Lourie, R. (1981), Developmental structuralist approach to the classification of adaptive and pathologic personality organization: Application to infancy and early childhood. *Amer. J. Psychiat.*, 138: 725–736.

———— ———— Nover, R. (1979), A developmental approach to the classification of psychopathology in infancy and early childhood. In: *The Basic Handbook of Child Psychiatry*, Vol. 2, ed. J. Noshpitz. New York: Basic Books, pp. 157–164.

———— Polk, W. (1980), A developmental approach to the assessment of adult personality functioning and psychopathology. In: *The Course of Life: Psychoanalytic Contributions Toward Understanding Personality Development*, Vol. III—*Adulthood and the Aging Process*, ed. S. Greenspan and G. Pollock. DHHS Publication No. [ADM] 80-786, Washington, DC: Government Printing Office, pp. 255–297.

———— Porges, S. (1984), Psychopathology in infancy and early childhood: Clinical perspectives on the organization of sensory and affective-thematic experience. *Child Develop.*, 55:49–70.

———— Sharfstein, S. (1981), Efficacy of psychotherapy, asking the right questions. *Arch. Gen. Psychiat.*, 38:1213–1219.

———— White, K. (in press), Conducting research with preventive intervention programs. *Basic Handbook of Child Psychiatry*.

———— Wieder, S. (1984), Dimensions and levels of the therapeutic process. *Psychotherapy: Theory, Research, and Practice*, 21:5–23.

Hartmann, H. (1939), *Ego Psychology and the Problem of Adaptation*. New York: International Universities Press.

Hellinger, F. (1950), Cost-benefit analysis of health care: Past applications and future prospects. *Inquiry*: 17, No. 3: 204–215.

Hibbs, E., Findikoglu, P., Lieberman, A., Lourie, R., Nover, R., & Wieder, S. (1983), Magical thinking and destructiveness: A comprehensive clinical approach to an infant and mother with multiple affective and developmental challenges. In: *Infants and Parents: Clinical Case Reports, Clinical Infant Reports: Report 2, ed.* S. Provence. New York: International Universities Press, pp. 247–306.

Hofheimer, J., Greenspan, S., Lieberman, A., & Poisson, S. (in preparation), The Greenspan-Lieberman interaction system; Reliability and stability studies. Division of Maternal & Child Health, HRSA, DHHS, Rockville, MD.

———— Lieberman, A., Strauss, M., & Greenspan, S. (1985), Short-term stability in observations of mother–infant interactions. Presented at 93rd annual meeting of APA, Los Angeles, CA.

———— Poisson, S., Strauss, M., Eyler, F., & Greenspan, S. (1983), Perinatal and behavioral characteristics of neonates born to multi-risk families. *J. Develop. & Behav. Pediat.*, 4, 3:163–170.

———— Strauss, M., Poisson, S., & Greenspan, S. (1981), The reliability, validity and generalizability of assessments of transactions between infants and their caregivers: A multicenter design. Working Paper, Division of Maternal & Child Health, HRSA, DHHS, Rockville, MD.

Hunt, J. (1941), Infants in an orphanage. *J. Abnorm. & Soc. Psychol.*, 36:338–358.

ICD-9 (1978), *International Classification of Diseases*—9. Vols. 1, 2, & 3. Ann Arbor, MI: The Commission on Professional & Hospital Activities.

Izard, C. (1978), On the development of emotions and emotion-cognition relationships in infancy. In: *The Development of Affect*, ed. M. Lewis & L. Rosenblum. New York: Plenum.

Kernberg, O. (1975), *Borderline Conditions and Pathological Narcissism*. New York: Jason Aronson.

Klaus, M., & Kennell, J. (1976), *Maternal–Infant Bonding: The Impact of Early Separation or Loss on Family Development*. St. Louis, MO: Mosby.

Kohut, H. (1971), *The Analysis of Self: A Systematic Approach to the Psychoanalytic Treatment of Narcissistic Personality Disorders*. New York: International Universities Press.

Lang, J. (1974), Planned short-term treatment in a family agency. *Social Casework*, 55:369–374.

La Vietes, R. (1974), Crisis intervention for ghetto children. *Amer. J. Orthopsychiat.*, 44:720–727.

Levine, R. (1964), Treatment in the home: An experiment with low income multi-problem families. In: *Mental Health of the Poor*, ed. F. Reissman, J. Cohen, & A. Pearl. New York: Free Press, pp. 329–335.

Lipsitt, L. (1966), Learning processes of newborns. *Merrill Palmer Quart.*, 12:45–71.

Lourie, R. (1971), The first three years of life: An overview of a new frontier for psychiatry. *Amer. J. Psychiat.*, 127:1457–1463.

Lowrey, L. (1940), Personality distortion and early institutional care. *Amer. J. Orthopsychiat.*, 10:546–551.

Mahler, M., Pine, F., & Bergman, A. (1975), *The Psychological Birth of the Human Infant*. New York: Basic Books.

Mazer, M. (1972), Characteristics of multi-problem households: A study in psycho-social epidemiology. *Am. J. Orthopsychiat.*, 42:792–802.

McCarthy, D. (1970), Manual for the McCarthy Scales of Children's Abilities. New York: Psychological Corporation.

McMahon, J. (1964), The working class psychiatric patient: A clinical view. In: *Mental Health of the Poor*, ed. F. Riessman, J. Cohen, & A. Pearl. New York: Free Press, pp. 283–302.

Meltzoff, A., & Moore, K. (1977), Imitation of facial and manual gestures by human neonates. *Science*, 198:75–78.

Minuchin, S., & Montalvo, B. (1967), Techniques for working with disorganized low socioeconomic families. *Amer. J. Orthopsychiat.*, 37:880–887.

—— Montalva, B., Guerney, B., Rosman, B., & Schumer, F. (1967), *Families of the Slums*. New York: Basic Books.

Murphy, L. (1968), The vulnerability inventory. In: *Early Child Care, The New Perspectives*, ed. C. Chandler, R. Lourie, & A. Peters. New York: Atherton Press, pp. 364–372.

—— Moriarity, A. (1976), *Vulnerability, Coping, and Growth*. New

Haven, CT: Yale University Press.

Olds, D. (1982), The prenatal/early infancy project: An ecological approach to prevention of developmental disabilities. In: *In the Beginning*, ed. J. Belsky. New York: Columbia University Press, pp. 270–285.

———— Henderson, C., Tatelbaum, R., & Chamberlin, R. (1984), Improving maternal health habits, obstetrical health, and fetal growth in high risk populations: Results of a field experiment of nurse home-visitation. University of Rochester, Dept. of Pediatrics, Rochester, NY.

———— ———— Chamberlin, R., & Tatelbaum, R. (1984), The prevention of child abuse and neglect in a high-risk population: Results of a field experiment of nurse home-visitation. University of Rochester, Dept. of Pediatrics, Rochester, NY.

Parmelee, A., Jr. (1972), Development of states in infants. In: *Sleep and the Maturing Nervous System*, ed. C. Clemente, D. Purpura, & F. Mayer. New York: Academic Press, pp. 199–228.

Pavenstedt, E. (1967), *The Drifters*. Boston: Little Brown.

Piaget, J. (1954), *Les relations entre l'affectivité et l'intelligence dans le developpement mental de l'enfant*. Paris: Centre de Documentation Universitaire.

———— (1962), The stages of the intellectual development of the child. In: *Childhood Psychopathology*, ed. S. Harrison & J. McDermott. New York: International Universities Press, 1972, pp. 129–137.

Poisson, S., Hofheimer, J., Strauss, M., & Greenspan, S. (unpublished), Inter-observer agreement and reliability assessments of the GLOS measures of caregiver infant interaction, NIMH, 1983.

———— Lieberman, A., & Greenspan, S. (unpublished), *Training Manual for the Greenspan-Lieberman Observation System (GLOS)*, NIMH, 1981.

Powell, M., & Monahan, J. (1969), Reaching the rejects through multifamily group therapy. *Internat. J. Psychother.*, 19:35–43.

Provence, S. (1983), *Infants and Parents: Clinical Case Reports*, Clinical Infant Reports No. 2. New York: International Universities Press.

———— Naylor, A. (1983), *Working with Disadvantaged Parents and Their Children: Scientific and Practical Issues*. New Haven, CT: Yale University Press.

Rachford, B. (1905), *Neurotic Disorders of Childhood*. New York: E. B. Treat & Co.

Reid, W., & Shyne, A. (1969), *Brief and Extended Casework*. New York: Columbia University Press.

Rheingold, H. (1960), The measurement of maternal care. *Child Develop.*, 31:565–575.

———— (1961), The effect of environmental stimulation upon social and exploratory behavior in the human infant. In: *Determinants of Infant Behavior*, Vol. 3, ed. B. Foss. New York: Wiley, pp. 143–171.

———— (1966), The development of social behavior in the human infant. *Mongr. Soc. Res. Child Dev.*, 31:1–28.

———— (1969), *International Encyclopedia of the Social Sciences*, ed. D. Sills. New York: Macmillan.

Riessman, F. (1964), Role playing and the lower socioeconomic group. *Group Psychother.*, 17:36–48.

———— Cohen, J., & Pearl, A., Eds. (1964), *Mental Health of the Poor*. New York: Free Press.

Sameroff, A., & Seifer, R. (1983), Sources of continuity in parent–child relation. Paper presented at Society for Research in Child Development meeting on "Stability and Change in Parent–Child Interaction in Normal and At-risk Children," Detroit, MI.

———— Seifer, R., & Zax, M. (1982), Early development of children at risk for emotional disorder. *Soc. Res. Child Dev.*, Monograph No. 7 (serial No. 199).

———— ———— Barocas, R., Zax, M. & Greenspan, S.I. (in press), I.Q. scores of 4-year-old children: Social-environmental risk factors, *Pediatrics*.

Sander, L. (1962), Issues in early mother–child interaction. *J. Amer. Acad. Child Psychiat.*, 1:141–166.

Seitz, V., Rosenbaum, L., & Apfel, N. (1983), Day care as family intervention. Paper presented at the Biennial Meeting of the Society for Research in Child Development, Detroit, MI.

Sperebas, N. (1974), Home visiting in family therapy. *Fam. Therapy*, 1:171–178.

Spitz, R. (1945), Hospitalism. *Psychoanalytic Study of the Child.*, 1:53–74. New York: International Universities Press.

———— (1965), *The First Year of Life*. New York: International Universities Press.

———— Emde, R., & Metcalf, D. (1970), Further prototypes of ego formation. *Psychoanalytic Study of the Child*, 25:417–444. New York: International Universities Press.

Sroufe, L., & Waters, E. (1977), Attachment as an organizational construct. *Child Develop.*, 48:1184–1199.

———— ———— Matas, L. (1974), Contextual determinants of infant affective response. In: *The Origins of Fear*, ed. M. Lewis & L. Rosenblum. New York: Wiley, pp. 49–72.

Stern, D. (1974a), Mother and infant at play: The dyadic interaction involving facial, vocal, and gaze behaviors. In: *The Effect of the Infant on Its Caregiver*, ed. M. Lewis and L. Rosenblum. New York: Wiley, pp. 187–213.

———— (1974b), The goal and structure of mother–infant play. *J. Amer. Acad. Child Psychiat.*, 13:402–421.

———— (1977), *The First Relationship: Infant and Mother*. Cambridge: Harvard University Press.

Suarez, M., & Ricketson, M. (1974), Facilitating casework with protective service clients through use of volunteers. *Child Welfare*, 52:313–322.

Tennes, K. (1982), The role of hormones in mother-infant transactions. In:

The Development of Attachment and Affiliative Systems, ed. R. Emde & R. Harmon. New York: Plenum Press, pp. 75–80.

———— Emde, R., Kisley, A., & Metcalf, D. (1972), The stimulus barrier in early infancy: An exploration of some formulations of John Benjamin. In: *Psychoanalysis and Contemporary Science*, Vol. 1, ed. R. Holt & E. Peterfreund. New York: Macmillan, pp. 206–236.

Thomas, A., & Chess, S. (1977), *Temperament and Development*. New York: Brunner/Mazel.

———— ———— Birch, H. (1968), *Temperament and Behavior Disorders in Children*. New York: New York University Press.

Tomkins, S. (1963), *Affect, Imagery, Consciousness*, Vols. 1 & 2. New York: Springer.

U.S. Department of Commerce (1980), *Statistical Abstract of the United States, 1980*. Washington, DC: U.S. Government Printing Office.

U.S. Department of Justice (1980), *Reports of the National Juvenile Justice Assessment Centers; A National Assessment of Serious Juvenile Crime and the Juvenile Justice System: The Need for a Rational Response*, Vol. IV. Washington, DC: U.S. Department of Justice.

Weikart, D., Bond, J., & McNeir, J. (1978), *The Ypsilanti Perry Preschool Project: Preschool Years and Longitudinal Results*. Monographs of the High/Scope Educational Research Foundation, No. 3. Ypsilanti, MI: High/Scope Press.

———— Epstein, A., Schjweinhart, L., & Bond, J. *The Ypsilanti Preschool Curriculum Demonstration Project*. Monographs of the High/Scope Educational Research Foundation No. 4. Ypsilanti, MI: High/Scope Press.

Werner, H., & Kaplan, B. (1963), *Symbol Formation*. New York: John Wiley.

White, K., & Casto, G. (1985), An integrative review of early intervention with at-risk children: Implications for the handicapped. *Anal. Intervent. Develop. Disabil.*, 5:71–98.

———— ———— Mastropieri, M. (1983), A meta-analysis of the efficacy of early intervention with the handicapped and at-risk child. Logan, UT: Early Intervention Research Institute.

———— Greenspan, S. (in press), An overview of effectiveness of preventive early intervention programs. *Basic Handbook of Child Psychiatry*.

Wieder, S., Jasnow, M., Greenspan, S., & Strauss, M. (1984), Identifying the multi-risk family prenatally: Antecedent psychosocial factors and infant developmental trends. *Infant Ment. Health J.*, 4/3:165–201.

Winnicott, D. (1931), *Clinical Notes on Disorders of Childhood*. London: Heinemann.

Zilbach, J. (1971), Crisis in chronic problem families. *Internat. Psychiat. Clin.*, 8:87–99.

Name Index

Subject Index

Abortion, 354
Abuse, 359-361
Affect
    affective relationship, 398-404
    cast study/Tom, 483-488
    developmental hypothesis on disorders of, 528-529
    disorders of, 528-529
    disturbance, 483-488
    gaze aversion, 492-495
    .regulation and control, 575-576
Age distribution of CIDP participants, 353
Aggressive attitude toward child, 162-163
Ambivalent mothers, 29-31, 40
    foster mother, 307-309, 312, 316, 318
    Mrs. M., 146-148, 160-161
Amy (child), 474-478
    assessment, 3 days, 476; 3 months, 476; 4 months, 476; 6 months, 476; 8 months, 154; 12 months/1 year, 159, 476; 17 months, 476-477; 18 months, 478; 24 months, 179; 30 months, 179; 3 years, 184-185; 3½ years, 477;
    birth, 475-476
    diagnostic impressions, 477-478
    first month of life, 138-142
    first 4 months, 142-144
    Infant Center, 164-165
    initial impressions, 127-128
    weight loss, 151-153
Anita (child) 478-481
    assessment, 3-day, 233-234, 478; 1 month, 234, 237, 478-479; 4 months, 246-247; 8 months, 254-256, 479; 12 months/ 1 year, 158-159, 481; 18 months, 271-272, 480; 24 months/2 years, 274-275, 282-283, 480; 30 months/2½ years, 281-282, 480, 481; last follow-up, 293
    birth, 231-233, 478
Andrew, 488-491
Anita (mother), 396
Antecedent variables, 356-358
Antipsychotic medication, 113, 118-119, 472, 473
Antisocial behavior, 365-366
Anxious mother, 489-491, 497-498
Attachment, 383, 398-404, 426, 438, 442, 451, 461
Autonomy of mothers, 35

Barbara, 399-400, 406-407
Behavior patterns
    patient's report of, 405-407
    regulation and control of, 575-576
Behavioral organization, initiative and internalization, 385-386, 440, 442, 453-454, 463, 464
Betty (child), 471–474
    assessment, initial, 91-92; 7 days, 471; 13 days, 471; 6 weeks, 94, 472; 4 months, 105-107, 472; 8 months, 113-114; 12 months, 120-121, 473
    birth, 90–92
    concern crystallizes, 92-94
    diagnostic impressions, 476
    foster care and return, 98-99, 100-103, 104-105, 108-111, 472
    intervention by infant specialist, 107-108, 110-111